AF361481

*William Gilmore Simms's Selected Reviews
on Literature and Civilization*

William Gilmore Simms Initiatives: Texts and Studies Series
David Moltke-Hansen and Todd Hagstette, Series Editors

William Gilmore Simms's Unfinished Civil War: Consequences for a
   Southern Man of Letters
David Moltke-Hansen, ed.

William Gilmore Simms's Selected Reviews on Literature and Civilization
James Everett Kibler, Jr., and David Moltke-Hansen, eds.

WILLIAM GILMORE SIMMS'S SELECTED REVIEWS ON
Literature & Civilization

EDITED BY

James Everett Kibler, Jr., and David Moltke-Hansen,
with Ehren Foley

The University of South Carolina Press

Publication of this book is made possible in part by the generous support of the Watson-Brown Foundation to the William Gilmore Simms Initiatives of the University of South Carolina Libraries and by those who established the William Gilmore Simms Visiting Professorship at the South Caroliniana Library.

Published by the University of South Carolina Press
Columbia, South Carolina 29208

uscpress.com

Printed in the United States of America

Library of Congress Cataloging-in-Publication Data
Simms, William Gilmore, 1806–1870.
  [Essays. Selections]
  William Gilmore Simms's selected reviews on literature and civilization / edited
by James Everett Kibler, Jr., and David Moltke-Hansen, with Ehren Foley.
      pages cm. — (William Gilmore Simms Initiatives: Texts and Studies Series)
  Includes bibliographical references and index.
  ISBN 978-1-61117-295-9 (hardbound : alk. paper) — ISBN 978-1-61117-296-6 (ebook)
  I. Kibler, James E. II. Moltke-Hansen, David. III. Foley, Ehren. IV. Title.
  PS2843.K55 2014
  814'.3—dc23
                              2013013549

CONTENTS

Part II: Civilization

REVIEW ESSAYS

ACKNOWLEDGMENTS

The editors gratefully acknowledge shared debts of gratitude to the Watson-Brown Foundation and to the University Libraries and the University South Caroliniana Society of the University of South Carolina. These institutions have provided financial and logistical support for the Simms Initiatives, the wellspring of this volume. Alexander Moore, of the University of South Carolina Press, gave crucial guidance. Ehren Foley transcribed most of the Simms reviews in part 1 and all the review-essays in part 2. In addition he wrote the headnotes to the four review-essays of part 2. Todd Hagstette facilitated many aspects of the project with patience and collegiality.

Individual thanks from James E. Kibler, Jr., editor of part 1, and David Moltke-Hansen, editor of part 2, follow.

Part 1: Literature

Edd Winfield Parks's *Simms as Literary Critic* provided a solid foundation. It is fitting that *William Gilmore Simms's Selected Reviews* was collected exactly half a century after the 1961 publication of this volume. *The Letters of William Gilmore Simms* pointed to still other essays. Simms himself collected two thick volumes of his "Reviews and Criticisms," passed down through his daughter Augusta and now in the South Caroliniana Library. These have proven indispensable in establishing the canon. For Simms's many reviews in the Charleston *Mercury* during the 1850s, masters' theses by Nancy Pantusa and Fred Greer, completed at the University of Georgia in 1975 and 1991, respectively, provided valuable assistance. In addition Greer gave me copies of the forty issues of Simms's *Mercury* book-review column, "Our Literary Docket."

Patrick Scott, Professor Emeritus at the University of South Carolina, in table talk throughout the summer of 2011, provided transatlantic context and information on English Victorians. How surprising to bring up in conversation a minor figure, only to have Scott report he had written essays on the subject. Such support can be found in the true community of scholars, which I experienced in

2011 when I was the Simms Research Professor. These included the South Caroliniana Library's staff: Allen Stokes, Graham Duncan, Brian Cuthrell, Lorrey McClure, John Heiting, and Henry Fulmer. Dean Thomas F. McNally and his staff at the Thomas Cooper Library provided office space and technical assistance. The dean's kindness was of particular personal significance, given that I recollected first entering the new undergraduate library (now part of the Thomas Cooper Library) as a freshman half a century before. The building was only two years old at the time. All the books were on open shelves and could be seen through the glass shell of the building, brightly lit at night. I had never seen so many books and had great respect for where they were housed. I still do. This respect extends to those who keep them.

Simms's great granddaughter Mary Simms Furman provided a sterling example and many kindnesses. Her mother, Mary C. Simms Oliphant, was my early encourager in Simms studies. She showed me unsurpassed hospitality at her home in Greenville and gave me the free run of the remnants of Simms's library there. I also recall many instances in which she shared her wisdom about Simms, gleaned from more than sixty years of hard scholarly endeavor. She said many times that the best way to know her grandfather was through his poetry and that if you did not know his poetry, you did not know Simms. After a life's study, I agree. Mrs. Oliphant was the inheritor of her grandfather's energy and spirit, no better exhibited than after a car crash that left her trussed in a steel back brace, but still traveling to Columbia to research Simms. She possessed, better than any scholar I have known, the trait southerners of a prior generation called *gumption*.

Others also provided guidance, perspective, and inspiration: the late Professor Charles Patterson; Professor Masahiro Nakamura, another example of energy and commitment, who, with his highly touted translations, has introduced Simms to Japan and also has written the first book-length study outside the United States; Karen Stokes of the South Carolina Historical Society; Martha Daniels of Mulberry Plantation; Alan Harrelson; and Clark and Clare Williams. Friends Wendell Berry, Fred Chappell, the late Shelby Foote, and the late George Garrett each presented the rare example in our time of the true man of letters. I often thought of them as standards by which to treat Simms as literary man, his gracious assistance to fellow writers, devotion to literature, and generosity of spirit. They all have shared Simms's long view and the sense that all writers in this tradition are contemporaries in the guild, no matter the century. It was Shelby Foote who often cautioned me never to forget that the profession of letters is "worth a grown man's time." The late Professor James B. Meriwether, mentor for forty-two years, taught me the basics of editorial practice and first assigned me to assist Mrs. Oliphant in 1966.

Part 2: Civilization

At the South Caroliniana Library in 1976, I found two bound volumes of off-prints of Simms's review-essays. These pieces struck me as remarkably revealing of Simms's thoughts and practice as a cultural critic and literary warrior. It is good to highlight the importance of the genre and Simms's deployment of it in the mid-nineteenth-century South. Several people have shaped my thinking on the subject. The late James B. Meriwether, founder of the Southern Studies Program, the late Elizabeth Fox-Genovese, Michael O'Brien, Patrick Scott, and David Shields, each in his or her own way critically focused my attention. My perceptions of the genre's contributions to developing romantic nationalism emerged even earlier, in Georg Heltai's College of Charleston seminars. Heltai was the refugee former deputy foreign minister in Hungary's 1956 revolutionary government. That training colored my approach to studying Simms's South and its antecedents, also framed by such professors as George C. Rogers, Robert Weir, and Clyde N. Wilson, as well as "Miss May" Oliphant. While director of the Southern Historical Collection at the University of North Carolina at Chapel Hill, I had many conversations with such distinguished colleagues and neighbors as James L. Peacock and John Shelton Reed, as well as with such friends of the collection as Tom Watson Brown, and these helped give those earlier engagements continued life. So have John Mayfield and Johanna Shields.

Nicholas Meriwether and Allen Stokes of the South Caroliniana Library obtained the grant from the Watson-Brown Foundation that launched the Simms Initiatives. Dean McNally prevailed on me to help conduct the initiatives in their developmental phase, while recruiting and training my replacement, Todd Hagstette. Of course, neither of these individuals nor my wife, Patricia Lewis Poteat (no mean editor herself), shares the blame for errors that have survived the close readings by many. Professor Kibler and I necessarily have that dubious pleasure all to ourselves.

NOTES ON THE TEXT, OR,
THE DEVIL AND NOAH WEBSTER

In 1850 Simms praised southerners for rejecting Noah Webster's dictionary of
1828 and wrote that John Walker was "still holding his ground in the South
against Webster" (*SQR* n.s. 2 [September 1850]: 32). The object of the enco-
mium was John Walker's *A Critical Pronouncing Dictionary, and Expositor of the
English Language,* first published in London in 1791. Simms saw Webster's
codification of northern spelling and pronunciation in *An American Dictionary
of the English Language* to be a form of veiled intellectual imperialism because it
sought to impose a conformist standard of language for all of the United States.
He resisted this movement in the same way he resisted other standardizations
to "Yankee" patterns, and he called Webster an enemy of the English language,
a "notorious offender of [the] tongue . . . who hath, through equal ignorance
and conceit, entirely overthrown the better English orthography, and who hath
corrupted half of this goodly nation in the art of spelling" (Charleston *Mercury,*
22 June 1859. See also the *Mercury* of 31 October 1855 and 4 August 1859.)

As it was for most southerners of his day, Simms's dictionary was Walker's,
not Webster's. It was arbiter for spelling, definitions, and pronunciations. Walker's pronounced *greasy* with a *z,* and *humble* without the *h,* defined *dinner* as
the "chief meal," *supper* as "the last meal," *lunch* as "as much food as one's
hand can hold," and *mamma* as "the fond word for *mother.*" Simms's embrace
of British spelling was another register of his transatlantic emphasis, particularly
with the souring of his relationship with the Young America movement of John
O'Sullivan's *United States Magazine and Democratic Review.* Launched in 1837,
it promoted Democratic politics, Manifest Destiny, and near-jingoistic American
culture.

The way Simms spelled was a literary and cultural statement in and of itself
and is no small matter. The texts presented here therefore have kept Simms's
preferred British orthography: *candour, chaunt, clamour, colour, endeavour, endeavouring, favour, favourable, favourite, honour, honouring, humour, labour,
mould, moulded, neighbour, pourtray, pourtrayal, succour,* and *vigour; lustre,*

metre, sombre, and *meagre; defence* and *offence; recal; develope* and *developement; amend* (for *emend*); *incumbrance; argueing; etherial; modelled, counselled,* and *equalled, marvellous* and *marvellously; fidgetty; practise; phrensied* and *phrensy; lowlily;* and *wilful, wo,* and *woful.* At times Simms omitted the period after *Mr* and *Mrs* in good British orthographical manner. The texts follow his practice, even when inconsistent.

The spellings from one magazine or newspaper to another were not always consistent, sometimes not even within the pages of a particular text itself. In the newspapers of the 1850s, Simms struggled especially hard against Webster's encroachments. There has been no regularization in this edition, however. The texts appear as they did when published with a few silent emendations: book titles have been italicized, although Simms either put them in quotation marks or, more often, in both italics and quotation marks at the same time. The initial *The* of a title, which Simms sometimes did not either capitalize or place in italics or quotation marks, has been gathered in (as in *The Æneid* rather than the "Æneid"). To prevent a clutter of footnotes, identification of persons, titles, and quotations has been limited to those not easily accessible. Such glossing has been placed in the headnotes. The few corrections of mostly typesetting errors have been entered silently. No effort has been made to regularize punctuation, which Simms and his contemporaries often used to indicate different kinds and degrees of pauses or emphases rather than primarily to clarify meaning.

Introduction

THE MAN OF LETTERS AS CRITIC

Why literary and cultural criticism? Examination of the career of the Charleston, South Carolina, poet and fictionist William Gilmore Simms poses the question insistently. Simms spent more than a quarter of his forty-five-year career between 1825 and 1870 editing journals that were largely but not exclusively literary in nature. He spent as many more years contributing to newspapers as a literary book reviewer, cultural journalist, and political commentator. In total he wrote criticism that would fill more than twenty thick volumes. The subjects of these reviews, notices, and essays were predominately literary, perhaps in the ratio of three to one. That does not suggest, however, that the nonliterary reviews were not an important focus—particularly in Simms's tenure as editor of the *Southern Quarterly Review* from 1849 to 1854, when the ratio became close to even. Less than five percent of Simms's reviews of literary and nonliterary topics are included here.

In these efforts Simms was participating in a broad culture of magazine and newspaper publication (Wells, *Women Writers and Journalists,* 57–75). That culture, and Simms, saw criticism as just one of the vocations of the man of letters. Poetry was the first both historically and personally. In that and other literary engagements, Simms insisted that the man of letters should discover, discern, and express, not merely describe. For Simms discernment carried spiritual connotations. He distinguished between what is essential to our nature and our enduring humanity and what is merely the fleeting, or, as Simms phrased the latter, of the "butterfly, bless'd in a bright caprice" (Simms, *Selected Poems,* 240). Simms insisted that the duty of the poet was to be "a minister to man," at once opening vistas and denouncing the "besetting" sin of the age, materialism, and its chief failing, literalism (Thierauf, "Ancient Wisdom versus Material Progress," 143; Simms, *The Wigwam and the Cabin,* 1: 1).

Because he understood his romances to be prose epics, these understandings also shaped his fiction. As fiction writer, he was to be realistic, lively, and genial, creating from experience so as to show rather than tell, and least of all to ride a pet hobby or encapsule truth in a preachy and "miserly little maxim."

As historian and as historical fictionist, Simms felt the man of letters should explore and explain his people's social, moral, and political development to help his people grow and succeed as a self-determined and progressively flourishing culture. As both literary and cultural critic in turn, he should demand respect for the highest and most refined literary and cultural values and judgments. If successful, he improved a reader's taste and deepened his discernments of human nature and what constitutes good and lasting literature. He fostered awareness of contemporary cultural currents and works, the traditions as well as topical circumstances informing those movements and productions, and the values vivifying them.

In all his work, the agenda was essentially Romantic, as was the age in which Simms exercised his sense of literary mission. One can see the evolution. The early Simms was precocious and already formulating views that stayed with him the rest of his life. His poetry and sketches reflected an exotic sense of the world under the influence of Lord Byron and other contemporary, largely British writers. Included among them, again precociously for an American, were Keats and Coleridge. Simms's lost drama of 1825 on the last Gothic king in the Iberian Peninsula apparently drew on Sir Walter Scott's 1811 poem and Robert Southey's 1814 epic, both created amid the struggle then against Napoleon's armies in Spain. From Scott and Southey, Simms understood early that remote histories influence present times and knew that the past merges with the present.

Simms learned early as well that literature can portray what makes a person human and, in so doing, deepen and preserve his or her humanity as a feeling, intelligent being. His criticism reflected these preoccupations. Soon, too, he focused on the idea, from Sir Walter, among others, that a people or ethnic group is often a central theme and inspiration of literature. In Scott the Scottish people emerged out of the mix of highlanders and lowlanders and the English out of the mix of Anglo-Saxons and Normans. In the eighteenth and early nineteenth centuries, the British were arising out of the mix of the Scots and the English (Moltke-Hansen, "Southern Literary," 11–12, 19–20).

Against this backdrop Simms the critic proclaimed: "the great moral triumph of recent times is the recognition of the race [or people] as well as the individual" ("Ellet's Women of the Revolution," p. 303). This is also why he thought "the cross of the Normans with the Anglo-Saxon race undoubtedly contributed to the improvement of both stocks" ("François Guizot, *Democracy in France*," 249). As his reviews of the two Carroll speeches show (p. 50 and p. 153), Simms was keenly aware that his own particular Scots-Irish lineage was important, not just to him, but in the South's formation. As the nineteenth century progressed, both American and southern identity emerged out of such mixing. The progression was the roadmap for Simms's personal and literary development of his ethnic identity and attachment. Earlier he had imagined southerners and northerners could be Americans together. Later, however, he decided that was not going to happen: growing cultural, ideological, and political differences made it impossible. Furthermore, he concluded, southerners were coalescing as a people and could and should become a separate nation.

Simms perceived that, like the literature it engaged, cultural criticism, when performing one of its functions, reflected and motivated a people and was profoundly political—that is, about, as well as from, the body politic. His enthusiasm for fellow Carolinian Andrew Jackson stemmed from more than his father's service under the General in the First Creek War and carried into Jackson's presidency. Old Hickory embodied the American spirit, the West, and the South. He also emobodied the Celt. Mary Ann Wimsatt declared that essentially Simms was culturally Celtic and that his art was influenced by this heritage (*Major Fiction,* 14, 183, 258). If the fact that Jackson and the elder Simms shared the same background has been largely missing from modern discussions of Simms, it was not hidden to the author. In describing Jackson fighting the English in the Battle of New Orleans, Simms wrote in 1828 that "the chieftains rejoiced as sincerely at the victory of Bannockburn, as their descendants did at that of New Orleans and for a like cause" (*SLG* n.s. 1 [November 1828]: 159–62).

For Simms later politicians were actually and symbolically less representative than Jackson. They were not like Thomas Carlyle's and Ralph Waldo Emerson's "Representative Men." Indeed, in his view, most politicians failed as representatives because they were too careerist and not sufficiently visionary and decisive—in other words, not statesmen. Leadership was about the future. One duty of the cultural critic was to point out what the politicians ought to do, but generally did not. This fact made editing and reading the news and opinion enormously frustrating for Simms, not just when he was twenty-five, but also when he was sixty.

Despite his alienation from the political arena—even his term in the South Carolina General Assembly in the mid-1840s was an exercise in futility—Simms wrote continuously, from the 1820s through to his death, for the newspapers as well as literary and cultural journals. He was seeking to influence—sometimes to change, sometimes to preserve the status quo—most often on behalf of literature, but also for cultural, social, and political development and enrichment. The number of reviews he wrote is a measure. At the peak of his literary reputation in the 1840s and 50s, the era of his most intensive work as editor of cultural periodicals, Simms's reviews were often extensive. The division of this volume into two parts (part 1 edited by Kibler, and part 2 by Moltke-Hansen with Foley) is a practical answer to these different kinds of reviews.

Simms's commitment to reviewing was both practical and ideological. It required that he keep abreast of the latest works for his own as well as his fellow citizens' enlightenment. He used the works he reviewed and placed in his

Woodlands Plantation library in his research and writing. He needed to fill his newspaper and magazine columns, and, rather than borrow from the pages of other periodicals, he used original items that interested him. In addition he sought to maintain positive relations with publishers who sent him works for review. From his literary and political associations, he knew personally many of the authors whom he reviewed.

The literary circle around Simms's mentor James Wright Simmons included the first writers with whom Simms was personally acquainted. Although centered in Charleston, this coterie was also connected to other circles that gathered around Lord Byron. In London, Simmons knew, for instance, Leigh Hunt and Edward John Trelawny. Hugh Swinton Legaré and Stephen Elliott were other Charleston editors and cultural critics important in Simms's youth. As Unionists, they were political mentors to Simms during the nullification controversy of the late 1820s and early 1830s. Loyal Jacksonians, like Simms, they resisted South Carolina's efforts, led by Vice President John C. Calhoun and Robert Y. Hayne, to nullify federal tariff laws.

The next circle to include Simms was the literary one to which Scottish immigrant James Lawson introduced him when Simms first traveled to New York in 1832. Many in the Lawson group, like Simms, translated their associations informally to the Young America movement. Simms sent numerous poems and review essays to the *United States Magazine and Democratic Review,* as well as other Young American organs, and he contributed four volumes to the Young America–inspired Library of American Books.

Simms in his turn became an axis of several circles of literary men and women. He took pleasure in the sociability but also considered his mentoring and encouraging of other writers a responsibility. Overlapping networks also reflected his evolving political involvements, his work as cultural editor, and his growing stature as a southern author and an often-acknowledged spokesman for the South. His political friendships eventually broadened far beyond the early Unionist circle.

In 1836 he wed Chevillette Roach, the daughter of Nash Roach. The Roach's plantations, midway on the railroad between Charleston and Augusta, were near that of his childhood friend Charles Rivers Carroll. Nearer Augusta, James Henry Hammond also had two plantations, part of his wife's inheritance. A nullifier and newspaper editor, this future governor and U.S. senator became friends with Simms after meeting in the late 1830s. Hammond contributed to journals that Simms edited. So did Professors George Frederick Holmes and Nathaniel Beverley Tucker in Virginia—other participants with Simms in what Drew Faust has called "a sacred circle."

As his status rose, Simms received an honorary doctorate and invitations to lecture and contribute to newly minted literary and cultural journals and societies across the South as well as in the North. These opportunities became the basis of additional friendships and alliances on behalf of the campaign to foster and strengthen southern literature and culture. Back home in Charleston, by the late 1840s, Simms presided over a group of writers, who often met in John Russell's bookstore. Notable among these were poets Paul Hamilton Hayne and Henry Timrod. These convivial and eager discussants visited Simms's home on Smith Street in Simms's old boyhood neighborhood, near St. Paul's Episcopal (the Planters') Church, to eat, drink port and madeira, smoke cigars, talk, and study German.

Simms continued to acquire new languages and literatures. Early on he studied Latin and Greek. French, Spanish, and Italian came next, then German. Even before he developed reading knowledge of a language, he familiarized himself with the literature by reading works in translation and contemporary criticism. This was how he knew Scandinavian and Irish sagas. Simms was at once mining sources and learning how other cultures evolved identity and expressed themselves. He also was considering the literary merits, accomplishments, and import of the works before him.

Simms thought poetry the ur-literary pursuit, defined himself as a poet, and used that standard in his criticism. When writing about his craft and assessing others' works, he was keenly interested in the technical, as well as the philosophical dimensions. Consequently he spent much of his review time in addressing what made successful writing, from proper meter to artistic vision. He often gave himself to the *Blackwood's* style of review essay, as in his pieces on Washington Allston, Lamartine, R. H. Horne, Wordsworth, American criticism, the poems of Henry Taylor, and *Richard III* as well as his essays "The Moral Character of Hamlet" and "A Chapter on the Supernatural."

The commentary on the nature of successful art might also come as brief asides or as miniature essays several pages long within the review of the work at hand. So, for instance, in his review of Elizabeth Sheppard's novel *Counterparts,* Simms foreshadowed E. M. Forster's distinction between flat and round characters. Novelists and critics erred, he contended, when "They seem to fancy that a subtle characterization . . . must be carried on through . . . long discussions of the abstract . . . in which the character argues" rather than acts. "Hence all the great masters from Homer down to Walter Scott . . . have dealt with the grand passions of humanity, and these in action. . . . Not one of them paused to philosophize"; neither did any ever indulge "in a single abstract thought or speculation of his own." The great writer must thus possess, above all things, "a wonderful universality" in order to enter his characters "so that each is at once individual, yet true to the common nature."

Simms provided the example of Sterne, who made "his captive silently notch on a stick, the simple record of the one day added to his captivity," and thereby "tells, in one sentence, the whole volume of his agonies and sufferings! Mr. Bulwer would have rambled through a whole volume with him, making him talk about it, and about it, in the prettiest set rhapsody and rhetoric, without compassing a thousandth part of that unutterable wo, too big for words or tears, which Sterne embodies in the simple action of his captive" (*Mercury,* 9 July 1859).

In the great body of Simms reviews, such commentaries on the practical nuts and bolts of literary creation, taken collectively, thus constitute a detailed and remarkably consistent artistic credo. In his extensive review of John Esten Cooke's *Henry St. John Halifax, Gentleman—A Tale* (Charleston *Mercury,* 20 January 1860), to take one example, Simms gave his clearest explanation of why the writer, "to be strong and successful, must be sectional"—that is, regional. He declared: "There is no strength, no success, unless he [the writer] be thoroughly master of his material; and it is not allowed any writer to be universally at home, equally in all regions. He should write, therefore, as Rob Roy felt and spoke, . . . 'I am on my native heather, and my name is Macgregor!'" Simms concluded that to disregard or be ignorant of the local "is really to become cosmopolitan" and thus "characterless." Here he called this placeless abstraction "the besetting infirmity of much that is called American literature." He referred to this yoking of "cosmopolitan" and "characterless" often. It was a critique that he shared with many in Young America of the conservative Mandarins of the *Knickerbocker* set (Perry Miller, *The Raven,* 11–35, 69–134).

Like other Young Americans, Simms was also deeply concerned with cultural, political, and social dynamics and developments. He wanted not just to understand, but to render powerfully vivid what makes a civilization, shapes a culture, gives identity to a people, informs a revolutionary movement, or reveals historical processes. He did this in the great majority of his romances. In his criticism he often addressed these weighty questions in review essays, in which the works before him of a political or cultural nature were not so much invitations to judgment as opportunities to reflect on various subjects and issues of a topical nature.

In "Tuckerman's Essays and Essayists," Simms drew on multiple sources. Brief, glancing treatments of literary works had been, he argued, a feature of Joseph Addison and Richard Steele's *Tatler* and *Spectator* magazines in the early eighteenth century. In his view the intention had been to avoid undue seriousness while promoting the appearance of wit, easy elegance of manner, and judgment. In a 1759 essay, "The Critic," Samuel Johnson explained one of the sentiments behind this approach: "Criticism is a study by which men grow important and formidable at a very small expense . . . ; and he whom Nature has made weak, and Idleness keeps ignorant, may yet support his vanity by the name of Critic" (*Idler,* no. 60, 9 June). Of course, Johnson did not practice what he preached. His *Lives of the Most Eminent English Poets* contains fifty-two essays that combine trenchant criticism with biography.

Simms had more regard for Johnson and other later Georgian writers than for the Augustans Addison and Steele. Yet he tended to treat Johnson the essayist as belonging to the Addisonian tradition; so, "still faintly," in his view, did Charles Lamb and William Hazlitt. The Augustan "occasional" essay and that style of writing belonged "to a contemplative rather than an active era." Simms's "age of steam" had no time "to pause and muse upon the mere forms of a season—the passing moods and fashions of society—the frivolous customs, the temporary tastes, the humours, or even the moral phases of a nice convention, or of ordinary life[,] . . . the topics for that class of writers whom we have, by common consent, recognized as the Essayists ("Tuckerman's Essays and Essayists," p. 266–72).

It was not just steam that powered Simms's new era. The writer of his day needed to "address himself to the higher objects of the masses, gradually rising into a political estate, and to recognise their wants." In consequence, "the Essay became an introduction to a stern examination of the characteristics equally of books, of arts, of politics, and men." The critic "grasped at loftier conceptions than the Essayist; cherished higher considerations of life, which were more important to humanity; opened new avenues to philosophy and history, and enlarged the boundaries of science and art." In true Romantic literary fashion, he "elevated narrative by analysis and suggestion, and borrowed from the imaginative in order to wing the contemplative." That was not all. "He helped to furnish better notions of what virtue demanded, as well from the citizen as the statesman; and, in the very choice of his topics, he opened the eyes of readers to a more just appreciation of what was required of life" ("Tuckerman's Essays and Essayists" p. 273). The diction and phraseology echo Coleridge.

Nevertheless, like Addison and Steele, Simms regarded "the essay . . . as an agent of civilization and refinement" ("Tuckerman's Essays and Essayists" p. 280). Yet Simms judged the demands on the writer and on the essay form very different in his day because of "the new *status* . . . under the encouraging auspices of gradually liberalizing institutions" (p. 267). Contemporary literature was "perhaps, more than ever, associated with the great business of life," having become "an active auxiliary, if not an actual leader, in the . . . toils of politics and statesmanship." At the same time, "History, under its new necessities, . . . assumed a higher rank, and share[d] the honours with Philosophy." He, however, still ranked both philosophy and history below great poetry in order of importance "in the discovery of truth" (Charleston *Mercury,* 23 December 1854, 12 January and 17 July 1855, 3 and 29 January 1856, and especially 20 February 1856).

In any event, having taken upon himself "the toils of the preacher," the critic deployed the language rather "of the prophet than the phlegmatic" or contemplative ("Tuckerman's Essays and Essayists," p. 267). In his view the poet or bard, as prophet or vates, proclaimed truths of the most important kind to universal humanity—of this time and of all times—irrespective of passing fashions and fads. The inspired, passionate essayist, as well as the best historian and philosopher, might partake in some degree of the poet's vatic, imaginative gift.

And passion, the central Romantic ingredient in the creative mix, was always essential.

The contrast between the critic of Simms's day and the Addisonian essayist owed its development to the emergence of the quarterly review. The first was the Whig *Edinburgh Review* (1802), issued by a copublisher of the *Encyclopedia Britannica*. Though a Tory, Scott was an early contributor. It focused attention on recent books, not just to assess their merits but to discuss issues that they engaged or, alternately, failed to treat adequately. The goal was to build critical discourse across the broad spectrum of intellectual interests covered by the *Britannica*.

The *Quarterly Review* began in London seven years later (1809) to offer a Tory counterweight. In 1815 the *North American Review* started in Boston. Stephen Elliott and Hugh Swinton Legaré launched the *Southern Review* from Charleston in 1828. Simms, James Wright Simmons, and Charles and Bartholomew Carroll produced a few literary magazines in the same period. Among them were the *Album* (1825–26, the first magazine in the South devoted exclusively to literature), the *Southern Literary Gazette* (1828–29), and the *Cosmopolitan* (1833, the year after the *Southern Review* ceased publication).

Feeling the need for something different, the editors of the *Southern Literary Journal* decided at the end of 1836 to transform this newest Charleston cultural magazine into "a Southern journal of literature" to "embody the opinions of those who are capable of giving a high tone and character to the literature of the South, and, consequently, to American literature." Fewer than two years after the launching of *Southern Literary Journal,* as well as of Richmond's *Southern Literary Messenger,* Simms cosigned the announcement with two dozen intellectuals from Charleston, including Mitchell King (one of his mentors) and members of the Literary and Philosophical Society. It informed subscribers that the *Southern Literary Journal* would in the future "embrace able and elaborate Reviews," while also presenting "the literary notices of recent works issued from the press," as a result of "arrangements . . . made with the largest publishing houses in the United States" ("Southern Lit." 16–17).

The next year John L. O'Sullivan began *The United States Magazine and Democratic Review.* "All history," he editorialized, "is to be rewritten; political science and the whole scope of all moral truth have to be considered and illustrated in the light of the democratic principle." This was the core of the Young America program. "All old subjects of thought and all new questions arising, connected more or less directly with human existence, have to be taken up again and re-examined" (quoted in Widmer, *Young America,* 3). Simms's long-time, if less than fully admired, acquaintance Cornelius Mathews gave the movement its name, speaking in mid-1845: "Whatever that past generation of statesmen, lawgivers and writers was capable of, we know. . . . Our duty and destiny is another from theirs. Liking not at all its borrowed sound, we are yet (there is no better way to name it), the Young America of the people: a new generation; and it is for us now to inquire, what we may have it in our power to accomplish and on what objects the world may reasonably ask that we should fix our regards" (57).

Chafing not only from the *Knickerbocker* circle, but from the Boston literary establishment that had (in Poe's words) "hag-ridden" American literature, Simms and Poe were the leading southern literary proponents of an essentially New York organ. Yet Simms committed to aspects of the program that did not engage Poe. Simms vigorously supported, for instance, the claim, articulated by O'Sullivan in a 27 December 1845 editorial in the *New York Morning News,* to "the right of our manifest destiny to overspread and to possess the whole of the continent which Providence has given us for the development of the great experiment of liberty and federated self-government entrusted to us." Yet manifest destiny would undermine "federated self-government" and, Simms eventually concluded, threaten southern "liberty." The Union foundered on the rocks of slavery's westward spread to new territories.

The threat, Simms felt, came from the growth of a northern majority. That meant that the concept of "federated" was becoming less essential to the new America that was forming; he concluded that unrestrained democracy would destroy the Republic. It was with that apprehension that he wrote to Hammond in mid-July 1847 that one reason to support the Mexican War, then underway, was to add territory for a future, separate, southern nation. This was because "a dissolution of the Union [was] inevitable" and "the acquisition of Texas and Mexico [would] secure . . . the perpetuation of slavery for the next thousand years" (*Letters,* 2: 332–3). This was important because "slavery will be the medium & great agent for rescuing and recovering to freedom and civilization all the vast tracts of Texas, Mexico &c." (*Letters,* 2: 332).

Just months before this comment, Simms saw through the press the two-volume set of his short stories, *The Wigwam and the Cabin,* and his *Views and Reviews,* also in two volumes. These appeared in Wiley and Putnam's Library of American Books. Simms's long-time friend Evert Duyckinck was series editor, as well as cultural editor of the *Democratic Review.* The library included typically two-volume works by such Young Americans as Herman Melville, Edgar Allan Poe, and Nathaniel Hawthorne ("Evert Duyckinck"). It also published a scattering of humorists of the Old Southwest, a genre that Simms discerned as vital and deserving recognition. Simms's works in the library were his last hurrah with Young America.

The shaking of the nation's foundations was growing in violence. The question of what turned Simms from American to southern nationalist has bedeviled modern scholarship at least since John Higham's essay on the topic. The question is misleading. It suggests a conversion rather than two sorts of gradual evolutionary paths to disunion. Simms concluded that southerners were growing sufficiently different from northerners in their values, manners, culture, and interests, to have a separate political identity. The principle that peoples, when they become sufficiently advanced, deserve their own polities had first been used to justify American independence and later would be used to support southern independence. By adhering to that principle, Simms did not change his views. In a similar vision, he perceived that northerners were becoming inhabitants of a different country—an alien and alienating, urban and industrial one.

Simms was increasingly frustrated by the difficulties of being a slave owner in a nation in which slavery was being delegitimized and slaveholders demonized by, as he saw them, unrealistic, vehemently meddling fanatics. He complained to Duyckinck, no friend of slavery, that he could not bring his wife and children north with him for the summer of 1847, because "we have a colored nurse," and "your vexatious abolitionists forbid that we should cross the Potomac" (*Letters* 2: 273). In Simms's eyes the northern denial of slavery broke the foundational compact of the Republic. It was not so much a case of Simms changing, but, as Simms saw it, of America's changing beneath him.

National foundational instability underlay Simms's reflections on the meaning of progress and revolution. Two long review essays, those on Guizot in 1849 and Ellet in 1850, gave him occasions to comment. Human progress of a certain sort, he maintained, was essential and inevitable: a people progressively developed from rude origins to a civilized state. If the people failed to progress, they were overrun by history, as were the Native Americans. Yet progress had to be carefully considered and carefully, intelligently, and vigorously managed. It also had to be of the right sort to be embraced. In Augustan England, as increasingly in the contemporary North, "the genius of the nation was too much in the market" to make for a healthy literature and society ("Tuckerman's Essays and Essayists," p. 266–67). Strict materialist progress was anathema to Simms, and anti-materialism an overarching and persistent theme throughout his work.

Simms asserted that the core of a people's health and future was not to be found in the market but in the home, nurtured by mothers and wives. Men made war and revolutions and settled the wilderness so women could make homes under their patriarchal oversight. Farms were centers of agricultural production, and homes centers of cultural reproduction, and these were intensely local activities. At the same time, the South had to grow in order to succeed on its own. To benefit civilization, Simms continued to believe, manifest destiny must not only claim, but also domesticate, the vast space and promise of the continent. This, he contended as well, should be under a slave regime. As he explained to John Pendleton Kennedy in April 1852, "slavery in all ages has been found the greatest and most admirable agent of Civilization" (*Letters* 3: 174). The South could not stay in the Union, which was denying slavery's role in human progress. It also meant that the South must look to the Caribbean to assure its future.

Such thinking shaped many of Simms's cultural review essays. Like the essays given here in part 2, his collected *Views and Reviews* pieces, nearly a dozen drawn from the late 1830s to mid-40s, were suffused with the belief that history and literature must reveal the condition, progress (or fate), and nature of peoples. No collection from the pens of Young America more insistently asked how Americans had come to be who they were or how that history should be used by the writer. Simms parted company with Young America when he decided that the South must emulate its revolutionary ancestors and claim a second independence in literature and politics. Simms's southern nationalism thus was a kind of refined American nationalism. That understanding of the purpose of literature would lose salience, at least in the United States. Yet the nationalist Romantic movement continued to influence the literary aspirations of Europeans from Ireland and Italy to Serbia and Poland.

One should not conclude that Simms read European or American writers simply to buttress his nationalistic preoccupations and commitments. The reviews here in part 1 reflect a remarkable breadth of literary interest and awareness. They reveal why Simms felt that creative literature, as opposed to didactic writing to persuade people of an idea of the moment, was worth a grown man's time and would last beyond philosophy, laws, history, specific religions, and even a people itself. After the disappearance of these, literature would remain to tell what the people had been and what their struggles for identity and freedoms were, when none of the rest continued to live. This is far from saying that fostering a people's identity did not matter. Simms was no alienated and disillusioned modern such as Matthew Arnold (whom he reviewed), not even after the South's defeat in 1865. He believed what literature does so supremely well is to preserve the paths of the past, so the future, if need be, might find its way by retracing them.

"An eye to the Universal" is a key phrase to describe Simms's focus. That literature was also a social enterprise was one reason why criticism mattered so much. However topical Simms got on occasion (and he definitely was passionately and intimately involved in his day, as the writings in parts 1 and 2 reveal), he never lost sight of what he deemed literature's lasting value. That value rose above the momentary, and also the momentary men on the stage of history, in their petty squabbles over power, wealth, religion, and even semantics. This understanding is summed up in the title of the introductory essay to part 1, "Literature's Long View."

Simms, the man of letters as critic, performed his critical mission nobly, as William Cullen Bryant observed in his New York *Evening Post* obituary of his old friend: "he was conscientious and consistent, always mindful of the dignity of his callings, uniformly honest, pure and high-toned" (1 July 1870). He upheld standards of gentlemanly behavior and good manners. Of these traits Edmund

Burke, whom Simms much admired, declared, with some Simmsian passion: "Nothing is more certain, than that our manners, our civilization, and all the good things which are connected with manners, and with civilization, have, in this European world of ours, depended . . . upon two principles . . . the spirit of a gentleman, and the spirit of religion" (Burke, "Reflections on the Revolution in France," 129–30). As Simms told the Ladies' Horticultural Society of Charleston in *The Sense of the Beautiful* just before his death, northerners and southerners had different values—material progress as opposed to beauty and a material standard of living as opposed to a standard of faith. In his last public presentation, he was thus remaining consistent with his earliest writings.

In being so, Simms understood himself at odds with emerging preoccupations. In 2011 Francis Beckwith and J. P. Moreland framed this opposition as follows: "there is no non-empirical knowledge, especially no . . . theological or ethical knowledge," no reliable or believable truth, goodness, or beauty to be found in literature in an era of scientific naturalism (series preface, 19). Beckwith and Moreland further insisted that such a view makes literature irrelevant, except as ideology, and its study meaningless. Perceiving a movement in this direction already in the mid–nineteenth century, Simms deemed it to be potentially dangerous for civilization. He declared, "The virtues of a people depend very much upon the incorruptible integrity of language" (Charleston *Mercury*, 20 August 1859), thus his commitment to the role and life of the man of letters as friend to man. The essential tool of the writer—language—stands at the heart of that vision. This is so, Simms insisted, only if one believes in language's ability to convey truth. Wendell Berry echoed him a century and a quarter later in a collection of essays, *Standing by Words* (1983).

Literature

Literature's Long View

James Everett Kibler, Jr.

A plague upon your knowledge—books and laws,
Sciences, theories, and doctrines cold,
Maxims and principles, and rules, and saws.

   Simms, "Sonnet," *Southern Literary Messenger*

As the literature of every nation constitutes its most enduring and honourable monuments, it follows that permanence and premeditation must enter largely into the spirit with which the labourer sits down to his task.

   Simms, *The Magnolia*

In his two-volume *Views and Reviews,* Simms collected eleven review essays in the manner of the British quarterlies. Hugh Holman, editor of volume 1, like Nathaniel Hawthorne in his 1845 notice,[1] saw that the volumes were significant literary criticism (xxxii–xxxiii). Written from 1837 to 1845, *Views and Reviews* provides a window onto the world of Simms the literary critic commenting on exclusively American subjects within an eight-year span. This was a period in Simms's career often reflecting the goals of Young America. Holman in fact called the work "a polemic in a literary war" waged by that literary coterie (xxxi). As such the essays do not convey the many transatlantic cross-currents in the much larger world of Simms's literary reviews. In order to get a reasonably full picture of Simms the critic, one must survey the complete range and broad interests of his criticism from throughout his career of nearly half a century.

The sixty-two literary reviews collected here in part 1 provide another way of understanding that career. While including shorter pieces, part 1 eschews all but a few of the elaborate review essays represented exclusively in his *Views and Reviews.* Simms always did things in a big way. He reviewed or noticed more than twelve hundred literary works. As book editor of the *Album, Southern Literary*

Gazette, the *Magnolia, Southern and Western Monthly Magazine and Review,* the *Orion,* and *Southern Quarterly Review* and as author of book columns for the Charleston *City Gazette,* Charleston *Mercury,* Charleston *Courier,* Charleston *Southern Patriot,* Charleston and Columbia *South Carolinian,* and Columbia *Daily Phoenix,* Simms was fond of writing compendium reviews that grouped several works by the same author or related ones—for example, recent women novelists, recent English fiction, or the latest works by G. P. R. James. A small sampling of these compendia appears in part 1.

Simms sometimes wrote closely considered literary analysis in a way that anticipated by nearly a century, the literary theory that would become known as the New Criticism. His careful reading of Dickens's *Bleak House* (p. 124) is representative of such an approach. Fully footnoted, it might have appeared in an academic journal in the twentieth century. Focusing on tone, speaker, plot, style, figurative language, diction, characterization, and unity, such reviews analyze the work of art as art. Simms was so precociously bold as to declare, in the fashion of the New Critics, that books should be judged "intrinsically . . . with no reference to the authorship" (Charleston *Mercury,* 29 October 1859). A fellow pioneer in these methods, Edgar Allan Poe, comes to mind.

Additionally, as it was for Poe, one of Simms's pet peeves in literature was didacticism, and he never failed to damn it when encountered. His reviews always brought to account the author of a poem or work of fiction that preached a lesson on the surface with an easy moral tag, thus oversimplifying life and relegating it to lifeless abstraction. He invariably criticized a writer for telling rather than showing. One particularly pointed statement on the subject of universality was Simms's observation that "stories should never be written with reference to a specific moral. Written with due heed to *general truth,* as they were designed to be, they carry with them a thousand wholesome morals, which are superior to maxims" (Charleston *Mercury,* 6 February 1856). In the *Mercury* of 13 April 1855, he declared poetry and didacticism to be incompatible. A work was moral in proportion to its truthfulness to life, simply that and nothing more. This became a central tenet of his theory of literary realism. He considered didacticism particularly prevalent in the works of New England writers and felt that the practice stemmed from preachy Puritanism, now secularized. He enshrined no sacred cows among the Boston Brahmins.

Simms at times wrote brief commentary, judging, as he saw it, the essence of the work under consideration. His role was to inform his readers about what was being published and what was going on in the literary world both at home and abroad. He often wrote reviews as if he were on the run, as he most probably was. It is relevant to note that Simms's habitual practice was to compose standing up or pacing before a stand-up desk. This may partly explain the dash and energy of his best literary reviews. But more significant are his penetrating discernments, in so brief a space, arrived at with such lightning speed. This achievement indicates keen critical ability. Simms's brief assessment of Elizabeth Gaskell's *Cranford* (p. 129) is a good example of this type of review. For that reason one might elevate the ranking of Simms the reviewer in Edd Winfield Parks's *William Gilmore Simms as Literary Critic* from consistently "vigorously and provocatively . . . good" to something at times better (110).

As Parks observed, it was unfortunate that *Views and Reviews* is devoted exclusively to American topics. Although giving the work unity, this approach does so "at the expense of a fair presentation of Simms's critical vision" (112). Parks accurately concluded that the volume creates a "warped" and "distorted impression" because Simms was not as narrowly focused as the work infers. The sum of his literary reviews, in fact, shows wide-ranging knowledge of past and present world literature, an understanding that was far from myopic or superficial.

Simms clearly understood that the taste he was shaping as reviewer involved more than particular dictates such as inveighing against didacticism. Even his friend William Cullen Bryant sinned in this respect. Instead Simms's concept of taste amounted to what Parks defined as an intellectual climate "based on international knowledge and cosmopolitan appreciation" (113). To provide that shaping for his readers, Simms knew that it was his responsibility to be as knowledgeable as possible himself. To this end it would not be too great an exaggeration to say that he read just about everything. He was certainly among the most well-read authors of his day.

By 1850, as his reviews of Carlyle's *Latter-Day Pamphlets* and Bryant's *Letters from the Continent of Europe* reveal, Simms had left behind the preoccupations of Young America, some of whose writers (such as Melville and Catharine Maria Sedgwick) marginalized and disparaged the South. In Simms's view of the Republic, regions could—and should—be distinctly different as long as there was mutual respect and none jockeyed to dominate the other, culturally or politically. He saw cultural domination as preliminary to political domination in the same way that he saw cultural freedom as necessary to political independence.

On the personal level, as William Cawthon has written, Simms "could not abide exclusion, or a sense of arrogant superiority on the part of the North, and this he increasingly saw" (17). Even among some of his associates in Young America, he found himself being treated as an outsider and thus effectively excluded. He was particularly attuned to what he called the "fanaticism and hatred" behind such portrayals as Melville's gratuitous creation in *Mardi* of "a loathsome picture of Mr. Calhoun, in the character of a slave driver, drawing mixed blood and tears from the victim at every stroke of the whip" (*Southern Quarterly Review* 16 [October 1849]: 261). Melville called himself Simms's friend in Young America, and Simms took this description of Calhoun personally. As he perceived in the 1840s that Young America was becoming more aggressive in its attitudes toward the South, he strengthened his transatlantic ties. For example, he became more interested in Irish literature, particularly that of the Irish freedom and Young Ireland movements. This and other shifts are chronicled in his reviews.

Simms reviewed Henry Giles's *Lectures and Essays* (*Southern Quarterly Review* n.s. 2 [November 1850]: 538), Henry Field's *The Irish Confederates, and the Rebellion of 1798* (*Southern Quarterly Review* n.s. 4 [October 1851]: 529–32), John Burke's biography of Robert Emmet (*Southern Quarterly Review* n.s. 6 [July 1852]: 278), Robert Shiel's *Sketches of the Irish Bar* (*Southern Quarterly Review* n.s. 9 [April 1854]: 558–9), and Henry Curran's biography of William Philpot Curran (Charleston *Mercury,* 20 November 1855). His essays on the Irish Nationalist poets James Clarence Mangan (pp. 163, 165) and Thomas Davis (p. 166) are perhaps his most significant. His essential essay, "Books from Ireland," and a review of John Savage's *'98 and '48: The Modern Revolutionary History and Literature of Ireland,* appeared in the Charleston *Mercury* of 29 January and 17 May 1856.

By 1870 Simms concluded, as his review of *Putnam's Magazine* (p. 191) made clear, that the South and Europe had closer ties, deeper affinities, and greater mutual respect than either the North and Europe or the North and the South. Some later European writers said the same. Oscar Wilde, in his lectures in Charleston in 1882, saw close cultural affinities between the defeated agricultural South and his own occupied Ireland (*Simms Review* 8 [Winter 2000]: 7). A half century after Simms's death, G. K. Chesterton wrote in *What I Saw in America:* "Old England can still be traced in Old Dixie. It contains some of the best things that England herself . . . has lost, or is trying to lose" (205). Irish writer "A.E." (George Russell) stated in his 1937 memoir after a visit to Charleston that he preferred "the Southern passion for rural life and culture" to the "machine civilisation of the New England industrialists." He added, "They are such nice human beings these Southern folk" (as quoted in Bellows, 139).

Parks's assessment of Simms's transatlantic breadth as literary savant is all the more remarkable today because a significant number of pieces collected in *Literature and Civilization* were not known when Parks published his study in 1961. Even with the incomplete record, however, Parks correctly revealed that Simms ranged widely over world literature at the same time that he was stepping up his fostering of the South's cultural identity as distinct from the North's.

Simms's letters provide supplementary, detailed information on the range of his reading. They show that he knew the works of German authors such as Goethe and Schiller in the original language and commented on whether a particular English translation was acceptable or not. In a recently discovered review of *Correspondence Between Schiller and Goethe,* Simms contrasted Goethe's "too majestic, too cold" nature to Schiller's "fervency of soul" and "passion and romance." Simms felt that Goethe, "except in his earliest writings, the *Werther* and the *Goetz von Berlichingen,* never went into his own heart for his fantasies, but wrote as if drawing from an external realm and nature, of which he is independent and to which he is superior" (*Southern and Western* 1 [June 1845]: 432–33; 2 [August 1845]: 139–40). Nevertheless, in his review of Goethe's *Essays on Art*, Simms called Goethe "emphatically the great artist of the age" (*Southern and Western* 2 [December 1845]: 423–24). In a review of *Wilhelm Meister*, Simms lamented that there was no good American edition of Goethe's works (*Southern Quarterly Review* 20 [July 1851]: 248). He elaborated on his earlier treatment by saying that the very "absence of intensity in the mind of Goethe . . . is yet one of the sources of charm and beauty in *Wilhelm Meister* which reconcile the reader to the wanderings equally of the author and the hero." Simms ranked the novel second only to *Faust* and considered it definitely his masterwork of fiction (Charleston *Courier*, 9 June 1868) because here the author made the domestic novel a work of profound political, social, and philosophical thought. Parks pointed out that for Simms "this was undoubtedly the highest praise to be given to a domestic novel" (28).

Simms and the group of friends who met to translate German authors (*Letters*, 5: 326) had as one of their projects the translation of Goethe's *Egmont*. Perhaps the best indication of the esteem in which Simms held Goethe was taking the epigraph for his novel *Confession* from *Faust*. He quoted Wagner's conversation with his master, in which Wagner says we would be happy if we knew more about the workings of the world, to which Faust answers that the few who did know and innocently gave their insights to the multitude, "were crucified or burnt" (title page). As Bettina F. Cothran has perceptively noted, the plot of *Confession* has striking parallels to Goethe's work. At the novel's end, a character who has caused the death of a young girl, contemplates suicide, but he opts for atonement by going to the wilds of Texas and (like Faust) vowing to live a life beneficial to others (102).

Surveying the critical reception of Goethe in antebellum Charleston, Cothran concluded that "readers in Charleston seem capable of a rather refined understanding of Goethe's thoughts compared to such a relatively simplistic evaluation as that expressed by George Bancroft of the *North American Review*." Bancroft stated that "Goethe's works would be infinitely more acceptable to American taste if they concentrated more on cheerful moral exhortation instead of self-inflicted sorrows or evils" (103). Cothran's assessment of Charleston's response in contrast to the moralistic tone of New England accurately describes Simms's critical judgment. She concluded, "The cosmopolitanism of Charleston seems to have eased the hold of a restrictive, moralistic norm" (103). This sophistication was reflected in Simms's frequent inveighing in his reviews against the moral tags he found pervasive in New England poetry. In critical essays such as "The Poetic Principle," Poe described it memorably as the heresy and cult of the didactic.

Other German authors Simms mentioned in letters and reviews include Bürger, Hoffman, Richter (see the reviews collected in this volume), Eichendorff, the Brothers Grimm, Uhland, Klopstock, Hoffman, Lessing, Tieck, Baron de la Motte Fouque, Körner, Freiligrath, and Zschokke. Such was his admiration for Bürger that Simms said he had a lyre, "a beautiful instrument once in the ownership of the celebrated German poet, the wild and mystical author of *Leonore*," from which he "has imbibed some of [Bürger's] mystical powers" and at "midnight, I frequently hear it sound" (Charleston *Mercury*, 9 September 1859).

Simms's translation of Dante's "Paola and Francesca" has been deemed highly creditable by Theodore Koch in his *Dante in America*. Simms considered Dante a master of characterization (Charleston *Mercury*, 9 July 1859). In correspondence to his friends, he mentioned translating other Italian poets (*Letters*, 4: 133), and he was a great admirer of Boccaccio's *Decameron* (Charleston *Mercury*, 10 January 1855) and had high praise for Alessandro Manzoni's novel *I Promessi Sposi*, whose originality he found beyond compare (*Southern and Western* 2 [November 1845]: 357–58). At one point he wrote a correspondent that he had been so busy of late with projects that "I so neglected my French and Italian that it is pretty hard for me to read a page understandingly without a dictionary" (*Letters*, 4: 40). He was also quite competent in the Spanish language and Spanish literature and history. As a student of language, for which he had a gift, he often commented in his reviews on the art of translation and whether this or that new edition was faithful and artistically rendered.

Unlike the early Thomas Jefferson, Simms was not a great admirer of French culture, but he, of course, had the French Revolution to affect his beliefs. He considered Balzac "one of the best of their modern tale writers" in his notice of *Père Goriot* (*Southern and Western* 1 [February 1845]: 150), and Simms defended him as a moral writer (Charleston *Mercury*, 22 Dec. 1860). Victor Hugo's poetic fancy and striking imagery were evident. However, his *Toilers of the Sea*, like "all his later books, is a violent and bitter assault upon society, religion, nature." Still its tremendous power made it the best of Hugo's works, including *Les Misérables* (Charleston *Courier*, 19 May 1866). There were other favorable mentions of Hugo and of Balzac, Rabelais, Montaigne and Alexander Dumas, but none of Gustave Flaubert. In a novel such as *Woodcraft*, Simms refused to join Flaubert's school of literary naturalism and flatly denied the philosophy of pessimistic determinism.

Simms's dislike of Voltaire was best summarized in two lines of verse. The iconoclast "broke all idols down, that he might leap / To all their pedestals, yet foul his own" (Simms, *Selected Poems*, 261). Simms considered the sentimental novels of Lamartine and George Sand perversions influenced, like so much of French fiction, by the malign example of Rousseau (*Southern Quarterly Review* n.s. 1 [July 1850]: 355–69). Rousseau he profiled as "All sentiment and syllabub" (Simms, *Selected Poems*, 261). Simms's discernment corresponded with Blake's depiction in "Mock on, mock on, Voltaire, Rousseau / Mock on, mock on, 'tis all in vain! / You throw the sand against the wind, / And the wind blows it back again" (Blake, *The Poetical Works,* 133). In his *Jerusalem,* Blake ranked Voltaire and Rousseau chief among the Deists and singled them out for biting criticism. Simms came remarkably close to saying with Blake, "You. O Deists! Profess yourselves the enemies of Christianity, and you are so: you are also the enemies of the Human race and of Universal Nature. . . . Voltaire! Rousseau! You cannot escape my charge that you are Pharisees and hypocrites" (Blake, *The Poetical Works,* 395).

Similarly, Simms ridiculed the unrealistic notions of "dear, delicate" Chateaubriand, who "finger[s] nature / With gloves of sentiment, and see[s] her features / Through opera glasses" while strutting "in costume of good Louis Quatorze" (*Selected Poems,* 261). His review of Atala declared "Chateaubriand was too much of a Frenchman, and quite too great a sentimentalist" (*Southern and Western,* 1 [April 1845]: 292). In general, Simms saw French culture as simpering and effete. His review of Tuckerman (p. 261) declared that Addisonian essayists were "mostly of a French and *finicking* kind; pretty and precise; . . . never deep, and never thorough, . . . expended chiefly upon the merest conventionalities, which . . . must die out in a brief season." These men thus lived in a superficial, time-locked present and had the butterfly mentality.

Even more significant, they had a destructive new manner of viewing the world that reversed the order of God and man. Simms's disdain for Voltaire and Rousseau reveals his rejection of Enlightenment philosophy. He did not enshrine the Enlightenment's reason as the new god of the world. This was clearly expressed in his essay on James Russell Lowell's *A Fable for Critics* (p. 95). Here he declared that he fully expected to see a Temple of Reason replacing that of Christ in the city of Boston, perhaps complete with a Reign of Terror in the manner of the French Revolution. Boston's progressive revolutionary tendencies were proved by such *isms* and *ologies* as Socianism, Fourierism, Communism, and Unitarianism, to name only four of a plethora. Simms went so far as to write in 1854, "Alas! for the world, it is so full of reformers now, that there is no chance of a single virtue!" (Charleston *Mercury,* 25 December 1854). As early as his 1829 review of James Hogg's *The Shepherd's Calendar* (p. 46), he declared that a simple man's rustic superstition is superior to Enlightenment coldness and scientific sterility stemming from a thoroughly empiricist mindset. He restated this belief over a decade later in the opening of his "Grayling; or, 'Murder Will Out.'" Here Simms declared that the people of the modern age have become "monstrous matter-of-fact in latter days," sadly believing "in every 'ology' but pneumatology." The culprit is "that cold-blooded demon called Science," for "the whole armoury of modern reasoning" is on the side of the materialist (Simms, *Wigwam,* 1).

Despite these strictures against most French authors, Simms felt Eugene Sue and Alexander Dumas to be underrated. He thought Sue to be the model for the lesser writers of English romance, such as W. H. Ainsworth—writers who did not "possess a tithe of his genius, his power, the skill with which he combines, or the courage with which he conceives" (75). Dumas may have been an equally important influence on the English romance and was also superior to his imitators in invention (Charleston *Mercury,* 3 February 1855). In the *Southern Patriot* (8 October 1845), however, Simms complained that Sue's *The Wandering Jew* contained a gratuitous and insidious attack on marriage and was popular in the United States owing only to its zealous crusade against Catholicism. In Sue's *The Female Blue Beard,* Simms found the main character a "flatulent monstrosity" (*Orion* 4 [May 1844]: 151). As for his reviews of the literary works of Lamartine the libertine, Simms had very little good to say, but he made frequent note of Lamartine's publications and passed the information on to his readers. In a review of *Atheism among the People,* Simms commented on the author's "intolerable egotism" (*Southern Quarterly Review* n.s. 2 [September 1850]: 254–55) Of his biographies and histories, Simms warned that Lamartine might be accepted briefly as a companion, but never as a teacher (Charleston *Mercury,* 29 December 1854; 31 May 1855.)

There is as yet no evidence that Simms knew the industrious and indefatigable William Blake, but the similarities between the two are striking. Kathleen Raine pointed out Blake's view of the Enlightenment as a foolish, destructive, and wrong-minded enshrining of Newton's Pantocrator as "demiurge of the mechanistic universe of science" (Raine, *William Blake,* 18). She further claimed that Blake "challenged the current fashion of the Enlightenment which held medieval Christendom in contempt." Blake's character Urizen (Reason, "cold and scientific") was the "self-deluded and anxious demiurge . . . imposing his 'ratio of the five senses' on rebellious life," which defied the "systemization of the rationalist." Blake thus saw Reason to be the "false God of the Enlightenment" and once again singled out French writers as that god's major disciples, particularly Diderot, Rousseau, and Voltaire (Raine, *William Blake,* 76).

Of all the authors of his day, Simms was perhaps closest to Blake in so adamantly placing God over man and man's reason and in the vehemence with which he denounced those who did not. There was certainly no American author with whom Simms was such a kindred spirit in this way, certainly not Bryant, Timrod, or Hayne, close friends though they were. Not even the much-revered Sir Walter Scott approached Blake in this particular affinity.[5] Only Coleridge, who admired Blake's poetry and had similar views about the Englightenment, rivaled him. No doubt all three felt that the more accurate term for the age was "the Endarkenment." For all three of these writers, the "Dark Ages" of medieval Christianity were considerably less dark and certainly more enlightened with spirituality.

In completely rejecting Deism, in the passionate manner of Coleridge and Blake, Simms thus struck at the root of what he called the "abominations" that grew from it: Unitarianism, Transcendentalism, Socianism, Empiricism, Positivism,[9] and the multitude of man-centered, egocentric *isms* that were to follow in their wake—programs such as Pragmatism and literary naturalism. He thus fought at its source what he deemed the primary great modern heresy. One of his several key elaborations upon the subject appears in "The Southern Convention" (p. 333). Simms observed that in attempting to be more than a man, he becomes less. A man-centered new world overthrew the teachings of both Christianity and the Classical understanding of humanity's subservience to the Deity.

Simms lamented the results: veneration gone, respect obsolete, reverence scorned and mocked. Unitarianism rejected the divinity of Christ; Fourierism attacked marriage; Socianism rejected scripture; Transcendentalism saw man as deity; atheistic Communism called religion the opiate of the people. In these schemes humanity sought to engineer a temporal paradise. Simms scorned the "sentiment and syllabub" that a person was born good and ultimately perfectible. No utopian program that only manipulated the surfaces would succeed. Humanity was thus not perfectible, but redeemable.

For critic and philosopher Richard Weaver, this understanding of man's fallibility was key to the success of the Southern Literary Renaissance. Weaver argued that unlike authors following *isms*, southern writers remained true to the vision of man as "the folly, jest, and riddle" but also capable of nobility and heroism (Weaver, *The Southern Essays*, 58–70). Simms's reviews show he understood the seriousness of departing from the old story of sin and redemption and the deleterious effect that this abjuring would have on literature.

As his reviews reveal, Simms's Latin and Greek were not of the little and less variety. He judged whether this or that new translation of the ancients either hit or missed the mark. This subject formed a significant area of his reviewing. In this context he called the classical Greeks "the most refined, intellectual race that the world has ever known" (Charleston *Mercury,* 25 December 1854)— so much for the idea that progress, despite all its technological advances, has brought modern mankind to the zenith of civilization. A particularly good essay contrasting Greek literature with that of early Rome is collected here ("Literature in Ancient Rome," p. 66)

These reviews show that Simms understood the role of the man of letters as defined in the highest circles of the literary world of his time. Their sum total from early to late reveals that he felt the key defining central trait of the true literary man was proper placing of the spiritual over the material in resistance to Positivism, Empiricism and Utilitarianism. Sir Thomas Carlyle came to that same realization in the 1830s with the publication of *Sartor Resartus*. Simms's many reviews and notices of Carlyle's works, and of Carlyle himself as heroic man of letters, attested to the kinship Simms felt with the author.

It has been said that "Carlyle was one of the very few philosophers who witnessed the industrial revolution but still kept a non-materialistic view of the world" (*Wikipedia*, "Carlyle," http://wikimedia.org/wikipedia/en/f/fo/August 2011). Carlyle understood the destructive effect of Blake's "dark Satanic Mills" on "England's green and pleasant land" and the world's green landscape (Blake,

The Poetical Works 370). For these writers, "Satanic" (or "demonic," to use the more common term in the Romantic era) would indeed be the right word to describe such mills. One of Simms's most powerful and prophetic essays, "The Ages of Gold and Iron," illustrates his adamant agreement. Simms used some of his most extreme language in his condemnation of industrial materialism when he noted that "the nation whose sons shrink from the culture of its fields, will wither for long ages, under the imperial sway of Iron, . . . may put on a face of brass, but its legs will be made of clay. . . . It may hide its lean cheeks, and all external signs of its misery under the harlotry of art; but the rottenness of death will be all the while revelling upon its vitals, and a poisonous breath will go forth from its decay which will spread its loathsome taint along the shores of other and happier and unsuspecting nations!" (*Ladies Companion* [May 1841]: 4).

In Simms's prediction lay the seeds of the history of modern wars. For Simms, exclusively material progress was counter to real progress. He concluded that so-called progress, if it destroyed anything of beauty, was the word's opposite. Doreen Thierauf recently treated the subject using Simms's poetry. She contrasts what she calls "ancient wisdom" with material progress. She finds that Simms concluded that the cardinal sin of the era was "the failure to see beyond the physical or material" (Thierauf, 143). The man of letters must warn humanity of that flaw, which he saw to be fatal to civilization. As it was for Blake, Simms saw the blighted industrial landscape to be only the shadow and logical result of a mechanistic view of the universe.

Simms diametrically opposed as dehumanizing the new era's belief in the exclusive role of money as measure, its neglect of tradition, and its "I-centered" vagabondage and rootlessness. He believed that the upshot of these egocentric "follies and vices" would be a wholesale destruction of nature eventually leading to man's own extinction. The central argument of Simms's defense of poetry, *Poetry and the Practical,* backs Thierauf's assumptions even more emphatically.

Simms's many reviews that presented a strongly anti-Utilitarian stance resulted from ideas he had developed no later than 1826, when he was nineteen years old. In his "Letters from the West," written in February 1826, the young author criticized the raw materialism and rootlessness of a progressive, money-as-measure mindset.[2] His 1829 review of Hogg (p. 46) also clearly stated his attitude toward "our dull and bank note world." These feelings were greatly strengthened by his sojourn in the swiftly urbanizing and industrializing North. He had gone there in 1832, contemplating relocation nearer the country's principal publishers, but rapidly returned home. His essay "The Philosophy of the Omnibus," published in the *American Monthly Magazine* of 1834 (revised for *Godey's* in 1841), criticized the out of control rush to destroy everything in the path of progress, imaged in the essay as a runaway omnibus smashing everything before it on the streets of New York. In *The Social Principle* of 1843, Simms wrote that railroads "are not virtues, nor duties, nor laws, nor affections" and "that all the steam power in the world" can never "bring happiness to one poor human heart." He concluded emphatically, "Still less can I believe that all the railroads in the world can carry one poor soul to heaven" (53). Nathaniel Hawthorne's "Celestial Railroad" may be indebted to Simms's piece.

In "The Philosophy of the Omnibus," Simms described the impulse to levelism as prevalent in the urban North. There it destroyed art and culture, miring the temples to the muses with the dross of the market-place. There existed no better single statement of why he was choosing the South as a place more congenial to his art. His homeland may not have had the agents and publishers or even the large body of readers, but he felt his people had the understanding that made possible the creation of literature of lasting import. His reasons were articulated in his reviews and correspondence. In one of his most telling letters, Simms wrote of his northern sojourn in August 1837: "I am heartily tired of this region. It is physically and morally a cold one" (*Letters,* I, 113).

Throughout the canon of his reviews, the words "cold," "cold-blooded," "frigid," "inflexible," "rigid in forms," and "arrogantly aloof" appear again and again in describing writers of the North, particularly New England (and sometimes Old England), whereas the literary attributes he admired are "warmth," "geniality," "tolerance," "flexibility in opinion," "energy," "passion," "spirit," and "liveliness." The latter he associated with southern literature and culture (and sometimes with the German and, more frequently, the Irish). The educated of the North were largely "sensible of the value of learning as an agent of social prosperity, but totally regardless of its uses, as a minister to the tastes and sensibilities" (*Social Principle* [1843], 39). It should be noted that this development and strengthening of his understanding had originated before his marriage in 1836, which gave him residence on a plantation far from a city's madding crowd. His move to Woodlands no doubt convinced him that the stand he had already taken was the correct one.

In the decade of the 1850s, Simms continued to refine his beliefs about literature and life. Echoing many of his reviews of the 1840s and 50s, *Poetry and the Practical* (1851–54) proclaimed that the materialist dealt with the surface, the selfish, the temporary, and the time-bound, while the literary man and true man of letters looked below the surface to truths, unselfishly served humanity, and was interested in the abiding universals rather than the "glandular" gratification of the moment. In other words the writers who mattered had the long view. Their bank accounts and stock in trade were the eternal verities. It was the true poet who was responsible for civilization's genuine progress. When the flash and dash of fashion and the rant of topical dispute had melted like mists before the sun, it was the true poet's work that would last. Simms portrayed the inspired writer as being always in advance, guiding that progress. Like Moses, he would lead, but he would never reach the promised land. His rewards, unlike those of "momentary man," would never be "of the day."

As pointed out in 1979, the struggle against the philosophy of John Stuart Mill and Jeremy Bentham, waged early by Coleridge and later by Carlyle, had its American counterpart in Simms (Kibler, *The Poetry of Simms,* 42). In his reviews Simms often referred to the epitome of misguided and American materialism: Benjamin Franklin's "miserly little maxims" that had stamped American character with a corrosive and fatal utilitarianism. His *Poetry and the Practical* has the most emphatic statements on the subject (30, 102–3), although many passing references critical of Franklin are scattered throughout his reviews treating both literature and civilization, several of which are collected here.

Simms's post–Civil War reviews became even more critical of a cash-nexus society, as he saw the horrific specter of a new age in which northern urban-industrial materialism had triumphed. In his last reviews, as it was for John Crowe Ransom in *God without Thunder* half a century later, the South is perceived as the last holdout in Western civilization from the "money-bag" mentality, the complete cash-register evaluation of every aspect of life. As for Ransom, Simms declared that spiritual disintegration can be stemmed by poets, novelists, and the true men of letters of the time and place. His advocacy of art in a torn and battered world that appeared hell-bent on destruction became even more insistent.

As a man of letters, Simms anticipated Walker Percy's "doctor of culture," who must do battle with the solipsism and empiricism responsible for the modern malaise that he diagnoses with his pen. Many of the reviews in part 1 also look ahead to Faulkner's insistence that literature is one of civilization's pillars and props, to help humanity endure and prevail. These reviews played variations on that theme and reflected a weltanschauung that is central to an understanding of Simms at his best, particularly his growth and development across the lines of genre. They are indispensable in achieving a view of the whole man, which Simms scholarship, owing to his large and diverse body of writing, has had such a difficult task accomplishing.

These reviews also demonstrate that Simms, unlike, for example, Thoreau and Ralph Waldo Emerson in his "American Scholar," felt that the literary man defined himself in terms of his community. One of Simms's clearest statements came in 1868, near the end of his life: "Material and mechanical progress . . . are erroneously assumed to be chief or main elements in a people's civilization. We are to teach what the Society of the South practised, that the virtues, chastities, the affections, are paramount duties and necessities of humanity, superior in value to all progress in mere material things, all of which are to be held subordinate to the needs of the soul—these alone being, of all things and influences, the best calculated to elevate man to the high developments which shall prepare him properly for humanity." Simms continued, "Utilitarianism, in its common sense, must be kept subordinate. The selfish instincts are all strong enough for their own preservation, and for the gratification of the mortal appetites. It is for the graces, the refinements, the sentiments, the arts, to refine society, and lift it into proper authority over all things which tend simply to worldly prosperity" (Simms, "Southern Society," scrapbook C, 33 r). There can be no clearer single statement of Simms's recognition of the value of art and literature and their role in civilization.

This declaration was also Simms's description of the role of the man of letters and a primary aim of the literature the true literary man champions or, better yet, creates. It was chiefly in this way that Simms understood that the literary review could play a part in shaping taste, discernment, and humane understanding. In order to pronounce meaning for the audience and guide readers' development, the reviewer must always be searching for the depths below the easy surface and the complexities that transcend the facile moral tag or the intransigence of faction. Superficialities are the province of the dilettante in letters, Simms often contended. And a dilettante Simms most assuredly was not.

One can usually rely on Simms for discernment and good sense in his literary reviews; and the wit, flare, and verve of his prose often make them enjoyable today. His style frequently distills in memorable lines and phrases. We have tried to include as many of these pieces as space allowed, but there are many more left uncollected. Perhaps at some future time, a larger volume exclusively devoted to the literary reviews might be gathered and published. Particularly of note is Simms's "Our Literary Docket" series in the Charleston *Mercury* of 1859. These forty, well-written, chatty, entertaining, sophisticated review essays deserve publishing in their entirety. Simms cast them in this form in order to engage the widest possible readership in a city newspaper whose readers were not all greatly interested in the latest books. That is why he often used wit and humor, as he said, "to honey our pills" and to "talk of books after the fashion of gentlemen in good society, over their wine and walnuts," and why, in doing so, he once received a reader's criticism for levity and lack of seriousness (Charleston *Mercury*, 29 October 1859).

Simms went on to say that he was not surprised by the complaint, for when one considers humanity's "prejudices, passions, preferences; the thousand cliques, sects, nations, interests, prejudices; the great consciousness of fault, or foible, or sin; the sneaking vanities that fill almost every heart, and which honest criticism must always offend—you must expect that there will be some to carp and cavil at the best wisdom." The advice Simms gave to the critic who was thus attacked was simply to "steer right on in your mission, looking neither to the right nor the left; neither to the praise nor to the blame; neither to the profit nor to the loss; assured only by your own conscience that you are working out your destinies, your deliverance, conscientiously, according to your endowment, and without malicious or evil purpose."

Throughout the literary reviews, Simms honestly followed his own advice, a fact which resulted in a more than competent discernment. For example, other than the reviews by the French critics such as Baudelaire and his followers,

Simms's writings, defining and championing Poe's genius, were rare in his day. He ranged over later canonized British writers such as Dickens, Scott, Charlotte and Emily Brontë, Robert and Elizabeth Barrett Browning, George Eliot, Thackeray, Tennyson, Wordsworth, and Trollope. He also treated Burns, Keats, Shelley, Coleridge, Byron, and Gray, as well as De Quincey, Lamb, Leigh Hunt, Thomas Hood, Goldsmith, Carlyle, Swinburne, Thomas Moore, and Matthew Arnold. Among the Americans he reviewed were Whittier, Cooper, Irving, Bryant, Longfellow, Melville, Hawthorne, and Emerson, to name only a few of the major writers.

His reviews of countless lesser-knowns often show him at his best, for here he was following few leads. An in-depth study of one such pioneering area might serve as an example of Simms's freshness and intuitive genius in discerning literary merit. This example came from his native South, of which Simms was always particularly mindful. The area was a developing genre completely unrecognized by the literary establishment of his day. In fact it was not until the mid–twentieth century that this group of writers began to be recognized as American literature's first realists. The genre is southern rustic humor, sometimes called the humor of the Old South. Both Parks and Holman (in 1961 and 1962) noted Simms's appreciation of the genre as legitimate and worthy, but did so in passing. Parks wrote of Simms's "The Humorous in American and British Literature," collected in *Views and Reviews* (second series): "The only true humor Simms finds in this country was our rapidly-developing frontier humor—a judgment that must have offended and horrified" the Eastern establishment (*William Gilmore Simms as Literary Critic*, 96).

The southern humor genre was in fact still horrifying the establishment in 1962 in Edmund Wilson's much-celebrated study *Patriotic Gore*. Wilson called Tennessee humorist George Washington Harris's character Sut Lovingood (appreciated by Mark Twain and much beloved by Faulkner) sadistic, a "dreadful, half-bestial lout," "repellent," and "a peasant squatting in his own filth" (509, 510).[4] It was not until 2004 that James H. Justus published the first full-length study of the genre in his *Fetching the Old Southwest: Humorous Writing from Longstreet to Twain*. Here Justus treated the writers as a kind of shadow canon in U.S. literature that led to Mark Twain and that remains vital, alive, and rewarding today. Simms had come to that conclusion nearly a century and a half before—and prior to Mark Twain.

The work in this genre that Simms most often praised was A. B. Longstreet's *Georgia Scenes* (1835). In his *Views and Reviews* in 1845, he described it as "rare, racy, articulate native humour," and he deemed it original, whereas the humor from America's eastern cities had been "denuded of originality." Simms, in fact, as editor of the *Magnolia,* successfully encouraged Longstreet to write a second series of *Georgia Scenes* for publication in the pages of this periodical in the 1840s.

Parks wrote that Simms felt "the English were not a humorous people" and the "slick city humour of the New Yorkers died with equal quickness" (95–96). Adding credence to his assessment, is Simms's review of Joseph Miller's *American Wit and Humor*. Simms reflected that Miller, "no doubt one of the melancholiest" of Englishmen, "has been the cause, a thousand times more than the British climate, of the tendency of Englishmen to suicide" (Charleston *Mercury*, 7 September 1859). For Simms, there was something very sad about a strained attempt to compile an entire book out of jokes and quips, having the final effect not of humor, but satiety, "disgust," and the "terribly lugubrious." The "professed joker" just tried too hard to be funny, for "to make a business of joking, is to destroy the merit in a joke, just as if one should make a meal of pudding, he would be sure to find his pudding nothing but a meal!" Simms wrote that Mrs. Trollope's "humor . . . is English only in its rudeness" (*SQR* 15 [April 1849]: 67)

In light of the many new reviews added to the canon, both Parks and Holman may have added that Simms saw the Irish and Scots-Irish, not the English, to be the primary influence on that broad rustic humor of the Old South frontier. Simms was later to make use of and display this understanding nicely in his own works—for example, *Paddy McGann,* in which an Irishman is the chief humorous character, and the tall yarn, "How Sharp Snaffles Got His Capital and Wife," which is set in the North Carolina mountains, appropriately a stronghold of the Scots-Irish in the United States. In his reviews of Irish writers, he often mentioned their humor and found it praiseworthy. Still, from the canon available in 1955, Parks perceptively came to the conclusion, in "The Three Streams of Southern Humor," that Simms belonged squarely in the tradition of the humorists of the Old Southwest (Parks, "Three Streams," 147–59). Mary Ann Wimsatt, in her "Simms and Southwest Humor," argued that Simms's use of backwoods humor began "early in his career" and lasted to its end (118–30).

Since Parks and Holman, the expansion of the canon of Simms's works has also added many notices that Simms made of southern humor. Owing to the lack of space in this volume, none of these has been collected here, but the following compendium might serve to supply the lack. Simms's first review of a work in this genre was of William Tappan Thompson's *Major Jones' Courtship* (*Magnolia* 2 [June 1842]: 399), which he found "full of life and spirit . . . very fresh and full of fire." The work "will doubtless gratify numerous readers, and persuade to broad grin and vociferous cachinnation." He compared "this sort of writing" to the great exaggerated caricatures of nature found in Dickens, a kind of valid realism that is not photographic, but in its own way just as realistic.

Simms met Thompson in Columbia in 1848. As remembered by rustic humorist O. B. Mayer, Mayer's friend A. G. Summer, also an author in the genre, invited Simms to dine with Thompson, Mayer, and himself at what Summer called his "Batcheler's Hall." Summer, as editor of the Columbia *South Carolinian,* made of his paper a kind of southern version of the New York *Spirit of the*

Times, in which he encouraged the writing of local humor and published the likes of Thompson, John Robb, Sol Smith, T. B. Thorpe, and Johnson Jones Hooper. Summer himself published in the *Spirit of the Times.* Mayer recalled that at the 1848 dinner, "when Major Jones attempted a story, and failed miserably, Simms annihilated him by telling a snake story such as I never heard before. The roar of laughter that followed the narrative was long and uproarious."[6] It is interesting to note that in 1846 and 1847 Summer was off and on coeditor and proprietor of the *South Carolinian* with Simms's long-time friend B. R. Carroll, Jr. Simms himself did a review of Cornelius Mathews's humorous work *Big Abel* in an as-yet-unlocated issue of the paper. He also treated Mathews in his essay on humor, included in the second series of *Views and Reviews.* Simms noted too that he contributed essays as well on the tariff and the *Knickerbocker,* pieces that are as yet unidentified (*Letters* 2 [9 Feb. 1846]: 134, 143).

A heretofore-unrecorded notice of Judge Hall's *Forest and Prairie* appeared in *Southern and Western* (2 [December 1845]: 428). Here Simms called Hall "one of the raciest, the freshest, and the truest writers of the great interior." In 1845 Simms was among the first to notice William Elliott's *Carolina Sports by Land and Water* in a piece that shows he knew of Elliott's volume before publication. He reported that Elliott "has now in preparation for the press a highly pleasant volume of miscellanies devoted to sports of the land and sea . . . with some of the sketches of which our readers are already familiar. He will make a popular book. He is at once a free, graceful and vigorous writer, and an admirable sportsman" (*Southern and Western* 2 [December 1845]: 422–23). In the Charleston *Southern Patriot* of 29 December 1846, Simms called Elliott "our excellent friend," who should be the man to prepare a general book of rules and manners for the establishment of local hunt clubs.

In 1847 Simms published a long review article praising *Carolina Sports* (*Southern Quarterly Review* 12 [July 1847]: 67–90). Here he reflected that "the sports of a country are somewhat akin to its ballads, and . . . of more importance than its laws. . . . An accurate description of their sports will continue to command attention when graver volumes, on what may seem to be more important subjects have been long forgotten" (67). Once again the literary prophet, Simms would not have been surprised to find *Carolina Sports* to be the only early American sporting book never to have been out of print since its publication. Simms recognized the volume's realism, its "accuracy of detail" made dramatic by "genuine reports of things actually seen and done." He said that its "truthfulness" and "faithful" description are "palpable" (67). In his praise Simms used the key terms of literary realism, words such as "veracious" (73) and "verisimilitude" (72). He concluded "that all has been looked upon and is drawn from nature—not seen and described through the spectacles of books" (85).

The dates of first serial publication of the majority of the sketches of *Carolina Sports* (between 1829 and 1838) show that even though Longstreet is often considered the pioneer of the genre, some of Elliott's sketches preceded Longstreet's. Because Elliott and Simms published in the same issues of the *Southern Literary Journal* in the 1830s, Simms no doubt knew these chapters before Elliott collected them in 1845–46. Simms also noted that the author had completed a five-act historical drama (*Magnolia,* March 1842)—likely *Fiesco: A Tragedy,* which Elliott privately printed in 1850 and gave "as presents to my literary friends."[7]

Simms briefly noticed Henry Clay Lewis's *Louisiana Swamp Doctor* (*Southern Quarterly Review* n.s. 1 [July 1850]: 587), bringing it to the reader's attention but warning against its morbidity. He correctly grasped the volume's nihilistic philosophy. In 1851 he commended Joseph B. Cobb's *Mississippi Scenes* as lively and "truthful in his portraiture" unlike the distortions that "so deform, disfigure and utterly pervert equally the natural and the humourous, in the writings of certain Yankee delineators of Southern life, whom it would be a monstrous stretch of fancy to describe as amusing, although they desperately labour to appear so" (*Southern Quarterly Review* n.s. 3 [April 1851]: 562). In another previously untreated notice, Simms called T. A. Burke's important humor collection *Polly Peablossom's Wedding,* "a collection of broad-grin, Southern and Western exaggeration—comicalities of the woods and wayside; such as will compel laughter if not reflection." He added that it is "just the sort of volume to snatch up in railway and steamboat, and put out of sight in all other places" (*Southern Quarterly Review* n.s. 4 [July 1851]: 272). It is clear that Simms understood this literature was not likely to be accepted outside its rough-and-tumble source and that it was for men only. It would never appear in the Victorian parlor of the Grangerford family in Mark Twain's *Huckleberry Finn* next to *The Pilgrim's Progress.* In this same issue of the *Review,* Simms called Alabama humorist Johnson Jones Hooper's *The Widow Rugby's Husband* "one of the best . . . singularly numerous collections of volumes of humourous literature of the South." He found it "very lively . . . roughly and adroitly told, and certainly compelling the broad grin of the reader" (272). He unsuccessfully advised including Hooper in Duyckinck's *Cyclopaedia* (*Letters,* 3, 437).

Simms also treated Kentuckian Charles W. Webber's *Romance of Natural History; or, Wild Scenes and Wild Hunters* in a recently discovered essay. "With enthusiasm akin to that of Aububon," Simms wrote, "he spared no painstaking, labour or money, when it was desirable to make the acquaintance of bird and beast; and he has the talent to describe, with glowing and lively pen, the groups among which it has been his fortune to fall." Simms again described a masculine audience desirous of realism and action, a world not seen through the spectacles of books or darkened with the soot of the student's lamp: "Webber is a frank, manly writer, full of impulse and movement, dashing, sketchy, free, versatile. . . . He is all life, and he justly conceives that action is as much the essential of the narrator . . . as of the orator." Simms liked the fact that Webber's "story never flags, his personages never drowse, his colours never lose their freshness. If he shows you the catamount, it is on the bound; the bird, it is on the wing, with its throat bursting with song; if the 'human varmint,' it is in the full flood of full fellowship, or in the mortal grapple, gladiator against gladiator."

Simms found Webber's work "true to the borders," a region Simms knew from experience. He thus felt able to judge Webber's accuracy of detail. In this respect, he declared, "A more spirited series of sketches, more piquant or life-like, cannot easily be found." He concluded, "Like most writers of much boldness, Mr. Webber is somewhat careless of the graces of style, but the very carelessness of a free and impulsive writer has a grace of its own, which the more finished art seldom reaches. We commend our hunter naturalist to the favour of our public" (*Southern Quarterly Review* n.s. 5 [July 1852]: 251). Simms again praised Webber as a naturalist and lively writer in the Charleston *Mercury*, 24 January 1856.

Liveliness alone, however, was not enough to draw Simms's praise. Just as informative about his artistic credo is Simms's critical notice of Samuel Cox's *A Buckeye Abroad*. It directly preceded the notice of Webber in the *Southern Quarterly Review*, and the pair provides a veritable dos and don'ts of writing. In the Cox review Simms judged that the author, although clever and "tolerably well educated," had only seen "surfaces," and thus all he had to say was "shallow and insignificant." Simms declared, "he is lively, but superficial; sees much but observes little, and fills his volume with all sorts of 'screeds,' in dilating upon all sorts of commonplaces" (251). The liveliness and dash that he described in both Webber and Cox must be accompanied by true "observation" rather than just seeing, and a discernment that goes beyond the superficial. Webber could do both; Cox could do neither. It was the role of the discerning man of letters to point out the difference.

Simms favorably reviewed T. B. Thorpe's landmark humor collection *The Hive of the Bee Hunter* as "quite a pleasant" series of realistic pictures "by a well known and highly successful sketcher . . . the writer showing equally a personal knowledge of the customs of people and places, natural and human history" (*Southern Quarterly Review* n.s. 10 [October 1854]: 525–26). Simms praised fellow lawyer James Glover Baldwin's *Flush Times of Alabama and Mississippi* as "full of fun and spirit" with "excellent analysis of character" and written in a "free and bold" style with "sentiment frank and genial" by an author "as hearty in his admiration, as he is unflagging in his merriment" (*Southern Quarterly Review*, n.s. 9 [April 1854]: 555). Simms again commended the volume in the Charleston *Mercury* (16 December 1854), as fresh, lively, witty, and "never tedious and always truthful," and remarked positively on it in his unpublished forty-one page manuscript "Wit and Humours of the Professions" (CCS, SCL). To his credit as critic, Simms distinguished Baldwin's genteel and genial wit from either the sometimes rough and racy "broad-grin humour" of Johnson Jones

Hooper or the grotesquely comic and incongruous situations of William Tappan Thompson or A. B. Longstreet. Baldwin and these other writers were two very different sorts of southern realists, and Simms, with his catholic taste, as long as the work had merit, obviously valued both camps. In 1855 Simms called for a mainstream anthology that would collect the works of these uncelebrated humorists (Charleston *Mercury,* 24 May 1855).

What one deduces from Simms's reviews of this genre is a steadily evolving theory of literary realism that anticipates Henry James and William Dean Howells by nearly half a century. In some ways, in fact, Simms's reviews show him to be more realistic than the realists of the 1880s and 90s, particularly such an author as Howells, whose famous dictum required a writer to write nothing that might cause a lady to blush. It may be said that both William Elliott in his early sketches and A. B. Longstreet in his preface to Simms's favorite *Georgia Scenes* had in fact blazed the path for Simms in this field of literary realism. It was a debt not forgotten. Simms returned to Longstreet in the Charleston *Mercury* of 12 July 1859, saying that he had learned that the author is now writing a new series of *Georgia Scenes,* which is "cause for rejoicing and taking up a bottle of wine for celebration." Unfortunately, apparently unknown to Simms, Longstreet's so-called new series of scenes was a didactic collection, to be entitled *Stories with a Moral,* which, like his later novel *Master William Mitten,* was to be a homily to indulgent parents against spoiling their children. As befitted his new professions of Methodist minister and university president, Longstreet had foresworn the gritty realism of *Georgia Scenes.* As president of South Carolina College, he may have declined Simms's invitation to take up a bottle in celebration, at least publicly.

Simms rounded out his reviews of the genre with a notice of Francis Bailey's *Life of William T. Porter* in the Charleston *Mercury* of 6 October 1860. As editor of the New York *Spirit of the Times,* Porter was an influential supporter and disseminator of the southern humor genre. Simms called him "a very clever man" whose periodical "did good." If one valued the genre as Simms apparently did, Porter "did good" indeed. To discern the value of the rustic humor realist in the face of near universal neglect by the literary establishment of the day is thus another reason to raise the evaluation of Simms the critic higher than merely competent and good.

In an allied area—because Simms was a hunter himself, it is not surprising to find well-written, intelligent reviews of sporting literature. The Henry William Herbert piece collected here (p. 107) serves as a good example. Simms's essays on Mayne Reid as hunter and naturalist are noteworthy. He reviewed *The Hunter's Feast, The Forest Exiles, The Bush-Boys of Southern Africa,* and *The Young Voyagers* (Charleston *Mercury,* 29 January 1855; 24 January and 27 May 1856).

Simms's essay "The Hermitage" details his first coming to the hunt and to the society of the local hunt clubs in around 1832, possibly at childhood friend

Charles R. Carroll's plantation, "Clear Pond," in Barnwell District. In a letter dated 28 October 1832, Simms in fact indicated that he was about to leave Charleston for the country to participate in a dove hunt.[8] "The Hermitage" praises "the hunter's song, and the hunter's story, and the hunter's joke" and declares "no objection to the fox chase or the hunt" in which he says he will still gladly participate in moments of leisure (Charleston *Southern Patriot*, 29 December 1846). Simms's description of the Old Hunt Club House is worth noting. It rings "with the cries of the dogs and the horns of the hunters, as the drivers were whipping in for dinner . . . in our monthly or semi-monthly reunion of friends and neighbours in every ten mile circuit." There is "the old Madeira and Sherry, and the more potent beverages," but they "added nothing to our exhilaration," for "the sport was enough for us; the meeting with old friends and cheerful faces; the frank and impulsive hospitality; the cheering defiance that was given to care, and the great good humour and good feeling, which added the richest sauces to the feast." He continued, "Half a dozen drives of a morning, through a country diversified by hill and dale, field and forest,—with a bright sun above, and a generous steed beneath us; some thirty hounds in full cry, and the deer breaking cover at the proper moment,—made dinner at five o'clock, smoking on a clean pine board, under the solemn shade of patriarchal oaks, a feast indeed." Beyond its enjoyment, however, Simms treated the social occasion of the hunt as a means of strengthening community, which in turn elevated civilization in a manner that books sometimes could not, for "graceful, spirited and elegant horsemanship imparts a nobleness and elevation to the character" and the "manliness of mind and body."

In a remarkable declaration, Simms insisted that books are not desirable for the great body of a people because "they are not always congenial, nor is it intended by nature that they should be so. The great hunter, the great warrior, nay, great statesman—may sometimes do very well with a small amount of literature. We are differently endowed and constituted." Simms insisted that he saw "nothing to disparage a farmer or planter in the frank profession that he prefers field-sports to the library." In his usual reasonable and tolerant way, Simms declared that if the planter who is not a great lover of books is only "as indulgent to the bookworm as I am to him, . . . we may sit at the same board, and join in the same festivities, with an equally cheerful temper."

In addition to their literary interest, the sporting book reviews are significant indications of a male audience for the periodicals in which they appeared, such as the *Southern Quarterly Review*. Although women contributors such as Louisa S. Cheves McCord wrote vigorous and sometimes ferocious essays on women's rights, Stowe, abolitionism, and political economy, they were not common. Simms's audience of intelligent readers did not exclude women, but, like McCord, Caroline Gilman, Mrs. Ellet, Caroline Lee Hentz, Mary Boykin Chesnut, and Susan Petigru King, they were exceptional.

Earlier, in the *Magnolia,* however, Simms clearly catered to a female as well as a male audience, so that the personality of each of his periodicals varied rather widely. He was a frequent contributor to gift annuals and *Godey's Lady's Book,* which primarily had women readers; but, like Young America in the 1840s, in the words of John Guilds, Simms "scoffed at the inanity of the matter in women's periodicals" and "was too much a realist to have much sympathy with the rising tide of sentimentality that was flooding America with magazines and literature especially designed for women" (Guilds, "Simms as Editor," 81). Hawthorne's barb about the damned scribbling tribe of women is pertinent here.

The *Magnolia,* which had begun in Macon and Savannah, Georgia, as the *Southern Ladies' Book,* changed dramatically when Simms took charge as editor. The emphasis shifted from literature that entertains and amuses to "literature that provokes thought" (Guilds, "Simms as Editor," 81). To this end the magazine began advertising itself as having a "manly tone" (*Magnolia* n.s. 1 [July 1845]: rear cover). Simms's "The Loves of the Driver," a realistic story about an attempted mixed-race seduction, was published there in 1841, two years before Simms became editor, as a sign of what was to come. There was absolutely nothing sentimental about the tale, a fact that raised the ire of "A Puritan," who, in a letter to the editor, called it a "low valley" and possibly wicked in intent (*Magnolia* 3 [June 1841]: 285–86). Clearly the U.S. magazine market was segmented in complex ways.

Such was the breadth of this man of letters, that with his focus on the great span of world literature past and present, Simms did not miss, belittle, demean, or ignore the realistic art of the commonplace—the homely familiar current literature being created at his own doorstep even when scorned or ignored by those who had the power to establish reputations. As a creative artist himself, Simms believed that all genuine literature, if it is to endure, must breathe the air of the local. Faulkner and other writers of the twentieth-century Southern Renaissance in fact did use the local as springboard to the universal in ways that Simms predicted in many of the reviews collected here. This credo, based on the primacy of the local, was also a part of his anti-Utilitarian stance, for with an obsessive and selfish focus on the material that blinds one to the things of the spirit, out of which true literature is made, Simms insisted that we lose "the sweet humility of our home desires" and that this thereby both diminishes and impoverishes our lives (Simms, *Selected Poems,* 130).

Simms called the opposite approach, in disregarding the local, the "cosmopolitan" in fiction, which he equated with the "characterless" (Charleston *Mercury,* 20 January 1860). The yoking of "cosmopolitan" and "characterless" is vintage Simms. He singled out this modern ignoring of place in favor of hedonism and various "isms and ologies" as "the besetting infirmity of much that is called American literature" (*Mercury,* 20 January 1860). As shown, for example, in his review of Mrs. Ellet (p. 294), Simms felt that civilization, like literature, began at the hearth and the *patria*, not the *palatia Romana*. By *patria* Simms meant the same as did Virgil in his *Georgics:* for Virgil it was that little plot of his father's fields running down to the Mincio beneath the beech trees with the broken tops. That specificity of attachment to the locally real was for Simms the bone, sinew, and soul of all lasting literature, and this understanding was frequently the standard by which he judged a work in his reviews. The place of the author's specific *patria* might be irrelevant to the reviewer, so long as it was not to the artist himself.

On this subject one of his last essays, written after the war, was on the importance of a viable local periodical literature. Simms contended that southerners, with their embarrassments of trade and life, had "suddenly arisen to the conviction that literature is an essential not only of society, but of liberty itself; the aliment most needful to a free people." He felt that "our people" should have come to this conviction long ago and that "the present condition of our country is mainly due to the singular and gross deficiency of public interest in literature and art." In other words political nationalism rested on a strong base of cultural nationalism. Furthermore, he concluded, in "Southern society, with its grace and polish, its tender regard to the sensibilities of others, its high moral sense, and its many generous tendencies, its hospitality, and the life so much exercised in social reunions, literature would seem to be a necessity rather than a luxury" (undated issue of the Baltimore *Southern Society*, scrapbook C, 21 Ra, SCL). Literature of the proper sort was thus a strong and indispensable pillar of that culture and necessary to the identity that makes possible political independence. Simms had often said so in the 1840s and 50s, and, after the war's loss, he was in essence saying, "I warned you."

Simms, as the literary reviews in this collection reveal, had come early to the view of the importance of literature to civilization. Literature stood at civilization's base and was not mere decoration. As he phrased it in a long article on Washington Allston's writings, the author should not consider authorship merely a pretty occupation to while away some pleasant hours. Realizing the crucial role the author plays in keeping mankind human and humane, he should devote his life to his calling without stint of energy and involvement, or as Simms himself put it, by "surrendering life to this one object," embracing his profession with passion and thus eschewing dilletantism (*Southern Quarterly Review* 4 [October 1843]: qtd. from pp. 381, 390). Simms's favorite phrase for the writer's proper commitment was that he should pursue his work *con amore*. This consideration of Allston's writings does as much to outline Simms's own theories of art as to elucidate Allston's own.

In a related statement on the importance of literature, Simms declared, in the Charleston *Mercury* of 20 February 1856, that philosophy, though well and good, "only does mole-fashion, what poetry does eagle-fashion." Similarly he wrote a friend, "Boccaccio undervalued his stories and built upon his treatises.

The last are forgotten and he lives by the former" (*Letters,* 5: 409–10). Simms continued, "A fine song or sonnet will make a reputation when a grave history will be forgotten. Contemporaries seldom see this. . . . It is through the poets of the Hebrew; Homer and Æschylus of the Greeks; Horace and Virgil among the Romans; Milton, Chaucer, Spenser, Shakspeare, among the English; Lope de Vega and Calderon among the Spaniards, etc., poets simply, and not through the historians" that later generations know and understand even the histories of their several countries.

In his review of Mrs. Ellet (page 303), Simms reflected on the proverb, "if a man were permitted to make all the ballads, he need not care who should make the laws of a nation," and he elaborated eloquently on the centrality of literature to civilization and the hearth as the place it begins. That is why he so often spoke of the household gods of various civilizations, from the Roman to the Hebrew— the teraphim, *lares familiares,* and *penates,* the gods of the hearth. In his first known poem, published at age sixteen in 1823, Simms declared of his books that "Nations may fade—but yours no endless date" (Simms, *Selected Poems,* 3). In his last poem he repeated that the poet's song stays "fresh for all the hills / That could not keep their cities," and he stated of Mycenae and Homer: "That a tale should live / While temples perish" (299). Perhaps his most emphatic comment on the elevated role of literature came in 1843 in *The Social Principle:* "next to religion, the business of Literature, is the noblest concern of human society. Nay, Literature is the religion of society" (25).

Simms never altered his view. Rather than being disillusioned with his profession, even in the last evil years when his own hearth at Woodlands was gone and he was penniless, when he had only a small and diminishing audience, and when he felt that writing was drawing water in a sieve, he remained firm in his commitment to the literary life as essential to maintaining humanity. It was after all more to him than a matter of window dressing, of pretty superficialities, or of congenial surface pleasantries; it was rather, as he often said, something essential to a person's core survival as a feeling being. That is why "passion" and "passionate endeavour" were such necessary words for the artist to understand and embrace and for the man of letters to praise and encourage.

As man of letters, Simms remained faithful to his calling as "minister to man." Parks wisely related, "When he mentions Homer and Æschylus, he is not talking of practitioners of an alien craft, but as in a sense his own direct literary ancestors" (11). Such was his broad understanding—the long view—as demonstrated time and again in his literary criticism. The fact that he attached the names of mythological Greek lyric poets as pseudonyms for his own lyric poems—names such as Linus, Alcæus, Tyrtæus, Arion, Sappho, and Musæus—shows just how immediately present in communion he was with his predecessors.

Simms's credo, expressed in passing in hundreds of his critical notices and put into practice in his poetry and fiction, is of a literature that keeps realistically to the essentials, the universal truths of human nature and high endeavor—in other words, the lasting, abiding element above the flash and dash of changing fads and fashions. Proper literature is for all time. It provides the essential continuities in the midst of the flux of change and the momentary. It lasts when temples and cities crumble. It transcends faction, intransigent ideology, polemics, the fanaticism of various reforms, and the distortion of abstractionist oversimplification.

When Simms's reviews take authors to task for betraying art by pushing various "isms and ologies" and thereby making the particularities of life into flat and vague generalities, he sounds very much like Eudora Welty in "Must the Novelist Crusade?" Here she placed the great writer and crusader "on opposite sides" and warns that such writers who preach a point are exchanging their honorable birthright for a pot of message (147). Restating Simms's warning not to crusade in literature, she proclaimed that in fiction "generalities" obscure truth, for "there is absolutely everything in fiction but a clear answer. Humanity seems to matter more to the novelist than what humanity thinks it can prove" (148–9). Welty's essay restates Simms's essential understanding of the attributes that constitute great *and lasting* literature.

Carlyle had first used the phrase "isms and ologies" in 1837, twelve years prior to Simms in his review of *A Fable for Critics* (page 95). The words may have been Carlyle's, but the concept was shared, not learned, as Simms's early reviews demonstrate. Simms understood and properly valued his relationship to his local community but, just as strongly, to his fellowship of writers.[10] In the latter community, those who labored centuries before were his contemporaries just as surely as Carlyle was in Simms's day, and Simms declared this to be, in the final analysis, the only real contemporaneity that matters. One day it may be possible to connect Simms properly to his fellowship, for that is most surely where he belongs, a truth of which he was fully aware. As proof of Simms's understanding, one need only read one of his last poems, "The Lions of Mycenæ," in which the poet-speaker merges with Homer, Horace, and Æschylus and sings with Electra in Apollo's morning chamber "of sorrows over" and the day now "dawning, glorious after a long night" (Simms, *Selected Poems,* 300).

Consideration of the complete corpus of Simms's reviews will be instrumental in properly placing him among his fellow laborers across the centuries. For now, at least, we have a beginning, and one which testifies to the fact that Simms successfully followed his sound advice to authors to be ever vigilant in steering "right on in your mission, looking neither to the right nor to the left; neither to the praise nor to the blame; neither to the profit nor the loss, assured only by your own conscience that you are working out your destinies, your deliverance, conscientiously, according to your endowment" (Charleston *Mercury,* 29 October 1859).

One implication of "deliverance" is release from the bondage of the mind, nicely summed up by William Blake's "mind-forg'd manicles" (102). When the mind is unaware of its enslavement, emancipation is impossible. Simms felt the man of letters holds one key to the manicles. In "deliverance" he connoted redemption, once again elevating the calling of letters to the spiritual. The mission of the critic, as for the writer in general, lies not in sermonizing but in leading to vision that sees beyond the myopic focus on the material and the time-bound present moment. One of Simms's key themes is man's fall from imaginative vision into Empiricism and materialism. Simms's prophetic urgency to return his world to the spiritual vision being lost with so-called progress is made clearest in his poetry and here in his literary reviews.

Notes

1. Hawthorne, review of *Views and Reviews,* Salem *Advertiser* (2 May 1846). Hawthorne wrote that the essays are able and "scarcely inferior to the best of such productions," but Simms was not a man of genius because his themes, "viewed as he views them, would produce nothing but historical novels, cast in the same worn out mould."

2. James Everett Kibler, "The First Simms Letters: 'Letters from the West' (1826)," *Southern Literary Journal* 19 (Spring 1987): 81–91.

3. "Sonnet—The Age of Gold," *Southern Literary Messenger* 10 (September 1844): 521; "Sonnet—Popular Misdirection," Aug. 1844, 485; "The Inutile Pursuit," Charleston *City Gazette* (28 October 1831); and "The Western Emigrants," *Southern Literary Journal* 2 (June 1836): 270–71. The first two are collected in Simms, *Selected Poems.*

4. Two celebrated current authors using Sut as models for characters are Fred Chappell and Cormac McCarthy. In McCarthy's *Suttree* the protagonist's nickname is itself Sut.

5. If, in the final analysis, as Moltke-Hansen has perceptively concluded, Scott failed Simms after the War because Simms could not use Scott's example "to shape the future through the fictive past" ("Southern Literary Horizons in Young America," 26), Carlyle, Coleridge, and Blakeian philosophy did not let him down, but instead became solace and renewed inspiration. After the loss of his library in 1865 it was for a volume of Coleridge that Simms begged his friend Lawson to haunt book stores in New York.

6. Letter of O. B. Mayer to Paul Hamilton Hayne, 4 February 1886, Perkins Library, Duke University. Copy in the Hardy Plantation Archives. From 25 to 28 November 1844, Simms served on William Summer's "Silk Committee" in the South Carolina State Agricultural Society (*Southern Cultivator* 3 [January 1845]: 2–3.) Although never showing open dislike, Simms and A. G. Summer, despite their work together in the State Agricultural Society in the 1840s, were never close. Simms criticized Summer for attacking Rufus Griswold. Summer, in a not-so-complimentary reference in the *South Carolinian* of 1 September 1848, wrote that he had recently seen Simms at a fashionable upcountry spa, Glenn Springs, where "the bard did eat, and eating did talk, and talking did slay Sampson-like his hundreds daily, in a most unsentimental way." Still Simms reported that Summer had invited the essay on Mathews in 1846; and in 1853 Simms reviewed Summer's *Anniversary Address, Delivered before the Southern Central Agricultural Society at Macon, Georgia, October 4, 1852* (Augusta, 1853) in glowing terms: "Col. Summer has not forgotten his agricultural lessons in his pursuit of law and politics; and we commend him for it. He shows himself, in this oration, to incline still to green fields, and the quiet contemplative life of the

good farmer." Simms reported that the oration was highly successful with its audience and "deserved to be so" (*SQR* n.s. 8 [October 1853]: 540).

For a treatment of Mayer, the humorist, see James Everett Kibler, "O. B. Mayer" *Dictionary of Literary Biography, Antebellum Writers in New York and The South* 3. (Detroit: Gale Research. 1979), 213–18; expanded in *Southern Antebellum Writers* 248 (2001), 227–35; Kibler and Edward Piacentino, "Orlando Benedict Mayer," *Encyclopedia of American Humorists,* ed. Steven Gale (New York: Garland, 1988), 315–20; Edward Piacentino, "Backwoods Humor in Upcountry South Carolina: The Case for O. B. Mayer," *South Carolina Review* 30 (Fall 1997): 79–85; and Edwin T. Arnold's excellent "The Good Doctor: O. B. Mayer and 'Human Natur,'" *The Humor of the Old South,* eds. M. Thomas Inge and Edward Piacentino (Lexington: University Press of Kentucky 2001), 199–211. The discovery of Mayer in Japan was owing to the circa-2004 work of Norio Hirose whose Japanese language article's title translates as "A Single-Hearted Search for Permanence: Orlando Benedict Mayer and His Distinctive Southwestern Humor" (interview, Hirose with Kibler, 2004).

7. Simms also noticed Elliott's various agricultural addresses. See for example, *SQR* 4 (October 1843): 527; 15 (April 1849): 262; and n.s. 2 (September 1850): 263. In the last he called Elliott a "spirited writer and a most efficient orator."

8. See James Kibler, "William Gilmore Simms," *Dictionary of Literary Biography, American Magazine Journalists* 73 (Detroit: Gale, 1988): 284.

9. For Simms's critique of Auguste Comte and Positivism, see Charleston *Mercury,* 3 January 1855 and 8 January 1956.

10. Simms's community of writers saw no national boundaries. His hotly-worded critique of R. H. Horne's *A New Spirit of the Age* lambasted the English editor for narrow anglo-centrism. Horne excluded continental writers like Goethe, Schiller,. Hugo, and Balzac from consideration "as if the spirit of the age were wholly framed and fashioned" by England. Simms considered that view myopic, "an injustice," and "in bad taste." It reveals "that arrogance in letters which has always marked her political temper." He added: "the world has other lights [than England], and wisdom will not wholly die from the earth in the hour which she sees her glories become extinct" (*SQR* 15 [April 1845]: 321–22).

Reviews

Sir Edward Bulwer-Lytton's
The Disowned and *Pelham*

Simms reviewed Bulwer-Lytton (1803–1873) throughout his career. He felt the popular author took "no higher aim than that of being the idol of the capricious and ever vacillating taste of the hour, to be set aside as 'fickle fancy changes,' after the manner of a toy or trinket." The novelist of the passing fashion must be ever furnishing forth new *Pelhams* to teach how to adjust a cravat, exhibit an opera glass, choose the right social club, or "edify the mind and heart with the conversations of 'Lady Patronesses,' and of 'stripling Dukes'" (*SLG* n.s. 1 [March 1829]: 384). Simms's fullest assessment was "Bulwer's Genius and Writings" (*Magnolia* n.s. 1 [December 1842]: 329–45), a detailed, balanced treatment that distinguished between fancy and the imagination and defined the proper uses of the real and ideal in fiction. Here Simms found Bulwer to be a writer of the fancy with two egregious flaws: a deficient, "oblique" moral sense that prevented the telling of right from wrong, and a boyish propensity for sensationalism in the use of vehement novelties. Other reviews appeared in *SQR* 7 (April 1845): 312–49; *SQR* n.s. 8 (July 1853): 266; Charleston *Mercury* (10 January 1855; 9 and 12 July 1859; 7 September 1859); and Charleston *Courier* (25 May and 24 August 1864; 9 and 29 June 1868; 22 September 1868; 9 December 1868). Simms concluded that Bulwer successfully blended the novel with the romance, but he was not "among the fathers of his time." Parks was accurate in saying that Bulwer fascinated Simms (27). Poe may have been correct in noting that Porgy in *The Partisan* is "a backwoods imitation of Sir Somebody Guloseton, the epicure" in *Pelham* (*Southern Literary Messenger* 2 [June 1836]: 117–21). Simms may have chosen the name of Major Bulmer, the lofty-mannered gentleman so proud of his English ancestry in *The Golden Christmas,* to recall the English author.

Jack Cade appears in Shakespeare's *King Henry VI,* part 2. See also "Bulwer-Lytton's Translation of *The Poems and Ballads of Johann Schiller*" at p. 78.

The Disowned. **By the author of *Pelham.***

This is a fashionable novel of much character. Written in a very graceful manner and quite a gentlemanly style, without much plot, but abounding in interest arising from situation. The author writes well, and is evidently a man of first rate genius. He is sometimes highly poetical in his sketching. Some of the passages in an episode, which involves the fortunes of a young, talented and ambitious painter are full of pathos. We think the conception of character generally, over-charged and extravagant, but the execution excellent. It is in this particular *only* that the writer falls short of Sir Walter Scott. Some of his personages are mod-elled upon others of this great novelist. The *English* fanatic, (a new creature by the way, Jack Cade excepted) who occupies an important place in this work, is but a poor imitation of that masterpiece of drawing, in the character of Burley, in one of the *Tales of My Landlord.* We recommend *The Disowned* to the reader, assured that he will rise from its perusal, without regretting, as we are frequently compelled to do, the unsatisfactory waste of time, employed in the performance.

Southern Literary Gazette n.s. 1 (February 1829): 321–23.

Pelham, or the Adventures of a Gentleman.

In reading *The Disowned* [1829] and *Pelham* [1828] we reversed the order in which they were published by the author; the latter having made its appearance some time before the former—we read *Pelham* last. Of these two excellently written novels, we are inclined, notwithstanding the voice of the public, to give the preference to *Pelham.* The same faults prevail in this work that we objected to in *The Disowned,* namely, extravagance in the conception of character and incongruity in the plan; but there is a vast deal of fine writing and excellent humour; a fund of morality and a perfect intimacy with the secrets of that "il-limitable vast," the human heart. We think the character of Glanville excessively overcharged. As a proud man highly gifted and possessed of that singular degree of sensibility, which the author has thought proper to bestow upon him, it was certainly out of character, to seek the poor revenge, afforded by the ruin of Tyr-rell, a low gamester, with a narrow vicious mind, whose only propensities were the gaming table, horse race, and brothel. A revenge too, so long delayed, to end at last in an abortive desire for a personal combat, which (to render more contemptible the character of his enemy) the latter very judiciously declines. The work throughout is excellently managed—the spirit of the dialogue seldom flags, and the interest is such that the reader is in no danger of becoming weary; ere he arrives at the end of his journey.

Southern Literary Gazette, 1 n .s. (February 1829): 321–23.

James E. Heath's *Edge Hill; or, the Family of the Fitzroyals, a Novel*

Heath's *Edge Hill; or, the Family of the Fitzroyals* (Richmond, 1828), set in Revolutionary War Virginia, was one of the earliest plantation novels. In this review Simms defined his regional concept of literature more than a decade before his statement in "A Passage with the Veteran Quarterly" and a quarter century prior to his declaration in the 1856 printing of *The Wigwam and the Cabin*. Simms's commitment to serve the South as man of letters is already apparent at age twenty-three.

The "Alps on Alps" quotation is from Alexander Pope's *Essay on Criticism*.

Edge Hill: a Novel in two volumes. By a Virginian.

This looks well; the South is not asleep, merely dozing, perhaps; we hope her nap will shortly be concluded. We like to see Southern books, though rough and uncourtly in outside, and wanting in those meretricious aids and ornaments which are the prevailing characteristic of English and Northern publications; and too frequently the only beauty they possess. A new era is commencing in the South. We have been taunted by Englishmen and Northernmen, and no men at all, so frequently, that we have at length really come to taunt ourselves, and question our right to the high names of our ancestors. We begin to think it time to do something for our own rights and reputation, and as a first step to these objects, we have begun to think and encourage those who do so. Let the good work go on, and we shall not tremble for the result. Let us only think that future days will receive as an inheritance from the present a set of *American Classics,* in which the North, East, West, all will have their representation but the South; and the niche which she should occupy, may be, (if we determine, not otherwise) like the monument of the decapitated Doge, all black, blank and barren.

We have skimmed over *Edge Hill, by a Virginian,* not to review it. We dreaded the effects of our Southern prejudices in favor of a Southern publication; but the journals generally, have already spoken a favorable doom and we are satisfied.

Let not this voice, however, satisfy the author. He must *toil* nor be 'weary in *his well doing'*, if he pursues his present vocation. An author should always be a discontented man. He should never rest satisfied with the honors already won, nor with the labors already over. Alps on Alps should continue to rise before him, and he should ever be told with a warning voice of stimulating encouragement, that 'Rome's beyond them.'

Southern Literary Gazette, 1 n. s. (1 June 1829): 33–34.

James Hogg's *The Shepherd's Calendar*

Simms read Hogg in *Blackwood's,* which he called "Ancient Ebony," that "bolder, cleverer, and more impudent magazine than all the rest" (Charleston *Mercury,* 12 July 1859). Simms, in declaring that he preferred the superstitions of men like Hogg to the empiricism of bald scientific fact in "our dull and 'bank note' world," continued one of his most prominent themes, begun at least three years earlier with "Letters from the West"—a view that was to become central to his poetry; speeches such as *The Social Principle;* essays such as "The Philosophy of the Omnibus"; his inspired defense of poetry, *Poetry and the Practical;* short stories such as "Grayling"; and his anti-Utilitarian novel *Woodcraft.* It is a sentiment that intensified after his visit north in 1832. Simms, before he encountered Sir Thomas Carlyle and his resistance to materialism, was already taking his own stand against empiricism and solipsism.

The "winter tales" mentioned in the review are Hogg's *The Winter Evening Tales Collected among the Cottagers in the South of Scotland* (1820). The passage Simms chose to reprint from Hogg indicates that he would later appreciate fully an agrarian life at Woodlands. This early review is one of Simms's most important.

The Shepherd's Calendar. **By James Hogg, Author of the** *Queen's Wake,* *&c.* **In two volumes. New York: 1829.**

The Ettrick Shepherd is now well known to the reader of *Blackwood.* To him, are we indebted for many of those fine off-hand graphic delineations of character; those phrenzies of wit and buffoonery which have made that journal what it is, though occasionally low and immoral, a rich receptacle of humor, and a perfect ark of varieties.

The life of Hogg, has been one of considerable interest. He has, amidst the fame acquired for him by his efforts in literature, still maintained the life of the Shepherd; and it has been in this capacity, that he has been enabled to gather up many of those touching and simple incidents that are always to be found in the life of adventure, common to the Scottish peasantry. The thunder storm in the mountains; the water-spout that breaks in the valley above the linn and rushes down to the destruction of the humble stock of the farmer; the frolic and festivity of a sheep shearing, and in that country of romantic and superstitious adventure, the fairy and brownie, the wraith and the second sight, have all contributed to the materials for *The Shepherd's Calendar.* The Shepherd appears as the narrator of what he has heard; the stories are generally such as naturally arise from the incidents of domestic and rustic life, and may be considered as illustrative of the life of the Scottish peasantry in particular. They have, generally, their moral, and the inculcation of meekness, humility and virtue; reproving with punishment, of the vicious, the vice; and where other and higher means are wanting, for refining and polishing the rough and uncouth peasant, by disposing his mind to the reception of that arcadian purity which delights not 'to throw the shadow of the storm' on the dwelling of its neighbor. Love forms a principal ingredient in these stories, and is, in fact, a fine instrument in the hands of the great moralist, who thus prepares the vulgar for the reception of hospitality and good will to men. But the Shepherd is more at home in the 'Tales of Faerie.' There is a bewitching simplicity, a something of nature about all the fiction that is wonderfully touching; considered too as a matter of rigid belief among the Scottish peasantry, the existence of these wanton creatures, gives a coloring to the national character which, while we smile at what we consider an absurd fondness for the idlesse of superstition, nevertheless, goes very far towards raising them in our esteem. For our own part, we feel a newer sensation of pleasure, at the recital of any of these tales of goblin. There is a freshness about them, a wildness, and occasionally, a deep and sweet pathos, that we feel to be irresistible. Besides this, we are disposed to believe, that however wanting in the sterner characters of intellect, the superstition of men will be found to be, that which is most characterized by tenderness, passion, and the sweetest and gentlest emotions. It is in fact a lofty aspiration, though commonly held a weakness, which directs us to seek in our dull and 'bank note' world for higher associations than truth is disposed to give us.

The following character of the Sheep, we give, as it stands unconnected with any tale, which could not be given entirely and would be injured by dividing.

'The *Sheep* has scarcely any marked character, save that of natural affection, of which it possesses a very great share. It is otherwise, a stupid, indifferent animal, having few wants, and fewer expedients. The old black-faced, or Forest breed, have far more powerful capabilities than any of the finer breeds that have been introduced into Scotland; and therefore the few anecdotes that I have to relate, shall be confined to them.

So strong is the attachment of sheep to the place where they have been bred, that I have heard of their returning from Yorkshire to the Highlands. I was always somewhat inclined to suspect that they might have been lost by the way. But it is certain, however, that when once one, or a few sheep, get away from the rest of their acquaintances, they return homeward with great eagerness and perseverance. I have lived beside a drove-road the better part of my life, and many stragglers have I seen bending their steps northward in the spring of the year. A twice; if he sees them, and stops them shepherd rarely sees these journeyers in the morning, they are gone long before night; and if he sees them at night, they will be gone many miles before morning. This strong attachment to the place of their nativity, is much more predominant in our old aboriginal breed, than in any of the other kinds with which I am acquainted.

The most singular instance that I know of, to be quite well authenticated, is that of a black ewe, that returned with her lamb from a farm in the head of Glen-Lyon, to the farm of Harehope, in Tweed-dale, and accomplished the journey in nine days. She was soon missed by her owner, and a shepherd was dispatched in pursuit of her, who followed her all the way to Crieff, where he turned, and gave her up. He got intelligence of her all the way, and every one told him that she absolutely persisted in traveling on. She would not be turned, regarding neither sheep nor shepherd by the way. Her lamb was often far behind, and she had constantly to urge it on, by impatient bleating. She unluckily came to Stirling on the morning of a great annual fair, about the end of May, and judging it imprudent to venture through the crowd with her lamb, she halted on the north side of the town the whole day, where she was seen by hundreds, lying close by the road-side. But next morning, when all became quiet, a little after the break of day, she was observed stealing quietly through the town, in apparent terror of the dogs that were prowling about the street. The last time she was seen on the road, was at a toll-bar near St. Ninian's; the man stopped her, thinking she was a strayed animal, and that some one would claim her. She tried several times to break through by force when he opened the gate, but he always prevented her, and at length she turned patiently back. She had found some means of eluding him, however, for home she came on a Sabbath morning, the 4th of June; and she left the farm of Lochs, in Glen-Lyon, either on the Thursday afternoon, or Friday morning, a week day afternoon, or Friday morning, a week and two days before. The farmer of Harehope paid the Highland farmer the price of her, and she remained on her native farm till she died of old age, in her seventeenth year.

There is another peculiarity in the nature of sheep, of which I have witnessed innumerable examples. But as they are all alike, and show how much the sheep is a creature of habit, I shall only relate one:

A shepherd in Blackhouse bought a few sheep from another in Crawnel, about ten miles distant. In the spring following, one of the ewes went back to her native place, and yeaned on a wild hill, called Crawmel Craig. One day, about the beginning of July following, the shepherd went and brought home his ewe and lamb; took the fleece from the ewe, and kept the lamb for one of his stock. The lamb lived and throve, became a hog and a gimmer, and never offered to leave home; but when three years of age, and about to have her first lamb, she vanished; and the morning after, the Crawmel shepherd, in going his rounds, found her with a new-yeaned lamb on the very gair of the Crawmel Craig, where she was lambed herself. She remained there till the first week of July, the time when she was brought a lamb herself, and then she came home with hers of her own accord; and this custom she continued annually with the greatest punctuality as long as she lived. At length her lambs, when they came of age, began the same practice, and the shepherd was obliged to dispose of the whole breed.

With regard to the natural affection of this animal, stupid and actionless as it is, the instances that might be mentioned are without number. When one loses its sight in a flock of short sheep, it is rarely abandoned to itself in that hapless and helpless state. Some one always attaches itself to it, and by bleating, calls it back from the precipice, the lake, the pool, and all dangers whatever. There is a disease among sheep, called by shepherds the Breakshugh, a deadly sort of dysentery, which is as infectious as fire, in a flock. Whenever a sheep feels itself sized by this, it instantly withdraws from all the rest, shunning their society with the greatest care; it even hides itself, and is often very hard to be found. Though this propensity can hardly be attributed to natural instinct, it is, at all events, a provision of nature of the greatest kindness and beneficence.

Another manifest provision of nature with regard to these animals, is, that the more inhospitable the land is, on which they feed, the greater their kindness and attention to their young. I once herded two years on a wild and bare farm called Willenslee, on the border of Mid-Lothian, and of all the sheep I ever saw, these were the kindest and most affectionate to their young. I was often deeply affected at scenes which I witnessed. We had had one very hard winter, so that our sheep grew lean in the spring, and the thwarter-ill (a sort of paralytic affection) came among them, and carried off a number. Often have I seen these poor victims when fallen down to rise no more, even when unable to lift their heads from the ground, holding up the leg, to invite the starving lamb to the miserable pittance that the udder still could supply. I had never seen aught more painfully affecting.

It is well known that it is a custom with shepherds, when a lamb dies, if the mother have a sufficiency of milk, to bring her from the hill, and put another lamb to her. This is done by putting the skin of the dead lamb upon the living one; the ewe immediately acknowledges the relationship, and after the skin has warmed on it, so as to give it something of the smell of her own progeny, and it has sucked her two or three times, she accepts and nourishes it as her own ever after. Whether it is from joy at this apparent reanimation of her young one, or because a little doubt remains on her mind which she would fain dispel, I cannot decide; but, for a number of days, she shows far more fondness, by bleating, and caressing, over this one, than she did formerly over the one that was really her own.

But this is not what I wanted to explain; it was, that such sheep as thus lose their lambs, must be driven to a house with dogs, so that the lamb may be put to them; for they will only take it in a dark confined place. But at Willenslee, I never needed to drive home a sheep by force, with dogs, or in any other way than the following: I found every ewe, of course, standing hanging her head over her dead lamb, and having a piece of twine with me for the purpose, I tied that to the lamb's neck, or foot, and trailing it along, the ewe followed me into any house or fold that I chose to lead her. Any of them would have followed me in that way for miles, with her nose close on the lamb, which she never quitted for a moment, except to chase my dog, which she would not suffer to walk near me. I often, out of curiosity, led them in to the side of the kitchen fire by this means, into the midst of servants and dogs; but the more that dangers multiplied around the ewe, she clung the closer to her dead offspring, and thought of nothing whatever but protecting it.'

We recommend these two volumes, with much earnestness to the reader. The simplicity of the title may deter many from a perusal, with whom a title is a matter of importance, and which they would otherwise enjoy with pleasure. The tales are short, natural and interesting, and all those who are familiar with his 'winter tales,' will do well to peruse the present interesting gleanings of the Ettrick Shepherd.

Southern Literary Gazette n.s. 1 (15 June 1829): 52–54.

Charles Rivers Carroll's *Address Delivered Before the Society of the Friends of Ireland*

Carroll (c. 1804–1875) was perhaps Simms's closest friend throughout his life. The following, on the art of oratory, takes the form of a review of a particular speech Simms heard Carroll deliver. Simms's father and Carroll's father (Bartholomew R. Carroll, Sr.) were both emigrants from Northern Ireland. Simms studied law in Charles Carroll's newly opened law office. They were neighbors in the Boundary (Calhoun) Street area of Charleston and attended St. Paul's Episcopal Church. In an essay in the *Southern Agriculturist* 9 (August 1836): 399–407, Bartholomew, Sr., refers to building a structure in 1835 on his son Charles's plantation in Barnwell District. Simms stayed with his childhood friend in Barnwell after his first wife's death and his sojourn in the North, and Carroll made it convenient for him to court his future wife at nearby Woodlands. Carroll in fact may have introduced the couple. John Guilds has surmised that in the summer of 1832 Simms left his young daughter, Augusta, with Carroll. (*Simms*, 376). In 1833 Simms edited the *Cosmopolitan* with Charles and his brother Edward.

This newly discovered essay reveals Simms's theory of public speaking, perhaps learned from Carroll himself. It gives his feelings about religious tolerance and proves his early interest in a shared Irish cultural inheritance, especially with regard to the inherent rights of an individual (shades of Jefferson). It should be read with Simms's important "Irish Remonstrance," published six months earlier (*SLG* n.s. 1 [November 1828]: 159–62), and his "Song of the Irish Patriot" (*SLG* n.s. 1 [December 1828]: 215). Simms began "Irish Remonstrance" by declaring "the Emerald is rather a favorite gem" and "we are fond of the refreshing tint, were it only for the lovely verdure of the humble Shamroc[k]." He recounted the fog-shrouded Irish history-myths of the *Tuatha da Danaan,* the *Firbolgs, Ollamh Fodltha,* Merlin, the Ulster Cycle of "the knights of the 'red branch,'" Partholan, and the Halls of Tara, seat of the ancient Irish kings. His focus, however, is a "later period" leading up to 1317, an "age when the remains of the venerable oak which gave to the Druid his shelter, his acorn and his missletoe [*sic*] existed only in the beams of some cathedrals."

In this later age Simms was "grateful at beholding the oppressed and persecuted chieftains of Ireland sending forward" a remonstrance claiming their rights as a people. Simms declared that, "in this state of things, the chieftains rejoiced as sincerely at the victory of Bannockburn, as their descendants did at that of New Orleans and for a like cause." He later linked the Revolution, the War of 1812, and the South's own war for independence as a continuing Celtic struggle against English and New English usurpation of rights. (See particularly the review of *Hartley Norman* at p. 159.) He traced the long history of England's perfidy in dealing with Ireland down to "King George IV's current treatment of [Daniel] O'Connell, McDonald, O'Shiel and the other Irish chieftains of our day." Columbkille and Edward Bruce are referenced, as well as "the O'Tooles, O'Briens, and "O'Carrolls [who] piped up such a jig, to use a true Hibernian idiom, as . . . brought tears, but not of joy, into the eyes of the Sassanagh." It is significant that Simms used the rare word "Sassenagh," a term of intense opprobrium reserved for the hated English oppressor. Simms's story continued through Robert the Bruce and Edward II, who called on Pope John XXII to admonish the Irish. The Irish answered the pope in their "Remonstrance," explaining their claims to sovereignty and "their own civil rights with which they will not permit interference." This was not rebellion, they said, because their rights were God-given and inalienable (*SLG* n.s. 1 [November 1828]: 166–67). There are close echoes here in 1828 of Simms's later wording of the South's position in 1861. This pair of reviews is among Simms's most significant.

See also Simms's "Address Written for the Benefit of the 'Association of the Friends of Ireland in Charleston'" (Charleston *Courier,* 21 April 1829), published in Simms, *Selected Poems* (312–14, notes at 435–36).

Address Delivered Before the Society of the Friends of Ireland on Thursday Evening, March 19, 1829. By Charles Rivers Carroll, Esq.

Nothing is more common than to render occasions, like that on which the above address was delivered, the means of affording opportunities to the young and ambitious orator, for the display of language and fine sentiment; too often a great deal is uttered, and yet, little or nothing is well said, either as regards the true objects for which the auditors have assembled, or the manner in which the subject should be considered. Like maiden speeches at the bar, or fourth of July harangues, the orators for the most part, are too much concerned for the *effect* they desire to produce, to bestow more pains upon themselves, than will well fit them for the populace; rather than aim at what is infinitely a pearl of greater price, an appeal to the good sense of mankind; and which, if anything can, will most assuredly advance or sustain their previous reputations. Tho' we are free to confess we regard this as not among the least defects of our southern friends, we cannot in truth or candor lay it to the door of Mr Carroll; on the contrary we discovered almost throughout his discourse an apparent indifference to any of the 'tricks of oratory,' and at the same time an earnestness and zeal, a warmth and seriousness, which, while they exhibit the sincerity and truth of the speaker, entitle him to much credit for a faithful discharge of his duty. He has, indeed, soberly and manfully defended the cause of his countrymen, as well as the principle upon which the 'Friends of Ireland' were established into body.

The subject of the address is one, which has for a number of years past, engaged the attention of a great portion of mankind; and within a short time back, has elicited some of the most passionate appeals to the sensibilities of men, as well as some of the most profound and argumentative discussions; nor have we been at all surprised at the general concern which seems to have been manifested almost everywhere for the result of this all absorbing subject; for if there be any question which touches, very nearly, every nation in every clime, if there be a matter which comes home to the business and bosoms of men, it is that which relates to the mode in which they shall be permitted to offer up their orisons to the God of their fathers. For ourselves, we have always regarded the question of religious toleration as one of those singular disputes which has only, not surprised us, because we could never bring ourselves to the serious belief, that, apart from *political considerations,* it admitted of any question whatever; how absurd to imagine that any human power should inflict punishment, or throw in the way of a freeman, at least, as far as his thoughts are concerned, disabilities and difficulties simply because his mode of belief is different from another's; how equally idle and unavailing the effort to make attacks of this sort upon the conscience of an individual, or of a nation, which is but a collection of individuals; but perhaps we do wrong to revive the question, it is, we trust, settled forever, and whatever may have been the *real* motives of the Duke of Wellington or Mr Peel, it is certain that Irishmen will not complain of the ends they have effected, though they may with some justice doubt the philanthropy of the motive which urged them to this vast undertaking.

We shall now present to our readers one or two extracts from the Address. The following language conveys much sound reasoning to show the *right,* and the propriety on the part of the people of maintaining an independent and untrammeled exercise of religious opinions and principles.

'It is, then, above all other considerations, the principle for which the Irish Catholics are contending, that we hold them in our communion, and esteem them to be our brothers indeed—brothers in a faith that recognizes no superior but God and the Laws—Laws which are impartial, resting on the Atlantean will of the people, whose influence is potent in preserving right.'

'Their religious emancipation is peculiarly interesting to us; for oftener do we boast of that than of any other article in our constitution, which tolerates all denominations of religion. We hold it to be the very best of these experiments in government which followed the Revolution of '76; and to us, it has long been a matter of exceeding surprise, why this distinction in the great charter of our rights, between a civil and religious obligation, now imitated by nearly all the Potentates of Europe, has not before this time been practised in England. In a country, from whose laws and institutions we have selected the wisest for our own, and which our young men are early taught to admire, for the many grains of popular influence they possess over those of all the other nations of Europe. Why cannot a citizen owe allegiance to the God of his own choice, and the state, at one and the same time? what liberal man will say he cannot? We here recognize two kinds of allegiance; the one to God, and the other to the Republic; and in like manner as we owe obedience to the laws of the land, because enacted by the administrative agents of the sovereign people, so do we owe obedience to the laws of God, or in other words, to a religion ordained by him to us in the light of reason, or by the wonderful mysteries of revelation. And for the reason that he who usurps the rights of the citizen is esteemed impertinent, and punished accordingly, ought public opinion to condemn any usurpation of a religious right to be impious and penal? The abstract opinions of a man, concerning any thing of theology, be they ever so absurd, so long as he obeys the laws of the land, and respects the purity of public morals, make him not the less a good citizen. This we can vouch for, when we say, that in the time of our trials, the Hebrew, the Protestant, and the Roman Catholic citizen, side by side, fought and saved this Republic; not for any ascendant religion, but for their homes, and the dear pledges of domestic love; for the honor of the Republic, and all its people; for its laws, and the benefit of its laws; for life, for liberty, and the very altars of one another.'

There is considerable eloquence, and great force of language in the claims made upon our sympathies for Ireland as every way worthy of consideration, especially when contrasted with that which proved so successful in behalf of suffering Greece.

'Do you not recollect the time? Sure, it is but a few months ago, and Greece was then the theme of all your tongues. Men ran up and down the streets, crying Greece, Greece, Greece. The school boy read his Xenophon with unusual pleasure; and scholars reviewed their classics. Matrons told their little ones the story of Epaminondas; and fair ladies sent their pin money to the Greek committees. The gray and hobbling aged, the grave and sprightly youth, the learned and unlearned—and the bigot, too, went into the temples of the Most High, and prayed for Greece. The mighty orators, in the halls of legislation, catching inspiration, from the enemy of Philip, rose in their places, and spoke for Greece. No one then said 'Greece shall not be free.' Warlike ships and food and raiment were sent over the waters to the beautiful Ægean; and even the iron-hearted sovereigns of Europe melted into sympathy, and warred for Greece. All Christendom was up with one voice declaring, that Greece must be aided—that the crescent should no longer flap over the cross—that the land of philosophy should not be the desolating murder-shop of the turbaned Turk! Who then heard of such things as breaches of neutrality and the like? We had not the Ottoman Porte to think of, nor did its anticipated, direful displeasure, haunt any of our sickly nerved old gentlemen, by day, or by night, in the form of a devilish ferocious fellow, with a long pair of shaggy mustaches and a prodigious Turkish scymitar, ready to behead the whole nation, at one fell swoop if we dared interfere between him and his subjects. No, Greece was oppressed, Greece was deprived of her rights, we felt for Greece, and we interfered for Greece. And wherefore should you, O! Americans, refuse to poor Ireland what you have done for Greece? Wherefore should not the same sympathies be awakened in your hearts? True, in Ireland the crescent is not flapping o'er the cross; yet there the cross is made to beat down the cross, and christians have been murdering christians for the *sake of the Lord!* True, Ireland is not the land of the school-men; nor was she inventress of the arts and philosophy; yet her people have improved on and embellished those things which were consecrated in the studies of Euclid, of Pythagoras, and in the Academia. If you tell me there is a fresh, bewitching originality in the character of the elder Greeks, that hold them up to be the models of after time; I will point you to the Irishman, in whom, there are striking casts of disposition, designating him in every age and clime. I will point you to his constitutional enthusiasm, to his proverbial hospitality, to his infinite humor, for which he is pre-eminent. The decided feature of Irish character is this enthusiasm; from which, I account for its conspicuous distinction, in all the provinces of labor, the arts, letters and philosophy.

Exertion without enthusiasm, or some stimulating motive, scarcely ever reaches those objects, exalted and difficult of attainment. The man warmed by an intense enthusiasm, fixes his eye on the prize, runs straight forward and takes it, while the little spirit, lagging in the rear, to pick up the golden apples, loses the race.'

Southern Literary Gazette n.s. 1 (July 1829): 83–85.

William Ellery Channing

This tribute to the Reverend Channing (1780–1842) shows Simms's ability to rise above faction. Channing, outspoken opponent of slavery and friend of the Transcendentalists, was a Boston Brahmin, a group which Simms rarely treated so magnanimously. Theodore Parker he called one of their "bright erratic stars . . . , a *mouvement* man, a progress man . . . [ranking] among that strange herd whom they dignify in that quarter with the name of transcendentalism." He concluded, "Our Southern topics . . . are usually calculated to make a monomaniac of the New England philosopher" (*SQR* 13 [April 1850]: 264). He later termed Transcendentalism "balderdash, and very bad balderdash at that" (*SQR* 17 [October 1852]: 544]. See also *SQR* 15 (April 1849): 260–61.

The nation has lost a strong man in William Ellery Channing. Whatever we in the South may think of his course on the subject of Slavery,—of its errors and its imprudence,—it must be admitted, we take for granted, that this venerable, and, in many respects, wise man, was governed by what he esteemed the purest and holiest purposes of humanity. We can forgive him his errors in this cause, and his injustice to us, in consideration of what was really noble, and intellectual, and worthy in his character. Without reasoning very closely, he yet reasoned profoundly, was a man of large and majestic vision, comprehensive thought, and earnest, penetrating enthusiasm. His style of writing was equally pure and forcible. His papers on Milton and Napoleon, are among the best models of American taste in composition. With the smoothness and sweetness of Irving, he possessed a strength, a force and fluency, to which Irving has no pretensions. That, thinking boldly on most subjects—launching out ever into new tracks of thought, he should, sometimes, suffer the audacity of his genius to lead him into false paths, and by false lights,—the *ignes fatui* of imagination, rather than the broad steady rays of its polar orb,—we can easily understand, and, as easily forgive. Aiming at the broadest sense of human liberty, it was, perhaps natural, that a mind like that of Channing, equally zealous and adventurous, should seize too hastily upon a subtle principle, and too earnestly pursue it, heedless of its thousand variations and multiplied and changing forms. Such we conceive to have been his mistake on the subject of Slavery—suffering himself to be confounded with words to the neglect of substances, and regardless, in consequence of any thing in a condition but its name. Hereafter, we shall endeavour to impart to our readers, some clearer idea of his intellectual stature, by a careful examination of his writings. We presume that a new and complete edition will follow, from the Boston press, his melancholy demise, which will give us a fitting occasion, to pay this becoming tribute, as well to his memory, as to a portion of the noblest specimens of moral and philosophical contemplation, which have ever found utterance in our country. At present our simple duty is to state an event which the literary community must every where deplore. A rich voice, that was equally copious and harmonious, equally strong and flowing, is hushed on earth forever. Did we set a proper estimate upon a great mind, this would bring a pang to the whole world's full heart.—As it is, while suffering much, it will only partially feel. The following sweet and graceful hymn, by Bryant, was sung at the recent celebration, in the Church of the Messiah, New-York, of the rites commemorative of his death.

> While yet the harvest fields are white,
> And few the tolling reapers stand,
> Called from his task before the night,
> We miss the mightiest of the band.
>
> Oh thou, of strong yet gentle mind!
> Thy thrilling voice shall plead no more
> For truth, for freedom, and mankind;
> The lesson of thy life is o'er.
>
> But thou, in brightness far above
> The fairest dream of human thought,
> Before the Seat of Power and Love,
> Art with the Truth that thou hast sought.

Magnolia n.s. 1 (October 1842): 327.

John Greenleaf Whittier's *Poems*

In his introduction to *Views and Reviews, First Series,* Holman generalized that Young America lavishly praised Whittier, and Simms echoed them (xxvi). Holman, however, must not have known the following review in which Simms recanted any earlier praise. He called Whittier's verse "very frigid" in continuing his critique of New England poetry as characteristically cold, abstract, and passionless. Simms said that heretofore he had not read Whittier for himself and his northern friends had misled him. In an 1845 review, Simms again resented Whittier's "abolition poems" but found that his verse, even though preachy and sadly running toward didacticism, also included an occasional "fierce lyric" (*S&W* 2 [November 1845]: 348–49). Simms again discussed Whittier's abolitionism in his *Literary Recreations and Miscellanies* in the Charleston *Mercury* of 8 February 1855. By 1843 it was clear that Simms already had serious questions about the views and abilities of Young America. Simms collected this previously unrecorded review in his "Reviews and Criticisms" (SCL).

Lays of My Home, and Other Poems. **By John G. Whittier. Boston: William D. Ticknor. 1843.**

Mr. Whittier is the writer of verses which it would be proper, in customary parlance, to describe as respectable. But in truth they rank in that class, which, we are told by unquestionable authority, is unendurable by gods, men or columns. The sin of mediocrity is at their doors. With tolerable smoothness of flow, and occasional energy of expression, Mr. Whittier's verses are distinguished by nothing so much as their wondrous frigidity. He is called the Quaker poet, and his poetry is very pink of broad-brimism. It lacks, very equally, tenderness and felicity. Its chief, or only, merits, are plain good sense, general correctness, and a very fair and commendable appreciation of morals and propriety. Beyond this, the volume is a blank. It possesses neither originality nor warmth,—unless, indeed, when the author falls into a fury (as he does) with Virginia, and for no better reason that we can see, but because our very excellent senior sister thought proper to adopt certain measures to prevent philanthropic persons from the Bay State—Quakers, in all probability,—from stealing and carrying back the slaves which they (or their ancestors) had previously sold her. These proceedings of Virginia do make our poet wrothy, and thus enable him to display—what otherwise we should scarcely have supposed him to possess—a due proportion of the *genus irritabile.* To confess a truth, we have been quite confounded by the perusal of this volume. Giving due credit to the lavish tongues of certain of the critics, and forgetting the monstrous penchant on the part of our Northern brethren, to mistake all their own geese as swans, we took for granted—in our own ignorance of Mr. Whittier's writings,—that he was a genuine son of Phœbus,—blasted, in very tolerable degree, with the poetic fire. But this volume throws cold water on our former faith. It proves that our author's claim to the divine afflatus is exceedingly small. He makes verses, it is true,—very tolerable verses, as the world goes,—but sadly deficient in glow and inspiration. We quote, as a very fair sample of his volume, the first piece in the collection. It is good rhyme enough, as the reader will see for himself, but very frigid, very monotonous and very common-place.

The Merrimack

"The Indians speak of a beautiful river, far
  to the South, which they call Merrimack."
    Sieur de Monts, 1604.

Stream of my fathers! sweetly still
The sunset rays thy valley fill;
Pour'd slantwise down the long defile,
Wave, wood and spire beneath them smile.
I see the winding Powow fold
The green hill in its belt of gold,
And following down its wavy line,
Its sparkling waters blend with thine.
There's not a tree upon thy side,
Nor rock, which thy returning tide
As yet hath left abrupt and stark
Above they evening water-mark;
No calm cove with its rocky hem,
No isle whose emerald swells begem
Thy broad, smooth current; not a sail
Bowed to the freshening ocean gale;
No small boat with its busy oars,
Nor gray wall sloping to thy shores;
Nor farm house with its maple shade,
Or rigid poplar colonnade,
But lies distinct and full in sight,
Beneath this gush of sunset light.

Centuries ago, that harbor-bar,
Stretching its length of foam afar,
And Salisbury's beach of shining sand,
And yonder island's wave-smoothed strand;
Saw the adventurer's tiny sail,
Flit, stooping from the Eastern gale;
And o'er these woods and waters broke
The cheer from Britain's hearts of oak,
As brightly on the voyager's eye,
Weary of forest, sea and sky,
Breaking the dull, continuous wood,
The Merrimack roll'd down his flood;

Mingling that clear, pellucid brook,
Which channels vast Agiochook,
When spring-time's sun and shower unlock
The frozen fountains of the rock,
And more abundant waters given,
From that pure lake, the "Smile of Heaven;
Tributes from vale and mountain side—
With ocean's dark, eternal tide.

Southern Quarterly Review 4 (October 1843): 516–17.

G. P. R. James's *Arabella Stuart*

Simms reviewed the chivalrous and prolific James throughout his career. In *Magnolia* n.s. 1 (July 1842): 53–56, he wrote a balanced essay on *The Jacquerie* and *Morley Ernstein,* in which he called James a "humble imitator" of Scott, but nowhere close to him in merit. Simms concluded that his main gift was as a storyteller, but otherwise "Mr. James has always seemed to us a dull man—a mere pen-peddler." In a review collected in "Reviews and Criticisms," Simms deemed *Rose D'Albret* "of average merit among his labors" and concluded that James, being no genius, "has not the resources of Bulwer and D'Israeli—but in the telling of a tale he is quite as good as either. He seldom attempts more. Nothing can be more insufferably tedious than his drawling didactics. We may add that his lovers, though very good persons in their way, are yet very silly, and do very silly things." Simms remarked that James was better in treating French characters than English, because the latter were dominated by "phlegmatic resolve and reserve" (*Orion* 4 [August 1844]: 296). Simms's notice of *Dark Scenes of History* was favorable without qualification (*SQR,* 13 n.s. 1 [April 1850] 237). In his review of *The Commissioner,* he again considered James to be "a *raconteur* simply. . . . But nobody looks to him for satire, or humour, or wit, or imagination, in any department. . . . Is it possible that, after writing more volumes than Lope de Vega, he needs to have this told him?" (*SQR* n.s. 4 [July 1851]: 267). When James was appointed British consul in Virginia in 1852, they became friends. When James turned to American settings with *Ticonderoga,* Simms felt he "lacked confidence in his American resources" (Charleston *Mercury,* 29 December 1854 and 10 January 1855). Simms also noticed *A History of the Life of Richard Coeur-de-Lion* (Charleston *Mercury,* 12 May 1855) and *The Old*

Dominion (Charleston *Mercury,* 22 May 1856). He corresponded with James in March 1857 (*Letters,* 6: 175). Simms collected this newly discovered piece in "Reviews and Criticisms" (SCL).

Arabella Stuart. A Romance of English History. By G.P.R. James, Esq. New York: Harper & Brothers. 1844.

We suspect that, for the present at least, the day of the historical romance is pretty well over. The taste for it naturally expires with the want of the necessary food. Not that there are not historical romances enough, daily issued from the press; but these seem not of the true antique fashion—they lack the genuine flavor—they smack not of that oily taste which came with the thing in former days—they lack the soul, the freshness of old times, and if they recall the commodity of which they bear the name, it is only to remind us of what we possess no longer. They wear the outer shape alone—it is the carcass only that is presented to us:—

> "The wine of life is drawn and the mere lees,
>   Is left this vault to brag of."

There is a day for historical romances as for every thing else. They were a novelty in letters for a season, and were duly honored while something of a novelty. They were not less legitimate because they were novel. It was indeed only while they were novel that they were legitimate. So with Byron's tales of vehemence and passion, and Scott's pittoresque ballads of feudal chivalry. A master hand first opens the way, lays bare the unsuspected vein, and the task of pursuing it is easy for the inferior laborer. The very fact that the performance has become easy is a sufficient reason why it should no longer excite wonder.

Arabella Stuart is not exactly a subject for the novelist. It would suit the poet better. Its facts are too well known—the restraints upon the novelist are too great and imperative. A great master hates such fetters. He requires of history but a few glimpses. The moment the narrative becomes full, and the record is copious of details, he stops. His privileges are derived from the meagreness of the chronicle. His wings grow out of the infirmities and deficiencies of history. Where the historian grows blind, he receives light. Where the historian trembles to advance, he takes courage. He shapes the dismembered fragments into forms and fancies of his own. And in the exercise of a creative and endowing faculty, he achieves an object equally wondrous in the sight of others and delightful to his own.

The story of Arabella Stuart left Mr. James with few such privileges. It was written to his hands. He had but to elaborate a known narrative, to spice it with occasional sentiments, and to throw in a few extra elements of passion and fear, and jealousy, and his romance was finished. The very fact that he seems pleased with his work—that he has danced in his fetters without misgiving—is proof against his genius. The slight addition which he has made to history, in the persons of his old knight, Sir Harry West, and his Italian girl, Ida Mars, are proofs of the little strain his labours made upon his genius.

Mr. James is a most tedious writer. His common-places are utterly unendurable. Take the first chapter of this novel, for example, and remark upon the dilations, whether of sentiment or description, in which truisms are labored for no obvious purpose unless to make it appear that the writer does some thinking in his way. When a novelist begins by describing minutely an old building, the grounds about it, the servants, the officers, the stud, you take for granted that the chief business of the work is done there, and a close knowledge of these particulars are necessary to your proper comprehension of what is to follow. When this is not the case, for what the deuse, you ask, are we troubled with all these nice details.

If Mr. James has to tell you of some long distant time—say two hundred and forty years—he is at some pains to tell you that "it is a long time to look back to"—and yet he says gravely, "the men and women of those days are much the same creatures that we see moving around us at present," etc. Then he exclaims—"Two hundred and forty years! What a lapse of time it seems"—and then follows another long stretch of common-places, the most ordinary of all human reflections, truisms without depth, and sentiments without even the charm of a graceful expression. If an old bachelor hurling his bowl at the pins, succeeds in tumbling them over—he says, like an old fool as he is—"Thus it is with human projects," etc., and so on, with such miserable gammon, to the end of the chapter.

It is not denied that Mr. James makes usually a book that will keep attention wakeful. This is the very summit of his powers as a novelist. His skill in combination is very good. The parts of his story are combined with patience and method. He is a tolerable literary joiner. His incidents are dove-tailed in proper order, and his fabric hangs together with a praiseworthy consistency of parts. For the reader who seeks amusement merely—who asks for nothing but to be kept from sleep—this is perhaps enough. But this is all. Mr. James rarely offers more. His invention is as common-place as his reflections. He has no fancy and less imagination. You are never made to rise in the contemplation of the subject—you are never made to feel that your author sees farther than yourself. He never requires you to lift your eyes to his elevation. He is a pleasant companion, but no teacher. He has no thoughts that compel you to exercise your own—no speculations that lead you from your world, into that vaster one over which he sways. This is the power of the original genius, which makes you follow in your own spite, and shows you empires which afterwards brighten in your dreams.

Mr. James is something of an artist. He is moreover a man of good taste and a proper understanding. He is well read in history. His knowledge of French

History is certainly very considerable, though the critics of France sneer at the uses to which he puts his knowledge. They are not prepared to recognize the felicity or truthfulness of his pourtrayals; and, indeed, how could this be expected of a citizen of Great Britain. We might as well expect truth and correct seeing from an English traveller in the United States, as from a British novelist when his theme is Jean Crapaud.

Mr. James, with all his cleverness, is not a man of genius. He lacks the creative power. He cannot group the unmalleable material and work it into new forms. He has none of the Promethean skill, though he sometimes strives desperately with a sort of Promethean daring. His fire is not caught from heaven, or if it is, it is the heaven of Mahomet—a sort of midway elevation which is occasionally fortunate in the reception of some straggling rays from far superior altars. This *Arabella Stuart,* which Mr. James thinks his best book, is a sufficient proof of what we say. It is a laborerd, not an inspired performance. Its mere external aspect, may remind us of better things from the hands of the masters. There is the shape, indeed, but it does not live. If it breathes it scarcely speaks. It is uninformed by the living soul, and glowing spirit of true genius.

Orion 4 (May 1844): 147–49.

Frances Anne Kemble Butler's *Poems*

This review recounts how Kemble "carried our heart away" when she played "the sweetest Juliet" and the most inspired Bianca. Simms was more gracious than Robert Browning, who found *Poems* "surprisingly poor" (Bell, *Major Butler's Legacy,* 286). Simms wrote one of his longest and most important review essays on Kemble's *A Year of Consolation* in *SQR* 12 (July 1847): 191–236. Here he commented variously on marriage, the roles of man and woman, the artist in society, and moral progress. Of the creative artist, he wrote, no doubt with autobiographical inference, that those who "labour in the imaginative arts, are those to whom sympathy is most precious. Their whole life is a struggle to be loved;—for what, after all, is the triumph which they seek, but the affections which they solicit with song, and at the frequent sacrifice of most other objects for which the worldling strives and sighs. They study and toil in secret, long days and weary nights, with brain always excited, under the impulses of a blood which, in the case of the imaginative mind, almost always takes this direction" (217). Frances Kemble had married Pierce Butler (of the South Carolina–Georgia Butlers) in 1834, and in 1845, after a stormy relationship, they separated. In

1849 they divorced. Miss Sedgwick is Catharine Maria Sedgwick. See the review of Sedgwick's *Home* (p. 73).

***Poems.* By Frances Anne Butler. Philadelphia: John Pennington. 1844.**

We have not the heart to deal unkindly with this volume. We have very pleasant recollections of its author, when, as Fanny Kemble, she first landed on our shores—the sweetest Juliet, the most inspired and inspiring of all Biancas. With admirable natural endowments for the stage, a quick intelligent perception of character—a feeling sense of the touching, the tender and the sublime—a well tuned and tutored voice, and an action, the grace and dignity of which were, perhaps, quite as much an instinct as an acquisition, she carried our heart away, with all the rest. We shall not forget those days, nor her former, in her present part. We dare not say that she is as good a poet as we found her an actress; but we will say that we believe her heart to be much more in the latter than the former character. We are pleased to think so. It is not so grateful a reflection to believe that she is not so happy in the more natural performance. Her song is almost uniformly a sad one. Her muse educes the melancholy from sights and sounds which are otherwise apt to fill young bosoms with less sombre sentiments. The star-light brings her thoughts of death and wo. Moon-light and moon-lit waters inspire sadness as well as tenderness; and there is a monotonous chaunt of sorrow in these pages, which should not be suffered to rest upon the souls of the young, the beautiful and highly endowed. The natural language of the young poet, is that, certainly, of melancholy, but it is melancholy of a pleasing description, and does not necessarily lead to lamentations. It is not to be encouraged. Such spirits are liable to frequent depressions. The moral nature, deriving much of its colour from the physical, is very apt to put on the caprices of cloud and climate, and wear them as a garment. This makes the curse of fugitive poetry, which is too apt to be the language of weariness rather than feeling, and which certainly produces a sad sense of weariness in the reader. We find too much of this sort of inspiration in the volume of Fanny Kemble—Mrs. Butler, we should say—though the first name sounds more naturally in our ears. Her verses are quite too occasional, and they share too much of the casual influence of the moment. Now, if she is ever to succeed, it is as an artist. Her "Star of Seville" was not successful, we believe, and her tragedy, which is not by us—*Francis the First*,—was, as far as we remember, very faulty in its plan. But we commend her once more to this field, in which we are of opinion that she may yet reap greener laurels than any of the past. Of the general merits of the book before us, we need but say that they are those of a graceful and well tutored mind, a lively fancy, and a rather too morbid condition of the feelings. Here is a pretty sonnet, with the truth of which we have no quarrel, unless it is with the thirteenth line, from which, we take it, Miss Sedgwick herself, to whom the volume is inscribed, might also dissent.

Woman's Love.

A maiden meek, with solemn steadfast eyes,
Full of eternal constancy and faith,
And smiling lips, thro' whose soft portal sighs
Truth's holy voice, with every balmy breath,
So journeys she along life's crowded way.
Keeping her soul's sweet counsel thro' all night;
Nor pomp, nor vanity lead her astray,
Nor aught that men call dazzling, fair or bright;

For pity, sometimes, doth she pause, and say
Those whom she meeteth mourning, for her heart
Knows well in suffering how to bear its part.
Patiently lives she through each dreary day,
Looking with little hope until the morrow;
And still she walketh hand in hand with sorrow.

Such verses teach sad philosophies indeed and do, as we are pleased to think, some injustice to life, which is not all so hopeless. It is the error of poets, having strong feelings, to generalize too largely from a single life, and possibly from a single period of suffering in life. That "joy cometh in the morning," should have been the subject of a second sonnet following just after the preceding. Here is another ditty of the same doleful school.

Lines for Music.

Loud wind, strong wind, where art thou blowing?
Into the air, the viewless air,
To be lost there—
There am I blowing.

Clear wave, swift wave, where art thou flowing?
Unto the sea, the boundless sea,
To be whelmed there—
There am I flowing.

Young life, swift life, where art thou going?
Down to the grave, the loathsome grave,
To moulder there—
There am I going.

Now these lines not only fail to give us the whole truth, but we should be at a loss to know in what circle their music would be agreeable. They would certainly overcast the young assembly as with a thunder cloud, and there were no kindly philosophy in that. Besides, we are constrained to say, that, as poetry, the sample is not to be commended. And what are we to say to these other—

Lines for Music

Oh, sunny Love!
Crown'd with fresh-flow'ring May,
Breath like the Indian clove,
Eyes like the dawnless day:
Oh, sunny Love!

Oh, fatal Love!
Thy robe is nightshade all,
With gloomy cypress wove,
Thy kiss is bitter gall,
Oh, fatal Love!

Mournful is it, indeed, very mournful, that young heart, and sweetly endowed mind should pour forth such gloomy strains. Let us hope that they fall rather from the fancy—an erring one we must say—than the soul and spirit of the singer. Here is a little song,—tender and pretty—but shadowed, like every page in this volume, with a most unhappy gloom.

Song

Never, oh, never more! shall I behold
Thy form so fair:
Or loosen from its braids the rippling gold
Of thy long hair.

Never, oh, never more! shall I be blest
By thy voice low,
Or kiss while thou art sleeping on my breast,
Thy marble brow.

Never, oh, never more! shall I inhale
Thy fragrant sighs
Or gaze, with fainting soul, upon the veil
Of thy bright eyes.

Orion 4 (August 1844): 291–92.

Literature in Ancient Rome

In contrasting Greek and early Roman literature, Simms also had an eye on his own day and the problems in creating a viable literature. The reason Rome did not have a literature early, he declared, was that it lacked the spiritual. Rome was too solidly utilitarian and materialistic, putting its energies into building roads, aqueducts, and other practical, progressive undertakings. Rome too lacked proper "veneration" (a key word in Simms) of both the past and the spiritual—in a too man-centered and now-centred society, a theme he again sounded five years later in "The Southern Convention" in part 2 of this volume. Literature was not considered a pursuit for any but the lowly. Simms was thus also clearly critiquing his own rawly materialistic American culture. This essay reveals close knowledge of Barthold Georg Niebuhr (1776–1831), Thomas Babington Macaulay (1800–1859), and Montesquieu (1689–1755) and their works on the ancients. The influence of Homer, Sophocles, and Æschylus remained pronounced to the end of Simms's career. See, for example, "The Lions of Mycenæ," published in 1870 (Simms, *Selected Poems*, 297–300).

The long prevalence of the Latin, as the written and spoken language of the educated classes in Europe, its constant employment in the services of the Roman Catholic Church, and its connection with the earliest developed of modern tongues as their root or principal element, are circumstances which have conspired to secure for it and its literature more general attention than has ever been devoted to the Greek. Moreover, the Latin had been for ages in the exclusive possession of all the honoured seats of learning, when the Greek was slowly and painfully introduced from the Eastern Empire; and being of easier acquisition and a more obvious practical utility than its new rival, it has always had other strong influences operating in its favour than those first mentioned. The general familiarity with the Latin, thus to be accounted for, and the consequent study and admiration of its numerous classics, have frequently led to a comparison of Greek and Latin Literature, in which, the latter has been elevated to an equal place of honour with the former. And thus, many have been seduced into a belief, that arts and letters were fostered and encouraged at Rome, by as generous a cultivation and as cordial a patronage, as were bestowed upon them in Greece. Yet no opinion can be further removed from truth;—constant difficulties and obstacles were thrown in the path of Roman Literature, the soil was unfertile, the culture scanty and injudicious, and the ground overgrown with briars and brambles, and other noxious weeds, through which, it had slowly to struggle into light and existence. It ought, accordingly, rather to be matter of wonder that the Latin language was enriched with so many treasures of intellect as it could undoubtedly boast, than that it should have fallen far below the riches of the Greek, from the baneful operation of so many unfavorable circumstances as retarded its birth, checked its development, and stunted its fair proportions. What the difficulties were, which Literature had to encounter at Rome, may be estimated, in some degree, from a few slight and rapid observations upon the condition of literature in Ancient Rome.

It is probable, that no rude people was ever yet so thoroughly rude and barbarous, as to have been utterly destitute, before any acquaintance with letters, of all songs and ballads, to serve as a substitute for historical tradition, and to kindle a generous emulation in the breasts of the living, by honouring the gallant deeds of the past, and celebrating the virtues of the heroes who had departed. The Bards of the Druids, and the Minstrels of the old Caledonians are sufficiently well known—the crags of Plinlimmon and the wilds of Morven echoed in days of yore to the note of the harper, and the voices of song. The rhymes of Roncesvalles—the spirit stirring story of the Cid—the dark Sagas of Icelandic Mythology,—the epic fire of the Niebelungenlied, furnish abundant examples in the history of modern nations; and if we go to remote periods, the Hindoos, the Persians, the Arabians, will afford a like illustration of the truth of the supposition: or, we may draw evidence of the same practice among people, of whom there is a more general knowledge. Many passages of Scripture will indicate its existence among the Jews: and we may discover it among the Greeks in the earliest times, by the traditions of Linus, Musæus, Orpheus, and Amphion, by an occasional allusion to it in *The Iliad,* and continual mention of it in *The Odyssey.* It seems, however, scarcely just, to introduce the Greeks as any illustration of this point, for the purest spirit of poesy was so closely wedded to all the developments of their intellectual faculties, that we can hardly conceive their existence without the accompaniment of song, and may regard them as forming a peculiar and honorable exception, in this respect, to the customary career of all other nations. But these facts would naturally lead us to the inference of a like condition among the early Romans, without the addition of any positive testimony to that effect, and may strengthen and confirm the scanty traditions of an early ballad poetry in Rome, to be gleaned from the writings of Cicero and the eloquent roll of Livy. From them and from other authors, we learn that it was long a custom in the old patrician families to have the praises of their ancestors and the poetic legends of the good old time sung in their halls and banquet rooms, at once for their gratification and improvement. It was an old custom, borrowed in all probability, from those Etruscans, to whom the Romans were indebted for so many of their best institutions and so much of their manners, to place round their *atria* the images of their distinguished ancestors, to be at once an honour to the dead and the pride of the living. These were their genealogical tables—these were their patents of nobility. And when a voice was added to the dumb and dusty images of their great progenitors by the habitual song of those antique ballads, which recorded their glory, the living had everything to inspirit them, to stimulate them to like deeds of renown, so that they might transmit, with new accretions of honour at each remove, that hereditary fame which had given to themselves power, place, and distinction among a highly aristocratic people. The origin and long continuance of the pleasing custom, as well as its existence, are thus accounted for and confirmed. These ballads, at first the private possession of the noble families of Rome, then chanted, it may be, by the ragged minstrel at the corner of the streets, or by the military companies over their watch-fires in the camp, at length became imbedded in the early histories of the nation, and the traces of them, have, at this late day, been detected in the flowing periods of their greatest historian. Indeed, Roman story, during the three first centuries of the existence of the City, is only a noble cyclic poem formed from these ballads, rhapsodically, and not always very dexterously linked together. Perizonius first discovered, in a dull age, the traces of them in the smooth cadences of Livy, Niebuhr proved the truth of the hypothesis, and built upon it the most ingenious and pleasing portion of his truly great work, and the brilliant Macaulay has made it the foundation of those spirited rhapsodies, which he has given to the world under the name of *Lays of Ancient Rome.*

The subjects of these ballads seem to have been principally confined to very remote periods of Roman History. The story of the foundation of the City—the legends of the Kings—the wars of Porsenna—the gallant deeds of the heroic Fabii—the invasion of the Gauls—the greatness of Camillus—the melancholy tales of the Decemvirs—appear to have formed the ordinary burden of their national songs. To these must be added the chaunts used in the services of their temples—the wild strains of the Sabian Priests—the rude hymns of the Fratres Arvales—and other 'psalmody' connected with the ministrations of their religion. But, after the burning of the City, sterner times and domestic broils, less favourable to the development of poetic talent awaited the Romans. Wars at home and abroad, dissensions within, and danger without, the strife of the privileged and the oppressed, the grasping avarice of the rich, the pinching misery of the poor, the engrossing pursuits of active life, the all-absorbing interest of political contention, the urgent demands upon their time of the Forum and the Camp, weaned away their thoughts and their affections from the siren strains of the Muses. Thenceforward, the Romans were busily engaged in doing deeds worthy of eternal remembrance; they had neither the time nor the disposition to record them; and the remark of Sallust on this point was as true as it was profound. Long centuries passed in the turmoil of stirring excitement before Scipio Africanus, towards the close of the Punic wars, introduced or revived the long forgotten taste for Literature, and endeavoured to add to the acknowledged glories of Roman arms, the more enduring and more peaceful fame of letters. Some few writers, probably over-estimated by subsequent generations from their rarity, had, indeed, preceded this attempt of Scipio; but the absence of all Literature at Rome was most obvious at the time when the undertaking was commenced.

In the long lapse of ages, which had intervened between Camillus and Scipio, the poetic element in the Roman character had either died out, from the want of fuel to keep the sacred flame alive, or had been violently extinguished by the hereditary devotion to pursuits, wholly foreign to the quiet seductions of the unwarlike Muse. The circumstances of the City, and of the citizens, during the period that had passed, had not been such as to foster or permit the growth of those qualities which give birth, and add grace and vigour to the more delicate productions of the intellect. A sterner nature than of old had been impressed upon the Roman mind, and the Roman heart had undergone that silent and gradual petrifaction, which rendered it senseless to all the beautiful creations of the intellect. The abysm of hebetude to which the Romans had been reduced, in all matters of taste, may be estimated from the well known speech of Mummius, to those who were entrusted with the transportation of the finest paintings of Corinth.

In the debates of the Senate House, the Romans had learnt the manly arts of Statesmanship and Legislation. In the angry quarrels of the Forum and the Comitia, they had acquired an habitual familiarity with the employment of popular oratory, a practical insight into the workings of the feelings amongst congregated masses, and an amazing tact in the management of the machinery by which they were to be moved. In the legal disputes before the Praetor and the tribunals, they had been taught the whole theory of jurisprudence and the interpretation of the laws. In the exercises of the Campus Martius, and the graver duties of the campaign, they had attained to that excellence in the arts of war, which gave them the dominion of the world. But none of these things was calculated to resuscitate the old poetic feeling, to give them a taste for those studies over which, the Muses presided, or to qualify them for appreciating or enjoying the pleasures to be derived from frequent and copious draughts of the pure waters of Helicon. The Roman might be a warrior, a statesman, a legislator, a jurist, a tactician, a plausible speaker, but there were no influences to inspire him with that deep poetry of the heart—that enthusiastic reverence and love for the ideal, which must form the basis of all high and genuine national literature. This is the more worthy of notice, as it is to be feared that the existence of analogous circumstances in these United States may retard, and, if timely care be not taken, may preclude the growth of any national literature here.

The religion of the Roman, and his mythology, were not qualified like those of Greece, to warm the heart, to kindle the imagination, to excite enthusiasm, to compel the soul to give utterance to its fervid conceptions, in the wild exuberance of lyric rhapsody. There were no lyric poets at Rome—Catullus and Horace—a spurious offspring from the Greeks, are the only names that could be mentioned. Quintilian deems Horace the only Roman lyrist, whose works were worthy of perusal—forgetting altogether Catullus, who was, in every respect, infinitely his superior. Yet, neither of these can be compared with their great Greek rivals, Niebuhr's opinion to the contrary, in the case of Catullus, notwithstanding. They had to contend with the iron rigidity of the Latin tongue; a difficulty, of which, Lucretius and Cicero continually complain. Where is the Roman Pindar? Where the names that they can array against Alcæus, Simonides, Anacreon, Sappho, and the rest of the glorious nine of Greece? What has Latin Literature to boast as an equivalent to the sweet and majestic choruses of Æschylus, Sophocles, and Euripides whose strains enchant, and ravish the soul in the labyrinthine wilderness of harmony? The songs of Greece were the noblest adoration of their gods. The Roman had no divinities presiding over literature, whom he could worship or propitiate by its cultivation. He had no Pallas, no Aphrodite, no Bacchus, no Apollo, no Muses, to render the pursuit of letters an act of positive veneration. These were all subsequently introduced from Greece, by the successors of Scipio in the task of *Hellenizing* the Roman taste. And, in the absence of these, he had no other stimulants to excite him to an earnest and sedulous devotion to literary pleasures. The atmosphere of poetry which hung around Greece, and peopled with bright etherial dreams, the hill, the valley, and the stream, giving to each its own peculiar divinity, never existed at Rome. The Romans had no Naiads, no Oreads, no Dryads, no Nymphs,—nothing which might fire an imagination, chilled by the bickerings of the Forum and the noisy turbulence of the Comitia. Their religion was cold, human, unimpassioned, artificial, at once uninspiring and uninspired. We brood over the glorious ruins of Greece with the feeling, that some portion of the old divinity lingers round them still, and sanctifies in their decay the relics which had been sacred in their prime. We wander amidst the shattered fragments of Rome, we witness the overthrow of the mighty works of man's hands, we are filled with the conviction of wonderful greatness and extraordinary power in those who had raised them, and are solemnly affected by the melancholy contrast between the present and the past; but the whispers of no celestial visitants breathe through the matted ivy and tangled weeds, which cling around the crumbling piles. Greece was a dream of heaven—Rome the colossal creation of man.

The absence of all art at Rome, in the earlier portion of her history, clearly attests the absence too of that artistic spirit, which, if existent, would not have suffered the defect to remain so long unsupplied. The poverty of the old Romans, their frugal habits, their sanctimonious avarice, their residence, principally on their country farms, may, in some measure, account for the continuance of this want; but they render the fact more obvious by explaining it. Much of Grecian excellence in art may be attributed to the beautiful forms of their idolatry—to the paintings and statues of their divinities, and to the architectural embellishments of their temples. But in those ages when the Roman character was moulded—and no one need be reminded how soon it hardened into stone—their gods were all invisible and bodiless powers, the rude block that stood for Terminus, being, perhaps, the only exception, if it can be deemed such. They were worshipped without the intervention of painting or sculpture; and those means, which, in Greece, would have been devoted to the erection of splendid fanes, were more profitably employed at Rome, in the construction of their imperishable roads, their vast aqueducts, and other stupendous works of public utility. In that day, grace, beauty, art, would not merely have been starved at Rome, but they would not even have received the cold tribute and scanty consolation of praise.

The same feelings and the same influences, which generate excellence in the plastic arts, give birth and encouragement to literature: and these different productions of the genius and imagination usually flourish or decay together. The age of Pericles, which has been immortalized by the fame of Thucydides and Sophocles, boasted of the works of Phidias and the erection of the Parthenon; the rule of Augustus was distinguished by the chaste proportions of the Pantheon, and the noble conception of the Laocoon, as well as by the works of Virgil, Horace, and Livy: the times of Leo X, are illumined by the triumphs of Michael Angelo, Bramante and Raphael, not less than by the verse of Ariosto and Tasso: the days of Elizabeth point to Inigo Jones, and that brilliant galaxy in which Shakspeare and Spenser were conspicuous: and the Georgian Era was ennobled by the great works of Canova, Thorwaldsen, and Chantrey, together with the splendid creations of Byron, Coleridge and Shelley, and the glory of so many other names which begun with stars, the heaven which has scarcely yet faded from our view. The paralysis of art, at Rome, was thus naturally, if not necessarily linked with the absence of that artistic spirit in other departments of human knowledge, which gives excellence and beauty to the master-pieces of literature. And the extent to which this want prevailed, may be inferred from the fact that, though the necessities of public life rendered the faculty of public speaking an ordinary accomplishment, it was not until the days of the Gracchi, subsequently, to the times of Scipio, that oratory could be said to exist at Rome as an art, or that any oration had been delivered worthy of being remembered in the history of Latin Literature. Previous to this, there might have been occasional bursts of eloquence, but no oratory—properly so called. Even this department of letters, in all times so necessary, and in after times so common, was purely an exotic—it was an off-shoot and scion of the Greek: and, without such splendid exemplars as Isocrates and Demosthenes, the public places of Rome might never have been ennobled by the flowing ease of Hortensius, the martial impetuosity and fire of Caesar, or the dignity, the grace, and the exuberance of Cicero.

To this enumeration of circumstances adverse to literature at Rome, two more remain to be added—the amusements of the people, and the class to which authorship was then almost entirely limited. The earliest records of Greece attest the existence of frequent poetic contests of that chosen home of all that most adorns the human intellect. The legendary contest between Homer and Hesiod, in which the latter is said to have borne off the palm; the more apocryphal fables of the rivalry of Marsyas and Pan, of Midas and Apollo, and other detractors of the gods, bear witness to this. We know, moreover, that the rhapsodies of Homer and the Cyclic Poets were sung in the cities of Greece on certain festival days, by minstrels, emulous of each other's powers; that the victors were publicly crowned, and probably honoured, with more substantial rewards of merit. And we are assured from the writings of Plato that this custom continued still to exist in his days. The dithyrambic and the lyric poets of Greece contended, in like manner, for the prize of victory. A bare allusion to the tale of Pindar and Corinna will be sufficient: nor will it be necessary to do more than mention the proud rivalries of the Tragic and Comic Poets of Athens. In Rome there was nothing analogous to all this. The Circensian Games and the shows of Gladiators were interchanged with the less reprehensible sports of the Campus Martius, as the sole recreations of the Romans, after the fatigues of the Forum or the duties of the field. Their tastes were thus not merely distracted from literary amusements, but their thoughts and their feelings were habitually diverted into a channel, which bore them ever further and further away from such pleasures, and, in a great degree, unfitted them for their appreciation, and precluded their enjoyment. What charm could song have for that people, which was wont to hang in ecstasy over the sights of the Circus, or to gloat with delight over the barbarous and bloody spectacles of the Amphi-theatre? From the fierce struggles of infuriate wild beasts, and the legalized butchery of their fellow men in the public arena, they could not hope to turn for gratification to those secluded glades of the Muses, when the charm to be experienced is calmly pure, and wholly alien to those baser passions which they had been but lately fostering and indulging. Thus, the amusements of Rome, equally with its active pursuits, were calculated to preclude the existence of a refined literary taste, and to prevent the growth of any national literature. The want of that solace which is to be derived from the cultivation of letters, was not felt among such a people, surrounded by such influences: and literature did not spring up spontaneously, because the necessity for it was never fully recognized.

We cannot be surprised if, under such circumstances as are here exhibited, the wealthy, the powerful, and the noble should neglect entirely, the cultivation of letters as an art beneath them, and thus, strange as it might otherwise appear, we have no reason to wonder that Literature should have been left in the hands of freedmen and slaves. With the exception of a few meagre annalists, the earliest authors of Latin Literature were of this class. And though Scipio Africanus and his friend Lælius amused themselves with literary pursuits, they thought it beneath their dignity, as consulars, to publish their productions in their own name, or to claim the honours, which they might have merited. Accordingly, they suffered the renown acquired by them, to settle on the brows of their familiar, Terence—a man originally of the lowest condition of life, and of servile birth. Even Cicero, in his day, thought it necessary to apologize for his devotion to philosophical recreations, and most of his treatises commence with an excuse for his wasting time in the humble labour of composition. Sallust, in like manner, commences one of his remaining works with a similar defence of himself and his occupation. It was not till Julius Caesar and Augustus, the first Emperors of Rome, had, by their own compositions, set the fashion amongst the crowd of adulators, that authorship became respectable at Rome, or was regarded as a liberal employment. In the time of Scipio, to which this paper is chiefly devoted, the Romans had scarcely any literature at all, and long after it continued to be esteemed an ignoble pursuit for a citizen, a statesman, and a warrior.

But, as if the poetic spirit was not sufficiently crushed and trodden down by the heavy weight of all these varied influences, positive legislative enactments were made more effectually to check its development. Fine and imprisonment were inflicted by the Laws of the Twelve Tables, on the poet who might have dared to irritate the sensitive nerves of the dominant patricians; and this early provision was afterwards re-enforced by a new statute, during the despotism of Sylla, whose own acquirements and undoubted literary abilities, ought to have prevented the enforcement of any such injudicious laws during his domination. It is somewhat singular that Niebuhr is ignorant of the existence of these legal prohibitions, though Montesquieu had referred to them, but both seem to have forgotten the passages of Cicero and Horace which attest it.

It need not be made more obvious, how unfavourable to literary excellence was the condition of Rome at that period from which the Latin Literature, preserved to our days, takes its rise. To trace the continuance or modification of the above influences may demand another and a separate inquiry.

Southern & Western Monthly Magazine and Review 1 (January 1845): 17–25.

Catharine Maria Sedgwick's *Home*

Simms reviewed Sedgwick's *Tales and Sketches* in *Southern & Western* 1 (March 1845): 223. He found the best of the tales, "read with pleasure many years ago," to be "so altogether superior in most respects to most of the female, and many of the male writers of our country," that he recommended her writings "without hesitation." In this previously unrecorded review of *Home,* he found her straying off course needlessly with "flings at the South" that had "been unnecessarily lugged in." He did not ask for things to be said "in our own favor," as these would be similarly pointless to the tale's progress. He found her nationalistic boosterism equally objectionable, as it fed "that already bloated pharisaical self conceit, which daily assures itself of those special smiles of heaven, of which other countries are not to be suffered to partake." He considered this the particular "folly in our country" that is the most "utterly loathsome . . . to good sense and to decency." Young America extolled her, however; and Simms declared that, despite her shortcomings, she is "one of our favorites." The review again shows fairness despite deep political differences. In *Letters,* 5: 388, he wrote that he would only "reproach her gently" for her "unnecessary flings at the South." From the account given in Malcolm Bell's *Major Butler's Legacy,* Sedgwick, Fanny Kemble's first and best American friend, did not regret the coming of the war because she wished "to see South Carolina humbled in the dust" (544). Despite such acrimony, which Simms gauged well, he praised *Redwood: A Tale* (*SQR* n.s. 1 [July 1850]: 540) for its expert "delineation of household events, the portraiture of the serene, the domestic, and the humble." He noticed Sedgwick's *Walter Thornley* as a "really pleasant tale of domestic life . . . with a fine current of just thought running through it." He judged it "a very charming volume, in remarkably good style." Of her general attributes, he said she is noted for "simplicity and grace . . . good sense, spirit and propriety." Simms gave few domestic novelists such unqualified praise or described their work in such glowing terms. To him she was a domestic novelist with a difference: her novels possessed an undercurrent of sound thought. He also placed her works *Alida* and *Allen Prescott* in the same category (Charleston *Mercury,* 20 August 1859). It is clear Simms had read the majority, if not all, of Sedgwick's fiction and did so with understanding. Despite her growing stridency in the antislavery movement, he continued to praise her publications. See also "Frances Anne Kemble Butler's *Poems,*" p. 62.

Home. By Miss Sedgwick

Miss Sedgwick is one of our favorites—one of those writers whom we find it always very safe to commend. This little story presents us with a very lovely picture of a well trained family, and, incidentally, and by way of contrast, with several very painful scenes occurring in families which lack this best of all blessings for the young. The importance of training is justly insisted on. We have an immense deal of teaching and but little training. Our young people will never grow to what they may be, and what they should be, until they rid themselves of much of the former, and, in its place, substitute a great deal more of the latter. But we despair of this, until we see realized the suggestion of Madame Campan to

Napoleon. We must begin with the education of mothers. They are responsible for all the training of the young. The character of a child is made in the first twelve years of its life. Its habits are formed and they constitute the character of the child. Attend to these habits—see that your young has good ones—and you need give yourself but little concern about their principles. Principles, indeed, are only names for habits. As there is no tyranny so inflexible as habit, the importance of such as are good, is obvious to the least considerate mind. This story inculcates this lesson, and, as is usual with our author, does so as effectually perhaps, as it could be done by the lessons of any writer. We are sorry to speak of blemishes in the writings of Miss Sedgwick. She is one of those women who are above ordinary prejudices. The occasional flings at the South, in this little volume, are in bad taste, and seem to have been very unnecessarily lugged in. Besides, she herself may reasonably doubt, upon reflection, not less the justice than the taste of her censures. It is by no means a proper lesson to teach a Yankee boy, that the Americans are distinguished for their good temper above the people of France, England and Ireland. The fact is by no means certain. But, even if true, the lesson is full of evil, as Miss Sedgwick ought to know, as it is coupled with the most outrageous self complacency and assurance. As little is it in good taste, or, we venture to say, according to truth, to insist that the Southern people must be excepted from the benefits of this eulogium. It saddens us to think that Miss Sedgwick only arrived at this conclusion, as it was necessary to discover the specially evil moral consequences of slavery. Her experience has scarcely been of that kind which would enable her to judge for herself, truly, so as to establish this broad line of division between our people. But the comparison was not called for by the lesson. It was an unnecessary and wanton fling at our institutions, and is farther objectionable, as it forbore to show to the reader, what are usually supposed to be the not ungenial, the not unfriendly, nor ungrateful fruits, growing out of the same institution. If slavery renders the Southern man more irascible than his neighbors—it is also supposed to increase his elevation of spirit and character, his hospitality, his courage, his disdain of meanness, his scorn of what is basely selfish, or sycophantic. We do not ask that this shall be said in our favor—but we do say, that, if one side of the picture is to be shown, a sense of what is just should call for an equally honest display of the other. But the whole reference to the subject was wrong and unbecoming—calculated to increase the vanity of our people—to increase the antipathies pervading the different sections of our country—to foster disgusts and dislikes of the one side, and to stimulate that already bloated spirit of pharisaical self conceit, which daily assures itself of those special smiles of heaven, of which other countries are not to be suffered to partake. If there be one folly in our country more utterly loathsome than another, to good sense and to decency, most certainly it is this; and it is with great sorrow that we see a person so enlightened as Miss Sedgwick, and so truly interested for the moral welfare of the citizen, contributing, in however slight degree, to stimulate and strengthen it.

Southern and Western Monthly Magazine and Review 1 (June 1845): 434–35.

—◄———————

Jean Paul Friedrich Richter's *Flower, Fruit and Thorn Pieces.* Volumes 1 and 2

Richter, while not as important to Simms as Goethe and Schiller, was still a favorite. Reviewing Elizabeth Lee's translation of *The Life of Richter,* he wrote, "Jean Paul, the spiritualist, the mystic, the humorist, is at once a study and a delight," but if you wanted to know him, you should look for him not in this biography but in his writings (*SQR* n.s. 2 [November 1850]: 539).

Flower, Fruit and Thorn Pieces. [Volume One] Boston. James Munroe & Co.

Jean Paul Frederick Richter, the author of this volume, is one of the most capricious, fantastic and playful of all the modern writers of Germany. With a wild and mischievous fancy, a capacious memory, and various reading, he subjects every thing which he lays his hands on to a garb and color of his own. You must not only see the particular thing that he beholds, but you must see it through his peculiar medium of vision; and his caprices are such, that, unless you are prepared, at the outset, liberally to allow for his sportive humour, the object which he seeks to show you is in danger of escaping from your sight altogether. He seems perversely resolved never to be serious—never, at least, to persevere earnestly to a profound finish with the object which he has in hand; and never to be really resolved on that to which he professes to call your, and confine his own, attention. Yet, take him with his humour, let him have play, yield yourself to his sports, and watch attentively his progress, and the method makes itself apparent through the madness, and there is a vein of wholesome thought and of becoming seriousness that rises to subdue and to qualify all his caprices and fantastics. Full of fancy, abundant in his comparisons, with a strong poetic impulse, and a peculiar richness of image and figure, he startles you ever and anon, with a grace and a beauty, growing out of his most grotesque associations. As it is the peculiarity of Retzsch's masterly outlines to endow all the auxiliaries of the scene with the gloomy and demoniac character which is its moving spirit, so it seems the merrier design of Richter to draw the pleasing and the bright, from the grotesque and the capricious. There is a story in this volume—but it is not by the story that the book is to be commended. That is purely subservient to the fancies and the philosophies of the author. Its sketches of domestic life are frequently happy and very naïve and natural. In little bits of pathos, gushing up every now and then like some struggling fountain that takes advantage of a chasm, to shoot upward from the earth into the sunlight, you will be occasionally reminded of the caprices, or if you please, the affectations of Sterne. But Richter is scarcely a person of affectations. His peculiarities seem natural to the genius of the man. They are at all events habitual. They give the peculiar character to every thing that he writes—soften his satire, elevate his humbler traits, and disarm of their solemn stiffnesses those features which, in other authors, we sometimes find unendurably tedious. Jean Paul is not a writer to be read as we run. We must go patiently along with him, listen respectfully to whatever he says, and sift it closely, for, however silly it may seem, on the first blush, it is not so certain that it does not embody something sharp at our expense. In plain terms, Jean Paul is a wit, who covers his darts in flowers, and looks so good-naturedly while he flings them, that one cannot be persuaded to believe that there is any mischief in the sportsman. The present translation is a good one.

Southern and Western Monthly Magazine and Review n.s. 1 (June 1845): 433–34.

Flower, Fruit and Thorn Pieces. [Volume Two]

The second volume of this delightful and fantastic book of Jean Paul, the most tricksy and original spirit of the literature of modern Germany, has just reached us, from the press of James Munroe & Co., Boston. This translation, made by Noel, is a good one. The book, itself, almost defies, while it delights, the critic— that is, when he has fairly reached the point of vision, which the author requires him to attain, before looking forth upon the landscape. Jean Paul is one of those writers who insist upon furnishing to their readers, an individual medium of survey. This, by the way, is one proof of his originality. He is not unreasonable in this. It is Pope who tells us, with absolute propriety,—

"In every work regard the writer's end."

You are not to know an author's object before hand,—not to know where he designs to lead you, or what he proffers to display. Even a preface, which is seldom read, can only furnish an imperfect hint of his purposes. In fairness, therefore, to read a work of original invention properly, you must yield your-self to its author implicitly—give him fair play, and leave him, unopposed by your criticism, to the end of the chapter;—then, if he has had no power to persuade you, or to carry you with him, at his will, you may throw him by, and dismiss him utterly from your affections. But, to set out with him, on *his* quest, having a will of your own, is only to thwart him in his objects, and, in most cases, to baffle your own pleasures. In reading Jean Paul, in particular, you must thus completely surrender yourself;—for a more wanton and capricious genius, with will more fantastical, does not exist any where. But you may enjoy this consolation from our assurance—that he will conduct you—thus submitting— to pleasant places only; show you none but agreeable sights, and tell you nothing which, saving first the usual limitations of fiction, you may not readily believe.

Southern and Western Monthly Magazine and Review n.s. 2 (September 1845): 207–8.

Sir Edward Bulwer-Lytton's Translation of *The Poems and Ballads of Johann Schiller*

Following the lead of Coleridge, Simms was deeply interested in Schiller. He translated Schiller's "Der Verbrecher" in 1828 and referred to him often throughout his career—most especially in his *Poetry and the Practical* (92–93, 112). In a previously unrecorded review of this same Bulwer-Lytton translation in 1844, Simms related that he had been familiar with portions as they had originally appeared in *Blackwood's*. He elaborated: "Partial collections have been given us by the Boston press, but the translations were generally made by very inferior persons—writers of verse, whose productions in the vernacular, would never pass the muster of an ordinary newspaper. Sir Edward has devoted himself, *con amore,* to his task. He is not himself a great poet, nor likely to become one, but he is an adroit machinist, who knows how to work out a clever and pointed verse to an epigrammatic conclusion. This collection, no doubt, exercised his industry and diligence in large degree." Simms concluded by calling Schiller "the author, who, more than any other, lies deeply enshrined in the very centre of the German heart" (*Orion* 4 [July 1844]: 243). In *Views and Reviews,* Second Series, Simms again expressed his dissatisfaction with the Bulwer-Lytton translation (151). He discussed a new translation of Schiller's *Don Carlos* in the Charleston *Mercury* of 9 July 1856.

The Poems and Ballads of Schiller. Translated by Sir Edward Bulwer-Lytton, Bart., with a Brief Sketch of the Author's Life. New York: Harper & Brothers. 1844.

The business of translation does not often commend itself to the man of genius, or only, we suspect, at the particular moment when he is acquiring the language of the original. Then, it is a help to his own progress in acquisition, and he acquiesces in the unproductive and unoriginal labor, as a means for exercising memory in tasks which might otherwise be his aversion. Our translations usually come from men of ordinary talent. The exceptions, in the case of Pope and

Dryden, do not affect the rule. The majority of translations are from inferior hands; and, that this should be so, is the natural consequence of that sense of mental independence, on the part of men of real genius, which makes them revolt at any performance, in which they are not permitted to give full and adequate employment to their native powers. Sir Edward Bulwer-Lytton would probably never have attempted the version before us, from Schiller, but that he has lately devoted himself to the German. In a different way, he is too much above the business of the translator, however seductive and superior may be his author. We cannot say that he has succeeded in his task. He is not, himself, a poet likely to acquire eminence. He is an artist rather than a creator. His strains are *strains,* in a sense somewhat more literal than that in which the word is used in poetical parlance. We see that he is toiling in an unusual occupation— working against the grain—in fetters, feebly striving at difficulties, which he scrambles through, rather than surmounts. His progress lacks ease, and grace and dignity. He puts the verses of Schiller into English measure, it is true, but his rhythm halts—lacks flow, freedom, energy, and felicity of expression. He may be correct, but he is cold and heavy. He may give us the ideas of Schiller, but where is the *verve,* the fruitfulness, the fluency—by which that writer is said to be distinguished in his own tongue? We do not find it in that of our translator. He has lost the purple coloring, the life-music of the song, in its transfusion, and we have, in place of it, in language coldly correct, elaborately tame, those otherwise wild, passionate, mystic and melancholy outpourings which are said to speak the true soul and spirit of the German muse. Yet this volume, and these translations, are not without their claims. The biography of Schiller is an agreeable piece of writing, which affords us as clear a notion of the career of the subject as we could glean from any source. The style is less pretending than that of Bulwer-Lytton generally, and there is much less straining after effect in his fancies and philosophies. The translation will afford to the reader, ignorant of the German, as just an idea of the mere thoughts and general design of the original, as can be gathered from any translation; and the collection is a complete one. In this, there is a more than ordinary recommendation. We can lay hands on numerous translations of individual and short pieces from Schiller, which are superior in all respects to those of our author—but the entire body of songs and ballads, from this great German writer, has never yet been given to the public. This collection, indeed, is somewhat essential to his biography. The soul of Schiller lived very much in his song. We may read the story of his mental progress, no less than of his feelings, in his verses. His was a nature to ally itself with his utterance. In this respect he differed from Goethe, who, except in his earliest writings, the *Werther* and the *Goetz Von Berlichingen,* never went into his own heart for his fantasies, but wrote as if drawing from an external realm and nature, of which he is independent, and to which he is superior. Schiller was the reverse of this. He speaks and sings ever from the heart within him, and it is for this reason that he enters so deeply into the German heart. We fancy that our translator would have been more successful dealing with the muse of Goethe. Her cold superiority, her capacity for abstraction, her artistical caution, and rigid propriety of carriage, would better have satisfied the artificial requisitions of Bulwer-Lytton's own genius. And yet, we doubt if he could have done any thing with the *Faust*—that inscrutable piece of mischievous authorship, in which we are at a loss to know if the author meant to mystify his readers, or was simply mystified himself.

Southern and Western Monthly Magazine and Review 2 (August 1845): 139–40.

Benjamin D'Israeli's *Sybil, or the Two Nations*

Simms collected this previously unrecorded essay in "Reviews and Criticisms" (SCL). The year before this review, he briefly noticed D'Israeli's *Coningsby* in *Orion* 4 (August 1844): 293, where he stated that the popular G. P. R. James had less than one-tenth of his genius (296). He devoted six pages to D'Israeli in his essay "R. H. Horne's *A New Spirit of the Age*" (*SQR* 7 [April 1845]: 312–49), where he took Horne to task for omitting him from his discussion. Simms noted, "D'Israeli belongs to the age,—is one of its informing spirits," and singled out for discussion *Coningsby, Vivian Grey* ("a sparkling achievement"), *The Young Duke, Venetia, The Wondrous Tale of Alroy, Henrietta Temple,* and *Contarini Fleming*. His balanced treatment praised D'Israeli's dialogue, "not often surpassed among novel writers," but criticized the novels as "deficient in cohesion and compactness." He again praised *Coningsby* in the Charleston *Mercury* of 28 May 1855.

D'Israeli.

Here is something from a writer of well known genius and ability. *Sybil, or the Two Nations* is the attractive title of a new political moral by Benjamin D'Israeli, M.P. It is a companion story, rather than a sequel, to the tale of *Coningsby,* from the same pen, published last season. That work, in the substantial respects of good sense, and excellent style and natural dialogue, was one of the best of the author's productions. If it showed less of genius and imagination, it was, at all events, much freer than usual of his accustomed vagaries. Besides, it gave us no imperfect glimpses of the condition of society among the leading classes, and enabled us to determine, for ourselves, upon several of the aspects in the political condition of England. *Sybil, or the Two Nations* aims at similar objects. It aims at something more, indeed, than mere description. Mr. D'Israeli is a member, and would be the leader, of a new party in Great Britain. He is supposed to represent "Young England" as one of the estates of that country, destined to have vogue, and to pass into the high places of power. Any catastrophe in England will probably bring about this object. Any disasters in India—any substantial commotion in Ireland,—a war with the United States, or with France,—may operate greatly to facilitate the hopes and prospects of "Young England." Whether Mr. D'Israeli will continue to be the leader, when the time of action shall have arrived—when real issues are in progress, and ultimate responsibilities are to devolve upon the politicians,—is a question, which, from the desultory career of this gentleman hitherto, will probably be answered by most persons in the negative. But of his book rather than himself. "Sybil" is the name of his heroine, and a fine creature she is. We congratulate him upon the felicity of the conception, and upon his success in its delineation. The *two* nations, are those which lie beneath the sway of Victoria. 'But what two nations are these?'—will be the question of the reader. The answer is distinguished, at this juncture of '*strikes,*' 'machinery,' 'low wages,' and 'Chartism,' with an abrupt significance. The two nations of Victoria are *the rich and the poor.* That Mr. D'Israeli has thus authentically set these two parties in opposition, is somewhat significant of his own political feelings and sympathies. We are not prepared to say or to believe, that he has fairly represented the character and condition of these opposing families. That the English nobility is about the coldest and most heartless in the world, we have every reason to believe. That they are quite as frivolous and silly, as they are cold and heartless, is not so very certain. Doubtless, they are silly and frivolous enough; that portion of them, at least, which live by, and have a faith in little else than, fashion and fashionable society. But we trust, for the sake of humanity, if not of England, that this class constitutes no leading portion of her aristocracy. Of the description which Mr. D'Israeli gives of the nation of the *Poor,* under the sway of Victoria, we have less reason to doubt the fidelity. His developments on this subject, may all find illustration, from a single extract which we make from these pages. Hear him:

"They come forth: the mine delivers up its gang and the pit its bondsmen; the forge is silent and the engine is still. The place is covered with the swarming multitude; bands of stalwart men, broad-chested and muscular, wet with toil and black as the children of the tropics; troops of youth—alas! of both sexes,—*though neither their raiment nor their language indicates the difference, all are clad in male attire; and oaths that men might shudder at, issue from lips born to bear the words of sweetness.* Yet these are to be—some are—the mothers of England! But can we wonder at the hideous coarseness of their language when we remember the savage rudeness of their lives? *Naked to the waist, an iron chain fastened to a belt of leather runs between their legs, clad in canvass trousers, while, on hands and feet an English girl, for twelve, sometimes for sixteen hours a day, hauls and hurries tubs of coals up subterraneous roads, dark, precipitous and plashy: circumstances that seem to have escaped the notice of the Society for the abolition of negro slavery. These worthy gentlemen, too, appear to have been singularly unconscious of the sufferings of the little Trappers, which was remarkable,* AS MANY OF THEM WERE IN THEIR OWN EMPLOY. *See, too, these emerge from the bowels of the earth! Infants of four and five years of age, many of them girls, pretty and still soft and timid, &c.*"

So much for this picture. Its truth is attested, not by the novelist merely,—not by the philanthropist, too apt to color his philosophies and facts with the feelings of his heart,—but by stern and calculating business committees of the House of Commons. The truth of this history is beyond denial. Mr. D'Israeli does not seem to be prepared with any specific mode of operations by which to relieve this misery. It is the worst feature in the domestic condition of England, that it baffles the judgment, and sets at defiance all the speculations of the statesmen. Nothing but a revolution—such a revolution as the English nobility are not willing to contemplate just yet,—can possibly save them,—if things continue thus much farther,—from insurrection and civil war. The nostrums of the politicians,—where they venture upon any,—are palliatives merely, putting off the evil day, and scattering, for awhile, those humors, which, gathering to a head at last, must find their relief in some fearful crisis. This romance deserves to be read. It is somewhat curious and worthy of remark, that the very condition of ancient England, when it was called, and deserved to be called "Merrie England,"—over which Mr. D'Israeli seems to gloat with the most hankering solicitude, was one in which the relation of the *feud* to his lord, was not greatly superior—nay, was very much like—to that of the slave, at this time, in the old established plantations of the South. Ours is in truth not so much slavery as feudality. Discard the ordinary terms of argument, and look at the intrinsic condition of things, and our bondmen appear in quite as independent,—and in fact a much more secure attitude—than that of the Commons in Harry the VIIIth's time. They enjoy better food, as much freedom, and greater security from injustice;—and, if not at liberty to exercise, in all respects, that sovereign will, which is but a poor substitute for the substantial necessities and comforts of life,—are yet secure from hunger and starvation, secure of protection, of tendance in sickness, and a shelter when the frosts of age come in.

Southern Western Monthly Magazine and Review 2 (October 1845): 284–85.

Poe's Poetry

Poe and Simms had much in common as literary critics. Both demanded close, methodical, analytical reading of a work. Neither "puffed" in reviewing (See Simms's comments on "puffing" in *Magnolia* 3 [February 1841]: 69–74). Both strongly rejected moralizing—the "cult" or "heresy of the didactic,"as Poe often phrased it. (See for example his "The Poetic Principle.") Both understood that the work of art is more important than the artist's biography. These are critical assumptions, about art for art's sake, for which Poe is praised as being ahead of his time in both Britain and the United States. Although the two men may have differed somewhat on the purpose of art, they agreed on its ascendancy. Neither, however, saw art or the cult of beauty as a replacement for religion, as did some of the English aesthetes. The two southerners' wit makes them readable. Simms, however, was rarely savage in his criticism; but when he was, he could rival Poe. In the following essay, Simms identified Poe's gifts as a critic, gifts he himself shared. As brothers in the literary wars against a powerful, exclusionist Boston establishment and the New York Knickerbocker Circle, the two stood together. The following review shows just how truly simpatico they were. Throughout their various commentaries on each other, they named weaknesses without bruising egos, committed as they were to the role of criticism. Simms was perhaps the most perceptive contemporary American critic of Poe's poetry. He quickly understood that concreteness in poetry was anathema to Poe. He spoke of "the music of [Poe's] verse, the vagueness of the delineation, its mystic character, and dreamy and spiritual fancies" (Charleston *Southern Patriot,* 30 July 1846). Simms anticipated Richard Wilbur's interpretation of Poe's poetry as the symbolic destruction of the physical.

Poe reprinted the piece in his famous "Boston and the Bostonians" (*Broadway Journal,* 22 November 1845) and called Simms one of his "*true* friends, and *tried*" who has taken "up arms in our cause." Poe added that Simms "cannot see (it appears) any farther necessity for being ridden to death by New-England." He concluded in characteristic fashion: "The Frogpondians may as well spare us their abuse. If we cared a fig for their wrath we should not first have insulted them to their teeth. . . . The fact is, we despise them (the transcendental vagabonds!) and they may all go to the devil together." In other reviews Simms shared Poe's dislike of the transcendentalists' poetry—as Poe put it, "the so-called poetry of the so-called transcendentalists." Simms considered the didactic verse of Emerson, Longfellow, Lowell, and Whittier to be the product of secularized Puritanism.

Simms's other significant assessment of Poe appeared in a review of Poe's *Tales of the Grotesque and Arabesque:* "We have read with delight the fine artistic stories of Mr. Edgar A. Poe, a writer of rare imaginative excellence, great intensity of mood, and a singularly mathematical directness of purpose, and searching analysis, by which the moral and spiritual are evolved with a progress as symmetrical, and as duly dependent in their data and criteria, as any subject matter however inevitable, belonging to the fixed sciences." Simms declared, "Certainly, nothing more original, of their kind, has ever been given to the American reader. Mr. Poe is a mystic, and rises constantly into an atmosphere which as continually loses him the sympathy of the imaginative reader. But with those who can go with him without scruple to the elevation which his visions are summoned, and from which they may all be beheld, he is an acknowledged master,—a Prospero, whose wand is one of wonderful properties. That he has faults is beyond question, and some very serious ones, but these are such only as will be insisted upon by those who regard mere popularity as the leading objects of art and fiction. . . . He is one of those writers of peculiar idiosyncracies, strongly marked and singularly original." Simms concluded that "The Gold Bug" unrealistically portrayed the topography of Sullivan's Island outside Charleston, and a "certain class of readers," the uninspired Enlightenment literalist-empiricists who read only for fact, would take issue; but he found it "a small matter," seeing that Poe's primary interest was to write a tale of ratiocination not dependent on geography. In other words, Poe's detractors should merely get a volume of statistics (*S&W* 2 [December 1845]: 426–27).

After Poe's death, in noting the publication of Redfield's new edition of Poe's work, Simms wrote, "Of the general merits of Poe's mind, curiously metaphysical and subtle, with something of the mathematical element, and much of the bizarre, there can be little question. His writings constitute a decided feature in our literature, and demand a prominent place" (*SQR* n.s. 8 [July 1853]: 284). Simms noticed a pocket edition of Poe's poetry in the Charleston *Mercury* of 9 July 1859, reiterating that, despite the fact he was "unquestionably one of the most morally wretched among gifted men," his work "will and should always find a place in the American library." Simms concluded in a poignant short eulogy that paraphrased Hamlet's comment on seeing the skull of Yorick, "a fellow of . . . most excellent fancy," who may have been prickly with others, but who rode Hamlet on his back when a little boy: "Enough that he sleeps at last. Let us hope a more peaceful sleep—for a happier waking—than he ever knew in life. . . . Alas! Poor Edgar! We knew him well." Simms found Hamlet's own tortured nature and his famous soliloquy's meditation on death appropriate to Poe and his work.

It took American criticism, "hag-ridden" as it was by an establishment that was decidedly anti-Poe, many years to reach Simms's judgment of 1853. Foreign critics of the calibre of Baudelaire and Thomas Hardy were early defenders. Allen Tate, T. S Eliot, W. H. Auden, and Richard Wilbur (perhaps, significantly, all poets themselves) would join the ranks of those recognising his genius. One final note: like Simms's grandfather and father, Poe's grandfather came from Ireland, and he was well aware of it, a fact Poe's standard biographer found significant in influencing his character and the kind of mystical poetry that he wrote (Quinn, 12–14). Simms was similarly aware of his own Scots-Irish background.

Poe's Poetry.

Mr. Edgar A. Poe is one of the most remarkable, in many respects, among our men of letters. With singular endowments of imagination, he is at the same time largely possessed of many of the qualities that go to make an admirable critic;—he is methodical, lucid, forcible;—well-read, thoughtful, and capable, at all times, of rising from the mere consideration of the individual subject, to the principles, in literature and art, by which it should be governed. Add to these qualities, as a critic, that he is not a person to be overborne and silenced by a reputation;—that mere names do not control his judgments;—that he is bold, independent, and stubbornly analytical, in the formation of his opinions. He has his defects also;—he is sometimes the victim of capricious moods;— his temper is variable—his nervous organization being such, evidently, as to subject his judgments, sometimes, to influences which may be traced to the weather and the winds. He takes his colour from the cloud; and his sympathies are not unfrequently chilled, and rendered ungenial, by the pressure of the atmosphere—the cold and the vapors of a climate affecting his moral nature, through his physical, in greater degree than is usual among literary men,—who, by the way, are generally far more susceptible to these influences, than is the case with the multitude. Such are the causes which occasionally operate to impair the value and the consistency of his judgments as a Critic.—As a Poet, Mr. Poe's imagination becomes remarkably conspicuous, and to surrender himself freely to his own moods, would be to make all his writings in verse, efforts of pure imagination only. He seems to dislike the merely practical, and to shrink from the concrete. His fancy takes the ascendant in his Poetry, and wings his thoughts to such superior elevations, as to render it too intensely spiritual for the ordinary reader. With a genius thus endowed and constituted, it was a blunder with Mr. Poe to accept the appointment, which called him to deliver himself in poetry before the Boston Lyceum. Highly imaginative men can scarcely succeed in such exhibitions. The sort of poetry called for on such occasions, is the very reverse of the spiritual, the fanciful or the metaphysical. To win the ears of a mixed audience, nothing more is required than moral or patriotic common places in rhyming heroics. The verses of Pope are just the things for such occasions. You must not pitch your flight higher than the penny-whistle elevation of—

> "Know then this truth, enough for men to know,
> Virtue alone is happiness below."

Either this, or declamatory verse,—or something patriotic, or something satirical, or something comical. At all events, you must not be mystical. You must not task the audience to study. Your song must be such as they can read running, and comprehend while munching pea-nuts. Mr. Poe is not the writer for this sort of thing. He is too original, too fanciful, too speculative, too anything in verse, for the comprehension of any but 'audience fit though few.' In obeying this call, to Boston, Mr. Poe committed another mistake. He had been mercilessly exercising himself as a critic at the expense of some of their favorite writers. The swans of New-England, under his delineation, had been described as mere geese, and those too of none of the whitest. He had been exposing the short comings and the plagiarisms of Mr. Longfellow, who is supposed, along the banks of the Penobscot, to be about the comliest bird that ever dipped his bill in Pieria. Poe had dealt with the favorites of Boston unsparingly, and they hankered after their revenges. In evil hour then, did he consent to commit himself, in verses to their tender mercies. It is positively amusing to see how eagerly all the little wittlings of the press, in the old purlieus of the Puritan, flourish the critical tomahawk about the head of their critic. In their eagerness for retribution, one of the newspapers before us actually congratulates itself and readers, on the (asserted) failure of the poet. The good Editor himself was not present, but he hammers away not the less lustily at the victim, because his objections are to be made at second hand. Mr. Poe committed another error in consenting to address an audience in verse, who, for three mortal hours, had been compelled to sit and hear Mr. Caleb Cushing in prose. The attempt to speak after this, in poetry, and fanciful poetry too, was sheer madness. The most patient audience in the world, must have been utterly exhausted by the previous infliction. But, it is denied that Mr. Poe failed at all. He has been summoned to recite poetry. It is asserted that he did so. The Boston *Courier,* one of the most thoughtful of the journals of that city, gives us a very favorable opinion of the performance which has been so harshly treated. "The Poem," says that journal, called *The Messenger Star,*

"was an elegant and classic production, based on the right principles, containing the essence of *true* poetry, mingled with a gorgeous imagination, exquisite painting, every charm of metre, and a graceful delivery. It strongly reminded us of Mr. Horne's 'Orion,' and resembled it in the majesty of its design, the nobleness of its incidents, and its freedom from the trammels of productions usual on these occasions. The delicious word-painting of some of its scenes brought vividly to our recollection, Keats's 'Eve of St. Agnes,' and parts of *Paradise Lost.*

"That it was not appreciated by the audience, was very evident, by their uneasiness and continual exits in numbers at a time. Common courtesy, we should think, would have suggested to them the politeness of hearing it through, though it should have proved 'Heathen Greek,' to them; after, too, the author had expressed his doubts of his ability, in preparing a poem for a Boston audience.

"That it was malapropos to the occasion; we take the liberty to deny. What is the use of repeating the 'mumbling farce' of having invited a poet to deliver a poem? We (too often) find a person get up and repeat a hundred or two indifferent couplets of words, with jingling rhymes and stale witticisms, with scarcely a line of *poetry* in the whole, and which will admit of no superlative to describe it. If we are to have a poem, why not have the 'true thing,' that will be recognized as such,—for poems being written for people that can appreciate them, it would be well to cater for their tastes as for individuals who cannot distinguish between the true and false."

The good sense of this extract should do much towards enforcing the opinion which it conveys; and it confirms our own, previously entertained and expressed, in regard to the affair in question. Mr. Poe's error was not, perhaps, in making verses, nor making them after a fashion of his own; but in delivering them before an audience of mixed elements, and just after a discourse of three mortal hours by a prosing orator. That any of his hearers should have survived the twofold infliction, is one of these instances of good fortune which should bring every person present to his knees in profound acknowledgment to a protecting providence.

Charleston *Southern Patriot* (10 November 1845).

Elizabeth Missing Sewell's *Laneton Parsonage*

English novelist Sewell (1815–1906) began as a children's writer; yet she transcended the genre in her later works such as *The Experience of Life* (1853), in part a repudiation of Brontë's *Jane Eyre* (Scott, "Genre and Perspective," 9). Simms erred in saying it was her father who helped her publish the books. It was rather her brother, the Reverend William Sewell, a Tractarian Oxford don, who in 1840 introduced her to the leaders of the Oxford Movement—Keble and Newman. Simms had earlier acknowledged the receipt of Sewell's *Amy Herbert* in *Orion* 4 (July 1844): 248, and he later noticed *The Earl's Daughter* in *SQR* n.s. 2 (September 1850): 271, and *Cleve Hall* in the Charleston *Mercury* of 17 October 1855.

Laneton Parsonage: A Tale. **Third Part. By the author of** *Amy Herbert,*
Gertrude, Margaret Percival, **etc. Edited by the Rev. W. Sewell, B.D.,**
Fellow of Exeter College, Oxford. New York: D. Appleton & Co. 1849.

The religious novel has been frequently condemned by the Purist, but with no
sufficient reason. The novel is only one of the forms and processes of art. It is,
by itself, totally objectionless; and, like every other human performance, which
exhibits the ingenuity and addresses itself to the tastes of men, it may be rendered, in proper hands, highly instrumental in promoting the objects of religion
and proper morals. The arts and faculties assigned to humanity, were intended
for the benefit of man. Whatever exercises his ingenuity may be made beneficial
to his welfare. Whatever appeals to his tastes may be made subservient to his
temporary affections and his eternal interests. If we had a scruple or a doubt
upon this subject, it would find its sufficient answer, in a thousand inspired authorities and examples. One will suffice,—Luther adapted the melodies of the
love-ditties of his day to his translations of the Psalms. The purists fell upon him
with reproaches for this alleged impiety. His answer is sufficient for our purpose.
"What," said he, "shall the devil have all the good music?" We have but to vary
the phrase, preserving the idea and the form of the novel, as applied to religious
instruction, is made legitimate for use. Shall fiction—which so sweetly appeals
to human fancies—which delights human ingenuity—which soothes human discontent—which provides against hours of weariness, when thought is no longer
willing to work, and nature demands equal remedy and respite—shall this large
attribute of humanity, be rejected as an agent of that superior love which pro-
poses to elevate the lowly nature from the bonds and blandishments of earth?
Shall the devil alone be permitted to monopolize an agency so capable of good,
and so frequently perverted to evil? There is but little wisdom surely, in rejecting
the use of an auxiliar, because it is sometimes abused by the ministers of evil!

The several stories which have issued from the hands of Miss Sewell and of
her father, are religious novels. They are not so much fictions as narratives of
life, in a pleasing form, aiming at the tuition of the heart, and the proper guidance of the passions and affections. There is in fact no tale at all, only a series of
domestic scenes and pictures, naturally described, with characters more or less
justly drawn, and under certain lights and shadows, which furnish the writer
with certain topics of rebuke, reproach, encouragement and reward. Good and
evil are set before us, through respective representatives, male and female. The
weak or vicious character—and all vicious characters are more or less weak—is
followed, watched and counselled through his career; is sometimes reformed
and rescued from vice by the moral influences brought to bear upon it; sometimes brought to shame and punishment by its own perverse moods, or by the
superior influence of evil associates, helped in their teachings by an early training which has been hostile to the good. The better nature is also watched and

followed—helped, where it shows itself feeble in the struggle with its natural enemy; and stimulated to perseverance when the native workings of the soul are favorable to virtue.

The interest of the story, *per se,* is never suffered to grow so intense as to make us forgetful of the religious lessons meant to be conveyed. It is not so much actions, as passions, sentiments, emotions and tendencies, which constitute the material of the work. They are kept always prominently in view, as the paramount consideration of the writer, who never forgets the moral in the scene, nor suffers the mood to unfold itself without the proper commentary. The degree of interest which the tale possesses, if wanting in excitement, is nevertheless not without its interest. To follow thoughtfully the progress of a single human experience, is to find food for thought, and necessarily of pleasure. To trace this progress through groups and families, acting together, though in an ordinary social progress, undisturbed by any events, those excepted which are of daily occurrence, is to increase this interest, and inform it with variety. This is the whole secret of such stories as the one before us. Their moral value is to be found in the principle, or text, which the author seeks to evolve in his progress, and in the illustration of the career and fortunes of his dramatis personae. In this tale of *Laneton Parsonage,* which is a third series of a class, former personages are brought to our view in new situations. The tale is perfect in itself without regarding the previous volumes. The object of this third part is to illustrate the training of several young ladies for the solemn rite of confirmation—the preparation of their hearts and minds, equally, for the awful, yet grateful responsibilities which they are about to assume, to themselves and to the Creator. In this task, the author ingeniously developes the workings of their several moods, their weaknesses as well as virtues; and employs such events and arguments, as will best produce the effect desired, of elevating their thoughts and affections to the higher rank which they seek to assume as responsible and religious beings. The work is equally pleasing and instructive; and, to young persons about to seek confirmation, it will be admirably suggestive of duties and studies of the closet, which cannot be too thoroughly understood and felt, as they cannot, with safety, or without presumption, be neglected or despised.

Southern Quarterly Review 15 (April 1849): 258–59.

John Motley's *Merry Mount; a Romance of the Massachusetts Colony*

As Simms reported, Motley (1814–1877) was also the author of *Morton's Hope* (1839). Both novels have as central character the non-Puritan Thomas Morton, deported in 1630 by Governor Winthrop from the elect community, self-styled ironically the "Modell of Christian Charity." Morton's house was burned, his property was taken, and he was shackled until banished. Morton later called the Puritans that "sect of cruell Schismaticks" and lampooned arch-enemy Miles Standish as Captain Shrimp. The Puritans established Boston on Morton's confiscated property. President Lincoln rewarded Motley with a sinecure in Europe for his essays favoring Lincoln's controversial policies toward the South. This novel reinforced Simms's views on Puritan intolerance and hypocrisy, as written by one of their own. The review continued to develop Simms's theme of coldness and lack of a broad sense of humor on the part of northern (especially New England) authors, a trait he felt they often shared with some of the stuffy lesser writers of Old England, and as distinguished from even the minor writers of Ireland.

Beverley Tucker (1784–1851), the Virginia novelist, was Simms's friend and correspondent. Poe agreed with Simms's assessment of *George Balcombe* (*SLM* 3 [January 1837]: 49–58). Miss Sedgwick is Catharine Maria Sedgwick. Simms's statement that she was more influenced by New York stems from her association with New York–centered Young America. See his review of Sedgwick's *Home* (p. 73).

Merry Mount; A Romance of the Massachusetts Colony. In Two Vols. Boston and Cambridge: James Munroe & Co. 1849.

It is not often that we receive any original literature from New-England. Its writers are mostly didactic in their character. They give us philosophies and sermons in abundance; criticisms and philosophies, history and homily. But they seem to lack invention. Even their poets are writers of moral and descriptive verses, rather than that which demands fancy and imagination; and Longfellow succeeds admirably in a chaunt where he fails wretchedly in a fiction. New-England has scarcely produced a single novelist, if we except Miss Sedgwick, whose influences are rather drawn from New-York than Massachusetts, and whose fine mind owes its successes to a graceful style, great good sense, and excellent descriptive powers, rather than to a capacity for grouping and combining. The imaginative faculty which is the great essential in all creative literature, is one in which New-England exhibits deficiencies rather than possessions. Most of the novelists of America, good or bad, it matters not, spring up in any other section. Brown, Irving, Cooper, Kennedy, Bird, Paulding, Tucker,* &c., owe their genius to a friendlier

---

* The Hon. Beverley Tucker, of Virginia, is understood to be the author of *George Balcombe,* an American novel published by Harper and Brothers in 1836, one of the most truly American, and one of the very best ever published in the country. It would be difficult,

climate; and were these sections as adroit, as diligent and eager in trumpeting their achievements to the world, as they have always thrown themselves in more northern latitudes, it would be difficult to say in what departments of art and fiction, the latter would not be excelled. It is, therefore, with a feeling of curiosity that we hail the publication of a romance, professing to be of New-England growth entirely. We are told that the author of the work before us has been in the field already. He is said to be the author of a novel called *Morton's Hope,* which we remember to have read with pleasure, just ten years ago. His name is Motley, a name which we must not allow to prejudice his productions. It would be rank injustice to impute to them any thing heterogeneous. On the contrary, his chief deficiency is rather a want of variety in his fiction; this want of variety implying a want of warmth and color. *Morton's Hope* was a work, showing considerable power, an ease and fearlessness of style, an eagerness in the action, and a purpose and life in the characters, which constitute much of the merit of prose fiction. But his story, if we do not now forget, was somewhat wandering, the action distributed over too wide a surface, and the interest of the reader distracted by a too frequent interposition of new characters. We are not able to recal his details, and cannot venture to be more particular. The present story possesses similar characteristics. It is marked by a good style and good sense, has some very marked characters, and considerable action. The events are numerous, and the actors sufficiently independent of the vulgar restraints of law and society. But we scarcely sympathize with them. If they have life, they lack warmth. There is no hearty conviction in our minds that we are dealing with genuine beings of flesh and blood; in other words, we are continually aware of the presence of the novelist, and this is grievously to the disparagement of the novel. It is perhaps one of the worst errors which the author has committed; that he has so freely employed those *extreme* characters—those personages so uncommon to the time—so unsuited to the scenes in America—persons warped in manners and modes of thinking from what is usual, by the ultra conventing of European civilization, as to fill the reader with continual doubts of their reality. In his preface, he seems to anticipate this objection by telling us that "the personages and scenes which may be out of keeping, are strictly true in their coloring and spirit." All this may be so, but it matters nothing to him who appeals to the reader as an artist. He is required to be in keeping, above all things. This is his great propriety. Careless of this, he must not be angry if the faith of the reader is reluctant to receive his history.

---

perhaps, to find a single New-England press which had ever accorded the slightest acknowledgment to this publication, or a single New-England citizen who had ever read it. It lacked the necessary *imprimatur* from the banks of the Charles. The saline flavor from the Plymouth rock, would have secured for it a thousand pæans.

Had he only ventured on one such extreme instance as Sir Christopher Gardiner, or the Suzerain of Merry Mount, we might have been more accommodating; but, we cannot yield credence to a world made up of these startling personages. Besides, the subordinates are made to partake too decidedly of the complexion of their superiors, and a uniform stillishness of character, among the dramatis personæ, produces a sense of weariness and monotony, which, even when the scene is a bright one, makes us look around with the desire for shade. The frigidity of our author is at variance with his character, as well as his scene, and the most brilliant of his passages are impaired by his coldness. He may shine, but his beams are wasted on the icebergs. Still, this narrative will be read with interest. Several of the scenes are highly spirited. Some of the persons of the drama, drawn with spirit and to the life. A brief glimpse of Miles Standish makes us regret that the author has made no more of him, and Esther Ludlow is a clever heroine enough,—for a Puritan.

Southern Quarterly Review 15 (April 1849): 260–61.

J. T. Headley's *The Adirondack; or Life in the Woods*

The Reverend Joel Headley (1813–1897) was a Presbyterian minister and author of *The Life of Oliver Cromwell* and *Washington and His Generals.* Simms wrote a long review of the former (*SQR* 14 [October 1848]: 506–38), of Headley's *Miscellanies* (*SQR* n.s. 1 [April 1850]: 249–50), and of his *Sketches and Rambles* and *Sacred Scenes and Characters* (*SQR* n.s. 1 [July 1850]: 507, 510). He commented on the "immoral," pirated publication of Headley's miscellaneous work. He supposed that "in some of the northern cities the great object seems to be to realize that condition of things, the Utopia of Communism, in which, in the language of M. Proudhon, "[La] propriété c'est [le] vol" (*SQR* n.s. 1 [April 1850]: 249). Proudhon (1809–1865), a socialist, anarchist friend of Fourier, asserted that property ownership is theft. Headley raised Simms's ire when he attacked South Carolina in his *Life of Jackson* for nullification's "treasonable course" and "how he exults in the anticipated spectacle of that fierce dragoon" (Jackson) burning the towns and villages of the state. "Peculiar Christian virtues for a parson," Simms observed. Simms found Headley's sympathy for Oliver Cromwell fitting, considering their shared militarism and religious zealotry (*SQR* n.s. 7 [January 1853]: 267–70). As a hunter himself, who had camped with the most experienced woodsmen of the Appalachian big woods, Simms mocked Headley's unrealistic and sentimental portrayals of wildlife, right down to the volumes's engravings, which he described as "sweet."

The Adirondack; or Life in the Woods; by J.T. Headley, author of Washington and His Generals, &c. New York: Baker & Scribner. 1849.

Mr. Headley is one of those light and lively sketchers, who, if he compels you to no deep reflections by his own profundity, at least embarrasses you by none of the impediments of heavy baggage. He travels post. He writes by express. He has a sort of telegraph at his finger's end, and his brain is so much electric fluid that is perpetually jerking and jumping along the wires. He claps his hands and you are off. He sees a lake, and he whips out his line and fly, as a trout fisher. Hark! a hound opens, and he gets his gun in readiness. In a moment, hit or miss, he blazes away in a fever of excitement, and as the deer bounds away in safety, he begins to moralize upon the length of his legs and the beauty of his antlers. Anon, a bird pipes up a merry carol, and he throws himself down to listen. It reminds him of his youth, and he meditates the flight of years and the vanities of life. The cry of his comrades startles him from his meditations, and he sings supper in full chorus with the rest. Thus he goes from morn to night and from night to morning. A mountain rises before him and he talks big about its majesty and sublimity. The river winds below, and he speaks of its serpentlike flow, glistening clear and sunnily throughout the plain. He launches into his boat, and he recollects and tells you of some glorious upset he has had or witnessed. He darts upon the silent shore, and its solitude reminds him that he is no longer in the crowded city, and that he has reason to be thankful for it. He makes an admirable cockney in the woods, and betrays himself at every instant; but he is so good natured, and so lively, so full of the neck or nothing temper, that goes forward, in devil-may-care fashion, no matter who pays the piper, that we slap him on the shoulder affectionately, even while we laugh at his absurdities, as we tolerate the shallowness of the stream in consideration of its transparency and liquid impetuous motion. His volume has little in it, but that is lively. It would be monotonous, for the incidents are few and of but one character, but that the author himself, with his pop, fizz, bang, sort of action and performance, is sufficiently full of transitions. The things that he sees, and which surprise him only, prove his cockney inexperience. They would surprise nobody accustomed to forest life. He should come South if he wants to see something of such a condition. Let him take the great back bone through Virginia and North-Carolina to Georgia. We should show him something to make him skip legitimately. His mountains are mere gopher hills to such as they might show him on the dividing line between South and North Carolina. He talks of Cheney, who is the great hunter, *par excellence,* among the Manhattan cockneys, and gives an account of his woful fights with a wolf. We know hunters to the manor born—men, who, at seventy, are still on foot, day by day, over the mountain in pursuit of the bear, deer and panther—men covered from head to foot with scars received in conflict with these varmints, each with a chronicle to make the particular cockney hairs stand on the head of our author, "like quills upon the fretted porcupine." He has seen nothing. Our readers will be amused at one of his discoveries. He records, *in italics,* with as much wonder as holy horror, that fish will eat each other, and that one trout was used for baiting his brethren! Of his mercurial temperament, by which his philosophies change at almost every chapter, we have some amusing illustrations. At page 101, he is about to shoot at a duck, when his companion, a professional hunter, arrests his arm. "She has young ones." "I stood rebuked," says our benevolent author;— "Not only by my own feelings but by the Indian with me. I was shocked that this hunter, who had lived so many years on the spoils of the forest should teach me tenderness of feeling. That mother's voice found an echo in his heart, and he would not harm one feather of her plumage, &c." Now, at page 133–4 the same humane hunter, actually goes out of his way, and takes the greatest pains, under our author's encouragement, as well as his own impulse, to shoot at a female eagle, who is watching *her* young. They *do* shoot at her, and, fortunately for her, their skill as marksmen is not more true than their humanity. In sparing the maternal duck, the hunter's feelings had no more to do with it than those of the man in the moon. He considered the duck as only taking care of *his* brood, and necessary to their growth for his future uses. A true hunter never kills anything out of season. It is your cockney sportsmen only who commit such blunders. Had our author but given himself time for reflection, he would have spared his eloquent pathos. He would have seen that the murderous attempt upon the eagle, in the same circumstances as the mother duck, as conclusive that any other than humane motives governed the proceedings of the hunter. The eagle was a bird of prey—a rival hunter—who would probably fasten his eye upon the same pretty little ducklings which the good hunter was willing to foster for his own uses. It was good policy to shoot *her,* the unfledged eaglets' claims to consideration being wholly out of the question. The mother slain, they would probably perish also. But the very same policy suggested the necessity of sparing the duck for her young. They *deserved* to be cherished—they *should* be fed—they would grow in growth, in beauty and fatness—and, another season, the hunter would then find his reward for his present forbearance. It is Mr. Headley's misfortune that he is always on the look out for something on which to expatiate with eloquent sentimentality. The practice is a bad one. The thing soon becomes overdone. The topic exhausts itself as well as the illustrative matter; and then all becomes laborious commonplace on stilts in the shape of pathos and reflection. The occasions for eloquent dilation must occur naturally. They must come to us—we cannot go to them. They *will* come to us, if we let ourselves alone. Had Mr. Headly suffered himself to pause and think, making the contrast that we have done, between his hunter's treatment of duck and eagle, in precisely the same circumstances, instead of dwelling upon the humanity and tender heart of the hunter, he would have been much more truly eloquent upon his deliberate, cold-hearted selfishness. He, Headley, in lifting his weapon to kill the duck, obeyed an impulse which was not inconsistent with humanity. The hunter, arresting his arm, obeyed an established law of self—a cool calculating policy, which lacked equally in impulse and humanity. But we must leave it to our author to be tedious. Taken at the hour of the *siesta,* in the warm of the afternoon, and these letters will be found sprightly and amusing, with all their absurdities. We must not forget that the book is well printed and illustrated with some very sweet engravings.

Southern Quarterly Review 16 (October 1849): 236–38.

James Russell Lowell's *A Fable for Critics*

In an 1845 notice of Lowell, Simms was favorable but felt him too bound by elitist Boston opinion (*S&W* 2 [November 1845]: 342–60). Simms wrote two reviews of *A Fable for Critics,* the one published here and an earlier one in the Charleston *Courier* of 30 December 1848, where he said Lowell's flings at the South were "not called for by the subject, but lugged in by the head and shoulders," words he had used in 1845 to describe Sedgwick's doing the same in *Home* (see p. 73). Simms's passage on Bostonian Oliver Wendell Holmes reinforced his statements at other places that he found Holmes "not ill-natured," like Lowell and Whittier, "and more humane" (*SQR* n.s. 3 [April 1851]: 563–64.) He read Holmes's work with much pleasure and wished to meet him. Theodore Parker (1810–1860), Boston clergyman, is said here to beat the Socinians at their own game and finally to believe in nothing at all—not even the Socinians. Poe would have appreciated Simms's wit. Socinian doctrine denied the divinity of Christ, the Trinity, and the natural immortality of the soul, explaining sin rationally, much in the manner of Deism and the Age of Reason. Simms's imagery of the French Revolution's Goddess of Reason and the erection of "a Temple of Reason" in Boston usurping that of Christ is pertinent social commentary. (See also Simms's review of Guizot in part 2.) Simms's phrase *sans culottes* refers to the violent methods and radical principles of the poor during the French Revolution. In a notice of Parker's *The Public Education of the People,* Simms wrote that he did not know him but correctly guessed his membership in "that strange herd whom they dignify in that quarter with the name of transcendentalists" (*SQR* n.s. 1 [April 1850]: 264).

Willis is N. P. Willis, founder of the *American Monthly Magazine* and a writer Simms came to dislike. Brownson is Orestes Brownson (1803–1876) of

Brownson's Quarterly. Alcott is Bronson Alcott (1799–1888), Boston philosopher. The *Hudibras* is Irishman Samuel Butler's mock-heroic poem of 1663–78, satirizing the English Puritans, and the model for Simms's poem *The Father Abolitionist* (1850), a scathing satire in hudibrastics on the Puritans' modern descendants in New England. Simms refused to publish it, however, perhaps because, as he said here of Lowell's poem, its malice rather outstripped its catholicity. Maintaining that New England poetry is ground out by "her sledge and trip hammers, her mills and machinery" is yet another of Simms's critiques of the progressive, urbanizing, Utilitarian machine culture of the North and the kind of cold, "teeth on edge" literature he felt that it was likely to produce. It bears repeating that Simms's disdain for the plethora of new "*isms* and *ologies*" in the North informed his canon, especially when these new abstractions took the ascendant over art. Here the enshrinement of pet secular crusades is placed in the context of what Simms saw as their opposite: orthodox Christian belief. Carlyle first used the words "*isms* and *ologies*" in 1837, and Simms may have been echoing his phrase.

A Fable for Critics, or a Glance at a Few of Our Literary Progenies, from the Tub of Diogenes; by a Wonderful Quiz. G.P. Putnam, 1848.

The above is only a portion of the fantastic title page of this slender volume. It is all that is written in black letter. Alternating with the black inscription are certain lines in red. The two, taken together, give us a string of doggerel verses, which afford no bad sample of the contents of the volume. We place, in due relation, the whole title page, that the reader may compass it without effort;

> "Reader! walk up at once (it will soon be too late)
>   And buy at a perfectly ruinous rate,
>   A Fable for Critics; or better—I like
>   As a thing that the reader's first fancy may strike,
>   An old fashioned title page, such as presents,
>   A tabular view of the volume's contents—
>   A glance at a few of our literary progenies,
>   (Mrs. Malaprop's word) from the tub of Diogenes:
>   A series of jokes by a Wonderful Quiz,
>   Who accompanies himself with a rub-a-dub-dub,
>   Full of spirit and grace, on the top of the tub.
>   Set forth in October, the twenty-first day,
>   In the year '48, by G.P. Putnam, Broadway."

The preface, printed as prose, is nevertheless written as the above, in rhymes, which are neither better nor worse than the preceding; and the strains that follow are woven after a like fashion, showing a painful industry in the manufacture of ingenious terminations, which, in some future year of grace, may make us forgetful of *Hudibras*. The satire is ascribed to James Russell Lowell, of Boston. We are inclined to doubt the truth of this suspicion. The writings of Lowell have given us no reason to suppose him guilty of such a production. His poems are rather more thoughtful and sentimental than satirical, and his verse usually has borne no sort of resemblance to that which is before us. This, however, is quite inconclusive as an objection. A writer of talent and facility, such as Lowell is, may readily assume new aspects and put on new disguises. But it is doubtful whether he would expend so much pains-taking and labor on such an object. Not that his satire lacks either point or merit. It is sharp and sometimes spicy, playful and fanciful, amidst much clumsiness and cumbrousness. But the fable is feeble, the point not often apparent, and the malice much more conspicuous than the wit. Its partialities and prejudices are of a kind seriously to discredit the claims of a real poet, to whose catholicity and justice, chiefly, we always look for the essentials of permanent authority. It is the misfortune of our fabler, that he adopts implicitly the vulgar parochial selfishness which disfigures so greatly the popular judgments of New England. This critic, for example, expends all his praise upon the children of the East. He finds no others in the country, or, if he does, he dismisses them with a scornful complacency that is rather more absurd and amusing than destructive or severe. Cooper, for example, is treated most contemptuously; though we should traffic unprofitably with the future to give his writings, loose and defective as they are, for all the pretentious literature of all New England. Irving is an exception. He is treated civilly, we might say graciously, but for a certain air of patronage which our satirist employs, and which, when addressed to a veteran like Irving, is sufficiently offensive, in spite of all the good things which are said. There may be reasons for this exception, by the way, in the fact that the works of Irving are now in course of publication by the same house which issues the satire. Besides, the reputation of Irving is no longer provocative of envy or rivalry. It is a settled reputation, at least for the present. It is no longer within the courts, and the tacit conclusion, among his contemporaries, is to leave his case entirely to the future. His genius was never of a combative character. He exhibited no salient points, in doctrine or imagination, about which opinion could quarrel; and he offended against no known proprieties. His style was at once sweet and unexceptionable, and he occupied a department which found him in nobody's way. The case is very different with such a writer as Cooper, whose faults are in due degree with his merits. His very originality must provoke questioning—his very audacity and courage excite spleen and anger. His career must necessarily have been a struggle, since, like the strong swimmer, he disdained to go only with the currents.—But to return to our muttons. Hear our satirist discourse on Emerson, whom he styles a "Greek head on Yankee shoulders," and you fancy him one of the most marvellous men that the world has produced. A parallel is run between him and Carlyle, greatly to the discredit of the latter. None less than Plato will content him for a comparison. "Carlyle's the more burly," but "Emerson's the rarer;" "Carlyle's the Titan," but "Emerson the clear-eyed Olympian;" "the one's two-thirds Norseman," "the other's half Greek," and so on through a long string of absurdities, in very clever doggerel. And all this said of a man who is really half-witted, and whose chief excellence consists in mystifying the simple and disguising commonplaces in allegory. One Mr. Alcott follows, of whom we know nothing, and our satirist does not much to enlighten us. He gives to this gentleman a chapter of homage, and shuts him up in a room with Plato, as a trusted brother, though, in all probability, from what is said, he has been pilfering from Plato's stores all his life already. Brownson has his chapter and Willis his—the latter being likened to Beaumont and Fletcher, and made the companion of Ben Jonson, though the flesh and blood of these stout quarter-staff men, would have shaken the very soul out of the cockney's breeches, at a single bout of the cudgel. Of Theodore Parker, we have a monstrous catalogue of comparisons, proving him to be every sort of a man, yet so much of a Jupiter Tonans in his way, as to be no man at all. He, it appears, is a Socinian preacher, who is too Socinian for the Socinians. He has beaten them at their own weapons, and, where they teach to believe little, he teaches them to believe nothing at all,—unless himself. We have long been prepared to believe that Boston would come to this. They have a school of teachers, possessing large popularity, intense self-esteem, and considerable ingenuity, who, with new *isms* and *ologies* daily, will some day contrive to throw down all their altars of belief. Were they a more inflammable race, with smaller bumps of caution, we might look for the advent among them of a Goddess of Reason, and a Reign of Terror, not imperfectly modelled upon those of the French. Their safety lies in their desire for the flesh-pots, and in the fact that they are already in possession of too large a share of worldly goods to venture much in dangerous experiments. Were they *sans culottes,* we should, in all probability, very soon behold a Temple of Reason in Boston, usurping that of Jesus Christ.

With one more name we must dismiss the catalogue. Oliver Wendell Holmes has written several spirited lyrics, and some small pieces of a pleasant and good-natured humor. It is probable that none of his own calmly, truly judging friends would claim for him a higher degree of credit than this. But here his songs are rated above Campbell's, and the "New Timon," (ascribed to Bulwer,) which possesses one quality, of invention—to which Holmes has no sort of pretension—and which is very good verse besides, is sneered at as "a huckleberry to Holmes's persimmon." This is a rare sort of fooling verily.

And now for a sample of this satire, in which the poet does honor to his mother State. We may forgive to a dutiful son the expression of an exaggerated tribute, particularly when this is a son of New-England, with whom such exaggerations are habitual. But we smile, nevertheless, when we find him appropriating, as peculiar, those possessions which not only did not originate with her, but which are very far from being confined to her territory. If her claims to poetry are to be founded upon her sledge and trip hammers, her mills and machinery, she may grind verses to all eternity, but will be suffered to set no one's teeth on edge with them but her own.

> "Here,—'Forgive me Apollo,' I cried, 'while I pour
> My heart out to my birth-place: O, loved and more and more
> Dear Baystate, from whose rocky bosom thy sons
> Should suck milk, strong will-giving, brave, such as runs
> In the veins of old Graylock,—who is it that dares
> Call thee pedlar, a soul wrapt in bank-books and shares?
> It is false! She's a poet! I see, as I write,
> Along the far railroad the steam-snake glide white,
> The cataract-throb of her mill-hearts I hear,
> The swift strokes of triphammers weary my ear,
> Sledges ring upon anvils, through logs the saw screams,
> Blocks swing up to their place, beetles drive home the beams.—
> It is songs such as these that she croons to the din
> Of her fast-flying shuttles, year out and year in,
> While from earth's farthest corner there comes not a breeze
> But wafts her the hum of her gold-gleaning bees:
> What though those horn hands have as yet found small time
> For painting and sculpture and music and rhyme;
> These will come in due order; the need that pressed sorest
> Was to vanquish the seasons, the ocean, the forest,
> To bridle and harness the rivers, the steam,
> Making that whirl her mill-wheels, this tug in her team,
> To vassalize old tyrant Winter, and make
> Him delve surlily for her on river and lake;—
> When this New World was parted, she strove not to shirk
> Her lot in the heirdom,—the tough, silent work,
> The hero share ever, from Herakles down
> To Otlin, the Earth's iron sceptre and crown;
> Yes, thou dear, noble Mother! if ever men's praise
> Could be claimed for creating heroical lays,
> Thou hast won it; if ever the laurel divine
> Crowned the Maker and Builder, that glory is thine!
> Thy songs are right epic, they tell how this rude

Rock-rib of our Earth here was tamed and subdued;
Thou hast written them plain on the face of the planet
In brave, deathless letters of iron and granite;
Thou hast printed them deep for all time; they are set
From the same runic type-fount and alphabet
With thy stout Berkshire hills and the arms of thy Bay,—
They are staves from the burly old Mayflower lay.
If the drones of the Old World, in querulous ease,
Ask thy Art and they Letters, point proudly to these,
Or, if they deny these are Letters and Art,
Toil on with the same old invincible heart;
Thou art rearing the pedestal broad-based and grand
Whereon the fair shapes of the Artist shall stand,
And creating, through labors undaunted and long,
The true theme for all Sculpture and Painting and Song!"

With a single farther word, we must dismiss this performance. It is disfigured by frequent reflections upon the slave institutions of the South, some of which are exceedingly brutal, exhibiting in the author a bad, malicious heart, and a temper that scruples not at a falsehood in the expression of a prejudice. We take for granted that the Southern reader will reject with indignation every such publication, while we counsel the publisher to be wary in perilling his interests in lending himself to the purposes of fanaticism and hate.

Southern Quarterly Review 16 (October 1849): 239–42.

Henry Wadsworth Longfellow's *Kavanagh*

Longfellow was a leading opponent of Young America. His pro-English sentiment is clearly stated in chapter 20 of *Kavanagh*. Given this fact, Simms's review was remarkably judicious. Elsewhere, as in his review of *Poems* (p. 111), Simms's primary complaint was Longfellow's didacticism. Of *Kavanagh* the didactic passages were said to be the poet's best lines, a statement that is doubly damning. Simms here restated Young America's usual criticism of Longfellow as imitative and passionless and continued to develop his depiction of the northern propensity for abstraction and crusades—epitomised in the bookish coldness of New England letters. In general Simms found Professor Longfellow to be like most other New England authors in his paucity of invention and lack of genialness and a sense of humor.

Kavanagh; a Tale; by Henry Wadsworth Longfellow. Boston: Ticknor, Reed & Fields. 1849.

Mr. Longfellow has a high reputation as a writer, and in some degree deserves it. He is a careful writer in the first place,—and in this respect he differs from the great body of American authors, who are very apt to write with their spurs on, and over their portmanteaus. He is a writer of exquisite delicacy, a sweet moral tone, delicate in his fancies, and very graceful in expression. As a poet, his successes have chiefly been derived from his ballads, which required little action or invention, and were the embodiments of sentiment chiefly, rather than passion. His school is the sentimental. He lacks passion. His invention is small, and the dramatic element is one in which he can neither dive nor soar. His prose consists of gentle and fanciful descriptions, to which a certain quaintness, borrowed mostly from the Germans, adds a considerable charm. He pursues a pretty thought very happily and seldom hunts it down. A choice and delicate conceit will afford him the materials for a chapter, in the perusal of which, if we are conscious of no excitement, or provocation to thought, we are at least secure from offence and annoyance. Mr. Longfellow's tastes are sufficient securities for the reader, while his limpid style, and gentle narrative, commend him particularly to that class of persons, who prefer the gratification of their tastes, to any appeal to the passions. The work before us does not differ from the previous prose writings of the author. It is of the same slender staple—with few thoughts, few incidents—unimportant action and a rather cold interest; but marked by his usual felicity and smoothness of style, the play of a gentle fancy, and a pleasant sentiment. *Kavanagh* must depend for its attractions on these agencies wholly. It is a bald village story, in which love appears somewhat of the school girl fashion and philosophy,—which seems to have fed on bread and butter all its life. Some of the scenes are prettily delineated, and the village priest and schoolmaster, are no doubt tolerable portraits, with, we suspect, some one or more elements of the character omitted. It is in his musings, and didactic passages,—where philosophy and fancy seem to meet on the confines of thought, that our author is mostly successful. He feels that this is properly his region and addresses himself to it with creditable pains-taking. Sometimes he succeeds excellently well in his fancies, and the quaint forms into which he throws his sentiments. But he too frequently and unprofitably labors to adapt the remote to the present—to illustrate the commonplace with the foreign,—and to make the familiar seem original by extravagance of comparison. His failures are sometimes sufficiently amusing. The ringing of a Sabbath bell is likened to the explosion of a brazen mortar (which the bell really is)—"bombarding the village with bursting shells of sound." The striking of the clock, reminds him "of Jael driving the nail into the head of Sisera, &c." This straining after fine comparisons for ordinary things, must commonly result in such absurdities. Sometimes our author has better success—though still too much on stilts—as when he describes the setting sun stretching "his celestial rods of light across the level landscape, and like the Hebrew in Egypt, smiting rivers, brooks, and ponds till they become as blood." But this ambitious sort of composition, scarcely repays by its occasional successes with the startled reader, for the labor which it demands from the author. We turn to a book of Mr. Cooper, a writer of very different order, and who takes no pains in the search after metaphor and illustration, and in the page under our hand—(the work is *The Sea-Lions,* just published)—we find one of those unforced comparisons which, however rudely expressed, are more grateful to the reader, because they occur unpremeditatedly, and without design, on the part of the author, than any of the more ambitious figures of Mr. Longfellow. He speaks of the departure of wealth and power from Italy "leaving in their train a thousand fruits, that would seem to be the more savory as the stem on which they grew, would appear to be approaching its decay." Here the propriety and beauty of the figure needs nothing but a corresponding grace and simplicity of expression to surpass most of the labored poetical efforts in *Kavanagh*. But we should be doing injustice to Mr. Longfellow not to admit the beauty and felicity of many of his passages. Some of his apothegms are marked by a delightful fancy, and much of his criticisms, on literature and society in America, is just and forcible. It is his invention that lacks. Nothing can be more bald than *Kavanagh* as a story; and for its design as little may be said. The author seems to have begun his book without fairly grasping his purpose. His moral is at once slight and commonplace.

Southern Quarterly Review 16 (October 1849): 245–46.

William Cowper's *Poems*

Simms felt Cowper was underrated and more than "merely a moral poet." Simms argued that Cowper, as a reformer of literature from the "false and meritritious school" of France and Italy and as nature poet, "deserves our homage" because he freed English poetry from the French (*Letters,* 1: 282). In *Views and Reviews* (First Series, 90), Simms praised Cowper for rejecting the French "clinquant of a false, for the hearty ring of the genuine English." He, not Wordsworth, rescued poetry from "the sway of French taste and authority in letters."

John Newton was the reformed British slave-ship captain and a Presbyterian reverend under whose zeal Cowper's melancholy over the Calvinist doctrine of the need of "assurance of salvation" turned to depression and then insanity. Cowper several times attempted suicide. With knowledge of such details, the reader can appreciate Simms's humor when he observed that Cowper's biographer was "no better prepared to be his biographer than Mr. Newton to have been his social and spiritual adviser."

Poems; by William Cowper. With a biographical and critical introduction, by the Rev. Thomas Dale: and seventy-five illustrations, engraved by John S. and Tudor Horton, from drawings by John Gilbert. In two volumes. New York: Harper & Brothers. 1849. Charleston: John Russell.

This is incomparably the most beautiful edition of the works of Cowper which has ever been issued from the American press. In point of typographical costume, and illustration, it will compare favorably with any British issues. It deserves general preference. Cowper is not so much read as he deserves to be by our people. We know of but one other American edition, and that was the wretchedest of all samples of mortal typography. Cowper was not merely a moral poet. He was one of admirable fancy, humor and wit. His imaginative faculties were strong if not discursive, and his mind, as an author, was singularly independent. He was, besides, in literature, a reformer. He was the first to strike at the false and meretricious school, borrowed from France and Italy, which, at the opening of his career, beset the poetry of his country. He led and taught the proper way to nature, and to that art only which is content to be the *accoucheur* of nature. He deserves our homage, and will reward our repeated study. His biography, by the Rev. Mr. Dale, will be read hesitatingly, though with interest. We doubt if Mr. Dale was better prepared to be his biographer than Mr. Newton to have been his social and spiritual adviser. It is very certain that Mr. Dale is but a doubtful judge of harmony. The criticism which he bestows upon certain lines of the author, only proves that the critic has no ear, and knows not well how to read or emphasize poetry.

Southern Quarterly Review 16 (October 1849): 260.

New Novels

This review of eight contemporary novels singled out Charlotte Brontë's *Shirley* as having the most merit though falling short of *Jane Eyre*. Simms treated Anne, Emily, and Charlotte Brontë in the announcement of Charlotte's death (Charleston *Mercury,* 1 May 1855). In 1849 he had lavishly praised *Jane Eyre,* which he preferred to *Wuthering Heights,* a novel that has "considerable shows of rough native power" but is "clumsy, inartificial, and frequently absurd" (*SQR* 15 [April 1849]: 78). Of Charlotte's *Villette,* Simms said it "scarcely rises to the standards of excellence" of *Shirley* and *Jane Eyre,* "not that it lacks in good characterization, good sketching, and in the exhibition of that masculine grasp of the subject, which particularly marked the mind of the author in her previous works." Although the novel has "excellent description" and "many scenes of lively and searching talent," it has "less concentrative power" and its main character "scarcely wins upon you, and the curious loves which she delineates between herself and the French Tutor, may be likened to those of a rabbit and a sturdy tom cat. M. Emanuel, however, though a strange creature in his wooing, is a fellow of excellent nature, and is wonderfully well painted throughout. But his love is very wolfish and devouring" (*SQR* n.s. 8 [July 1853]: 267). The other novels are Catharine Sinclair's *Sir Edward Graham,* Mrs. Catharine Gore's *The Dowager* and *Mothers and Daughters* ("silver fork" novels of the English aristocracy), *Constance Lyndsay* by a still-unknown author, Mrs. Elizabeth Grey's *The Duke and the Cousin* and *The Belle of the Family,* and Count Philippe Jarnac's *Rockingham; or, the Younger Brother.* Simms's copies of the novels by Jarnac and Mrs. Grey (including *The Gambler's Wife*) are preserved in the remnants of his library at SCL.

New Novels. 1849.

We must exercise a sort of summary process jurisdiction in respect to this collection. There is no reason that we should do otherwise, where there are no peculiarities in the novel of a character to take it out of the general rule—where, in fact, there is no absolute originality. *Shirley,* necessarily occupies a first place in our regards as a work which has attracted more than common consideration. The name of Currer Bell, given as that of the author of this and previous romances, is now understood to be a *nom de plume,* and the newspaper gossip ascribes them to a Miss Brontë. If, indeed, a lady, she employs a very masculine pen. *Shirley,* though less successful as a story than *Jane Eyre,* is quite as full of the proof of power. Its merits consist rather in the development of character and in highly wrought scenes than in its combinations. Its portraiture is much more vigorous than its invention. Shirley herself, is a highly spirited portrait, with some striking faults, and some of the scenes are very excellent—that in especial, where Moore relates to Yorke the manner of Shirley's rejection of his hand. This is equal to anything in *Jane Eyre. Sir Edward Graham* is by Catharine Sinclair, a lady formerly known by several other writings. Its portraiture is generally inferior. The arts of Miss Percival were too transparent to deceive any by the most consummate flat; and the contradictions in her character are not less offensive to *vraisemblance* than to good taste. We have found the book a dull one. *The Dowager,* and *Mothers and Daughters,* by Mrs. Gore, are pleasant specimens of a class with which that lady has made us almost too familiar. They are quite readable, however, if not rememberable. To Mrs. Grey, we owe *The Duke and the Cousin,* and *The Belle of the Family,* tales more sedate and less spirited than those of Mrs. Gore, but of the same order: things that amuse us while they last, like certain companions, but whom we never miss, and never recall, after departure. *Constance Lindsay,* seems to be by a new candidate. It carries us back a century, and riots in old materials which we had fondly fancied were forever buried with the ancient rubbish of a day of extreme bigotry. We have the arts of the Jesuits brought back,—the snares of Rome, and the martyrdom of brave spirits, who, under recovering consciences, have broken away from thralldom. The book is without probability, and, unless to feed ancient grudges, and prejudices that ought to be suffered to die out, we see no policy in the employment of such material. Portions of the story are interesting, but as a whole it will be found tedious. *Rockingham; or, the Younger Brother,* is a work of more real power than any of these stories, *Shirley,* perhaps, excepted. It is life-like, full of action, and of an interest well sustained to the close.

Southern Quarterly Review n.s. 1 (April 1850): 255–56.

Sir Thomas Carlyle's *Latter-Day Pamphlets*

As one of the few philosophers who witnessed the industrial revolution but still kept a nonmaterialistic view, Carlyle (1795–1881) reinforced Simms's early rejection of the cash nexus he had expressed by 1826 (Kibler, "Letters from the West"). Carlyle's stand against Utilitarianism and the commercialization of society and his questioning of the naive claims of a strictly material progress struck particularly responsive chords, as did his depiction of the active man of letters as true hero. In this notice Simms revealed the move he had been making for some time from the American nationalist viewpoint to the broader transatlantic tie. Here he noted (and later reiterated in his January 1870 review of *Putnam's,* p. 191) that the South and Europe had closer ties and deeper mutual respect than either the North and Europe or the North and the South. He continued to strengthen his transatlantic interests and connections as his acquaintances in Young America grew increasingly aggressive against the South. (See Bryant review, p. 142). For example, he followed current Irish literature more closely, especially that of the independence movement, a topic that had interested him since his early years, but now from an additional impetus. Some of the particular American bores whom Carlyle had in mind were the Boston and New York City set. Simms's declaration that "The American people as a race of bores" would try the patience of the "best tempered person" is a good indication of his new attitude. Simms reviewed *Sartor Resartus; On Heroes, Hero-Worship, and the Heroic in History; Past and Present;* and *Critical and Miscellaneous Essays* in an excellent compendium review essay in *SQR* 14 (July 1848): 77–100. He had *Latter-Day Pamphlets* reviewed at length by George F. Holmes (*SQR* n.s. 2 [November 1850]: 313–50). Simms's review of Carlyle's collected writings (Charleston *Mercury*, 22 June 1860) was his final eloquent tribute: "Perhaps Mr. Carlyle has never done more good to mankind than in the steadiness with which he has concentrated his great powers upon the inculcation of the one grand absorbing moral law of sincerity."

Father Mathew was Father Theobald Mathew (1790–1856), Irish temperance reformer, who toured the United States after this review was written. Despite his earlier sympathies, Mathew refused to endorse abolition and thus enraged his former northern abolitionist friends and supporters, who savaged him personally and in print.

Latter-Day Pamphlets. By Thomas Carlyle. New York: Harper & Brothers. Boston: Phillips, Sampson & Co. 1850.

Here are two very neat editions of Carlyle's *Latter-Day Pamphlets,* one of those publications which cannot be dismissed in a single paragraph. We must reserve it for a future moment of greater space and leisure. Carlyle has offended the people of the North, since he has come out, sensibly, philosophically, and like a man, superior to cant and false philanthropy, in favour of negro slavery. They now discover that he is a fool, a twattler, and, like Father Mathew, has lived just a year too long. We perceive but little falling off, in these pamphlets, from the stern, old, prophetic Carlyle whom we have known before. "He repeats himself!" cry aloud the donkeys of literature; as if they did not repeat themselves, day after day, to the eternal sickening of all good men's stomachs—as if Isaiah, and all the prophets had not need, hourly, to repeat themselves, since the wretched communities to which they addressed entreaty and imprecation, in vain, were also repeating themselves, with increasing vice and venom, with neither remorse nor understanding. But the wonder is, to see so many of our Southern presses— not having read these pamphlets—actually repeating the clamours of their Yankee file-leaders—actually denouncing, in their abominable blindness, one of their best friends and champions. What if Carlyle does sneer at the American people as a race of bores: we need not be solicitous in the defence of the Yankee part of the nation. And, it is this part which has been boring him, and all other English writers, by visit and letter, until the best tempered person in the world might well be angry.

Southern Quarterly Review n.s. 1 (July 1850): 509.

Henry William Herbert's *Frank Forester's Fish and Fishing of the United States*

This Englishman living in New York was an early admirer of Simms's fiction. He ranked *Guy Rivers* above the works of Cooper and even Scott (*American Monthly Magazine* 3 [July 1834]: 295–304). Herbert placed Simms first among American novelists in a review of *The Yemassee* (*American Monthly Magazine* 4 [February 1835]: 367–68), and again he found the novel "above any romance of native production on a native subject" (*American Monthly Magazine* 5 [May 1835]: 171–81). The following year, Herbert wrote of Simms, "There is no author whose abilities we deem more highly" (n.s. 1 [January 1836]: 101–4). Simms contributed important essays such as "The Philosophy of the Omnibus" and "The Progress of Civilisation" to Herbert's *American Monthly Magazine* 3 (May 1834: 153–59 and August 1834: 361–72).

Although Parks made no mention of Herbert, Simms noticed his works often. In 1836 he wrote that Herbert's *The Brothers* is a "spirited romance" with a plot both "impetuous and exciting" (*SLJ* 2 [July 1836]: 395). In 1849 he called Herbert's Irish novel *Dermot O'Brien, or the Taking of Tredagh* "defective in invention" and possessing a "meagre" plot. Although Simms observed that Herbert here makes use of a deus ex machina, he "never outrages the sterling rule of the poet: '*Nec deus intersit, nisi dingus vindice nodus*'" (*SQR* 16 [October 1849]: 256). The quotation is from Horace's *Ars Poetica:* "Never use a god to intervene unless the situation is so knotted up that only a god could untwist it." In 1853 Simms found Herbert's *Chevaliers of France* "a world of stirring adventure." Of Herbert's writings in general, he judged: "He is always respectable— too respectable, perhaps, since he is always on stilts. His style is too elevated for the quiet and domestic portions of his story, and he does not seem to perceive that the effect of this is to impart frigidity to a narrative which would otherwise possess a force and a passion such as the incidents seem to require" (*SQR* n.s. 7 [January 1853]: 272). No doubt the southern author whom Simms had in mind to do the counterpart of *Fish and Fishing* was William Elliott of Beaufort, whose *Carolina Sports, by Land and Water* Simms noticed on two occasions: *S&W* 2 (December 1845): 422–23, and at length in *SQR* 12 (July 1847): 67–90.

***Frank Forrester's Fish and Fishing of the United States and British Provinces of North America.* By Henry Wm. Herbert. New York: Stringer & Townsend. 1850.**

There are few of our writers so variously endowed and accomplished as Mr. Herbert; of a mind easily warmed and singularly enthusiastic, the natural bent of his talent inclines him to romance. He has accordingly given us several stories abounding in stately scenes, and most impressive portraiture. Well skilled in the use of the mother tongue, as in the broad fields of classical literature, he has written essays of marked eloquence, and criticisms of excellent discrimination and a keen and thorough insight. His contributions to our periodicals, have been even more happy than his fictions. With a fine imagination, he inherits a *penchant* and a capacity for poetry, which has enabled him to throw off, without an effort, some of the most graceful fugitive effusions which have been written in America. His accomplishments are as various as his talents. He can paint a landscape as sweetly as he can describe it in words. He is a sportsman of eager impulse, and relishes equally well the employments of the fisherman and hunter. He is a naturalist, as well as a sportsman, and brings, to aid his practice and experience, a large knowledge, from study, of the habits of birds, beasts and fishes. He roves land and sea in this pursuit, forest and river, and turns, with equal ease and readiness, from a close examination of Greek and Roman literature, to an emulous exercise of all the arts which have afforded renown to the aboriginal hunter. The volume before us—one of many which he has given to this subject—is one of singular interest to the lover of the rod and angle. It exhibits, on every page, a large personal knowledge of the finny tribes in all the northern portions of our country, and well deserves the examination of those who enjoy such pursuits and pastimes. The author's pencil has happily illustrated the labours of his pen. His portraits of the several fishes of the United States are exquisitely well done and truthful. It is our hope, in future pages, to furnish an ample review of this, and other interesting volumes, of similar character, from the hands of our author. We have drawn to them the attention of some rarely endowed persons in our own region, who, like our author, unite the qualities of the writer and the sportsman; from whom we look to learn in what respects the habits and characters of northern fish differ from our own, and thus supply the deficiency of the work before us. The title of this work is rather too general. The author's knowledge of the fish, and of fishing, in the United States, is almost wholly confined to the regions north of the Chesapeake, and he falls into the error, quite too common to the North, of supposing this region to be the whole country. Another such volume as that before us will be necessary to do justice to the Southern States, whose possessions, in the finny tribes of sea and river, are of a sort to shame into comparative insignificance all the boasted treasures of the North. It would need but few pages in our review, from the proper hands, to render this very apparent to the reader. Meanwhile, we exhort him to seek the book of Mr. Herbert, as a work of much interest and authority, so far as it goes.

Southern Quarterly Review n.s. 1 (July 1850): 527–28.

The Life and Letters of Thomas Campbell

Simms's connection to the English literary scene was more than tenuous. Campbell himself reviewed Simms's *Atalantis* in his London *Metropolitan Magazine* 9 (January 1834): 12. Albany William Fonblanque (1794–1872), a man of some literary authority in his day as editor of the London *Examiner* from 1830 to 1849, had pronounced *Atalantis* worthy of the author of *Comus*. Simms's *Southern Literary Gazette* coeditor and mentor, James Wright Simmons, had returned from London in the mid-1820s. There he knew Leigh Hunt and was a friend of one of Byron's circle. Byron's friend and compatriot in Greece, Edward John Trelawney, visited Charleston in 1829 and no doubt met Simmons and Simms (*Simms Review* 8 [Winter 2000]: 20–21). Participation in Young America seems to have narrowed Simms during the decades of the 1830s and 1840s, when the group strongly insisted on a distinctively American literature cut loose from England and Europe. Some scholars have emphasized Simms's retreat to things southern in the 1850s; but perhaps what might be more fruitful to consider is his earlier turn from a transatlantic connection to the parochialism of Young America, and a shrinking into an American box from which he has never recovered. Then, Simms's rupture with the North, confirmed by his northern lecture tour in 1856, left him without true influential friends in either sphere. Campbell's high praise and Fonblanque's comparison to Milton marked the height of Simms's recognition abroad as poet, even though by 1834 his career as poet had just begun in earnest. Simms continued to ask James Lawson to send his books to the *Edinburgh Review* in the late 1850s, but this did not happen.

In a previously unrecorded review of Campbell's *Letters from the South, Written During a Journey to Algiers,* Simms paid respect to the poet's genius and noble qualities (*SLJ* 3 [December 1836]: 239–48). He thought highly enough of the essay to collect and bind it in "Reviews and Criticisms" (SCL). In the 1840s, after Campbell's death, Simms placed him with Thomas Moore in his poem "Heads of the Poets," one of a select few authors to be so enshrined. In *Poetry and the Practical,* he listed Campbell as a minstrel like Ariosto, Virgil, and Tasso—good company indeed. For Simms, Campbell's death in debtor's prison in 1844 was an indication of the "heartless indifference of the world to the fate of its most noble intellects" (94). "Noble," in fact, is a word he often used with Campbell.

Of Capt. Frederick Marryat (1792–1848), Campbell's replacement as editor of the London *Metropolitan,* Simms had written earlier, "his talents are considerable," with "a coarse sense of humor, which gives a healthy relish to his ordinary scenes . . . a stout, rough writer of plain English,—a sort of William Cobbett in fiction" (*SQR* 7 [April 1845]: 335). Simms had met Marryat around 1840–1844; he mentioned Marryat's rivalry with Campbell in the Charleston *Mercury* of 28 September 1859, where he described Marryat thus: "Personally, he is rude of manner, coarse of speech, as of look, and with such a strong relish of the fore-mast man in all that he says and seems, that the wonder is how he ever got upon the quarter-deck" (*SQR* n.s. 2 [April 1845]: 335. In short Marryat was no Campbell.

Life and Letters of Thomas Campbell. Edited by William Beattie, M.D., one of his executors. In two volumes. New York: Harper & Brothers. 1850.

These volumes furnish a very affecting history of the career of a man of genius, of whose private griefs and trials, our American world hitherto has known but little. Campbell has usually been regarded as a successful man of letters. It was, perhaps, his worst misfortune, as a literary man, that he should have been so rapidly successful—that, at a single bound, he should have placed himself so conspicuously, almost on the highest rounds of fame. He could scarcely have gone higher at any succeeding leap: yet the natural expectation required that he should do so. His own elevation embarrassed him; his courage faltered at the reflection that any future effort involved quite as much chance of loss as prospect of gain; and the apprehensions thus provoked by success, acting upon tastes naturally fastidious, and a temperament singularly susceptible to external influences, restrained and delayed his efforts, and lessened the number, if not the vigour of his performances. *Gertrude of Wyoming,* "O'Connor's Child," the martial and naval lyrics, and some two or three isolated pieces, which remain unclassed—"The Last Man," for example—are admitted fully to have sustained and enhanced the reputation which their author had won by *The Pleasures;* but after these, his muse obtained no successes with the public. It is still a question whether she did not deserve to obtain them. We are not prepared to believe that there is less *real* poetry in *Theoderic* than in *The Pleasures of Hope;* on the contrary, there is, we are persuaded, a great deal more;—but there is less pleasing and swelling declamation, and this is the more *popular* quality in verse. We shall endeavour, at some early day, to review the whole of Campbell's poetry, with the view to the proper development of what is excellent, and to be cherished, in his less appreciated performances. To one who reads these volumes, there will be no surprise that he achieved so little. The wonder will be that he achieved so much. His private and literary history, as traced here by a friendly biographer, is a touching and instructive one. We are afraid that our biographer has passed, however, with too much tenderness over the private errors of his subject. There is no policy in this forbearance. It is not properly due to the author, and the opposite course is due to the world, and to succeeding poets. We have no doubt that Campbell's habits were deplorably bad. We remember the almost brutal answer, concerning them, which Capt. Marryat, when in this country, made to ourselves, in answer to a direct question, "Yes, d—n him, drunk on gin every night!" His biographer touches upon this frailty with extreme tenderness. It was probably under this sort of inspiration that Campbell uttered his absurdities with regard to the United States and the slave institutions of the South. His sonnets and speeches, where these are the subjects, are equally maudlin. But we have no pleasure in dwelling upon the failings of superior intellect. We commend these two volumes to all the admirers of Campbell the poet, in the day of his strength and purity. They afford a painful history of griefs and weaknesses, of ambition, too frequently looking round for the crutch, when it should have seized the staff; and of pride, lacking that proper tone and consistency, without which the results were inevitable in disappointment and humiliation. Campbell seems to have been quite too fond of looking about him for assistance—to have been quite too ready to borrow money from his friends, and even newly-made acquaintance—in brief, to have lacked the manhood, which resolves, from the first, on self-reliance. Dr. Beattie is not much of an artist, and—perhaps prudently—has left the subject to speak as much as possible for himself. The correspondence is very copious, and contains numerous small pieces of verse, which have never before appeared in print; but these letters nowhere impress you with the idea of a man of large and commanding powers.

Southern Quarterly Review n.s. 2 (September 1850): 248–49.

Henry Wadsworth Longfellow's *Poems*

Simms reviewed Longfellow as early as 1845 (*S&W* 2 [December 1845]: 347–49) and then throughout his career. An arch-enemy of Young America, Longfellow was no friend of Simms. The following gracious treatment of his merits provides a balance and evenness that is typical of Simms the reviewer. Simms always strove to divorce faction from art, a trait that he says Longfellow could not do in his "moment of folly and fanaticism." This objectivity became more and more difficult for Simms as the political rhetoric of the 1850s became more extreme on both sides. The memorable final sentences of the following review summarize nicely both Simms's view of truth as the basis of poetry and his intense dislike of didacticism. Later, in the Charleston *Mercury* of 22 December 1855, Simms deemed *Hiawatha* "dreary, irredeemable nonsense" and *Evangeline* very little better. His last known review of Longfellow was in the Charleston *Courier* of 19 November 1869. Privately Simms made clear his position on Young America's accusation of the poet's propensity for plagiarism: Longfellow "stole from everybody" (*Letters,* 5: 263–64). See also Simms's review of Longfellow's *Kavanagh* (p. 100).

Poems. By Henry Wadsworth Longfellow. In two volumes. A new edition. Boston: Ticknor, Reed & Fields. 1850.

Longfellow is confessedly one of the most charming poets of the present generation; his merits as a writer of grace, of fancy, and of exquisite taste, are beyond question, and almost beyond comparison. His verse flows, rarely limpid, in the pleasant sunlight, and among the shady woods. It is a bird song, speaking of the free, generous and bouyant nature; of morning and its dews; of evening and its flowers; of night and its unclouded stars. He is a moral poet, without being an ascetic; a fanciful poet, without being flippant and capricious; and a thoughtful poet, without obscurity or crudeness. He is not profound as a poet; is not imaginative, or only in moderate degree; we cannot urge his originality, nor can we speak of him as possessing voice of much power or intensity; but for purity, grace, sweetness, and consistency of tone, the charm of manner, the delicacy of his fancy, and the melody of his strain, it would be scarce possible to find his equal among living poets, and still more difficult to assert that he has any superior. That he is largely imitative is unquestionable; but he certainly possesses the happy faculty of improving in some respects upon the materials which he appropriates. The present edition is the best for the library that we have seen. It is beautifully printed, on the best paper, in the best style. Here we have said every thing that we can conscientiously say in behalf of the author and his publishers. We regret that what we have yet to say, must be in a different temper. These volumes contain matters which are by no means contemplated in any thing that we have just said. They contain sundry gross and coarse verses, which Longfellow, in a moment of folly and fanaticism, has devoted to slavery subjects—brutalities and falsehoods, coined from the abolition mint, and which not even the genius of the author, his otherwise pure taste and graceful utterance, can possibly elevate with any of the characteristics of poetry. Here his fancy leaves him,—here his grace departs—he flounders heavily along with the falsehood, and experiences, in the ill success of these articulated strains, the full truth of the maxim of the artist, that, unless the soul of the fiction be truth, there is no life in it—nothing by which it can live. The poet never so trifles with his fame as when he lends his genius to the purposes of a faction.

Southern Quarterly Review n.s. 2 (September 1850): 255–56.

Robert Browning's *Poems*

Parks remarked that Simms knew Browning's poetry as early as July 1848, when he sent a poem to Caroline Gilman that mentioned him (52). Simms grouped Browning with Tennyson and R. H. Horne in his "Heads of the Poets" in *Graham's* 33 (September 1848): 170–71, and *The Cassique of Accabee* (New York: Putnam's, 1849): 80–88. In 1854 Simms wrote an essay on both Robert and Elizabeth Barrett Browning, placing them in the "sensuous and fanciful school of poetry." He gave the laurels to Robert, despite Elizabeth's greater popularity, and singled out *Poems* and *Sordello* for praise (Charleston *Mercury*, 20 and 22 December 1854 and 13 January 1855). His assessment of Browning was ahead of its day. For an extended treatment of Simms and Browning, see Jason Johnson, "A Southern Victorian: William Gilmore Simms's Reconstruction of Robert Browning," *Simms Review* 18 (Summer/Winter 2010): 35–44.

**Poems. By Robert Browning. In two volumes. A new edition.
Boston: Ticknor, Reed & Fields. 1850.**

This very beautiful edition is worthy of the author whom it enshrines. Browning is no common verse-maker. He is a writer of thought and genius, of peculiar and curious powers as an artist; subtle, spiritual, and singularly fanciful, and, though as yet perhaps unacknowledged, is one of the master minds of living European song. He is obscure, however, and will scarcely ever reach that degree of popularity which follows only the limpid and transparent Sonnetteer. He will grow slowly in public esteem, and, finally, when his peculiar phraseology shall become familiar, to the ear, it will compel an admiration which is very far from general now. The singular deficiency with Browning, at present, seems to be that his power of utterance is inadequate to the thought with which he is burdened. It will need more years of practice before he will find a fit expression for the phrenzies of his muse. Hence his obscurities and roughnesses, and the frequent wrong done to his fancies by the halting and ungainly measures in which he clothes them. We shall probably review him at length hereafter. Meanwhile, let us briefly say, that his claims to the regards of those who require a deep and earnest thought, in verse, as well as music and fancy, is beyond question. All such persons must take him to their studies, if not to their hearts. It is only through the one, indeed, that he can find his way to the other. Why, let us ask, have the publishers of this very fine edition, omitted *Sordello* from its table of contents?

Southern Quarterly Review n.s. 2 (September 1850): 256–57.

Alfred Lord Tennyson's *In Memoriam*

Contrary to John Eidson's standard *Tennyson in America,* which stated that the *Southern Quarterly Review* "did not like *In Memoriam* at all" (79), the notice is balanced in Simms's usual way. Eidson also wrongly implied that the *Southern Quarterly Review* notice of April 1853 was by Simms. It was actually by Robert H. Nelson. Eidson called it another of the magazine's "depreciations of Tennyson." In fact Simms referred to Tennyson as "one of the greatest poets now living in England" (*SQR* n.s. 2 [September 1850]: 21). Simms's evaluation of the poet was on the whole favorable, sound, and reasonable, especially when compared to reviews in some other American periodicals. For example, Orestes Brownson, in *Brownson's Quarterly,* called *In Memoriam* tiresome and Tennyson "a poet for puny transcendentalists, beardless boys, and miss in her teens." Simms favorably reviewed *Maud* in the Charleston *Mercury* of 12 November 1855 and then *The Princess, Maud* again, and other Tennyson works in the *Mercury* of 16 June 1859, where he called the author "a frank, earnest, and simple poet."

In Memoriam. Boston: Ticknor, Reed & Field. 1850.

This volume is understood to be by Alfred Tennyson, though there is nothing on the title page, and there is no preface to assure us of the fact. It is a tribute to the memory of A. H. Hallam, a son of the historian, who was united to our author by the sweetest and strongest bonds of friendship, and who was destined to be united in marriage with his sister. But the one union was ruptured, and the other was prevented by the premature death of Hallam, at Vienna. This is all that we learn of the subject, and this is only gathered from the verses of the volume. Tennyson is now confessedly at the head of the English poets. The death of Wordsworth, recently, and the condition of Moore, render this claim for him indisputable. His genius unites, in degree, the peculiarly spiritual endowments of Shelley, without his intensity, and the contemplative nature of Wordsworth, warmed by much more of enthusiasm and passion. We shall, in future pages devote ourselves to an examination of his genius and performances. For the volume before us a few words will suffice. It contains undoubtedly a considerable proportion of excellent verse; sweet fancies and subdued thoughts, in a mournful strain, such as the title might lead us to expect. But the plan of the volume is monotonous,—more than two hundred pages, in verse, upon a single general topic, however diversified by varieties of rhythm, and broken into small pieces, each addressed to some one of the phases of the theme, could scarcely be otherwise. But Mr. Tennyson has not employed a varying rhythm. His verse is not only uniform in measure and structure, but it is one which does not readily commend itself to the ear. Though marked with frequent rests and pauses, the only change which it shows, is in the transition from one sentiment of the same subject to another. Death, loss, change, privation; memory of the past; hope of the future; recollection of dear scenes, hallowed by the presence of the lost one; the presence of dear sufferers who still weep; the tree where the poet and his friend lay together in the noon-tide; the studies which they mutually pursued, the endowments, hopes, qualities, performances of the lost one,— these, and many other incidental themes, naturally educed from the main topic, furnish the material of the volume, and afford many passages of tenderness, and mournful but grateful contemplation. We give a single one as a specimen:

> How pure at heart and sound in head,
> With what divine affections bold,
> Should be the man whose thought would hold
> An hour's communion with the dead.
>
> In vain shalt thou, or any, call
> The spirits from their golden day,
> Except like them, thou too canst say
> My spirit is at peace with all.
>
> They haunt the silence of the breast,
> Imaginations calm and fair,
> The memory like a cloudless air,
> The conscience as a seat of rest:
>
> But when the heart is full of din,
> And doubt beside the portal waits,
> They can but listen at the gates
> And hear the household jar within.

Southern Quarterly Review n.s. 2 (November 1850): 535–36.

William Wordsworth's *The Prelude, or Growth of a Poet's Mind*

In his maturity Simms considered Wordsworth the greatest living poet and un-questionably "the greatest contemplative poet that has ever lived" (*Views and Reviews*, First Series, 37). Simms felt that his friend William Cullen Bryant was the greatest contemplative poet in America, but one who fell far short of Wordsworth. Simms mentioned Wordsworth scores of times and used him as the standard by which to measure all other contemplative poets. "Contemplative" for Simms was not an altogether positive term, however. In *Views and Reviews,* he discussed the nature of the contemplative writer, "usually a phlegmatic in temperament" who lacks "the blood and the brain in common" (First Series, 37–40). Great as Wordsworth was, Simms felt that Chaucer, Shakespeare, Spenser, and Milton far outstretched him in every way. Simms deemed *The Prelude* Wordsworth's best achievement, a discernment with which many Wordsworth afficionados would agree. For Simms this poem was the real biography of the man, which "tells us all we need to know." Simms correctly called *The Prelude* the history of the author's mind. (Columbia, S.C., *Phoenix,* 21 June 1865). For a book-length treatment of the similarities between the poetry of Simms and Wordsworth, see Matthew Brennan's *The Poet's Holy Craft: William Gilmore Simms and Romantic Verse Tradition.*

The Prelude, or Growth of a Poet's Mind. An Auto-biographical Poem. By William Wordsworth. New York: D. Appleton & Co.

We owe it to Wordsworth to bestow the most elaborate consideration upon this last and admirable effort of his genius. We shall do this hereafter, at a moment when we can command the necessary space and leisure. It must suffice, for the present, that we say that this poem is quite worthy of his muse, and absolutely essential to the history of his progress and career. It is full of passages marked by his earnest sweetness, the grave delicacy of his mood, his habit of musing contemplation, and the rare philosophical simplicity which makes the analysis of his mind and writings a study so interesting. We take for granted that every one who has ever sympathized with the previous writings of our author, will soon put himself in possession of this volume. It is due to the publishers to say that they have given it to us in excellent library costume; a large new type, fine white paper, and a beautiful impression on every page, commending it to the eye worthily, as becomes the noble strain of meditative and narrative verse, which the author so gratefully commends to our minds.

Southern Quarterly Review n.s. 2 (November 1850): 540.

Nathaniel Hawthorne's *The House of the Seven Gables*

When Simms reviewed Hawthorne's *The Marble Faun* in the Charleston *Mercury* of 7 June 1860, he gave an extended, balanced appreciation of the author as "a man of genius, a man of fine original conceptions; of a taste at once delicate and masculine; of a nice blending of the sanguine and the spiritual, of exquisite sentiment; and a just recognition, along with it, of the sensuous and human. . . . His readers . . . will always, in spite of all failures, feel themselves in the keeping of one who not only thinks for himself, but will require them to do some thinking also." Simms concluded that *The Marble Faun* would richly repay readers whose views are "somewhat metaphysical." Simms also gave favorable notices of *Tanglewood Tales* (*SQR*, n.s. 9 [January 1854]: 256) and *The Snow Image* (*SQR*, n.s. 5 [January 1852]: 262), the latter of which, "quiet, gentle, fanciful," clothes "naked facts in pleasing allegory, and beguiling to truths and virtue, through the pleasing labyrinths of fiction." In the following he gave a perceptive general analysis of Hawthorne's art. See also his review of *The Blithedale Romance*, p. 122.

The House of the Seven Gables. A Romance. By Nathaniel Hawthorne. Boston: Ticknor, Reed & Fields. 1851.

Mr. Hawthorne is rapidly making himself a high reputation, as a writer of prose fiction. He is a tale writer, rather than a novelist, and exhibits some very peculiar endowments in this character. He has a rare and delicate fancy, with an imagination capable, in particular, of that curious distribution of light and shade—"that little glooming light, most like a shade,"—which constitutes the singular faculty of some of the most remarkable of the Italian painters. He is truthful, also, in his delineations of character, though his range is a limited one. He enters, with the art of Sterne, into the heart of his single captive, and, with exquisite adroitness, unfolds to you, and to the victim's self, the hurts of the secret nerve, its morbid condition, and how it operates upon, and affects by sympathy, the whole system. In these revelations, our author shows himself a minute philosopher. He goes farther than the simple delineation of the sore and secret places—he shows you why they became sore, and how they failed to keep their secrets from him. As a writer of prose fancies, fresh and delicate, of simple truths of the heart, which are obscure, in other hands, only from the absence of those exquisite antennae which he employs, he exhibits a grace and felicity which show him to be a master. His province is peculiarly this fine one of the heart, with its subtler conditions, its eccentric moods, the result of secret weaknesses or secret consciousnesses, which it dare not confess and dare not overcome—its aberrations of soul or temper—its morbid passions, which fester without action, and are thus quite as vicious as if they had become developed by the actual commission of crime. Of the particular story before us, we have only to add that it exhibits happily the characteristic faculty of the author, in the delineation of morbid and peculiar conditions—in the curious distribution of light and shadow, and in the utterance of graceful and happy fancies, in close connection with moral philosophies and mental feelings, which are at once true to nature and agreeable to art. As a story, *The House of the Seven Gables* will probably prove less attractive to the general reader than *The Scarlet Letter,* as exhibiting a less concentrative power; but it is a more truthful book, and, if less ambitious in plan and manner, is not less earnest of purpose, nor less efficient in the varieties of character.

Southern Quarterly Review, 4 n. s. (July 1851): 256.

Christopher Wordsworth's *Memoirs of William Wordsworth*

Bishop Christopher Wordsworth (1807–1885) was the poet's nephew. As Simms had said in his 1845 review of Richter, if one seeks the author, he should look for him in his work, for Wordsworth's "life was in his poetry entirely." In the final analysis, for Simms it was the work, not the life of the author, that mattered.

Memoirs of William Wordsworth. **By Christopher Wordsworth. In two volumes. Edited by Henry Reed. Vol. I. Boston: Ticknor, Reed & Fields. 1851.**

The personal life of the literary man, as commonly written, is not often an interesting or instructive one. That of the poet is still less likely to be so; and that of a man like Wordsworth—a recluse—in the last degree shy, reserved, exclusive—living wholly *within,* if not wholly *for,* himself—must, of necessity, require the most singular endowments on the part of the biographer, to render the smallest justice to either subject or reader. Wordsworth's life was in his poetry entirely. He is a remarkable instance of a person dedicating himself, at the earliest period, to the service of the Muses. He set himself apart, as a priest, at their altars, directing all his thoughts, sympathies, aspirations, studies, to the single object of his choice, eschewing every other form of life, all the attractions of the outer world, and living wholly in the subtle atmosphere—which most men find quite too thin and cold—of the fancy and imagination. Such a life needs a biographer, who can breathe at ease and with pleasure in the same atmosphere. Wordsworth has not found this biographer in his excellent kinsman, to whom the work was confided. The memoir, thus far, is simply one of facts—baldly given; meagre facts, unwarmed by eloquence, and wanting in that double faculty of mixed spiritual and philosophical, which is, over all other qualities, the one necessary to pursue the inner being of a creature like Wordsworth, and analyze at once his character and genius. The subject needed a philosopher, and has found a chronicler only. But the work is one of integrity—affords us details of newness and interest—makes copious extracts from the correspondence and the prose writings of Wordsworth, and is, altogether, a still valuable acquisition, though falling greatly short of our hopes and expectations. For such a work, we need such a writer as De Quincey. The perusal of the extracts from Wordsworth's political pamphlets moves us to desire that some of our publishers would make a complete collection of his prose writings. They would, like Milton's, afford a noble support to the monument which his verse has consecrated to his genius. They are at once pure in purpose, vigorous in spread and stretch of thought, and chaste and eloquent of style. We commend the suggestion to the consideration of the enterprising publishers, to whom we owe the present volume.

Southern Quarterly Review n.s. 4 (July 1851): 246–47.

Margaret Fuller's *Memoirs*

In 1846 Simms found Fuller "a woman of thought, who *feels* her subject, and is one of our most human and genial philosophers" (Charleston *Southern Patriot,* 9 July 1846). Parks has Simms "personally on friendly terms" with her (*William Gilmore Simms as Literary Critic,* 127). She was strongly influenced by Horace Greeley of the New York *Tribune.* A member of Brook Farm, the socialist utopian experiment, she was also influenced by Charles Fourier, the French socialist, and his New York publisher Albert Brisbane. Fuller was likely the model for the unfortunate Zenobia in Hawthorne's *The Blithedale Romance.* After Fuller's death at sea in July 1850, *Memoirs of Margaret Fuller Ossoli* was published in February 1852, edited by Ralph Waldo Emerson and William Henry Channing, the socialist Brook Farm Unitarian clergyman. Her editors, believing her works would not be of lasting importance, censored and reworded her manuscript, leaving out all references to her love interests. They had not foreseen that the book would be the bestselling biography of its decade in the United States. By 1852 it was obvious that Simms's opinion of Fuller had changed dramatically. His final notice of her came in the Charleston *Mercury* of 26 May 1856 in reference to her brother Arthur Fuller's edition of her *At Home and Abroad.*

Simms often noted Greeley's "cold-blooded" and vehement attacks on the South. As Mary Boykin Chesnut declared in 1861, "Greeley says in his *Tribune,* 'South Carolina is the meanest and the vainest state in the Union . . . and nobody will feel any compunction at laying it waste'" (*Mary Chesnut's Civil War,* 264). In 1850 Simms reviewed Greeley's *Hints Towards Reform,* where he called its author an egocentric reformer after the school of Fourier and "a wrong-headed man of considerable parts, who suffers under the conviction that the burden of American reform has developed particularly, and by special decree of heaven, on his shoulders" (*SQR* n.s. 2 [November 1850]: 542–43). Simms grouped Greeley, Fourier, Brisbane, Channing, and Fuller among those "cold-blooded fanatics" who in good Enlightenment, Deistic manner would perpetrate revolutions as mere interesting experiments on humanity "for the sake of science."

Memoirs of Sarah Margaret Fuller (Marchesa Ossoli.) Edited by R.W. Emerson and W.H. Channing. In two volumes. Boston: Phillips, Sampson & Co. and Charleston: John Russell.

The Marchesa Ossoli, *née* Fuller, was one of those clever, and somewhat pragmatical female writers, whom our Yankee friends are apt to regard as domestic prodigies. She was certainly a prodigy of self-esteem. She had considerable and various talent, no doubt; but seems to have laboured under an evil social training, that tended to confirm this self-esteem,—which, largely developed from the beginning, grew, finally, into a despotism, at once, for herself and her neighbours. A flippant society of self-constituted philosophers, creatures at once pert and dull, ministered daily to this infirmity, and did much to prevent the proper application of her power, and to defeat the just performance of her faculties. She had a good deal of the practical talent, more than she employed; and was shrewd and smart, at the same time, in discussion; but always argueing in a circle, or from falsely assumed premises. She ranked as a reformer, after the schools of Fourier, Brisbane, Channing, Greeley, and that tribe of cold-blooded fanatics who regard revolutions only as interesting experiments upon the race, for the sake of science. Her writings were mainly contributed to *The Dial Magazine* and to *The Tribune*. Her collected papers, as far as we have seen them, are contained in the volumes entitled *Women in the Nineteenth Century*, and *Papers on Literature and Art*. She perished at sea, on her return to this country. The two handsome volumes before us contain portions of an Autobiography, selections from her Correspondence, and brief passages from the pens of her editors, supplying the gaps in the narrative. The book will prove interesting as a study of a being, singularly constituted, and thrust by circumstance, and education, into a false and really unfriendly position. Margaret Fuller was wrong-headed, no doubt; but this was rather her misfortune than her fault. Such company as she seems to have kept, would have driven the common sense out of the brains of any woman. We perceive, by a London paper, that her Journals,—supposed to have been lost with her, at sea,—are likely to be recovered;—or, rather, that duplicates of them, are said to have been left by her—a proper precaution—with a lady friend in Europe.

Unidentified Newspaper Clipping, circa 1852. Simms's Scrapbook B, folio 6b, CCS, SCL.

Herman Melville's *Moby-Dick*

Simms reviewed at least six Melville novels from 1846 to 1854. In the Charleston *Southern Patriot* of 9 and 25 April 1846, he found *Typee* curious but interesting. Simms saw that Melville's "fiction takes the form of allegory rather than action" (*SQR* 16 [October 1846]: 260). That he was unaware of Melville's penchant for symbolism (as stated in Holman, ed., *Views and Reviews, First Series,* xxxvi) is disproved by this notice. Simms said that *Redburn* stands in contrast to *Mardi,* "being rather cold and prosaic, while that novel was wild, warm, and richly fanciful" (*SQR* n.s. 1 [April 1850]: 259). Simms allotted five pages to *White Jacket,* which he saw to be more an effort at reform of the navy than art. Calling it "a history, and an argument, not a story," nevertheless he saw Melville himself to be "a shrewd, sensible, well-informed man, thoughtful and practical." He was offended by Melville's monstrous character, named "Nulli" (*SQR* n.s. 1 [July 1850]: 520). Simms felt Melville's sensibleness completely left him with *Moby-Dick* and *Pierre.* This must have been a painful concession because both were allies of Young America, and Simms's friend Evert Duyckinck was one of Melville's closest friends and promoters. Melville scholars have as yet failed to ascribe this review of *Moby-Dick* to Simms.

Melville's *Moby-Dick*. Harper & Brothers.

In all those portions of this volume which relate directly to the whale, his appearance in the oceans which he inhabits; his habits, powers and peculiarities; his pursuit and capture; the interest of the reader will be kept alive, and his attention fully rewarded. We should judge, from what is before us, that Mr. Melville has as much personal knowledge of the whale as any man living, and is better able, than any man living, to display this knowledge in print. In all the scenes where the whale is the performer or the sufferer, the delineation and action are highly vivid and exciting. In all other respects, the book is sad stuff, dull and dreary, or ridiculous. Mr. Melville's Quakers are the wretchedest dolts and drivellers, and his Mad Captain, who pursues his personal revenges against the fish who has taken off his leg, at the expense of ship, crew and owners, is a monstrous bore, whom Mr. Melville has no way helped, by enveloping him in a sort of mystery. His ravings, and the ravings of some of the tributary characters, and the ravings of Mr. Melville himself, meant for eloquent declamation, are such as would justify a writ *de lunatico* against all the parties.

Southern Quarterly Review n.s. 5 (January 1852): 262.

Herman Melville's *Pierre, or the Ambiguities*

The dark, nihilistic world of *Pierre, or the Ambiguities* elicited an extreme response. Simms seemed to be gauging accurately Melville's severe depression, bordering on the suicidal. He knew Melville personally and no doubt read his character perceptively. Simms apparently remembered Melville affectionately in 1867, when Simms wrote that although very ill, he would, for Melville's sake, have gone to visit his brother Allan while in Charleston (*Letters,* 5: 55).

Melville's *Pierre, or the Ambiguities.* (Harpers.)

That *Typee, Omoo,* and other clever books, should be followed by such a farrago as this of *Pierre* was not surely to be predicted or anticipated. But, verily, there is no knowing when madness will break out, or in whom. That Herman Melville has gone "clean daft," is very much to be feared; certainly, he has given us a very mad book, my masters. His *dramatis personæ* are all mad as March hares, every mother's son of them, and every father's daughter of them; and that too, without needing that we should take any pains to prove their legitimacy. The sooner this author is put in ward the better. If trusted with himself, at all events give him no further trust in pen and ink, till the present fit has worn off. He will grievously hurt himself else—or his very amiable publishers.

Southern Quarterly Review n.s. 6 (October 1852): 532.

Nathaniel Hawthorne's *The Blithedale Romance*

Simms's comments on Zenobia are particularly interesting considering his review of Margaret Fuller's *Memoirs.* Hawthorne is said to have at least partly modeled the character on her. See Hawthorne's *The House of the Seven Gables* (p. 116) and "Margaret Fuller's *Memoirs*" (p. 119).

Hawthorne's *Blithedale* (Ticknor.)

We are inclined to think this very pretty story quite as successful, as a work of art, as any of the preceding volumes of our author. It has all their defects, and these defects are such as seem inseparable from the writer's mind. These lie chiefly in the shaping and conception of the work, and in the inadequate employment of his characters. Their results do not co-operate with their natures; and the events are not always accommodated to the moral of the personage. The catastrophe rarely satisfies the reader, and seldom accords with poetical propriety. Instead of

Zenobia committing suicide, an action equally shocking and unnecessary, he should have converted her, by marriage—the best remedy for such a case—from the error of her ways, and left her, a mother, with good prospects of a numerous progeny. Apart from faults such as this, the book is full of beauties. The character of Hollingsworth is admirably drawn in most respects.

Southern Quarterly Review n.s. 6 (October 1852): 543.

J. V. Huntington's *The Forest*

Jedediah Huntington (1815–1862), Episcopal clergyman of New York, converted to Roman Catholicism in 1849, as Simms correctly related. His *Lady Alice* appeared in the year of his conversion; his autobiographical *Alban, or the History of a Young Puritan* was published in 1851. This review presents another facet of Simms's antididacticism: his rejection of an author's placing a "theological hobby" over art. In many additional reviews, Simms criticized a work in which any other "pet hobby," "cant," "faction," reform, or "fanatic *ology* or *ism*" took the ascendancy. Here Simms also fleshed out and elaborated on his credo of "art for art's sake" before its English popularization. He never advocated art as religion, however, but as its aid and strong reinforcement.

Mr. Huntington, the author of *The Lady Alice*—a book which caused some sensation by its equal talent and voluptousness; and *Alban,* which, while it showed, perhaps, less art, showed no less talent and voluptousness than its predecessor—has now given us a third story, entitled, *The Forest* (Redfield)—a pleasing fiction, having the characteristics of the author of *Lady Alice* in general, but without pushing to such an extreme, as in his former writings, his peculiar modes of opinion and religious belief. Mr. Huntington having, we believe, been converted from Protestantism to Catholicism, has been too much disposed to carry his religion into his fictions, and, possibly, his fictions into his religion. A religious novel is, *prima facie,* a solecism in language no less than morals. To make a truth depend upon a fiction, or to argue a truth by means of fiction, or to endeavour to inculcate a body of moral opinion through the agency of a tale which requires the invention of facts, is a very doubtful, if not dangerous, practice. Art will sway, and should sway, in a work of art; and the truth will become as clay in the hands of the potter. It is very questionable, if we can safely pass beyond the wants of parable and allegory in any endeavour to make fiction a medium for the inculcation of morals. All *good* fiction may, and must, inculcate good morals; but to employ art, as subservient to morals simply, is greatly to degrade the medium in behalf of the object had in view. It is in consequence of these objections, that most religious fictions are frigid and ineffective. Art is paralyzed when coerced to inferior duty; and the very design of the author—that of making truth attractive to his readers—is defeated by the process. It seems to be written, that all lessonings for truth shall be studiously simple and direct. There is no royal road to morals any more than to education. Both require painstaking, unwearied application, care, anxiety, constant watchfulness, and a pursuit of the object for its own sake. The sweets are to follow, and to grow out of, the acquisition, and are only to be won while making it. Mr. Huntington's religious elements in his fictions, have invariably lessened their attractions as works of art; nor have his stories, by the degree of interest which they really possess, been of any help to his religion. We trust that he will hereafter keep them separate. Let him inculcate his theology by publications which shall show no false colours. Let him not endanger his religious argument, by urging it through a medium, the very success of which is fatal to any interest which the reader might otherwise take in the inculcated moral. We owe it to Mr. H. to say, that *The Forest* is quite an interesting narrative, which shows what he might successfully do, by dismounting from his theological hobby, and taking entirely to the *destrier* of romance.

Southern Quarterly Review n.s. 7 (January 1853): 266–7

Charles Dickens's *Bleak House.*

Simms noted that he received the first, third, and fourth parts of this novel in July 1852 (*SQR* n.s. 6, p. 266). In July 1853 he wrote that the novel "drags its slow length along" in the exasperating form of serial parts and found Dickens using "some shocking expedients . . . to get rid of troublesome characters," while at the same time using sensationalism to horrify the reader. "The destruction of a sot by spontaneous combustion" is balderdash; and, per Simms, "the probability is that the drunkard merely fell into the fire place" (*SQR* n.s. 8 [July 1853]: 267.) Simms commented on the pitfalls of serial publication of novels in *Views and Reviews,* Second Series, 159–60: lack of unity and consistency of tone and harmony of parts, neglect of the main purpose, no symmetry of outline, no compactness of plan and execution. He listed Dickens as one whose art suffered greatly from serialization.

Simms first noticed Dickens with the initial part of *Martin Chuzzlewit* (*Magnolia* n.s. 2 [April 1842]: 209–10). In 1845 he gave sound and balanced assessments of the novels to date (*SQR* 15 [April 1845]: 333–35), placing Dickens "very highly, as a genial and truthful writer, with very great powers of humour and fancy." Simms concluded, however, "we are no blind worshipper of his genius, affecting an admiration because it has become cant." He found *A Christmas Carol* "probably one of the fairest and highest specimens of [Dickens's] several attributes of fancy, art, humour and pathos" (334). A previously unrecorded notice of *The Chimes!* appeared in 1845 (*S&W* 1 [March 1845]: 222–23). Simms noted getting the first installment of *Dombey and Son* in 1846 (*Letters* 2: 204). He declared that if *The Haunted Man* had "been issued by an unknown writer," "it would have been generally pronounced a wretched piece of drivel" (*SQR* 15 [April 1849]: 270).

In 1851 Simms felt that Dickens, at his best in *David Copperfield,* revealed a mixed quality of characterization "inimitable in particular cases and unexceptional in most. . . . The 'Child Wife' portrait is very happy, and Micawber, in his miseries, extremely so" (*SQR* 19 [April 1851]: 568). Simms saw Dickens's strength to be in the delineation of characters. Of *Hard Times,* he wrote, "Its portraiture is mournfully true and terribly human throughout. The story is painfully pleasing; the softening features . . . contrasting with the iron of the age" (Charleston *Mercury,* 29 December 1854). By "the iron of the age," Simms meant industrialization, urbanization, and the consequent oppression of the poor and helpless by heartless empiricists such as the character Gradgrind. (Compare Simms's Millhouse in *Woodcraft.*) The following year Simms wrote admiringly of *Household Words* in the Charleston *Mercury* for 3 April and 19 May 1855. (See also *Letters* 4: 428–29 and 5: 255.) In 1860 he found *A Tale of Two Cities* less artistic and less profound than Dickens's earlier novels but, at the same time, judged that Dickens "cannot make a dull book, though he may sometimes lead the readers into the meshes of a tedious one" (Charleston *Mercury,* 9 May 1860).

"Lugs" in the essay's final sentence is Scots and Scots-Irish dialect for "ears."

Dickens's Bleak House. (Harper & Brothers.)

This new novel of Mr. Dickens, which promised to be interminable, going through the press as a serial—and which, indeed, according to the plan of the author, might have been made so, has, at length, been brought to a conclusion. In the case of a work which contemplates rather the development of character and incident, than any definite design,—and depends for its merits upon the interest excited by particular scenes, rather than upon the unique development of a single leading purpose, or the progress of any one superior personage to the complete triumph or over throw of his fortunes, there is no good reason—while the good public are content to buy and read,—why it should ever be brought to a close. It is easy, with such a desultory plan, and with new personages perpetually brought in to increase the resources, and the expedients, and to multiply the events in the power of the writer, to prolong the narrative, and find materials for the action, till doomsday. But the advantages of such a plan exist only while the work is published in detail. They cease to be advantages when the story is rendered *whole* into the hands of the reader. Then it is that he finds that tedious which he has read with interest and pleasure in its successive parts; and that he looks to the entirety of the action, as the source of the attraction, rather than to the effect of successive scenes. The completed work requires a degree of unity and simplicity, which was not essential to its success in its *serial* progress; and the reader, intent upon the development of the story, and the career of the leading persons of it, in whom the author has awakened his chief interest, grows vexed and impatient at the tedious interruption of the narrative, and the perpetual obtrusion of new persons upon his attention, whom he is not prepared to admit to his regards. It matters not that these new persons are well drawn, or that the scenes in which they appear exhibit the author in so many successful portraitures from the life. We are willing to admit the claim, but we feel that the interruptions are vexatious, obscuring, while delaying the action, and constantly breaking the clues, and tangling the threads, which connect the several stages of progress. It is in this respect that our author's stories differ so greatly from those of Scott, Cooper, James, Bulwer, Porter, and the other great masters of the modern novel; and, indeed, from writings of such romancers as Fielding and Smollet, to which they have a nearer resemblance. Even in these latter writers, who were less compact of design usually than the novelists above mentioned, there was still a greater simplicity of plan than with Mr. Dickens, a more unique development, and a far smaller number of persons engaging our attention.

The characteristics of Mr. Dickens are human geniality, great closeness of detail, a familiar acquaintance with lowly habits, low virtues and low vices, and an immense knowledge of the minutiae of low life, in such a various and vicious world as London. Give him full range in close alley, and foul cellar, and cumbered garret, in the tavern and the chop house, in the dirty purlieus of starving poverty, in the dens of vulgarity, and among those classes in which vice and passion, cunning and fraud, stupidity and simplicity, congregate perforce, and in a perpetual warfare with one another for the spoils which are common to the desires of all, and under the presence of a dreadful necessity from which none of them can make escape—and it is wonderful how his knowledge of details, in such provinces, or his appropriate invention, will carry him on, from progress to progress, until one fancies there is no end to it—until he looks about him, with a horrid fancy that there is in the world nothing but filth, and fraud, pestilence and crime, and cunning and stupidity—until he feels his garments saturated, as it were, and reeking with fumes and horrors; an atmosphere from which there is no possible escape to pure air, and through which no genial gleam of heavenly sunshine can ever penetrate. In each corner of the wall you behold some great tumid black spider, snugly environed with his artful fortress, from which his snares extend in every direction, leaving no opening for the escape of the victim upon which he sets his eye. And, all the while, the horrid orgies are going on below. Some blindly game, some madly drink, and, ever and anon, some life is going out in smoke and blackness and pestilential vapor, as, in the work before us, one of the wretched creations of his art is made to perish in a snuff—to go out in stench, and slime, and fatty vapor, in spontaneous combustion.

To relieve this too prevailing characteristic of these fabrications, we are brought to a knowledge of strong contrasts. There is, always, some poor, single-hearted, silly boy or man—some pretty idiot of a girl child—gentle, loving, dependant, very ignorant, but very susceptible—whose sorrows, as they fall the victims of these bloated spiders in the corners, are meant to soften and inspire our sympathies. We see them suffering all manner of tortures while they live, and dying very christian and delightful deaths, in all sorts of horrors at the close; and while the manner of their death compels our sorrows at their fate, it increases necessarily our loathing of the great black spider, to whom we are to ascribe it all. Or if the good, and the humble, and the loving, are permitted to survive, and, by surviving, to triumph over hate and despotism, it is only after they have gone through such trials, and suffered from the gnawings of such worms of torture, as must leave their hearts sore and scarred for the remainder of their days.

It is not denied that these constitute legitimate materials for works of fiction of every sort, but it is to the exaggeration of certain features that the objection lies. The exaggeration, in the portraiture of Mr. Dickens, is sufficiently indicated by the uncouth nomenclature which he employs. As in his names of persons, so in his portraits, there is always a laborious toil in the distortion of images and aspects. His books are always full of deformities and monsters—men and women half made up—dwarfs—men with hideous attributes—horrid from age, decay, bad passions, bad habits, gestures, protuberances, and personal monstrosities of sundry kinds, too numerous to particularize; so that we find his volumes a very museum, such as Barnum loves to accumulate, in the collection of which the whole world seems to have been searched through, in order to bring together the scattered varieties of the ogre, the reptile, the foul, the hideous, and the ridiculous; the combination of the hideous and the ridiculous, being a favorite process with Mr. Dickens, in the creation of some of his most favorite portraits.

All of these characteristic features are strikingly exhibited in *Bleak House,* in a greater degree, perhaps, than in any other of the previous writings of the author. We take leave to say, that these are, by no means, his most successful portraits. The Detective Inspector, Bucket, is an admirable portrait; so is the gentlemanly vagabond, Captain George. Miss Summerson is a sweet young woman, and Caddy Jellyby a uniform and gradual development, from the infant germ to a perfect womanhood, such as rarely grows up under the hands of any author. The sketches—for they are only sketches—of Miss Flite, the little woman, brain-touched—of Guppy, of Richard and Ada, Jobling and others, are all, more or less, graphically hit off. The useless agency of Boythorn might have been dispensed with in the story, as might many others—but he stands out fairly as a character. Joe is one of the fortunate victims of our author, who perishes that he may obtain a good character. Tulkinghorn is a conceited ass for all his pains, whose ambition—if there ever were a person with so much power and pretension, who entertained so paltry an ambition—to hold and keep the secrets of his neighbour, is a half formed conception only—an abortion, in fact, and a monstrous bore besides. He reminds us of the "long passages" in Mrs. Radcliffe, "which lead to nothing." He dies, as he lived, for no useful purpose to the story. Sir Leicester and Lady Dedlock are lay-figures rather than actors. The vague conception of a character, which our author seems to have had in the delineation of her portrait, seems to have been utterly disordered and distracted in his mind by external causes—possibly by the very difficulty of "keeping the run" of all his characters and customers. This is one of the dangers of this panoramic sort of writing. He speaks of her strength, but he shows her only feeble; and never more so than in the last concession which she makes to Tulkinghorn, when she visits his house fruitlessly on the night when he is murdered. Mr. Dickens here sacrifices all that he had done towards creating her capital of character, in the stale fetch of art, by which he seeks to render her obnoxious to the suspicion of the crime. Her flight and death are as fatiguing to the reader, if not so fatal, as to the lady herself. The events in this connection are infinitely more tedious than touching. The whole story of the lady is a failure—as inconsequential as it is studiously obscure. Of the pompous Sir Leicester we can only say that he is a very common-place person in conventional buckram. He is, briefly, a bore. Mrs. Jellyby is another, but of a more natural school; the portrait, however disgusting and ridiculous, must yet be acknowledged as the type of a considerable family—particularly in these days of woman's rights. Prince Prettyman—Turveydrop we mean—and his father, are both excellent in their way. In Richard Carstone, the weak, we have a too truthful, though a humiliating portrait of a large class of silly creatures, who are as the moth to the candle, the fly to the spider. We cannot reproach him for the weaknesses of a nature not trained to the encounter with its certain foes— though we must needs despise him. The "Furrener Woman," Hortense, is good as a portrait in some respects, but the motive to her commission of the murder of Tulkinghorn, is totally inadequate, and seems to us to be an after-thought of the author, when, tired himself of the prolonged labour, he sought to unwind himself of his threads of connection as fast as possible. It is true she is "a devil for spirit," but how, with such a spirit, so easily fired by such provocation, did she never pistol any body before? Why leave it to her twenty-fifth year before she cuts throats, in maintenance of her self-esteem? Besides, there is a manifest inconsistency between such phrensied passions and such deliberate and coolly contrived malice, which could only have been met and foiled by that inimitable master of fence, Mr. Detector Bucket. Of the Rouncewells, Carboys, Kenges, Krooks, Vholes, Chadbands, Coavinses, and others, we have few words to say. Vholes is probably the best of these sketches; Chadband's too much over-done. But what shall we say of the cruel mistake which Mr. Dickens has made in the case of Harold Skimpole, changing his character completely from that of his first conception, and destroying one of the happiest ideas of unique and perfect portraiture, that ever grew beneath the pen of an artist. Nothing more suicidal has ever been done in fiction. In respect to the story, we may add that the result of the case, Jarndyce *vs.* Jarndyce, in Chancery, while it will disappoint everybody, was yet what everybody might expect, and was, perhaps, the best finish that could be given to such a beginning. The error of Mr. Dickens is in allowing his *satire* to get the better of his *fiction*. The joke, which concludes two such monstrous volumes, should have been a more pregnant one. We see that there is a terrible satire in the finale to a case which has had so many victims; but we feel how pointless and ineffective it is, when addressed to the ears of a Lord Chancellor, whose big wig must effectually keep it out; and how utterly without echo it is in the lugs of Mr. Vholes, whose duties to his family counsel him, the moment that death relieves him of Richard Carstone, that he must now look around him for another victim of the same susceptible type.

Southern Quarterly Review n.s. 9 (January 1854): 224–28.

Mrs. Elizabeth Gaskell's *Cranford*

Simms often noticed the domestic novel and praised it if realistic and both entertaining and thought-provoking. Such was the case with *Cranford*. Gaskell's presentation of the village of Cranford's "state of simplicity" pleased him especially, for it viewed the local as the center of the world. Simms found this attitude "perfectly delightful to behold" and saw Cranford's place-centered setting mirrored in his traditionalist Charleston. He also reviewed Gaskell's *North and South* in the Charleston *Mercury* of 12 April 1855.

The Little Pedlington is John Poole's *Little Pedlington and the Pedlingtonians* (1839). Like Gaskell, Poole created an insular village to which Londoner Mr. Paul Pry flees to find "a very paradise," only to encounter Major Boreall and Colonel Dominant. (Simms again referred to Paul Pry in the 1860s.) The Greenland fog may have had its origins in any number of sources: Coleridge's "The Destiny of Nations" (from which Simms borrowed his definition of poetry as "winged thought"); from *Jane Eyre,* with its images of this mysterious land; from Hogg's Ettrick Shepherd; or from Gaskell herself, whose character Sylvia loses her husband to the Arctic ice. It was a popular motif for Romantics, as in Poe's *Pym,* or the "ultimate dim Thule" of his poetry.

Cranford. (**Harper & Brothers.**)

By the author of *Mary Barton* and *Ruth,*—both very interesting social stories, presents us with the grave and graceful picture of a little old-fashioned village, occupying a little nook of God's earth which has been left wholly unnoticed by the railroads. There, the people have grown up pretty much after the fashion of their fathers, enjoying the vulgar virtues and vices, just as they were relished in the same region, two hundred years ago; and never once fancying that there is a progress any where—still less that there is any place or progress half so wonderful as their own. Their state of simplicity, in this conviction, is perfectly delightful to behold; and reminds us very much of what is the case still, with a certain portion of the people of our own good city of Charleston, who really believe that we are favoured above all the sons of earth, and occupy, in fact, the original site of the Garden of Eden. They look out upon the Ashley, and they say, "this surely is the very river that went out of Eden to water the garden." It a little troubles them when they are told that the river aforesaid divided itself into four heads; but they soon recover from this difficulty, and point successively to the Cooper and the Wando. For the fourth, they go back to the Ashley, and push a little dug-out through Wappoo, for the purpose of exploration, and are satisfied. When they rise at morning, looking out East and West, they thank God, saying, "surely we see all that is precious in the world." Where the horizon circumscribes their vision, they say—"Ah! all beyond is Greenland fog, and Norwegian ice and darkness." Of this very sort of stuff are the people of *Cranford* made. *Cranford,* in fact, is another *Little Pedlington,* but drawn without the asperity of Thackeray, by a female hand, and the portraits are mostly female Pedlingtonians.

Southern Quarterly Review n.s. 9 (January 1854): 245.

Anthon's Manual of Greek Literature

In a previously unrecorded notice, Simms said Charles Anthon's new school edition of *The Æneid* is part of his classical series that "promises to supersede all others. It is making its way in Europe, and, we believe, occupies the highest ground every where in America" (*Orion* 4 [July 1844]: 247). He reviewed Anthon's *English-Latin Lexicon* (*SQR* n.s. 1 [April 1850]: 244–45), ranking the author "among our best American authorities in Latin." He noticed Anthon's edition of *Ciceronis de Officiis* as a work which improved the text of the Reverend Ashton (Charleston *Mercury,* 5 August 1859).

Grote was George Grote, English historian (1794–1871) and author of *History of Greece* (1846). Simms's close care in reviewing Anthon included his searching out the footnote in Grote with which Anthon disagreed and not finding it in "either the English or American editions." Simms's knowledge of Greek and Roman literature extended to the scholarship they inspired. In his essay on the subject (p. 66), he again refers to Niebuhr.

Anthon's Manual of Greek Literature. (**Harper & Brothers.**)

Mr. Anthon is rather an erudite man than a man of letters. He is no doubt an admirable compiler and a fair editor, with more industry than art, and more learning than discrimination. The volume before us will be found highly useful. It embodies all the essential facts of the history, and gives very fully and sufficiently, for such a work, the detail of the subject. And, so far, we accord our approval to the labours of the editor. It is to his literary judgment that we mostly object, and there are sundry instances, in this volume, in which we happen upon points of dissent and difference which occasion us surprise. Thus, for example, when speaking of Plato, Mr. Anthon tells us of his "scheme for a community of property and wives," he overlooks what is the conclusion of most critics in regard to *The Republic* of that writer. This work is now conceded to be an allegory, having for its object man, rather than government. Any deductions, in regard to this work, therefore, which are founded upon assumptions of an entirely different kind from those of the author, must necessarily result in error. The judgment, at all events, of Mr. Anthon, is quite too abruptly and incautiously rendered. There is another matter. We observe that Mr. Anthon, in a note, speaking of Grote upon Niebuhr, ventures to apply the terms "flippant and unfair" to the former. This will hardly do. It is a boldness of which we had not thought Mr. Anthon capable. We make free to say to him that it is a rashness, and in very bad taste, for Mr. Anthon to speak of Mr. Grote as "flippant," and of no less questionable propriety to describe him as "unfair." No European critic, of any eminence, would venture to use the first epithet in connection with one of the profoundest of all the modern Grecians, and no writer, of any candour, could possibly conceive of such a vice as unfairness in a writer, who is confessedly the frankest, most careful, and most modest of all historical critics. In regard to the *note* of Mr. Grote, which occasions this remark of Mr. Anthon, we are still at a loss, having failed to find it in either the English or American editions of Grote, in the volume and page referred to.

Southern Quarterly Review n.s. 9 (April 1854): 536.

Thomas Campbell's *Specimens of the British Poets*

First published in seven volumes in London in 1819, the work, as Simms related, ends with Cowper, Beattie, and Anstey. See also Simms's review of *The Life and Letters of Thomas Campbell* (p. 109).

Campbell's Specimens of the British Poets. (Henry C. Baird.)

The selection from the British poets, made by Thomas Campbell, is acknowledged to be the best that we have, so far as it goes. But it is brought down only to the names of Beattie and Anstey; in other words, only to the close of the last generation. The glorious constellation of the present century, including such names as Byron, Moore, Wordsworth, Southey, Keats, Shelley, and a glorious host besides, only second to these, do not here find a place; and we submit it to the American publisher of this beautiful volume, whether he does not do injustice to himself, in suffering the work, however valuable in itself, to remain incomplete! Though perfect as the work of Campbell, and though it might be difficult to procure the aid of so eminent a taste and judgment, in supplying its deficiencies, yet we submit that an approach to this desirable consummation might be made, and, for the sake of the reader, ought to be made. An addition of three hundred pages would enable him to give favourite specimens of all the British writers from 1800 to 1850, which would include the living authors of Great Britain also. Could he happen upon a good editor, we should take leave to counsel him to exercise a severer privilege than Campbell has done, and exclude from the collection sundry names that now occupy undeservedly a place in these pages. We trust that he will meditate this suggestion in season to make this volume one of the gift books of next Christmas. In the hands of a good editor, such a volume would constitute one of the most beautiful and appropriate for holiday presentation; as, indeed, it does now. The publisher has performed his part of the work with a due regard to the beauty and value of the contents. It is rich in illustrations on steel, and is put forth on the best paper, and with the clearest type.

Southern Quarterly Review n.s. 9 (April 1854): 537–38.

Thomas De Quincey's *Writings*

Parks does not mention Simms as a critic of De Quincey, but Simms considered the English writer an essential essayist. In 1851, in an excellent review of the earlier volumes of De Quincey's *Writings,* Simms called the author "the most profound of the recent psychological writers of Great Britain" (*SQR* n.s. 4 [July 1851]: 243–44). In a notice of *Essays on Philosophical Writers and Other Men of Letters,* Simms stated that De Quincey treated his subjects in "his own wayward fashion—always with thought and keenness, but always with desultory temper, which provokes quite as often as it diverts. . . . To those to whom our author is unknown, we urge his acquaintance. They will find him mingling the reminiscent, the poet and philosopher in an odd manner; but they will never find him a dull companion, though sometimes a capricious one" (*SQR* n.s. 10 [July 1854]: 243). Simms again recommended De Quincey's collected writings, singling out *Klosterheim* and *Confessions of an English Opium Eater* in the Charleston *Mercury* of 8 February 1855 and 27 May 1856 and *Suspiria de Profundis* in the *Mercury* of 8 February 1855. He pronounced De Quincey a "remarkable essayist endowed especially with the Poetical and the Metaphysical faculties" (8 February 1855). In 1859 Simms declared De Quincey to be "one of the most piquant of modern English writers. . . . His mind is curiously constituted, with some remarkable anomalies. We rarely find fancy so free, easy, excursive and fond to wander, in the case of one who is so ingeniously thoughtful, and in some respects so severely logical" (Charleston *Mercury,* 19 October 1859).

De Quincey's Writings. (Ticknor, Reed & Fields.)

Of these highly piquant and thoughtful miscellanies, we have three additional volumes, comprising the essays on the poets, and historical and critical essays. We do not know that these volumes conclude the series of our author's works, which it is the design of the American publishers to give us; but we hope not. De Quincey is still alive, and still, we believe, at work in his vocation. His characteristics are quite well known, by this time, to the generality of our readers, and we need not do more than say, with regard to the volumes before us, that they are to the full as instructive, curious and interesting as any of their predecessors. The genius of the author delights in the metaphysical, and is marked by a subtlety which leaves nothing of his subject unfollowed. It is enough for him that the light gleams through a crevice. He will trace it out. But, in these toils, he does not pursue the subtlety so intensely, or narrowly, as to deprive himself of the liberty to note and survey, whatever is incidentally curious in his examination, and a judicious introduction of all the natural relations of his subject, enables him to relieve with variety, and group for picturesque effect, and thus escape the monotonous. There never has been a writer yet, so thoroughly metaphysical in his tendencies, who is yet so thoroughly free from the reproach of being tedious.

Southern Quarterly Review n.s. 9 (April 1854): 538.

Charles Kingsley's *Hypatia*

Simms later reviewed Kingsley's *Alton Locke, Hypatia,* and *Yeast* in an important essay, "Charles Kingsley and His Writings," Charleston *Mercury,* 14 April 1855. He treated *Westward Ho!* in two reviews (8 May 1855 and 27 May 1856). Notice the similarity of Simms's title *Southward Ho!* He wrote about *The Saint's Tragedy, Poems, The Heroes,* and *Hypatia* (once again) in the *Mercury* of 27 May 1856.

Simms always recognized Kingsley as a serious writer. His fullest tribute occurred in a review of his brother Henry Kingsley's "fine masculine novel," *The Recollections of Geoffry Hamlyn,* where Simms judged that Henry shared some of his brother's talent. Charles possessed "heartiness, thoroughness, boldness, freedom and dramatic ability" (Charleston *Mercury,* 3 August 1859.)

Hypatia; or New Foes with an Old Face. By Charles Kingsley, Jun., Recor of Eversly. In two volumes. Boston: Crosby, Nichols & Co. 1854.

Kingsley is the author of some well known, bold and popular volumes, *Alton Locke, Yeast,* &c. He belongs to a new school of reformers, with perhaps rather vague notions of civil liberty and the rights of man, and somewhat cloudy, in striving to be clear with new lights, on the subjects of religion and the church. His mind is one of audacities, which, in a time of much mental stagnation, are likely to be wholesome, however occasionally wandering. At all events, we have no reason to doubt the benevolence and integrity of his intentions. As little reason is there to question his ability. He is shrewd, excursive, thoughtful and imaginative; with a fearless reformer-like tone, yet marked by frequent modulations, such as give sweetness and softness to his utterances. His fancy shows itself at times, delicately and persuasively, lighting up an otherwise gloomy and stern aspect. *Hypatia,* the work before us, is an historical romance, illustrative of the sort of christianity which prevailed in Alexandria, under the fierce and cunning dominion of Cyril, the patriarch. The portrait of the christians under this rule, is no less true to history than revolting. "Hypatia," the heroine, is also an historical personage—a beautiful Greek, the teacher of a school at Alexandria, who standing in the path of Cyril to power, was torn in pieces by the christians. The story is full of variety and interest, terrible and startling situations, such as naturally belonged to the period and country, and many of our author's scenes are depicted with dramatic power and effect.

Southern Quarterly Review n.s. 9 (April 1854): 539.

Hudson Gurney's Translation of *The Works of Apuleius*

This review again reveals the depth of Simms's erudition in the classics. Hudson Gurney (1775–1864) and Mary Tighe (1772–1810), Irish poet and novelist, published the translation in 1800. The edition by John Lyde Wilson (1784–1849) is *Cupid and Psyche; a Mythological Tale, from the "Golden Ass" of Apuleius* (Charleston: Hussey, 1842), which, as Simms said, supplied many additions to the expurgated London edition of 1800. Wilson, buried at St. Paul's Episcopal (Simms's church in Charleston), was governor of South Carolina from 1822 to 1824 and an ardent secessionist. This review demonstrates both Simms's knowledge of the long tradition of poets' uses of "Cupid and Psyche" and his editorial philosophy in criticizing expurgation.

***The Works of Apuleius.* London: H. G. Bohn. 1853.**

The writings of Apuleius, complete, are here collected in a compact volume; a new and well prepared translation, comprising *The Metamorphosis, or Golden Ass, The God of Socrates, The Florida,* the defence of Apuleius on a charge of magical practice, in which he discourses of magic, and gives us its history to the period in which he writes and in the region in which he lived. The work is one of those helps equally to history and philosophy, which he must necessarily study who would be thoroughly informed of the faith, the social practice and the height to which the popular mind and cultivation had reached in his time and country. It is rich in other respects, as a development of the highly imaginative genius of the author. *The Golden Ass* is the work by which Apuleius is best known to fame. This tale, which is quite too free for the use of the sex, is, at the same time, distinguished by its poetic beauties and the brilliant episodes in which the author exhibits his grace, his fancy and his invention. Among these, *The Allegory of the Soul, or Cupid and Psyche,* is the most remarkable. It has furnished a theme for succeeding poets and artists, through whom, rather than its original author, it is chiefly known to the moderns. The volume contains the poetical version of this story as made by Gurney and Mrs. Tighe. The latter poem is a somewhat cold, tame, diffuse paraphrase, which is commended to us only by its delicacy and correctness. The version of Gurney is more loose and less finished; but more free, and, in modest quatrains, unfolding the fable with more spirit and simplicity than the more elaborate effort of Mrs. Tighe. Gurney's poem, however, omits many portions of the original; the versifier seeming to be governed in this omission by a desire rather to tell the story itself, than to display its poetical beauties, and the mere sentiments of the author, as they rose naturally out of its situations. Something, therefore, was lost to the reader of the original—some passages of fancy and description which readers of taste would not care to lose. These passages ought to have been supplied by the present translator or editor, and we could have wished that he had known of the version made by the Hon. John L. Wilson, formerly one of the Governors of this State, who published an edition in Charleston several years ago. Mr. Wilson's volume may be found in our libraries by the curious. He was a man of taste, talent and education, a lawyer and politician, who relieved his public labours by an occasional indulgence with the Muse, and who, in supplying the gaps in Gurney's version, showed himself fully equal to an original translation, which would have been quite as worthy as Gurney's of the public eye. But Bohn's volume will supply all that the reader desires. It is undoubtedly the best and most complete edition of Apuleius that has yet been given to the English tongue.

Southern Quarterly Review n.s. 10 (July 1854): 235–36.

Caroline Lee Hentz's *The Planter's Northern Bride*

Simms first reviewed Hentz's drama *De Lara* in two previously unrecorded pieces (*Magnolia* n.s. 2 [June 1842]: 209–10; and *SQR* 4 [October 1843]: 521–22). He recognized her gift for realism. In his review of *Rena* (1851), Simms commended the "much esteemed" author for "an easy, graceful style," and he deemed it one of her best novels. Its "very successful portraits and spirited scenes" make it "a natural and lifelike picture" instead of "a strained and extravagant romance." Still, Simms explained, "It is a defect to exhibit two or three rescues from the ice-ponds; and the catastrophe is precipitated, in a manner which shows careless characterization, and an impatience, in working out the conclusion" (*SQR* n.s. 4 [July 1851]: 264.) Simms in the following notice judiciously contrasted Hentz and Harriet Beecher Stowe. Stowe has more power, but Hentz is more truthful—that is, realistic. Returning to his frequent critique of didacticism, he admired the fact that she "has no hobby to ride, no crusade to promote," which made her novel more true to life than Stowe's. Simms praised her ability to see the world "with her own eyes, without green shades of any sort." The notice gives valuable insight into Simms's theories of realism and reveals how he could bestow proper credit to writers whose philosophies he did not approve. His dislike of abolitionism did not prevent him from speaking of "the passionate power" of *Uncle Tom's Cabin*. Further his prediction in 1854 that Stowe's "pleasure in maintaining an argument" would bear fruit in "the destruction of a nation" was prophetic.

The Planter's Northern Bride (Hart), by Mrs. Caroline Lee Hentz, is a pleasantly written story, picturesque, and with much dramatic force, designed as a foil to the work of Mrs. Stowe. It has not the passionate power of *Uncle Tom;* in other words, Mrs. Hentz has not the power of Mrs. Stowe; but she is more truthful, more pure, and imbued with a more becoming Christian spirit. She has no hobby to ride, no crusade to promote, and she does not promise herself any particular pleasure in maintaining an argument by the destruction of a nation. She is a better witness, in all respects, than Mrs. Stowe; is a Northern woman by birth, and has seen with her own eyes, without green shades of any sort, the society which she describes. She has lived in close communion with the institution, which she has accordingly learned to love and honour, and desires to sustain. She has veneration, one of the most precious of moral virtues, in which the feminine Uncle Tommys are marvellously deficient. Her book will be found of grateful reading in the South, and may become of great Christian utility to the North.

Southern Quarterly Review n.s. 10 (July 1854): 255.

Phoebe Carey's *Poems and Parodies*

Sisters Phoebe (1824–1871) and Alice (1820–1871) Carey moved from Ohio to New York in 1850, where Simms met them. Simms correctly described Alice as sickly and Phoebe as energetic and lively. Phoebe championed women's rights and was a friend of Susan B. Anthony. Whittier championed her poetry. In Carey's poem, quoted at article's end, Simms inserted the bracketed "are" to provide grammatical accuracy, hence the reference to Lindley Murray (1745–1826), author of popular English grammars. That Murray became a depressed recluse in old age explains Simms's description of "poor old Lindley Murray." Simms said that Carey's errors in grammar were not tweaks of his nose, but major head poundings. Simms gave his lecture on proper rhyme and the necessity of polishing one's verse to many young writers and followed the advice himself.

Poems and Parodies. By Phoebe Carey. Boston: Ticknor, Reed & Fields. 1854.

We had the pleasure, some months ago, of meeting, in society at the North, with the two poetic sisters, Alice and Phoebe Carey—one, sad apparently, and in somewhat delicate health—Alice, we believe—the other buoyant, and looking as buxom as if she had never suffered once from the blasts of Apollo. Certainly, she did not wear that sad, sighing, sentimental expression which the vulgar world is very apt to anticipate always in the aspect of the damsel who lisps in song. These young ladies have acquired much American celebrity in a very short time. The value of this sudden American celebrity we are not called upon to decide; but, valueless or not, the very possession of it by our fair sisters imposes upon them the necessity of elaborating well before they publish. Poetry is art which, beyond all others, perhaps, demands the *labor limœ;* unless, indeed, the genius be of a character so audacious and grand as to legitimate its own outlawries. This is not the case with either of our sisters, who must establish their claims by assiduous art, and dutiful study, and the exercise of a fancy carefully regulated and counselled to wing the thought—not fly away with it. Whatever the merits of Miss Phoebe Carey, as shown by the verses in this volume, we must, *in limine,* take occasion to say that she has *not* been sufficiently heedful of the pruning of her rose-tree. She has not done quite enough of clipping and filing, polishing and perfecting. Here, for example, in the very opening verse of the volume, there is a grammatical error:

> "Softly part away the tresses
>   From her forehead of white clay,
>   And across her quiet bosom
>   Let her pale hands lightly *lay,*" etc.

Now we are prepared to subscribe fully to the opinion which insists upon the imperative character of rhyme; but, unless the necessity is shown to be absolute, we cannot, for the life of us, consent to the sacrifice of the grammar to it. We are really of the notion that our author has not just right, and quite as little reason, to use her stylus with such mangling ferocity upon the mazard of poor old Lindley Murray. Had she simply taken his proboscis between her taper fingers, and wrung it gently by way of giving emphasis to a sense of dove-coloured agony, we might have suffered the case to go by default. But the proceeding here is quite too public, too audacious, too extreme—on the very first page—at the porch of the volume! Really, our poet betrays a shade too much of poetic outlawry; and we dread lest she brings upon herself some harsh judgments hereafter. It is to spare her this danger that we look grave, and lift a solemn finger before her eyes. "Phoebe," we say, "take heed to thy grammar, look to thy verses, see that thy rhymes do not trespass upon thy rhetoric, to the utter confounding of thy fame!" As for devouring the damsel, after any savage critical fashion, Heaven forefend that we should be guilty of such gracelessness. Is thy servant, gentle reader, a dog that he should do this thing? No. We prefer rather to encourage where there is merit, and to show to our young beginners how to tread firmly along the unaccustomed way. And Phoebe Carey has a good deal of merit; and with hard working, and constant devotion, fasting, prayer and study, she may take rank with the best of the sweet singers in this our Israel, and make songs which shall serve for the singing of less gifted damsels for a hundred years to come; but there must be much work done first, and the study of much better models than those to which our author seems accustomed. Fugitive verses are dangerous exercises to those who deliberately undertake them as *works*. It scarcely seems proper that they should be works; and yet, if they lack the finish that can be supplied by work alone, we are apt to be more severe upon the poet than if he had failed at an epic. In great works, one is often forgiven for failure. In small works seldom. He who undertakes humbly betrays a very humble sort of talents when he fails in his effort. Hence, fugitive poetry involves a superior danger. We, at least, require the fugitive to make his toilet before he takes the highway. Better that our young authors should propose to themselves *works*—subjects and forms of composition which demand design, and exercise *all* the faculties— invention, thought, grouping, as well as fancy and good taste—than content themselves with small endeavours to illustrate by new fancies and rhymes an ancient common-place. In the one case, even failure commands our respect, if we see that there has been painstaking, with a certain amount of talents and knowledge. In the other case, grant that all has been won that has been aimed at, and how small is the result? To sing, in tolerable verses, what has been sung a thousand times before, will hardly avail for amaranthine triumphs. Now, Miss Phoebe Carey is a very clever woman. This volume sufficiently proves it. But it proves more—that she has nowhere *tasked* her cleverness;—unless, indeed, in the parodies of popular poets, which constitute one half of her volume; and which, at best, are very clever *parodies!* Of the first—the original half of her volume—the first *thirteen* pieces relate to *death,* the *dying* and the *dead!* Now, if anything could disarm the hostility of criticism in respect to fugitive poetry, it must be its various and capricious changes—the beauty of its caprices—its rapid transitions from grace to grace—and the joyous impulse, and airy brightness, of that fancy, which hovers about the realms of feeling and sentiment, and crowns them with hues of the rainbow, dipt in the freshness of dew and morning. To give us *thirteen* fugitives, consecutively, all draped in black, and sprinkt with ashes, is a little too sombrous for the season of rabbits and pairing doves. In plain terms, Miss Carey, if she will sit down to depict fugitive emotions and sentiments, must take care to group them after such a fashion as will render the procession picturesque and attractive. To array all her folks in funeral guise, is to make us weary of the monotonous spectacle. But we must not dwell upon these dreary difficulties. Our purpose is not to censure so much as to improve, and, contenting ourselves with the objections already urged, we give a single sample from the little volume—one of the best in it—which will sufficiently prove that the mind of Miss Phoebe Carey is worth quarrelling with—and this is no small compliment from a Reviewer. The piece which follows is simple and pretty, and the rhyme is neat and elastic.

Drawing Water

I had drunk with life unsated,
Where the founts of pleasure burst;

> I had hewn out broken cisterns,
> And they mocked my spirit's thirst:
>
> And I said, "life is a desert,
> Hot, and measureless, and dry;
> And God will *not* give me water,
> Though I pray, and faint, and die."
>
> Spake there then a friend and brother,
> "Rise, and roll the stone away;
> There are founts of life unspringing
> In thy pathway every day."
>
> Then I said,—"My heart is sinful,
> Very sinful was my speech;
> All the wells of God's salvation
> Are too deep for me to reach."
>
> And he answr'd—"Rise and labour—
> Doubt and idleness is [are] death;
> Shape the one, a goodly vessel,
> With the strong hands of they faith."
>
> So I wrought and shaped the vessel,
> Then knelt lowly, humbly there,
> And I drew up living water,
> With the golden chain of prayer.

Southern Quarterly Review n.s. 10 (July 1854): 245–48.

The Poetical Works of Alexander Pope

This review might be considered scholarly, so careful are its details about editing. Here Simms went into minute analysis of the editorial process. One might expect this expertise of him, given his credible job of editing Shakespeare's apocrypha, an edition of southern war poetry, a volume of Revolutionary War correspondence, collections of the papers of political friends, and a biography of Nathanael Greene. As a magazine or newspaper editor for nearly half a century, Simms clearly took an interest in such things, was practiced at it, and had a discerning eye. Of his assessment of Pope from the 1820s onward, little needs saying beyond the fact that Pope was a model for Simms's first book of poetry, *Monody* (1825), and Simms often quoted him from memory, perhaps the highest compliment one writer can pay another.

***The Poetical Works of Alexander Pope.* Edited by Robert Caruthers. In four volumes. London: Nat. Cooke. 1853.**

The writings of Pope will be among the last to stale in the estimation of the readers and students of English literature. His wit, taste, propriety and humour, the general excellence of his moral, the beauty of his versification, his strong common sense, constitute essentials of authority in art and literature which no generation will venture wholly to depreciate. With little of the spiritual or the intense in his poetry, he rarely allows us, while we read, to feel their deficiency; and he appeals to us from so many strong points, that we readily forgive and forego, and, while in his hand, rarely feel the want of other essentials of the great poet. An edition of his works, such as the present, is a desideratum. Three out of the four volumes promised are now before us, in very beautiful style for the library, on the finest paper, in excellent print, and teeming with such illustrations from the hands of the engraver, as tend greatly to the satisfaction of our curiosity with respect to the distinguished persons, his contemporaries, the friends he loved and honoured, and the enemies and subjects whom he victimized. We have here, among other heads, those of the heroes of *The Dunciad.* But the chief value of this edition consists (apart from its mechanical beauty and cheapness of cost) in its completeness. It contains the latest biographical intelligence; in providing which, the editor possesses, at this day, a vast deal more of material than could be found fifty or even twenty-five years ago. The text has been carefully revised, and the variations distinguished; and the emendations of different editions, at different periods of time, so compared and contrasted, as to show us the varying moods of the author, and the growth and decline of his friendships and antipathies. Altogether, the present is probably one of the most acceptable of all the editions of Pope, leaving little to be supplied by future editors, and giving us all that is valuable in the labours of preceding ones.

Southern Quarterly Review n.s. 10 (July 1854): 249.

Henry David Thoreau's *Walden*

Simms caught the book's thoughtful, speculative nature. He respected the author's intellect and found its Spartan philosophy to be "the antique Puritan" carried "to its proper results, in all social matters." Simms would indeed find it "queer" (a word he used twice in the two short paragraphs) not to dispense hospitality lavishly in the southern manner. He singled out the fact that the book was well-written and saw immediately it was not just a book by a naturalist. Word for word, this notice is among the most pregnant analyses of *Walden.*

Of our native essayists, the same publishers have recently given us several volumes of interest and merit. Among these is a somewhat queerly conceived narrative of a Yankee philosopher, whose question is upon how little he can live and be virtuous; feed and be charitable; clothe himself and others; and test both parties; first as to what they can endure in the way of privation, before he bestows upon either of them a shirt or a supper.

The conception is that of a pure Yankee. It could be made by no other. It is carrying out the antique Puritan philosophy to its proper results, in all social matters. This queer, well-written book is called *Walden; or Life in the Woods.* It is by Henry D. Thoreau; whose intellect we should greatly wrong, did we not describe it as one well calculated to inspire the respect and compel the watchful consideration of yours. His book is full of a speculative interest, such as results from the continued exercise of thought in practical affairs.

Charleston *Mercury* (8 February 1855).

Our Literary Docket—New Publications: William Cullen Bryant and Lady Morgan

In the usual manner of his "Our Literary Docket" series, Simms here judged in the court of books two more "offenders," Bryant and Lady Morgan. Bryant was indeed an "old offender" because he had been brought before this docket many times. Their relationship had begun in 1827, when Bryant reviewed Simms's *Lyrical and Other Poems,* declaring that Simms possessed "no ordinary degree of poetical talent" (New York *Evening Post,* 14 August and 4 September 1829). In 1828 Simms pronounced Bryant "the first American poet" when no one else had said so (*Letters,* 1: 157, *SLG* 1 [November 1828]: 157–58, 192). Bryant praised *Atalantis* effusively in 1832. Simms was aware that Bryant had closely borrowed from one of his poems, but when his friend Lawson noted it, Simms wrote to keep the information strictly to himself. Such was the depth of Simms's regard. Simms, however, still understood that the United States was in too big a hurry, with "bustle and excitement," to create a great poem that would last, like Spenser's *Faerie Queene* has (*Magnolia* 4 [February 1842]: 65–67.) Simms's long personal tribute to Bryant (*Magnolia* 4 [April 1842]: 193–201) described the times he had heard his friend read poetry "indoors and out." Despite their friendship Simms said he was presenting a just and balanced appraisal. Bryant "could never become a passionate poet," Simms wrote, owing to his "calm, contemplative philosophy" (199–200). In reviewing *The Fountain and Other Poems,* Simms concluded that, even though the volume contained no "grand Miltonic hymning, Mr Bryant is almost the only one of our poets, who does not give us the occasion to say that he writes too much" (*Magnolia* n.s. 1 [September 1842]: 191–92). As Parks noted, possibly Simms's "finest tribute" came in 1859, after the two had disagreed politically (58). The Richmond *Enquirer* had published an editorial mentioning Bryant's "mean doggerel." Separating faction from art, Simms asked why the editor should "attack Bryant the Poet when his sole business is with Bryant, the black Republican editor" (Charleston *Mercury*, 13 December 1859). The latter was "a most laudable object" of attack; but the former (that is, the attempt to malign the poetry owing to the author's politics) was "supremely ridiculous." Parks felt that this treatment of Bryant was "a fine example of Simms' objectivity in judging literary works" (58).

The subject of the following essay is not poetry, however, but Bryant's travel letters, *Letters from the Continent of Europe*. The previous letters to which Simms referred were published as *Letters of a Traveller* (New York: Putnam, 1850), in which Bryant described his visit to Woodlands in 1843. At Woodlands, Bryant found the "blacks of this region" to be a "cheerful, careless, dirty race, not hard worked, and in many respects indulgently treated" (81–89). In 1970 Mary C. Simms Oliphant recalled to the editor from family tradition that Mrs. Bryant incensed the house servants by lifting their skirts to see if they had been given proper undergarments. It was still talked of by these women and their children fifty years later. Simms's cryptic comments that Bryant ridiculed certain European countries and spied out "the poverty of their several lands" for possible later appropriation hinted at his friend's growing imperialism. The reference to taking lands, plantations, and "Negroes" may have been Simms's oblique way of hinting that the South may also be included in these aggressive designs. See also the review of *Hartley Norman* (p. 159).

At Simms's death in 1870, Bryant paid his friend a touching tribute: "In all [Simms's] writings, from first to last, during a literary career of more than forty years, he was conscientious and consistent, always mindful of the dignity of his callings, uniformly honest, pure and high-toned" (New York *Evening Post*, 1 July 1870). Additions of the words "blessed with a sense of humor," "fair," and "possessed of great energy" to Bryant's list might also be a good description of Simms the reviewer.

The brisk little woman of "very uncertain age" is Lady Sydney Owenson Morgan. She was likely born around 1776 rather than in the 1780s, as she claimed. She also claimed blue blood, but Simms thought this exaggerated. Her works were praised by Scott, Byron, Shelley, and Moore, all favorites of Simms. Trollope and Thackeray borrowed from her life and work. Morgan's Irish nationalist novels and themes of Irish independence kept her and her house in Dublin under permanent surveillance by the English secret police. That would be enough to make her "fidgetty." The English government backed vicious critical attacks in the quarterlies to undermine her popularity (Brophy, introduction, viii–ix). Simms created characters at the Docket from the titles of her novels: *The Wild Irish Girl* (1806), *The O'Briens and the O'Flaherties: A National Tale* (1827), *Woman, or Ida of Athens* (1800), *Miladi* (decade of the 1800s, specific year unknown), and *The Princess; or, the Beguines* (1835), about the Catholic lay order of that name. Lady Morgan died in 1859. Mary Campbell, her biographer, characterized her much as Simms did, as a woman of great spirit and vivacity. Here the book under review is *Passages from My Autobiography* (New York: Appleton, 1859). That she, her father, and her husband financed most of her writing perhaps explains the court's verdict that she be allowed to amuse the public—"but always at her own expense." Simms noticed Morgan's *Book of the Boudoir* in Charleston *City Gazette,* 18 December 1830, and her fiction at *SQR* 14 (April 1849): 69.

Wm. C. Bryant, an old offender is brought before the court by Appleton and Brother, charged with a body of *Letters from the Continent of Europe,* in which he says certain free things of Spain, Italy and other countries, with which this confederacy is under treaty of peace and amity—altogether in very agreeable relations. Bryant has been frequently before our tribunals. He is well known as a poet, one of a class of offenders who are always sure of conviction. He has been guilty of publishing letters like the present, on sundry previous occasions. It is proved, in his favor, that he writes gracefully and well—prose as well as verse; that no exception, on this score, can be taken to the present volume; that it is quite as good as those preceding it. But it is shown that he speaks very freely of the said nations with which this confederacy is at peace; that he has gone spying out the poverty of their several lands; that he scandalously reproves and ridicules them on sundry occasions; and has photographed their cities and countries, their society and scenery, in such a manner that, in the event of our future annexation of their territories, it will not be difficult, from said Bryant's descriptions, for each of us to choose his favorite plantation, or farm and niggers. Such developments are justly held to be inconsistent with the comity of states and nations; and the charges are fully brought home to the prisoner; who, entering no defence, and standing obstinately silent, his books have been decreed to be scattered along the highways, through the hands of the common booksellers. The prisoner, an old offender, did not show himself at all mortified by this most humiliating sentence.

The next case called, brought before the court a brisk fidgetty little woman, of very uncertain age, who persisted in dressing herself in the fantastic costume of a *Wild Irish Girl,* and claimed close relationship with the ancient families of the *O'Flaherties and O'Doherties.* She was attended by a muse of the order of *Beguines* on one hand, and by a bright blue-eyed girl, in Greekish costume, whom she called *Ida of Athens,* on the other. She, herself, claimed to be of the *pur sang azul,* and was named in the indictment as *"Miladi* Morgan." Her offences consisted in publishing *A Diary,* and the agents of her arrest were, again, the Brothers Appleton. It was charged against this little lady, that she had lived quite too long for her own reputation and the public peace; that she was *passé,* and no longer tolerable; that she was a creature of the most inordinate self-conceit, who mistook pretty compliments, of good-humored people, for fame and celebrity; that she had done some clever things in her youth; but that she had done nothing half so good in her age; that, however, she might deny this fact, it was certain she was no longer young; that she had made no progress to maturity in spite of her years; and that, in the present volume, her senility had led her to make quite too free with really great people; that the book was, in some degree, a scandalous chronicle; perhaps more ridiculous than scandalous; that it was written in no particular language; that in acquiring French and Italian she had forgotten her English and her native tongue, the Irish, and could no longer wag the vernacular; that her writings were a hotch-pot of all of these languages, and so larded with French that her vocable might as well have been all lard. The prosecuting attorney further urged the necessity of dealing severely with the offender, as she had threatened the public with a repetition of her offence—that is, with other volumes from the same *Diary.* The counsel in defence urged the merits of her youth at a remote period, and brought forward the fair *Ida of Athens,* the *Wild Irish Girl* and others, as witnesses, who averred her to having been once young, beautiful and winning. The muse of the *Beguines* also gave testimony in her favor to the like effect, and some of her details made the most favorable impression on the Court. It was admitted that she was garrulous, but her age and sex were urged in extenuation; and, as respects the *Diary,* it was pleaded that, in spite of her garrulity and vanity, she had certainly spoken the truth of others if not of herself. That she had given us pleasant re-unions with many remarkable people; and such spirited photographic impressions of them, as redeemed her book of its absurdities. The argument in defence had its weight with the jury, who, after a five minutes absence, returned with a special verdict; upon which the Judge discharged the prisoner, with full permission to amuse the public with her *Diaries* as often as she thought proper, but always at her own expense. She was at liberty to be read and laughed at.

Charleston *Mercury* (20 May 1859).

Our Literary Docket—Novelists, George Eliot, James Hungerford, and Charlotte Mary Yonge

In the Charleston *Mercury* of 3 October 1860, Simms declared *The Mill on the Floss* to be inferior to *Adam Bede,* but he held George Eliot "incapable of a positively bad book—incapable of a book which shall not interest, and in which there shall not be picturesque development and fine characterization." He regretted her use of the flood as deus ex machina because this was contrary to literary realism. In his fullest, most perceptive treatment of her career, when he reviewed *Felix Holt,* Simms lamented "her deterioration as a novelist," but he concluded, "as a woman of genius, a master of strong, graphic, good English, a keen appreciation and delineation of scenery and character, she still holds the high position which she reached almost at a bound." *Felix Holt,* with its "long side issues of local political discussion, its impossible plots and improbable personages," does not bear comparison to *Adam Bede, The Mill on the Floss,* or *Scenes from Clerical Life* (Charleston *Courier,* 31 August 1866). In the *Courier* of 11 November 1869, he called *Romola* a work of "exquisite characterization." The friend, George Elliott, is George P. Elliott of Beaufort, lawyer and fellow writer for the *Mercury* (31 January 1859).

Simms was correct in saying that James Edward Hungerford (1814–1883), Maryland novelist and poet, had published in the *Magnolia* in 1842–43. Hungerford became editor of the *Southern Home Journal.* The North Carolina "renegade" is unidentified but may be the abolitionist Daniel Reaves Goodloe (1814–1902), author of *The Southern Platform* (Boston, 1858), or, even more likely, Hinton Rowan Helper (1829–1909), whose antislavery tome *The Impending Crisis* appeared in 1857. An oblique reference is made to Frances Anne Kemble Butler's *Two Years on a Georgia Plantation.* Hamlet's *miching malicho* means *sneaky mischief.* Simms's mispelling remains here as he wrote it.

Ben Sylvester's Word is a moral tale for children by Charlotte Mary Yonge, whose *The Heir of Redclyffe* (1853) became one of the most popular works of the age.

We continue the reports of cases on our literary docket. Quite a group of offenders, charged with the heinous crime of novel and romance writing, were next brought before the court. The jury consisted of a body of grave old gentlemen and evangelical spinsters, who showed themselves instantly alert in respect to this class of criminals.

George Eliot (not our friend of the Port Royal city and railway) was charged with a volume of domestic fiction called *Adam Bede,* from the press of Harper & Brothers. *Adam* underwent a searching examination; but he went through the fire without flinching, and with only a few feathers singed. His book received the "well-done" of the critical jury; was pronounced a good moral story; *Adam* was declared to be an admirable fellow, and to have worked out his mission in society with credit to himself and family; and George Eliot, to whom we owe the creation of this *Adam,* was bade go and make as many more of the same sort of persons as he pleased. It was held that George could be trusted to fashion men as well as books, much more beneficially to society than many of the professing teachers.

James Hungerford, brought up by Harper & Brothers, charged with the writing a book called *The Old Plantation, and What I Gathered There in an Autumn Month.* This was a very suspicious title for a book. It looked, to southern eyes, like "*michin malico.*" Plantation life—a month or two—only a month or two, and on a southern plantation! Folks began to smell an abolitionist in Mr. James Hungerford, and every eye was down upon him with forty-microscope power. It did not matter to be told that he was from Maryland. Is not Baltimore, itself, a half-abolitionized city? Has not a renegade from North Carolina, the venerable old North State, been recently taken up by the abolitionists as a great bell-wether, to ring their clatter and clamors in the very ears of the South! No! no! Birth place no longer offers assurances of safety, and truth, and honesty, and patriotism; and it is clear that James Hungerford, though hailing from Maryland, may be an enemy, in disguise of a friend. Now, we too, observed James with more than ordinary closeness; but for reasons purely our own. We happened to know something of him *lang syne*—less than a hundred years ago—as a contributor of very pretty verses to the *Magnolia Magazine.* We thought favorably of the accused and suspected: and, in our sympathy, were willing to take for granted that all would turn up right with him. And so it did. His book was subjected to a most thorough drilling, and pronounced quite harmless, and utterly free from censure on the tabooed topic. So far from being objectionable on this score, it presented a very genial portraiture of the pleasant relations existing on the southern plantations between Ebony and Topaz. And, besides, was quite a readable domestic volume; sketchy, lively, good humored, and symmetrical; without much invention or power; but sly—very sly—clever—a fair fireside and family volume. James Hungerford, released from custody, departed with the friendly countenance of his late accusers; and we hope to shake hands with him again, over a still better volume.

Ben Sylvester's Word proved to be a very interesting story of a boy who loved the truth for its own sake; whose instincts were truthful; and who triumphed over all his trials and troubles simply by his truth. The story is well told, and just the sort of tale for young people. It is, by the way, from the pen of a writer who has been found repeatedly able to delight old heads as well as instruct young ones—the author of that very popular novel, *The Heir of Redclyffe.* We need not say, after this, that the verdict of the jury, corresponding with the charge of the judge, authorized the free circulation of this little book among the juveniles, as one well calculated to interest their minds and help to strengthen their hearts and morals.

Charleston *Mercury* (31 May 1859).

Our Literary Docket—Lord John Campbell's *Shakspeare*

The 1848 work to which Simms referred is his own *Supplement to the Plays of William Shakspeare.* Simms was arguably the best Shakespeare scholar and critic of his time in the United States. See his extended analysis of "The Moral Character of Hamlet" (*Orion* 4 [March, April, May, June 1844]: 41–51, 46–89, 105–19, 179–94) and "Shakspeare—'The Tempest'" (*SLG* n.s. 1 [15 September 1829]: 202–4). He clearly did not accept the Romantic era's sentimental stereotype of Shakespeare as a simple, common man of little formal learning, untutored by all but nature.

Lord John Campbell, well known for his admirable *Lives of the Lords Chancellors,* has suffered himself to be brought up before one of the *pie-poudre* courts of literature, charged with an argument to prove "the *legal acquirements*" of William Shakspeare, long known as dramatist and deer-stealer; hitherto recognized as a poet; now also expected to have been a pettifogger! My Lord Campbell hopes to show this, by reason of sundry quotations from Shakspeare's writings, in which the dramatist delivers occasionally, and correctly, the technicalities of the law courts—and is not unfamiliar with that barbarous jargon, mixed Latin, Gothic, and Gaulish—that strange

> "*tria juncta in uno,*
> But a worse 6—than Juno,"

Which Lord Coke used most gustily, even while he abused most lustily! But, to the assumptions of my Lord Campbell, we oppose a *non sequitor.* It may be quite true, and we think it probable, that William Shakspeare did serve an apprenticeship in a law office;—(of this hereafter)—but that we should hope to prove, or be justified in assuming this, because he knew the value of a *capias,* or could define the writ *ne exeat,* is mere absurdity. As well assume, from his knowledge of the Scriptures, that he was Pope or Parson. A great poet is apt to be a little of everything—and to know a little of everything! His genius is as near to being universal genius, as it is possible for mental genius to be! He has a peculiar power of acquisition—by absorption—and picks up knowledge where other men pick up—simply money! and he finds flowers where ordinary men find fares! Shakspeare's knowledge of the law (as educed from the evidence in his writings) proves only that he made use of ordinary opportunities. He could easily have picked up all his law phrases, numerous as they are, by a three months attendance in any Court of *Oyer and Terminer.* A quick ear and mind, and an eager curiosity, would enable him not only to do this, but to employ all that he thus acquired, with the legitimate meanings, in any future writings. And so, no doubt, he picked up—as such minds generally do—a thousand odds and ends of science and philosophy, from occasional readings, from the conversation of others, and from a thousand unsuspected sources of society. What we call self-education is, really, in most cases, of this very sort and character; and this mode of acquisition is predicable of all that class of minds which possess native powers of absorption; not an ordinary class, to be sure; but, when found in the individual always significant of equally strong powers of use and application in new, bold and peculiar forms. But even supposing Lord Campbell to be right in his conjectures, we must add that he only repeats what others have said and shown before him. The opinion is an old one, that Shakspeare not only was better taught than people have supposed, and his early biographers have written, but that he had, in some degree, a legal education. The notion was broached in England some twenty years ago. It is possible that Lord Campbell had something to do in originating it, but his name does not occur among those which were at first associated with the idea. Even in this country we find, in the "general introduction" to the only edition that we have of the plays imputed to Shakspeare, but not included in his writings—a work edited by Mr. Simms—this language: "The earnest activity of such workers as Dyce, Collier, Knight, and the gentlemen connected with the Shakspeare Society in England, will continue to make discoveries, such as they have already made, which will most probably lead us to such an approximation of the true, in Shakspeare's career, as, at least, to relieve his biography of the great exaggerations and errors which have disfigured it. We shall probably learn, as in fact we do already, that his family was one of good repute and condition, though somewhat reduced in fortune, and not so much stinted, but that his education was quite as good as could be afforded in that part of England during his boyhood;—that he was not only somewhat informed in Greek and Latin, as Johnson, indeed, tells us— (though the wilful biographers of Shakspeare have perversely construed the line—'And though thou had'st small Latin and less Greek'—into the possession of neither) but that he was probably, in some degree also, acquainted with French and Italian—and visited the Continent at some early period of his life; making a personal acquaintance, at Venice, with the Rialto; and receiving his prompting, for the most perfect of all love stories, at the very tomb of the Capulets, in Verona. It is highly probable that, on leaving the Grammar School of Stratford, he passed into the office of an attorney, and there picked up that familiarity with legal phrases, which his writings betray to a greater extent than those of all his contemporary dramatists together." This was printed in this country in 1848. But, whether well or ill founded, whether original with Lord Campbell or not, the suggestion is one that well deserved the illustrative volume (by examples) which we here owe to his lordship. The instances quoted are equally numerous and curious, and this *brochure* is one to reward curiosity. We commend it to the faculty, as well as the general reader. The profession may well rejoice, quoting as they do so commonly from Shakspeare, to discover that he has first been freely employed in quoting from them.

Charleston *Mercury* (3 June 1859)

Our Literary Docket—Charles Lever's
Gerald Fitzgerald, the Chevalier

Simms considered this prolific Irish novelist badly underrated by the English. Two early previously unrecorded notices of Lever's *The Nevilles of Garretstown* and *St. Patrick's Eve* appeared in *S&W* 1 (March 1845): 223 and 2 (October 1845): 288. Simms judged the novels to be well-constructed and alive with action (*SQR* 15 [April 1849]: 70–72). His *Roland Cashel* was lively and "melo-dramatic," very much like his "usual performances" (*SQR* n.s. 1 [July 1850]: 539). *Sir Jasper Carew* was "stirring and interesting," though "not quite so clever" as *The Dodd Family* (*SQR* n.s. 1 [October 1854]: 527). While the novel is "not altogether satisfactory as a story" with too much "purposeless wandering," Lever was a writer who could not "wholly fail in any subject which he undertakes." Simms praised *Harry Lorrequer* and *Charles O'Malley, the Irish Dragoon* in the Charleston *Mercury* (8 January 1855). In the Charleston *Courier* (4 November 1868), he favorably reviewed *The Bramleighs of Bishop's Folly*. Parks perceptively concluded that Simms "had a higher regard for contemporary Irish romances than their British fellows" either from pro-Irish and anti-English sentiment or "unprejudiced critical standards" (27). Simms praised William Carleton's stories of Irish life and Samuel Lever as a "rare good fellow" who "succeeds in depicting

Irishmen who are true to life" (Parks, *William Gilmore Simms as Literary Critic*, 27). William Maginn (pseudonym of Morgan O'Doherty) was also a favorite (Charleston *Mercury*, 5, 17, and 24 May 1855).

Simms's depiction of Talleyrand (1758–1838) as a sneering Mephistopheles and Mirabeau (1749–1791) as juggler and "prince of diableries" reflected his intense disapproval of these French revolutionists. See also the review of Guizot in part 2.

Charles Lever, a rollicking Irishman, of portly presence and the usual national bashfulness, is brought up to answer for a book, entitled *Gerald Fitzgerald, the Chevalier;* a work of which but a single instalment was brought into court, and of which we are to judge only in reference to the promise which it conveys of good or evil hereafter. It is just possible that the offender, the author, relies somewhat upon this fact to escape present conviction.

It was shown by the prosecuting attorney that the said Charles Lever had been frequently before the Courts, and was, in short, a very notorious personage. To this it was answered, as promptly as pertly, by the defence, that, if so, he had always hitherto escaped conviction, and had, in fact, gone off with flying colors.

The accuser urged that the said Lever was a sort of Proteus in authorship, leaving his readers half the time doubtful where, or in what humor to find him;—that, as under the wand of a magician, and with the mere cry of "Presto," he could change his hues and character—become grave as a portly Carolina Chancellor, and anon as merry as a starving Italian mountebank. That he had changed his deportment in almost as many books as he had written; at one moment appearing as a "Bould Dragoon;" at another as a sentimental fighting Hamlet or Romeo; now dashing into broad farce, fun and comedy; now as full of horrors as Macbeth or Richard Crookback. To illustrate this impudent versatility of our author, quoth the accusing attorney, here is one of our own city papers which refers its readers to this very *Gerald Fitzgerald* for fun and frolic, roaring and rollicking, when its chief merit lies in its being a tragedy under most momentous circumstances.

Between the fires of the opposing counsel, our Irish friend, Charley, found it as hot as the French at Marignano, in the days of Bayardo. But Charley himself maintained a most incrutable visage under all this fire. He looked on and lied without winking.

The Judge, meanwhile, had been reading through the book, and paying but little attention to the sharp-shooting of counsel. Before the close of the discussion, however, he looked up to ask of the contending parties if either of them had read the offensive volume; a question to which, as honest critics, both answered in the negative.

"Then," saith his Honor, "release the prisoner, and go home and read his book. It is a thing of good things; may be true or not; that matters little. 'Si non e vero, e ben trovato,' which means, gentlemen, that if not true it ought to be. Read it, gentlemen. It contains, among other good things, most lifelike portraits of Alfieri, the great Italian poet; Mirabeau, the great Gallic juggler and prince of diablerie; and of Talleyrand, the best representative on earth of the sneering devil, Mephistopheles. There are many other portraits of less famous people besides, quite as admirably sketched. Go home and become familiar with these several legal models, for they had all legal minds, even Alfieri, though they never filed their minds with the profession—at least in vulgar courts. Dismiss the prisoner, and if you can get him to go home with you for the night, you may be brighter wits, if not better lawyers, to-morrow morning."

Charleston *Mercury* (21 June 1859).

◄━━━━━━━

Our Literary Docket—Anthony Trollope's
The Bertrams and *Doctor Thorne*

Trollope (1815–1882) was never Simms's kind of writer. Words such as "sometimes forcible" and on the whole *possibly* "truthful" did not offset the damning with faint praise of "charming." Neither did Simms's characterization of Trollope's fans in Charleston as likely to be "thirteen old maids and forty or fifty fashionable ladies . . . sighing in secret." In a survey of English prose writers in 1845, he was quick to place D'Israeli "far above" Trollope (*SQR* 15 [April 1845]: 344). When he defended Trollope's *Phineas Finn* as "not liable to objections sometimes urged, that of giving false views of life and characters," he again raised the question of Trollope's realism (Charleston *Courier*, 13 April 1869).

Mrs. Trollope is Frances Trollope, Anthony's mother. The wordplay on the tub's large bottom is a humorous twist on her nickname "Fanny." She was obese, and Simms here was uncharacteristically unchivalrous in his levity. In *SQR* 15 (April 1849): 66, Simms writes, "Her nose is ever in the pantry" and "she possesses better digestion than brains." He included his essay on her *Domestic Manners of the Americans* in *Views and Reviews,* Second Series. Russell and Courtenay were Charleston booksellers.

Anthony Trollope, a person of very equivocal name, but of no bad presence, brought up as guilty of uttering a book, classed as a novel, and called *The Bertrams.* It was shown by the prosecuting attorney that Trollope was a very bad name *per se;* that it was especially evil in American eyes, as having been borne by one who, perhaps for the better maintenance of her name, had greviously slandered the American people; that the said slanderer was a Mrs. Trollope; a gross, fat, coarse woman, who never said her prayers but after a hearty meal, and was then too plethoric to say them with grace, or intelligibly.

The accusing attorney evidently labored to produce the impression that the said Mrs. Trollope was the mother of the said Anthony—the author of the book under consideration—and that he, Anthony, was of like kidney with the mother! But this fact was not made out by the evidence.

The defendant's counsel joined the general issue, and denied everything, and put himself upon the country. He avowed that he was a Trollope, but not the Trollope; that he was not merely, because of name, to be amerced for the slanders of the woman in question; that every tub must stand on its own bottom, even the tub of a Trollope, and that he himself was only answerable for a tale of a tub! And so forth.

It was shown by the evidence that Anthony Trollope was not now, for the first time, before the courts;—that he had erewhile been guilty of one or more volumes of fiction; that his *Doctor Thorne* was a charming work of fiction; and that this of *The Bertrams* is even more charming. The Judge, however, ruled otherwise. He did not think the *Bertrams* quite so clever a book as *Doctor Thorne;* did not find it so generally amiable and clever; the interest might be as great, but was not so agreeable. It was interesting, however, and this is the *sine qua non* in every work of fiction. It was not dull; not tedious; was sometimes forcible and touching; and, on the whole, might be held truthful. Anthony Trollope escaped conviction, and almost censure, on the promise of still better books, with which, according to his counsel, his brain was already teeming. He left the court, supported, one one side, by Mr. John Russell, and, on the other, by Mr. S.G. Courtenay, who had been the sureties for his appearance, and who were quite happy at his passing through the ordeals of criticism so luckily. On the strength of it, they forthwith ordered new supplies of *The Bertrams,* for which thirteen old maids and forty or fifty fashionable ladies were even then sighing in secret.

Charleston *Mercury* (22 June 1859).

Our Literary Docket—Bartholomew Rivers Carroll, Jr., Hayne, and Timrod.

Bartholomew Rivers Carroll, Jr. (born 1807), was the son of an emigrant from Northern Ireland and the younger brother of Charles Rivers Carroll (p. 50). An early neighbor of Simms and a childhood friend, he was a schoolmaster, author, editor of the *Southern Literary Journal* (1835–38), to which Simms contributed, the *Southern Agriculturist* (1835–1840, 1842–1846), and the Columbia *South Carolinian* (1846–1847). He collected and published documents of early Carolina history and was an orator of distinction. Like his brother Charles, he was a local activist for Irish independence. His *An Address Delivered before the St. Patrick Benevolent Society and Irish Volunteers* (Charleston: T. J. Eccles, 1838) and *Speeches Delivered before the Association of the Friends of Irish Independence in Charleston* (Charleston: Burges & James, 1848) furthered a cause that Simms also favored throughout his life and in which he became even more vitally interested as he advocated the South's own independence and began considering the means and methods to achieve it. As usual Simms was using his broad knowledge of world history to provide precedents and to learn from those who had walked similar paths before him. The reference to Simms's son, who was to be educated by Carroll, is to Govan Simms, whose nurse was indeed Statira, as the piece reveals. Simms was a mentor for the two young Charleston poets, Henry Timrod and Paul Hamilton Hayne. The books they had in press were Timrod's *Poems* and Hayne's *Avolio,* both published in 1860 by Ticknor of Boston. William Henry Hurlbut (1827–1895) was a Charleston poet, essayist, and Unitarian minister who made a living writing for the New York press. Keitt was South Carolina congressman Lawrence Massillon Keitt (1824–1864), a foe in the House of Representatives of Galusha A. Grow (1823–1907), a free soiler representative of Pennsylvania. The former sheriff Carew was John E. Carew.

The court room—our snuggery—was in admirable literary confusion—strewn with books, papers, pamphlets and manuscripts, when Mr. B. R. Carroll entered, in full dress, bringing with him a new edition of his excellent *Catechism of United States History.*

Judge *Mercury* was in the best of humor.

"Mr. Officer, hand Mr. Carroll a chair, if you please!—teachers of the young must not only have place, but state! We must habitually show them reverence. They have, in their keeping, the souls and minds, the passions, the principles, fancies, feelings and affections, of unborn generations! And in this community, especially,—which is famously prolific; and where wives, loving their lords according to the rule laid down in Shakspeare, seem annually resolved to bestow upon them fresh, living presentments of their own beloved images—and this, too, without any considerate regard to their several incomes;—in such a community, we say, the obligations of society to the teachers of the young, demand that we treat them with all honor, and requite their services by—a prompt payment of their quarterly bills!

"So shall our little Bills—ay, and Johns, and Toms, and Neds, Dicks, and Harrys—all prosper exceedingly in future years.

"Please take a seat, Mr. Carroll, in that high-backed Elizabethan chair, which stands upon the right covered with crimson velvet. Be seated, sir; pray remove your hat—take off your coat, if you will! It is, I see, of professional black, and a little too hot for such weather. Mr. Officer, pray find a cool linen overall for Mr. Carroll, and a cigar.

"What! you don't smoke? You are, perhaps, right. You are of the order of the *Leankinites,* and the mechanical effects of smoking may be too exhaustive. But here, sir, having all about us famous teacher-men, and of great physical devel-opement, we all smoke!

"You are aware that, in the Courts of Judge *Mercury,* we keep our poets especially on sherry and cigars! Were you a poet, now, instead of teacher and historian, we should commit you for contempt, for refusing that cigar. Poets must smoke! Smoking induces that abstract, dreamy mood in which the imaginative mind luxuriates. Fancies, purple and golden, rise up on every curling vapor, edging it with beauty to the half-shut eye; and the mind, in a delicious reverie, realizes all those felicitous discoveries in cloud-land which make it temporarily forgetful of the dull mundane sphere, and the gloomy condition which always hangs about mere earth. Then it is, sir, that we realize, though in broad daylight, such fairy visions as grand old Milton describeth:

> 'Visions
> Of these gay creatures of the element
> That in the colors of the rainbow live,
> And play i' the plighted clouds.'

"Yes, our poets all smoke! You will, anon, see them popping in upon us—Hayne, Timrod, Hurlbut, and half a dozen of the still younger brethren, each with a cigar in his mouth!

"Hayne, who has quite a Shelley aspect, with a considerable cast of Keats—whose face would make a fine picture for the boudoir of Sappho, and of whom we must certainly get a photograph for our own sanctum, is peculiarly choice and delicate in his cigars! He uses a nice, tiny little Cabanas, such as *Oberon* would use, approximating these *cigaritos,* which lie so naturally between the pulpy lips of the Cuban damsels when they are divided between cigar and *siesta.* I suspect he is half afraid of a big cigar, such as Timrod puffs with formidable ease and confidence! Such would fuddle Hayne; and he prudently confines himself to the most modest dimensions in the choice of his cigars; and he smokes with the greatest deliberation—never makes any effort to throw out a volume of smoke—never puffs out his cheeks—and his lips are scarcely lifted at all for the insertion of the slenderly curled up weed.

"You can almost tell, too, by the manner in which he smokes, whether he meditates a lyric, a sonnet—a gush of fancy, or a passionate song! His eyes will enlarge with one class of subjects, and his lips will quiver over another, while the eye half shuts, like those of a young damsel, for the first time listening to love-assurances from young Whiskerando, her first cousin! Now Timrod smokes like a Zouave going into battle! You can see that he is in dead earnest. He is in no humor for trifling. He shows as much *élan* in smoking, as the Frenchman in fighting! and he is not content with overcoming and bringing a single victim to the dust; he consumes one after another, as if he had been sent into the world for this purpose and no other.

"I suspect he learned his lesson when a boy, and probably smoked a couple at a time, in learning! And like the Zouave, he is best pleased when his victim is of the biggest and strongest! And, strange to say, it is when with one such—a Regalia of six inches, at least—crunched between his jaws, that he writes his most sentimental verses! Then it is that he thinks of dark, languid eyes; with diamond darts and drooping lids, and tender hearts and juicy quids; as smoke persuades and fancy bids.

"It is wonderful, Mr. Carroll, to see, and feel, and know and hear; and how to reconcile the sentiment and song, so tender and so fanciful, with such monstrous big cigars and such formidable demonstrations, is beyond any philosophy in our system.

"Now, sir, we have dwelt upon these, our poets, and their innocent practices; as we happen to know that, in your school practice, you heedfully inculcate among your pupils a proper taste for poetry and other fine arts. We have heard your boys, sir, at their public exhibitions, and they do you honor, sir—they do! You do them a great service by your lessons in elocution; and have done them more by inspiring them with a proper taste for pure sentiment and fine poetry! And, sir, it is magnanimous in you, not claiming to be a poet yourself, that you love the poets; that you are not jealous of them; as is quite too apt to be the case with that large herd of pretentious whipsters about town, who, incapable of their divine speech, indulge in contemptuous sneer at their diviner art! Teach it, sir, when you can. Every boy whom you can imbue with delicate sentiments, and noble aspirations, and beautiful fancies, and tender sympathies, is a man saved from the stews!

"And while we are on this theme, it will give you pleasure to hear that both Hayne and Timrod are in the press with new volumes of poetry. They will be refreshing volumes, as we trust and believe. You will be able to find in their pages many noble ballads, which your boys will declaim with unction to the big wigs, the little wits, the congregated sires and dames of our venerable city. And having spoken their public speeches, your boys aforesaid such as begin to feel a downy incumbrance on chin and cheek, will seek out for themselves, from the same pages, some tenderer ditties, which they will not deliver in public, or to the same auditors. There will be a whispering in moonlighted groves, Mr. Carroll, and lessons given and taken there which are not to be found in all your curriculum. And Hayne and Timrod will provide the books!

"Ah! thank you, sir, for this nice copy of the second edition of your school *History of the United States.* We see that you have put our name in it, with your compliments—an author's presentation copy.

"This shall go into our library. We have had one already from your publishers. That shall go into the hands of our boy—a fellow of infinite promise, though but two years old! You may have him in your hands, as pupil, some few years hence. May you live long enough, sir, and continue your labors long enough, to do him good service.

"He is a fellow of head, and has pat on his tongue some of the favorite pet phrases of popular eloquence, as used in Congress and other select menageries. Why, but last night, when we said to the nurse, 'take that urchin off to bed!'— his response was quick and sharp as a Parthian arrow.

"'No, sirree, Bob!' he cried; and with one little mutton fist, he drove into the ribs of *Statira*, the nurse, while he shook the other at ourselves with as much fury as our Col. Keitt exhibited when he took Pennsylvania Grow by the throat.

"You see, from this anecdote, the most encouraging promise in the boy, and the most interesting prospect for the future teacher. How that chap's eloquence will flow; how those little mutton fists will grow; how manfully well will they plant each blow; and (possibly) make the future teacher know! He shall have your book in his hands, and he shall go into yours, as soon as his growing becomes sufficient for his knowing;—ay, and for his blowing!

"Let us now say, Mr. Carroll, that we have reexamined your volume with the greatest satisfaction. The book itself, in the first edition, met our fullest approbation. We approved the plan very highly. Your revision of it, we see, has been painstaking and careful. You have made many useful additions. Briefly, it is surprising how much matter you have succeeded in condensing into so moderate a space.

"With this manual, our boys have a more complete summary of our history, as colonies and as a confederacy, from first to last, than is to be found in any similar work in the country. It is an ample and admirable book; and the plan, by question and answer, grows upon our preference from reexamination.

"We do not see that you have omitted anything of importance to be known; that you have put in anything not proper to be shown; that you have made any mistakes or errors of your own!

"Stay! We have seen, in some of the papers, that your facts are questioned, in one particular, touching the early laws of New York. You state that the religious intolerance of that colony caused the passage of a law commanding that every Roman Catholic entering the province shall be hanged, while Dissenters among the Protestants—Non-Conformists—are to be punished in other ways. This fact has been denied, and we cannot, at this moment, help you with any evidence or opinion of our own. But, as a question of mere fact, we presume that it is one which may be easily settled. We have little doubt of it ourself. It is quite in keeping with the spirit of that age. The laws of all the colonies at that time, and before and after it, were more or less cruel, brutal and intolerant. You would be quite safe in saying that there was hardly a colony which did not exhibit religious intolerance. But, get the five volumes of *Documentary History of New York,* and you will probably be able to settle the question decisively. And yet, you may have to look further, for there is little doubt that in some of the colonies a feeling of shame has prompted the descendants of the ancient persecutors to do a very shameful act—to mutilate the records! Still, the evidence may be had.

"In our dear little State, where the people now constitute one large, loving family—where the lion lies down with the lamb—where the frog and the crane sup together—where the snake goes to bed with the chicken, and the hawk is on friendly terms with the partridge, and the eagle with the hare—it was very far otherwise in colonial times! Ah! we can rub our hands with delight at the change! We are now so linked together and loving that we are only not living in common; and we have no doubt that you or we, growing hungry, might walk, unarrested, into our neighbour's kitchen, and carry off his chicken from the gridiron; and the owner would send his cook after us to say—'Maussa beg you come back and git de rice and tatter, too!' A blessed time, surely—almost the millennium!

"And now, dear Mr. Carroll, we have a question for you. You have given us a whole volume of questions and answers, and we have pronounced it excellent. Now, pray, answer this one question. Are you of that tribe of authors who require the critic to say—'Thou art perfect!'—who will not be satisfied with less;—who, whatever your approbation, yet vexed with it all, if you happen to say—'there is a grain of salt too much, or of pepper too little, in this soup? But for this, it would be perfect.' Who, like the French cook, when so told, will kick over the whole pot, and perhaps rush to the garret and hang themselves, or rush to the highway and blackguard the critic? Tell us, Mr. Carroll, whether you are of this Sir Fretful order.

"Ah! you laugh, and shake your head. No! we could have sworn it! Well, then, there are some small errors of style which we would have you amend in a future edition. They are few, and proof, rather of carelessness and haste, than of any deficiency of knowledge or judgment. Here is one example which shall suffice: On page 179, speaking of Burr and Hamilton, you say—'He (Burr) was opposed by Hamilton, who associated with him on friendly terms in public, but secretly denounced him in private.'

"It strikes us that the sense will not be hurt, and the sentence may be improved, by omitting that world 'secretly.' Perhaps a re-construction of the whole sentence would be advisable.

"We would also counsel you to omit, or to rewrite, the whole of the passage on page 260, entitled, 'Conclusion.' Your muse has been evidently drowsy during the performance of this portion of her task. It needs only that we should call your attention to it; your own good taste and good sense may be relied on, to suggest all the objectionable matter in the passage, and to amend it, with better style, and a closer regard to its sequences.

"These are all small matters, Mr. Carroll; but, dealing with a teacher, they are important still. And it is better that a friendly critic should point them out, than that they should exercise the venom and wit of a malignant one. You remember, nobody better, the reply of Brutus to Cassius, in the famous quarrel scene:—

> 'Cassius—A friendly eye would
> Never see such faults.
> Brutus—A flatterer's would not, though
> They did appear
> As huge as high Olympus!'

We may add—

> And the malignant's tongue
> Would swell them to a mountain vast of bulk,
> To which all Ossa, upon Pelion piled,
> Would show but as a wart!

"Mr. Officer, will you order us a couple of tumblers of that patent ice-wedded sangaree, from that dozen claret, which we had the honor to receive yesterday from Ex-Sheriff Carew. Very graceful, is it not, Mr. Carroll, that a gentleman going out of office should so amiably distinguish the event, by making parting gifts to his friends?"

Charleston *Mercury* (9 August 1859).

Our Literary Docket—Allen Hampden's *Hartley Norman*

This review became the impetus for assessment of the state of literature influenced by faction over art and for damnation of all hypocrisies, especially in the use of euphemistic language, that would work counter to literary realism. Simms here linked New England imperialism and hypocrisy to Old English imperialism through the figure of Oliver Cromwell. He predicted this new Cromwell-style zealotry would "burn us Southrons out" or "kill us off." Simms was specific in saying "the puritan fanatic is the source of our modern Yankee" in his review of J. T. Headley's *The Life of Oliver Cromwell* (*SQR* 14 [October 1848]: 519).

Simms quoted imperfectly from Pope's *An Essay on Man,* epistle 2, lines 217–19. Allen Hampden is unidentified.

"Call up the next case!"

"*Hartley Norman, a Tale of the Times,* said to be written by one Allen Hampden —*a nom de plume,* of course—from the press of Rudd and Carleton, New York; new publishers, your Honor, who put forth their books in very handsome style."

"What's this penciling here, in the title page, Mr. Attorney?"

"A 'd—d cramp hand,' your Honor;—quoting from Oliver Goldsmith. I suspect it to be Mr. Gordon's chirography, sir,—in the office."

"My spectacles! Can you make it out!"

"I think I do, sir."

"What is it, then?"

"It is a most audacious piece of irreverence, your Honor! I am surprised, sir, that Mr. Gordon should have done such a thing! He is such a mild, placid person, by no means an acid person; yet, your Honor, by my troth, he here indulges in an oath!"

"Read, read, sir!" impatiently.

"Well, sir, he has here written these very awful words, by way of commentary upon the book which he tells me he has glanced at in parts.

"The words, sir—decypher."

Mr. Attorney reads solemnly—

"A d—d Anti-slavery Book!"

"A most awfully delivered judgment, Mr. Attorney."

"Horrid, sir! And for a person so mild, gentle, amiable and little given to bad words, as Mr. Gordon!"

"It argues a remarkable change for the worse! Be so good as to advise him that, in future, the Court will do its own swearing! The Court has privileges which it must not part with. Swearing, sir, unless officially, is a very bad, pernicious habit. Judges, distinguished politicians, Quakers—these may be permitted to swear."

"Dragoons, too, sir. The privilege is proverbial with them."

"A dragoon, sir, is scarcely to be held human. His vocation implies inhumanity. Soldiers are not human. They are merely destructive machines. Their swearings may be classed with the belchings of cannon when they vomit balls upon the enemy."

"Does not your Honor use rather strong language? Belchings and vomitings! Such words distress very nice people."

"Do you remember what Dean Swift said of very nice people?—they are people who have very nasty ideas!"

"Nasty, sir, is also a very censurable word with some people."

"So is hell, sir. What says the poet—

'Never mention hell to ears polite.'

"Sir, it is the peculiar faculty of some people, who pretend to great niceness, that they are the first always to discover the latent vice and immorality in everything, and where simpler people find no offence. This is due, sir, wholly to the fact that the nastiness is innate in their minds, and glossed over in a subdued phraseology. The vulgarity and sin are in their conception, not in your or my expression. It is this sort of people who call a sot a gay man; who call a gambler a sporting gentleman; who call a—a fast woman. Names are things, sir. When you get to distinguish a vice by some vague, namby-pamby, meaningless phrase, you strip the vice of what is repulsive in it. And this is one of those sad compromises with vice, which this age, under the notion of delicacy, is perpetually making. The practice finally reconciles us to the vice! It loses its horrid characteristics when you dress it up daintily in purple and fine linen. Nobody sees it fairly—or only sees it fairly (when you should see it fondly)—when you mask it with some lacka-daisical, meaningless phraseology. We grow, as Pope says—

> 'Familiar with its face—
> And first endure, then pity, then embrace!'

"I do not know anything which has done more mischief to virtue, and youth, and innocence, propriety and good manners, than this nice tampering with language in regard to the otherwise hideous immoralities which prevail in society.

"Now, Mr. Attorney, we wish it to be distinctly understood that, in this Court, we have no compromises with vice in behalf of convention! We mean to call things by their right names; we shall not surrender the good strong vernacular of *old* England to any mincing, wordy, flatulent, affected and really vicious habit of society. We shall do nothing to corrupt the language with *Euphemisms*, appealing to petty tastes, conceited fashions and licentious practices in disguise. We have some rods in pickle now, specially designed for that large class,—teachers, preachers, professors, socialists, authors—who have done incalculable mischief, by their circuitous habit of reaching a vice or a truth—a crime or a morality! The virtues of a people depend very much upon the incorruptible integrity of language; and, just in degree as we avoid the use of the right words in regard to human conduct, and substitute fanciful, or conventional words for them, will cant and hypocrisy prevail throughout the land. Look at the books of the old authors, sir; look at the paintings of the old painters,—Hogarth, for example;—nay, look at the sermons of the old priesthood, including 'the fathers,' if you would comprehend the stern, marrowy, manly manner in which they dealt with those vices of men which, now-a-days, we hear called by such pet and indulgent phrases! We could show you, Mr. Attorney, some ancient sermons which would shake your fashionable congregations with such terrors, as would take the stiffening and starch out of all their linen, shrink up hoops and corsets, till they should feel like fiery cinctures, burning into the very soul; and make the soul itself grow conscious of winged dragons, bearing bolts of doom, which no sudden burst of penitence and prayer would be likely to avert.

"But to the book, sir,—what of the book? Do you see any thing in its pages to justify Mr. Gordon in his most irreverent judgment?"

"Not exactly, sir! I suspect Mr. Gordon has got his impression from a hasty glance at a single chapter of the story! In that we are indulged in an episode, which relates the story of a fugitive slave. This *Sambo* had an excellent Charleston master, whom he loved very much, according to his own account, and for whom he would have died! But the unreasonable slaveowner never required *Sambo* to die, but died himself; leaving *Sambo* virtually free—that is, verbally free! And, here, the story tells rather against the abolitionists! The heir of the property is a northern man;—the case is substantially that of Sumner, the brother of Charles, the cudgelled; who came on, sold the negro, without respect to his future fate; pocketed the money, and vamoosed back to the free New England! *Sambo* did not like his new master; he, too, vamoosed; but, instead of sheltering himself in free New England, that paradise of the negro, he made his way to the Isthmus of Panama; and hence he sent back the money, paying for himself, to the late purchaser;—a sort of honesty which the abolitionists do not encourage or approve. This is pretty much all that is said on the subject, and does not constitute a sufficient justification of Mr. Gordon's vehement judgment! *Sambo,* educated by a southern gentleman, becomes a model gentleman himself;—altogether a very good model gentleman for the mongrel tribes that flock to the gold regions—Yankees, Gothamites, Chinese, Mexican, Hittites and Sodomites!"

"And what of the story, sir!"

"It is one of tolerable spirit and interest—perhaps, I should say, considerable interest sir,—for the judgments of our Court are indulgent ones."

"Very merciful!"

"There is variety, keeping, a fair presentation of character in the tale, and some lively and salient action."

"Well, sir, let the booksellers have it; Russell & Jones, Courtenay & Brothers, Sam'l Hart, Sr., and the rest; and let our enemies know that we, in the South, quarrel with nobody for the simple exercise of his opinions. We only cry aloud, and spare not, when there is a show of malignity, and when the party sets forth on a malicious crusade against us! We can listen patiently to Old England man and New England man, in the discussion of an abstract principle. We do not desire to prevent any man's opinions. Let Bull or Jonathan think as he pleases: We care not a button for the opinion of either blackguard. But we will not suffer Bull or Jonathan to run us through with a hot poker, and, at the same time, demand from us full payment for the operation! The worst of this class of works of fiction is the art objection.

"When they resort to elements, drawn from the negro condition of the South, it shows that they only seek a popular *fetch,* to help them out in their invention. It shows that true art is wanting; and that their hope of sale lies in the appeal to a vulgar fanaticism. Such books, perhaps, are not so malignant as stupid. They are monstrous stupid and vulgar to boot. Even Mrs. Stowe, who has a great deal of cunning talent—genuine serpent—seems to have exhausted her capital. At first it was all wool, and then there was a great cry over it;—now the author gives a great cry, and there is very little wool! *Cuffee's* wool is at discount. People sweat severely, after giving their sympathies to such woolly subjects; and as they refuse to sweat any longer, to please philanthropy, it is remarkable how the sympathy declines. The northern world has a world of sympathy always in the cause of inferior people; but you mustn't draw upon its sixpences as well as its sympathies. You will note that New Englanders never sympathize with their equals—perhaps they fancy that such are not; but it is certain they never sympathize with any race in whom the world recognizes an approach to equality. Its sympathies are only given to the inferior, whom it can patronize; and these must be at some distance, and it must only be some such case as will enable it to patronize some one race at the expense and to the annoyance of another. The New England people, from the time of Oliver Cromwell, must be annoying somebody—Red men or Quakers, or Manhattanese Dutch, and Southrons, after they have fairly overcome all the others! They have exterminated the Red men—abolished the Dutch—burnt out the Quakers—stole and sold the negroes, till they could steal and sell no longer; and the question now is, by what process shall they kick or burn us Southrons out, or kill us off! When they have done with us, they will try and sell all our *Cuffees* and *Sambos* to the Cubanese, by way of keeping down a too excessive philanthropy."

Charleston *Mercury* (20 August 1859).

James Clarence Mangan's *Poems*

John Mitchel (1815–1875), a member of Young Ireland whose *Jail Journal* is a classic of the Irish liberation movement, escaped to New York in 1853 after his deportation to Bermuda and his political imprisonment there. Carlyle, who had earlier met and encouraged him, accurately predicted this punishment would come. In the United States, Mitchel championed the works of his fellow Irish nationalists by editing and publishing. One such author was poet James Clarence Mangan (1803–1849), son of an Irish nationalist hedge school teacher. After the Great Famine his poetry had a strong nationalist bent. His verse was later admired by both Yeats and Joyce. It was Yeats who wrote, "To the soul of Clarence Mangan was tied the burning ribbon of genius." Mangan's "Kathaleen Ny-Houlahan" became Yeats's famous "Cathleen Ni-Houlihan." John Montague suggests Mangan may have influenced Poe (32).

Like Simms, Mangan taught himself to read German and translated German lyrics. Simms accurately gauged Mangan's translations to be free translations rather than transliterations. Mangan was the first to render the Irish poets into English. In 1840 he began translating from Turkish, Arabic, and Persian. He suffered from mood swings and depression and became increasingly paranoid and eccentric. He often wore green spectacles, a long cloak, and a blonde wig. As the South was contemplating her own liberation, Simms understandably became even more interested in the current works of Irish revolutionary poets— the Irish Confederates, as they called themselves. In this important previously unrecorded review, Simms expressed the reader's difficulty in learning of these Irish writers owing to the British press's refusal to notice them. His appreciation of Mangan's poetry is among the most astute assessments of the author written during the time. This review was discovered only after the publication in 2009 of Kibler, "Simms's Celtic Harp," and provides significant reinforcement to the essay's argument.

Poems. By James Clarence Mangan: with biographical introduction by John Mitchel. P. M. Haverty, New York: 1860.

We owe this very remarkable volume to the editorship of Mr. John Mitchel, the famous Irish patriot of recent periods. He has introduced us to an Irish poet of singular power, and of very eccentric genius, of whom few in this country ever heard a syllable before. Mr. Mitchel gives us a well-written biography of the poet, with a review of his career and life, and a thoughtful analysis of his genius. Mangan united the poet and the patriot with the usual proportions of patience and poverty. His life was humble, his resources more so; his fame without comforts; his career without distinction; yet his heart full of his country, and his head full of poetry. He was especially a lyrical poet; possessing all the necessary enthusiasm, fancy, pathos, and fine faculty for free versification in all measures. There is a wild, inartificial gush in his verse—frequently eccentric and irregular—which realizes for us the idea of the audacious vivacity of the mocking bird, in his moments of original inspiration; a hearty frankness; a piquant eccentricity; sudden flights of song, that defy all ordinary metrical barriers; and, while frequently sounding gratingly on the ear, just as frequently realizing that fresh invention which "snatches the grace beyond the reach of art." In his war songs, he is a genuine Britisher. In these of Irish and patriotic character, there is a savage intensity—a rush of the emotions, which rouses the spirit, to use the prose of Sydney, speaking of the Chevy Chase, as with the sound of the trumpet. But he does not confine himself to Irish themes. Mangan was a man of education—of learning, etc., in certain provinces; such as give the imagination play, and provoke the fancy. He was a librarian. He gives us a German anthology, which is singularly copious, as well as an Irish anthology, which is fresh and rich;—and we half incline to think, that none of the translations of Schiller, Uhland, Tieck, Körner, Bürger, Goethe, Freiligrath, Fouque, etc., have shown themselves so free, so bold, so true to their originals, yet so nearly original themselves, as our poor Irishman, Mangan! Rude and careless, at times, he shows himself, however, singularly capable, when he pleases, of uniting the utmost grace of delicacy with the utmost vigor and freedom of versification. How is it that the British press has suffered us to remain—nay, shown itself—so long ignorant of this poet's writings? We repeat our thanks to Mr. Mitchel, for bringing us to the knowledge of so bold, so spirited, so free and wild a singer in the groves of the Irish Agarippe.

Charleston *Mercury* (16 February 1860).

Current Irish Literature from Haverty

As Simms stated, John Mitchel (1815–1875) was an important editor of Irish poets Thomas Osborne Davis (1814–1845) and James Clarence Mangan (see previous review). Davis was the chief organizer of Young Ireland and founder of the *Nation*. His poem "A Nation Once Again" became, for a time, the Irish national anthem. His role in the Irish Confederation was to build up Irish identity in preparation for independence. He provided a good poet model for Simms, himself soon to be a major poet of the new Southern Confederation, employing "the *Past* to incite and inspirit the *Present* to proper action."

Daniel O'Connell (1775–1847), a charismatic Irish statesman, gained concessions from England, but he fell short of demanding sovereignty. Simms referred to him in his "Address, Written for the Benefit of the 'Association of the Friends of Ireland'" (Charleston *Courier,* 21 April 1829, and collected in Simms, *Selected Poems,* 312–14). Mitchel himself was to become a public voice for the South in the 1850s and 60s. He equated the South with Ireland, both being agricultural societies in a predatory union dominated by "the commercial, manufacturing and money-brokering power . . . greedy, grabbing, griping and groveling" (*Jail Journal,* 111). He blamed international free-trade capitalism for the current miseries in India, the Great Hunger in Ireland, and Lincoln's war upon the South. Mitchel argued early that the abolition of slavery was being used as a pretext to wage what he deemed to be a war of imperialism dominated by industrial power and for industrial interest. He founded a newspaper, *Southern Citizen,* which highlighted what he saw to be abolitionist hypocrisy and sought to demonstrate that southern slaves were better treated than Irish cottiers and industrial workers in cities such as Manchester. Two of his sons volunteered and were killed as soldiers in the Confederate army. Mitchel once again found himself imprisoned near the end of the Civil War, this time by the U.S. government, but he was released through the work of the Fenians. He left the United States in exasperation at Reconstruction policies and returned to Ireland in 1875, where he was closely followed by the English secret police until his sudden death that year. His statue stands at Newry, County Down, at John Mitchel Place. Several of the Irish volumes that Simms noticed in this review and elsewhere were printed by his own publisher J. S. Redfield, likely a fruitful topic for future investigation. For a more detailed treatment of Simms's reviews touching on the Irish struggle for independence, see Kibler, "Simms's Celtic Harp."

New York, September 20. To those, my dear *Mercury*, who desire to procure a fresh and charming body of Irish literature, such as is but little known in this country, and such as we never receive any report from English or Scottish periodicals, we commend them to a series of publications from the press of P.M. Haverty, of New York. Mr. Haverty is rather an obscure publisher, taking no rank with those lordly publishing houses, the Appletons, the Harpers, the Derbys & Jackson, who dwell in great places of Gotham, and feed on the brains of authors, foreign and domestic, even as the maggot is said to feed on the brains of the elk. Mr. Haverty's shop is a mere cellar in an obscure street, and, in addition to his cellar, which is large and full of books, he has several vast bookcases or shelves, occupying a permanent place on the sidewalks, on both sides of the street, near his cellar. He is, besides being a publisher, a collector of old books; and persons who seek for rare and curious volumes—collections for libraries—and who fail to find what they desire in grand, new and gaudy establishments, may be frequently much more successful here, in the dingy cellar of Haverty, and turning over his dusty old volumes.

His publications of Irish literature are quite numerous, and include all the best productions of young and patriotic Ireland. Your columns have already noticed the admirable poems of Mangan, that most remarkable and eccentric of men and poets, whose effusions combine some of the most exquisite qualities of fancy and feeling, passion and tenderness, love and patriotism, that have been given to us by the muse of any country for many years. It is introduced to us by the editorial hands of John Mitchel, the patriot, who has written a fine life of the poet, and made a judicious estimate of his qualities as a writer. To the same accomplished gentleman we owe another collection from one of the youthful and patriotic poets of Young Ireland—*The Poems of Thomas Davis*—a lyrical poet, also of great affluence, warmth, fire, enthusiasm and energy. He has made the history of Ireland, her struggles, sacrifices, defeats and triumphs, tributary to modern song, in the hope to unite and to arouse the Irish people to the proper efforts at independence.

But Davis is now a historical name, and to those who know anything of those conflicts between Great Britain and Ireland, in recent days, his career must be generally familiar. He wrote for the famous *Nation,* and in his premature death, which happened in 1845, the paper, to use the language of Mitchel, "lost its strength and inspiration." Davis was one of those patriots of the Young Ireland party, whom the British Government punished for his patriotism by imprisonment, in 1844. This was the period of O'Connell's power. Mitchel says boldly, that at that period, "one movement of O'Connell's finger—for only he could give the signal—and within a month no vestige of British power could have remained in Ireland." Mitchel adds—"For his refusal to wield that power, then unquestionably in his hands, may God forgive him!"

Davis died at the early age of thirty-one. His lyrics are wholly devoted to Ireland—its cause, character, genius, rights, and histories. He employed the *Past* to incite and inspirit the *Present* to proper action. His lays are bold, free, vivacious, and warm—not much characterized by mere grace, and not often by simple tenderness; but distinguished by a rude inspiration, a gushing force and impulse, a wild enthusiasm, an ardent passion for glory and liberty! He may be distinguished as the Koerner of Ireland, but will be found to be very far superior in energy, vigor, and a fresh native impetuosity, in which passion blends happily with tenderness, to his German predecessor. Let me commend your readers to provide themselves with that, and the other Irish publications of Mr. Haverty. Of these I may send you other advices hereafter as they are severally read.

Davis' prose essays, by the way, from which Mitchel frequently quotes, are warm and vigorous, and marked by the fanciful and the forcible in every equal degree. This volume closes with an Appendix, containing several very interesting notices of Irish history. The "Life," and "Introductory Essay," which precede the volume, are well written, and also of much instructive interest.

Charleston *Mercury* (2 October 1860).

Martin Farquhar Tupper's *Poetical Works*

Simms reviewed Tupper's first work, *The Crock of Gold* (1844), with glowing praise in a previously unrecorded notice. He declared: "Tupper is no feeble writer. He has large sources of originality. His *Proverbial Philosophy* proved that; and this story . . . does much to confirm our confidence in his strength. We take it, he will do yet better things" (*Orion* 4 [July 1844]: 246). Apparently Simms was gravely disappointed, for in the following review, he is irritated sufficiently to issue a blast in the form of a memorable extended metaphor. Although Simms as reviewer was known for balance and graciousness, he could at times be prickly. *Proverbial Philosophy* (1838) was the book for which Tupper was known throughout his life. That his career was one of sinking reputation and quality thereafter, Simms was making clear. In this Simms was like his English counterparts, for as Patrick Scott has written, "even in his lifetime his reputation fell into eclipse, and by the 1860s smart young reviewers were finding 'Tupperish' a handy term of critical abuse" ("Tupper," 289). Trent reported that Tupper's cousin in Charleston said the English author "expressed a warm admiration for Simms's romances" (320). Correspondence between the Tupper cousins and the English author is at the South Carolina Historical Society, Charleston.

N. P. Willis was the founder and early editor of the *American Monthly Magazine.*

The Poetical Works of Martin Farquhar Tupper, including Proverbial Philosophy, A Thousand Lines, Hactenus, Geraldine, and other Poems. 2 vols. New York: W.J. Widdleton, Publishers, 1865.

It is a thousand pities that a man who has such an "alacrity in sinking" as Tupper, should not permit himself to subside quietly to the bottom. Lying there five fathom deep, with his singing robes decently composed about him, a placid smile on his face, and a sort of pearly cloudiness about his lack-lustre eyes, he might hope to "suffer a sea change into something rich and strange"—as happens frequently with a diseased oyster. But Tupper will not down at any man's bidding. Buoyed up on the bladders of an amazing self-conceit, albeit no swimmer, he kicks and founders about like a dying grampus, spluttering out inarticulate cries, gulping wind and water whenever he opens his mouth, unable to save himself, and yet refusing either to drown or to be dragged out.

N.P. Willis had the honor of first fishing him up, and holding him out limp and dripping to the American people. The credulous public taking Willis' word for it that this was a veritable Merman, accepted his drivel as oracular, and forthwith the *Proverbial Philosophy* of Tupper rose to the dignity of Delphic utterances. At home his name, up to this time, was alike unknown and unhonored, but the publishers seeing the reverence paid it in these Western wilds, introduced the new worship into their own island, and thenceforth, like England's drumbeat, Tupper circled the globe.

Had he been content to rest on the laurels thus won, the *Philosophy* would still have kept its place on the tables of sentimental grocers, and have furnished the inspiration of gushing school girls. Profits, too, would have accrued. No small matter this to Tupper—with his large family, one of whom he describes as "the last, an infant toothless one, now prattling on my knee," showing how early the Tuppers talk—for he was one of the few who, being exactly on a level with the reading public, sold—them and his book. But he could not let well enough alone. Having been told that he was a poet of the first water, he thought it incumbent on him to maintain his grip on the Parnassian seat, and so he must go on dealing out his bottled thunder, until—at last—the worshippers found out that it was not the Olympian Jove, but only a very mild imitation of that terrible cloud-compeller.

Furthermore, the transcendent genius of the father, incapable of repression, burst out in the triple strains of those charming daughters whom he has described, with all parental fondness, in "A Family Picture." Due justice has been done them in an article on the Tupperides, published in the *Spectator,* from which it appears, that although this beautiful triad even in their totality cannot give us the measure of his full orbed grandeur, they have discovered to the world the transmissibility of his genius, and leave us grounds for hope that, through all the changes of future civilization, his voice may still guide us from the grave, mingling with that of generations yet unborn, through the diffusive power of his multiplied descendants.

Lost in the contemplation of his own surpassing excellence, and swelling with pride at the thought that when Wisdom was dead she would still be justified of her children, one would imagine that his cup was full; we never dreamed that, having drunk it to the dregs, he would have the greedy impudence to hold out his bowl for "more." But Byron has told us of a fever which

> "But once kindled, quenchless evermore,
>   Preys upon high adventure, nor can tire
>   Of aught save rest."

To use the more glowing and truthful language of Tupper,

> "There is a sordid imitation, a feverish thirst for notoriety,
>   Waiting upon vanity and sloth, and utterly regardless of deserving;
>   And then fame cometh as a curse; the fire-damp is gathered in the
>   mine;
>   The soul is swelled with poisonous air, and a spark of temptation
>   shall explode it."

Thus swelled, thus inflated, with the most mephitic gases, Tupper has come in contact with a spark—and burst.

Moxon, with a delicate irony which Tupper could not appreciate, published a selection from the works of Martin Farquhar, among his "Miniature Poets," and Tupper not relishing the rotten eggs and decaying cabbages which his quondam idolaters have been pelting him with ever since they found him out, seizes the opportunity to sound his own trumpet, in hopes to drown the penny whistles of the piping critics. For Tupper need not deny that he is the author of the eulogy on himself in a late Saturday Review, called the *Public Opinion.* There is not another man in England capable of the same moral platitudes, nor could its bold imaginative flights and audacity of assertion have had another source, unless it was from the pen of that imp of song, his own true Margaret-Elenora.

We agree with him that if censure killed, Tupper would have been as dead as a door nail. Men have died of poisoned arrows before today, and worms have eaten them; but the immortal Tupper, "in self-adoring pride securely mailed," is proof against all shafts. Nor does he need the Moorish javelin nor the death-bearing quiver. Under the scorn and sneers of this malignant world he describes himself as quite cheerful, and ready to treat all who have censured him with pity and contempt. Nay, he rather likes it. "Despise me," says he with Mawworm, "I love to be contemptible." It sells my books, it noises my name abroad, it creates jealousies, heartburnings, quarrels among the publishers as to who shall have the honor of embalming me, like a fly in amber. My poetry is never beyond comprehension, like Browning's. It is filled with no dazzling metaphor, no brilliant fancies, no daring imaginings. (Mr. Tupper is too modest here to be truthful); it is all plain, homely, commonplace, and this causes it to be so heartily appreciated. (Mr. Tupper is both modest and truthful here.) The great world of humanity likes the feeble and the prosaic, (true again); it dotes upon turgidity, and is intoxicated with vapid sentiment, (a Daniel come to judgment), and hence my kindly and healthy moralizings in language always temperate, but never deficient in force, are both pleasing and successful. And this great world, in spite of all the critics of all the schools, will crown me Vates, and I shall strike the stars with my lofty head; while the mere mechanical poet, with his high-sounding and pompous rhapsodies, shall pass into oblivion.

Not content with this self-commendation, Mr. Tupper actually proceeds to self-quotation, and cannonades his enemies, as he styles all those who do not award him the lyric crown, as follows:

"Bravo Detraction! libel worse and worse:"

This is in the true Tupperian style, plain, homely, unmetaphorical, and one is left in a pleasing uncertainty at the same time whether "libel" is a noun agreeing with "Detraction," or an active verb governing "me" (Tupper) understood; but at any rate he proceeds.

"Blessed is he whom you delight to curse;"

A condensation of the whole sermon on the mount, whose moral tone is unfortunately lowered by what follows:

"Go on, go on—you serve my purpose so,
    The more you slander me the more I grow;"

Like the Cammomile, the more it is trodden on—

"Spit scorn, spout hate! I glory in your blame,
    These dulcet whispers do but help good fame;"

The confusion of metaphor, whenever Tupper *does* indulge in a trope, marks the master's hand at once. None but this bard would have ventured on so bold a figure, made up of the trick of the Llama when provoked—Tupper is doubtless a frequent visitor to the zoological gardens, and has seen this savage salivator stirred up by the small boys—and the habit of the right whale. All doubts as to authorship vanish when being squirted upon and spit upon is shaded down into a dulcet whisper, such as a lover might breathe in a lady's ear.

> "One envious foe stirs up a million friends—
> A wasp attacks me, and a world defends."

Unfortunate Tupper! had you lived in the age of *The Dunciad,* that line alone would have given you immortality. Pope, with the instincts of genius, would have hailed you Prince of Grub-street, and Settle's numbers would have flowed unheeded amid the buzzing of your wasp and the *clamor incertus* of a world in arms.

Tupper! you have done enough for posterity; more than enough for an ungrateful and viperous generation. Leave to the blissful triad who bear your name, to the realistic Mary Frances, the tender and susceptible Ellen-Isabelle, and the vigorous, almost masculine Margaret-Elenora, the thankless task of pouring their distilment into the dull ears of the unheeding multitude. But do you, while your fancy is still fresh and warm, while your brain is still seething with thoughts which the world cannot let die, before your hand has forgot its cunning or your ink has given out, do you—we beseech you, Tupper—write for *Punch.*

Charleston *Courier* (24 February 1866).

Leigh Hunt's *The Book of the Sonnet*

In this review Simms once again defined poetry as "winged thought," an oft-used phrase gleaned from Coleridge's "The Destiny of Nations" (line 29). (See Kibler, *Poetry,* 11–15, 33.) James Wright Simmons had known Hunt in London before coediting the *Southern Literary Gazette* with Simms in 1828 (15). Simms complimented Hunt's poetry elsewhere and recommended his "admirable translation" of Francesco Redi's "Bacco in Tuscany" (*Letters,* 4: 133). See also Charleston *Mercury,* 20 November 1855. Clearly Simms understood the sonnet and its tradition. Trent's statement that he did not know how to write a sonnet, or even what one was, is obviously incorrect (145–50). Parks accurately concluded that Trent, in claiming so, was trying hard to "illustrate the defects of Southern poetry" (124) and, by extension, the culture that produced it. For a treatment of Simms's facility in the sonnet, see Jason Johnson, "Dazzling Outlawries."

The Book of the Sonnet—Edited by Leigh Hunt and S. Adams Lee. Boston: Roberts Brothers. 1867.

Here are two very charming volumes, very beautifully issued from the press, a handsome edition for the library, and rich in the interior with the beauties of the best poets of Europe and America, as expressed in that peculiarly constructed verse which is called the Sonnet—a word borrowed from Italian. The structure of the poems is also of Italian origin. In that language, its law requires a special combination and concurrence of rhyming lines, developing a single leading idea, to be compressed within fourteen lines. To comprehend fully the degree in which the structure of the Italian Sonnet is arbitrary in its requisitions, we have but to hear what Mr. Leigh Hunt—who was undoubtedly, one of the best English authorities on the subject—has to say upon it. "The fourteen lines of the Sonnet *proper*," he tells us, "or what is called the *legitimate* Sonnet, * * * * are divided into two distinct portions, *major* and *minor,* each of which is divided into two also. The major division consists of eight lines, called the *Octava* which possesses but two rhymes; the minor, of six lines, called the *Sestette,* which possesses never more than three; and the sub-divisions or halves of these eight lines, are called *Quatrains;* and those of the six lines *Tarzettes.* The two rhymes of the major division almost invariably occupy the same places; the two or three rhymes of the minor may be varied at pleasure, but seldom close with a couplet."

The Sonnet of the Italian was probably due to the desire to avoid monotony, which is the danger and the defect in a language so very soft and musical as the Tuscan. It is really the *setting of the five vowel sounds in a single frame work.* We are told that the gondoliers of Venice and the peasantry will sing snatches and a single verse or so from Tasso—the whole poem being quite too much sweet and soft for any long session even of song.

The English Sonnet is commonly a thing of more freedom. Much of it, and much of the best of it, belongs to what is somewhat improperly styled the *Illegitimate* Sonnet—i.e., it does not knowingly adopt the arbitrary Italian model. It recognizes simply two rules, viz: The employment of a single leading idea, which, like the Italian, is to be condensed into fourteen lines. It is, accordingly, susceptible of more various uses, and of the exercise of a still higher power. The Italian Sonnet is, in fact, a subtle refinement of art, more possible to the flexible Tuscan than to the stern, savage and eagle like utterance of the English. As more flexible, it is more easily moulded into form than the English, and perhaps, with less loss of vigor. But pure art in poetry, while it recognizes those laws which demand *harmony* as an essential of verse, does not regard with much esteem the dexterity which delights to multiply its fetters, in order to show how deftly they may be danced in.

There are some *moral* differences also, if we may so phrase it, between the Sonnatteers of the two kingdoms. The Italian's Sonnet, from Petrarch to the present day, is given mostly to themes of tenderness, love and fanciful sentiment. But English and American Poets cannot make love in Sonnets. The very severity and rigidity of the rule of art in the Sonnet is unfavorable to the expression of an earnest passion. We find, accordingly, that a large portion of the Sonnets, whether Italian or English, dedicated to love, are mostly crowded with mere conceits, fanciful plays with thought, rather than the expression of an earnest feeling or an honest passion. Even Shakspeare's Sonnets are seriously infected by this weakness, though, aside from Shakspeare, Sidney, Wyatt, Spenser, and a few other Poets of the Shakspeare era and beyond it, very few English writers have ever used the Sonnet as a medium for love utterances, and they have rarely proved successful when they have done so.

Our modern and recent poets, such as Milton, Wordsworth, Southey, Bowles, &c., in English literature, and most of the writers in American literature, have used this form of verse for sterner purposes; as a trumpet to blow the blast for liberty; as a medium for political opinion; as a compact mode of giving expression to bold moral sentiment, fearless pride and patriotism; the keen speech of scorn; the sting of satire; the passionate lament, or the outbreak of a passionate indignation! The Sonnet, in brief, is one of the best forms of the English epigram; and some of the very best of those that we have belong to what Mr. Hunt calls the *Illegitimate* Sonnet. Illegitimate under Italian law, it is perfectly legitimate as the *English* Sonnet, and so the critic will have to recognize it. It is a bolder, braver, manlier thing than the Italian, and you cannot in all the collections of Italy find any Sonnets to compare in thought, grandeur, dignity, a sonorous emphasis, or masculine majesty, with many of the grand performances, in this field, of Milton and Wordsworth.

Leigh Hunt, one of the most charming and picturesque of the recent English essayists, has given us, in these volumes, a copious introduction of foreign sonnets which he has made. He has, in fact, very warmly exhausted his subject. It was one peculiarly suited to his genius, which was light, airy, fanciful, graceful, and *dilettantish*. He delighted in all those topics in which his fancy could have free play. This was his *forte,* province and predominant faculty. He had no passions; was lacking in depth and earnestness; was of mercurial temperament, and his genius, which was considerable, was greatly impaired by the levity and probity of his temperament.

But in the essay—in such writings as those contained in his *Indicator* and *Companion,* he was usually excellent. His reputation as a writer will depend almost wholly upon his performances as an Essayist. He was good at short flights. His fancy could carry him up at a bound, in air, but he had not the wing to remain poised long in that ethereal and upper empire. His imagination was feeble; his invention was small; and he had no cavernous depths of thought, from which he could bring up at will, the hitherto unsunned treasures of the mind. His essays are light, graceful, sportive, and fanciful. His tastes were delicate and proper;

his style, though somewhat diffuse, possessed an admirable flow, great flexibility, ease and sweetness; and some of these essays are equal to anything of the sort in the language. In the copious essays which conducts us to the contents of these beautiful volumes, he has done his spiriting as gently and gracefully, as fully and pleasantly, as in most of his previous performances. When he wrote this essay he was a very old man, and yet he writes with a gleesome spirit, and a gaiety and glibness of tone, such as he cohabited in his most *riant* days of boyhood, and such, by the way, as has been the chief characteristic of most of his writings. He has probably done enough in this essay and the selections which he has made, to afford the American reader as full a knowledge of the European Sonnet, and Sonnetters, as they may need or desire. The conception of the book and its arrangement are equally excellent, and the execution perfectly satisfactory.

Mr. Hunt was fortunate in his coadjutor, Mr. S. Adams Lee, who has taken for his province the Sonnets produced by the American Poets. We believe, indeed, that the plan of the work originated with Mr. Lee. We remember, many years ago, to have had a correspondence with him on the subject. The work was one of considerable labor, and necessarily required considerable time. The field which Mr. Lee had to explore was almost as large as that which Mr. Hunt had charge. Most of our poets have tried their hands on the Sonnet, and many of them with great success. Some of them have written numerously in this province, and few of them, but with some degree of success. Many of our Sonnets, those of Mr. George H. Boker, of Philadelphia, for example, are equal to most of European origin, and may well take their place in any foreign company. Mr. Boker, by the way, is, perhaps, the most really able, various and powerful of all the poets which the Northern States have produced. He has more depth and breadth of thought, more imagination, more variety of material, and more concentrated vigor of expression than any we can now call to mind. He has written several of the best dramas, whether for stage or closet, that this country has ever produced; and in the lyric, the ode, the narrative, and especially the sonnet, his poems will take rank among the highest and noblest specimens of art and genius, with any of the more notorious of his contemporaries.

Yet he by no means shares their popularity, because he does not share their lucidity. His standards are pitched upon heights too lofty for the present approach of his people. He is too deep for them—his flight is too wide and far—they must read as they run; and all that contemporary readers usually demand of the poet is that he shall provide them with pleasant, portable and melodious commonplaces, which they may murmur as they go. In brief, he has not only art but genius. Genius is, properly, the spirit of discovery. It seeks the depths, whether of earth, or air, or sea, and brings down its wings, or brings up its pearls and treasures from empires never found, as never sought before. Poetry, in its best sense, is winged thought. It must imply originality of suggestion or idea, a wing for flight, and a verse of melody as it pursues its way. The minds which grasp—the eyes which painfully strain only in ancient avenues of routine—which pursues none but the axe marks of a thousand years ago—will never be able to follow such a flight, or comprehend the glories of that wing, which bathing, eagle like, in the very ardors of the sun, is beyond the reach of every blear and contracted vision.

To return to Mr. Lee. He, too, has written an essay, introductory to his selections, which is not unworthy of association with that of Mr. Hunt. He is sufficiently comprehensive; as genial of mood; sympathizes heartily with his subject; is sufficiently appreciative for nice discrimination; and writes in a style of grace and neatness, which disarms criticism. His opinions, if not always just, are such, evidently, as he believes to be so. We might take exceptions to some minor matters, here and there, in respect to his decisions, but these are so tentatively delivered, that they do not provoke any hostile issues. Enough, then, to say that the editors have wrought successfully, and have given to their readers a full opportunity, not only to gratify a fine literary taste, but to form a just literary judgment.

Charleston *Courier* (5 April 1867); Clipping in Simms's Scrapbook C, folios 24 v, 25 r, CCS, SCL.

John William De Forest's *Miss Ravenel's Conversion from Secession to Loyalty*

De Forest (1826–1906) was the son of a wealthy Connecticut manufacturer of cloth made from southern cotton. In New Haven he organized a company of volunteers and became a captain during the Civil War under Phil Sheridan, the general notorious in the South for his war on civilians and in the West for his slaughter of native peoples. Most critics of *Miss Ravenel's Conversion* have argued that the romanticized plot mixed poorly with the grisly battle scenes. Few books angered Simms more. In 1859 he had written kindly of De Forest's *Seacliff,* encouraging him at the beginning of his career to "do better things" (Charleston *Mercury,* 8 July 1859). But by 1867 Simms denied knowledge of him, perhaps owing to a failure in memory. It may also be that he was doing the equivalent of disowning a disappointing son who had shown such promise. Simms seems to have been hurt on a personal level; and, as he stated, with North and South forced to reunite, it served no purpose for the victors to malign their former adversaries, especially with the profession of an "avowed desire of the Northern people to conciliate rather than to stab or wound." Simms apparently felt stabbed, and in the back at that.

Miss Ravenel's Conversion from Secession to Loyalty, is the title of a new novel by J.W. De Forest, which we owe to the courtesy of Holmes & Co., Booksellers, King-street. The work is from the pen of a writer who seems to have done other works, of which we know nothing. Of this, what we have need to say, shall be dispatched briefly. It is the embodiment of all the brutal malignity Northern writers have ever conceived, or reported, to the slander and misrepresentation of the South. With none of the art-faculty of Mrs. Beecher Stowe, the writer endeavours to *outbeecher* her in his gross and infamous disparagement of the characteristics and the people of the South. His book is remarkable for nothing but the intense malignity, which has blackened every page with a slander, and pointed every paragraph with a lie.

But the venom is baffled by the unmitigated dullness of the volume. It consists of a long string of lugubrious dialogues between very silly or very stupid people; only spiced by the malignity which poisons all its pages. There is no story, no art, no invention. There is no decent characterization. The heroine (Miss Ravenel) is a silly and vulgar chit, who is converted from secession to loyalty, by appetite rather than argument; her father is a raving and ridiculous blockhead; one of her lovers is a blackguard, the other a snob; which is being a peg or two below the English standard of snobbism. Briefly, with the exception of a good masculine style, and a smart epigrammatic facility in rounding a period with a sting, the book is wholly without merit. As a work of art in fiction, it is bald, utterly and below criticism; as a narrative, pretending to facts, it is as false in its design throughout, as an ingenious malice and a viperous hate could make it, in the hands of one whose morals suggest no scruples when slandering a whole people, either for the gratification of a passion, or the earning of a penny. Why such books should be put forth now, with what object and to what good end, it is difficult to conceive. They are in direct conflict with the avowed desire of the Northern people to conciliate rather than to stab or wound. They are in conflict with the avowed policy of the Government, they are in conflict with the needs as well as the morals of society, and they are utterly damnable in the sight of Christianity. In such publications as this, the press becomes a panderer either to the greed of gain, or to the roused malignity of individual hate, which is too strong equally for public policy or private morals. We trust that the Holmes' Book Store will keep its counters unpolluted with all such writings.

Charleston *Courier* (4 June 1867).

John Conington's *Æneid*

This important review illustrates Simms's understanding of metrics and its significance in the long tradition of English versification.

The *Æneid of Virgil;* translated into English verse, by John Conington, M.A., Corpus Professor of Latin in the University of Oxford. New York: W.J. Widdleton, 1867.

This work is a novelty—quite a surprise, indeed, to the British public; the hexameters of Virgil rendered successfully into English octo-syllabics.

The old translators were content with the ordinary English heroic line. And that was good—a famous verse, indeed, in the hands of such masters as Pope and Dryden—flexible in the hands of one—very smooth and musical, though a trifle monotonous, but occasionally very grand and powerful; and, in the hands of the other, also; varied, happily, as was Dryden's habit, with the occasional Alexandrine.

The octo-syllabic was not unknown to the old English verse-mongers. It is a mistake to ascribe this verse to Walter Scott. He was by no means the originator of it, though, it must be confessed, he made himself the master of it. It became a powerful instrument under his fingers for heroic song. So, also, with Coleridge and Byron,—in passages rising at times to a higher pitch, in the fanciful and the passionate, than was ever attained by Scott; but none has ever surpassed him in flexibility; none has ever equalled him in his prolonged, consistent flights, or in his narrative; and never approached him, in those portions of his poems, in which he was *most truly Homeric*—we mean in his battle-pieces. There are, in fact, no descriptions of battle in the whole compass of British verse to compare with those of Scott. He wrought the ballad of the medieval period into the epic, and thus added a new string to the modern lyre. His ballad-epics were original discoveries in rhythmical narrative, though the verse itself is older in English poetry than Milton.

Scott gave us a reason for his adoption of this form of verse for such purposes, that it precluded the unnecessary use of adjectives and expletives, which always, more or less, were employed to eke out the burden of the full line in the English heroic. He thought that, in our ten syllable line, there were usually *two* syllables, at least, that might be dispensed with, without doing any hurt to the sense, and with some natural increase of energy and strength. And there is, no doubt, much truth in the opinion.

But the octo-syllabic verse itself, might become monotonous in any long poem such as "Marmion," or "The Lay of the Last Minstrel;" and he varied it, accordingly, with happy effect by sundry alternates; passing from eight syllables to six; from the distich to the triplet or the quatrain; and, occasionally, diversifying all these, especially at the close of a stanza, by some irregular, lilting verse, usually a quatrain, which wound up the whole paragraph trippingly to the ear. But the variation was one which demanded rare judgment in its use, and was required to be perfectly consistent with the tone and tenor of the sentiment and situation.

It was in the due consideration of these and other points in the management of this measure, in the wonderful ease and flexibility with which he wrought it out, and in the rapidity of his movement, and the fire and life in his narrative, that Scott has completely identified himself and muse with the octosyllabic.

It was a quick wit on the part of Mr. Conington to conceive the peculiar uses of this form of verse in rendering the great poem of Virgil. The measure is admirably adapted for the rendering of a long narrative poem, abounding in details and particularities, and not perhaps any where rising to that degree of sublimity and grandeur which the more imaginative muse of a Milton would exhibit.

The English heroic verse is one of the noblest that we have, and accords with the genius of our language; but unless the poetry itself is very noble, and pitched to the highest uses of thought and imagination, it palls finally upon the ear, and fatigues by its monotonies.

To say that Mr. Conington has succeeded excellently well in the management of the octo-syllabic, and in his free and facile rendering of Virgil, so as really to commend him more favorably to the English reader than has ever yet been done by the translator, is not, however, to acknowledge that he has achieved the same mastery over the verse that we accord to Walter Scott. This, perhaps, is not to be expected. The ear of Scott was exquisitely attuned to this measure. It was his natural utterance. It served better the purposes of his genius than any other form. Compare it, in his case, with his heroic rhyming couplets—compare it with his blank verse, as shown in his dramas, such as *Halidon Hill*—and there is a grace, ease, spirit, and flexibility about the one which you fail to note in any other of his forms in poetry. His genius literally revels, in this one province, as a bird, high-mounted, on ever rising wing, with the glow and ardor of one making loving salutation to the dawn.

Mr. Conington is easy, harmonious, forcible, correct, and, we repeat, has made a very successful translation, commending Virgil anew to the English reader, in spite of the many great and gifted translators who have gone before him. But he has not yet acquired the exquisite natural facility of Scott, and rarely rises into those passages of an indescribable grace and beauty, such as Scott so frequently gives us whenever he becomes thoroughly warmed with his subject; when he flames out with the passion which it inspires, or when he toys with it under the impulse of a newly born and mercurial fancy.

But Mr. Conington labored under the disadvantage of being a translator. His own muse was, to a certain degree, hampered and fettered. He was bound to obey the directions of that of Virgil, and his own fancies were not suffered free play. Doubtless, if in the utterance of his own, and warmed by the fresh fires which they kindled in the brain, there would have been a more eloquent gush of expression, and a more easy and rapid flow of song, and we should not be made to see, as we now do, in this translation, that the strain is felt by the translator; that he *labors;* does not always seize upon and secure the right word, and fails in that art which, to enjoy a perfect success, must always conceal itself.

But, while we do not admit of any very near approach of Mr. Conington to Walter Scott, in the mastery of the octo-syllabic, we cannot question the excellence of this translation, nor deny the judgment which has selected the present form of verse for the purpose. We have no doubt that *The Æneid* will, as it should, commend itself anew to the reader, through the graceful medium of Mr. Conington's translation.

Charleston *Courier* (29 June 1867); Clipping Simms's Scrapbook C, folio 18 r, CCS, SCL.

The Late Henry Timrod

Timrod died 7 October 1867 at the age of thirty-eight. This tribute appeared twelve days later. Simms must have taken pen in hand soon after he heard the news. Timrod was the most talented young writer of Simms's circle that met in Charleston at Russell's Bookstore. Simms perceptively gauged Timrod's genius in this important essay. Timrod's sister Emily was offended by the comment that "his hope was small," as reported in Walter Brian Cisco, *Henry Timrod* (124). Simms's comment that Timrod's father published a "volume of poems in Charleston some fifty years ago" is accurate: *Poems on Various Subjects* (Charleston, S.C., 1814).

We had but just published the name of Henry Timrod, of South Carolina, as one of those fine contributors of the South upon whom we should rely in making our work a just type and representation of Southern intellect and society. We are now painfully required to record his premature death. Cut off in the prime of life, by the inexorable shears of Fate, he is lost to us and to the country. But not without having left a beautiful and worthy record. His memory is preserved to us in harmonious verse, in chaste thought, in the music of a fine fancy, and an ingenuous nature. As Milton sings:

> —Lycidas is dead; dead ere his prime,
> Young Lycidas; and hath not left his peer;—
> Who would not sing for Lycidas? He knew
> Himself to sing and build the lofty rhyme:
> He must not slumber on his lowly bier,
> Unwept,—
> Without the meed of some melodious tear!

Literary men, in the South, have always laboured under great difficulties in finding an audience. An appreciate audience, rather than a numerous one, was what Milton craved.

> Give me audience *fit* though *few*.

Henry Timrod necessarily laboured under all the disadvantages of his people. An agricultural population is rarely susceptible to the charms of art and literature. He had his audience, however, and it *was* fit, capable, appreciative—though few. There were thousands that felt quickly and keenly his chaste sentiment, always pure; his gentle and winning thought; his beguiling fancy, his delicate art, and his ever fond and virtuous intercourse with nature. Such was his genius. He was not passionate; he was not profound; he laboured in no fields of metaphysics; he simply sang—"sang as the birds do when they would rejoice"—with a native gift, of the things, the beauties, and the charms of nature. He belonged, in the classi-fication of literary men, to the order that we call the contemplative; and without the deeper studies and aims of Wordsworth, he yet belonged in his school.— He was observant, meditative, and amiable. He avoided all strifes of parties and politics—all strong and gusty passions. The fields, the wayside, the evening twi-light, stars and moon, and faint warblings of the birds in green thickets—these were the attractions for his muse. These he meditated in song and sonnet, and his songs emulated all the gentle institutions of nature.

Yet he could be lyrical, as well as contemplative.—His verse was smooth and soft, with gentle cadences of rhyme and rhythm. His fancies were lively, with most felicitous turns of thought and expression, and he was never monotonous and never dull. Nor was he overstrained in the measure, either of thought or expression. He possessed the most exquisite sense of propriety, and, whether he dealt in song or sonnet, his thought was always appropriate to the theme, and his Fancy, a happy page, was always obedient, waiting upon the thought, and nimble in attendance. Such was the muse of Henry Timrod, and whether he sang of his own or the loves of others, the open purity of his genius refined equally the thought which he expressed and the verse in which he clothed it.

His genius was, in some degree, inherited. His father—William H. Timrod— was a poet before him. He was a man whom we knew well, and whom we met, for many years, almost daily, in the intercourse of life. He was a strong man, of quick intellect, at once sparkling and sensitive. He conducted a literary paper in Charleston more than forty years ago, which he enriched with bold thoughts and generous fancies, taken from the rough of the mine, careless perhaps of art, though sometimes her absolute master. He wrote freely and frequently. He pub-lished a volume of poems in Charleston some fifty years ago, the general char-acteristics of which somewhat resembled those of his son. He, too, was a lover of nature, and his poems were meant frequently to illustrate her phases. He was finely musical in his writings. His rhythm was perfect, while his utterance was frequent and copious. His musings were so many genial and generous aspirations to the superior nature, the pure tastes and generous affections. We remember some of his *dramatic* fragments, published in the Charleston magazines, which were marked by a singular grace as well as power. His works, with those of his son, would form a valuable and beautiful contribution to the library of the South. Why should they not be blended in a new edition?

Henry Timrod received a good education at primary schools, and (we believe) finally, at the Charleston College. He attracted attention at an early period, by his proficiency of attainment and by the development of his poetical genius. Not that he showed himself precocious; not that he exhibited himself frequently, or in ostentatious exhibitions of performance. His muse was rather reticent. She required soliciting. As Mr. Timrod has frequently told us, he wrote with great pains-taking and labour. He lacked in that readiness which belongs solely to a different temperament. His temperament was morbid. It was diseased from the beginning. He belonged to the lymphatic temperament, or rather to that which the medical men describe as the scrofulous. He was slow, timid, sensitive, and always suffering. Give him a good condition, under any circumstances, and this temperament would always work to his discomfort and disquietude. His hope was small. He had none of the sanguine in his system. His blood worked languidly and gave no proper support, stimulus, or succour to his brain.

But, that he *should* work, was the necessity of his condition. He was poor, and his brains, and the acquisitions of his brains, were required to be put in requisition for his support. He became a teacher of the young. He prepared lads and young men for school and college. He taught in schools and in private families. He was a good Latin scholar, something of a Grecian, and possessed a fair general acquaintance with some of the Continental languages.—But, whatever his acquisitions, he was always slow in asserting them. His temperament made him modest—made him distrustful of himself—and he undertook all his educational tasks with fear and trembling. How long he laboured in these fields we do not now remember. He passed from them into those of pure literature, and in 1860—as we think—a volume of his poems was published (nominally) by Ticknor & Fields, of Boston. This was published at the request of friends, and by the aid of friends. The publishers did nothing for the work, as they rarely will do where they are not themselves proprietors. Recently a copy was sought for at the shop of the publishers, and, for awhile, they knew nothing about it. It was finally discovered on an obscure shelf, and that it was so found was owing, no doubt, to the pertinacity of the applicant.

The contents of this volume sufficed, or should suffice, to establish the fame of Timrod as a pure, chaste, graceful, fanciful, and most exquisite writer of felicitous verse—verse far superior to anything that could or can be done in Boston, by any or all of the sweet-singing swans of that American Olympus. But, save with the friends of the author, his book may be said to have fallen dead from the press. It yielded him no returns in money. Northern criticism was silent.—New England criticism is always silent in respect the swans of other regions. Its own geese are its sufficient swans. The parish absorbs all the praise which its naturally costive character is able to bestow.

But Timrod had many admirers in the North as well as in the South. He had friends, also, who were quite willing to expend money in his behalf. At a certain period in the war he was an assistant editor in the office of the Charleston *Mercury*. About this period Mr. Vigateley, an employee of the British press, was in Charleston, and employed in taking notes of the events of the war. He was engaged to produce a volume of Timrod's poems, handsomely illustrated, in England. Money was subscribed for this object here, but the scheme, we know not why, came to nothing. Money was raised for it, we know. Subsequently to his employment on the *Mercury,* Mr. Timrod became a joint editor, in charge of the *South Carolinian* newspaper at Columbia, and funds for which paper were also largely subscribed in Charleston. His assumption of the duties of this charge was coeval with his marriage. He married Miss Goodwyn, a lovely English girl, the sister-in-law of his widowed sister. By her he had one lovely child, who died prematurely.—The death of this child affected the sensitive nature of the father to a very serious extent—far more than usual with men. His muse poured forth some of his most mournful lamentings on the subject, and his genius, never remarkable for its playfulness, acquired a more sombrous tinge from this visitation of death in his little family. His own health was impaired, and gradually he began to exhibit those shows of feebleness which awakened the liveliest fears among his friends. For the last three years he had been struggling with the adverse influences of poverty and physical prostration. His friends, themselves most generally overborne by the cruel fortune which has prostrated all the South, could do but little for his relief; and though the philanthropic and able physician watched and waited by his bedside, with liberal and scientific service, it was probably, all the while, with the most painful misgivings that all effort would be made in vain. Day by day found him feebler; his vitality, always feeble, did not readily rally to the relief of nature; and his letters to his friends were imbued with a gloomy tone which indicated his own unexpressed convictions of his certain decline. It was in this mood that he gave out a beautiful and touching little fancy, which prefigured the hour of parting and escape for the over-wearied soul. The reader of this little poem needs not that its delicate grace and fine fancy, and the sweet spirit of resignation which it embodies, should be pointed out to him. The picture, so exquisitely touched in the lines which follow, has been realized, and the whispers of beloved ones by his couch of dying, have murmured mournfully and lowlily the sad, unavoidable words—"He is gone!" Was there a single moment of breathing consciousness left to the moribund, in which the senses, at such a moment, perhaps, singularly acute, might enable the escaping spirit to take in the sounds? Did his darkening eyesight take in the melancholy aspects of the loved ones weeping around him?

> Somewhere on this earthly planet,
> In the dust of flowers to be,
> In the dew-drop, in the sunshine,
> Sleeps a solemn day for me.
>
> At this wakeful hour of midnight,
> I behold it dawn in mist,
> And I hear a sound of sobbing
> Through the darkness—list! oh, list!
>
> In a dim and murky chamber,
> I am breathing life away;
> Some one draws a curtain softly
> And I watch the broadening day.
>
> As it purples in the zenith,
> As it brightens on the lawn,
> There's a hush of death about me,
> And a whisper, "He is gone!"

The last poem from his pen, a sonnet, written literally on his dying bed, embodied a graceful tribute to the memory of a friend, in which it will not be difficult to trace the working of a thought, shadowing the presage of his own approaching fate. It will be read now, irrespective of its pure poetic merits, with a sad interest, by all those who loved the man and esteemed the genius of the poet.

In Memoriam—Harris Simons.

> True Christian, tender husband, gentle sire,
> A stricken household mourns thee, but its loss
> Is Heaven's gain and thine; upon the cross
> God hangs the crown, the pinion and the lyre;
> And thou hast won them all. Could we desire
> To quench that diadem's celestial light,
> To hush thy song and stay thy heavenward flight,
> Because we miss thee by this autumn fire?
> Ah, no! ah, no!—chant on!—soar on!—reign on!
> For we are better—thou art happier thus!
> And haply from the splendour of thy throne,
> Or haply from the echoes of thy psalm,

> Something may fall upon us like the calm
> To which thou shalt hereafter welcome us.

We have before us a few of his later poems, the last croppings of that bright field of cultured thought and fancy from which our Southern society gathered so many lovely flowers. They indicate no decay or decline of the poetic vein. The verse flows freely and triumphantly. The fancies are sown thick upon the groundwork of the thought. They have all the airy grace and animation which distinguished his lyrical poetry in its hours of best strength and enthusiasm. What more full of freshness, life and spirit, grace and tenderness, than this spontaneous lay upon so simple a subject as

A Summer Shower

"Imbres Deducunt Jovem."
  Welcome rain or tempest
  From yon airy powers:
  We have languished for them
  Many sultry hours,
  And earth is sick and wan, and pines with all her flowers!

  What have they been doing
  In the burning June?
  Riding with the genii?
  Visiting the moon?
  Or sleeping on the ice amid an arctic noon?

  Bring they with them jewels
  From the sunset lands?
  What are these they scatter
  Which such lavish hands?
  There are no brighter gems in Golconda's sands!

  Pattering on the gravel,
  Drooping from the eaves,
  Glancing in the grass and
  Tinkling on the leaves,
  They flash the liquid pearls, as flung from fairy sieves!

  Meanwhile, unreluctant,
  Earth like Danæ lies;
  Listen! is it fancy,
  That beneath us sighs,
  As the warm lap receives the *largesse* of the skies?

Jove, it is, descendeth
In those crystal rills;
And this world-wide tremour
Is a pulse that thrills
To a god's life infused through veins of velvet hills!

Wait, thou jealous sunshine;
Break not on their bliss!
Earth will blush in roses
Many a day for this,
And bend a brighter bow beneath thy burning kiss!

What more dainty and felicitous than the string of triplets in the following—
the fancies so happily wedded to the most delicate of human sensibilities?

The Rosebuds

Yes, in that dainty ivory shrine,
With those three pallid buds, I twine
And fold away a dream divine!

One night they lay upon a breast
Where Love hath made his fragrant nest,
And throned me as a life-long guest.

Near that chaste heart they seemed to me
Types of far fairer flowers to be—
The rosebuds of a human tree!

Buds that shall bloom beside my hearth,
And there be held of richer worth
Than all the kingliest gems of earth.

Ah me! the pathos of the thought!
I had not deemed she wanted aught;
Yet what a tenderer charm it wrought!

I know not if she marked the flame
That lit my cheek, but not from shame,
When one sweet image dimly came.

There was a murmur soft and low;
White folds of cambric, parted slow;
And little fingers played with snow!

> How far my fancy dared to stray,
> A lover's reverence needs not say—
> Enough—the vision passed away!
>
> Passed in a mist of happy tears,
> While something in my tranced ears
> Hummed like the future in a seer's.

Of a sterner mood and character is the following poem, having its birth, most probably, in the melancholy condition of his native land, borne down by a brutal tyranny, which threatens the moral as well as political atmosphere with the upas of degradation as well as death; the putridity of the worst corruption, prefacing the pangs of a prolonged dying.

Storm and Calm.

> Sweet are these kisses of the South,
> As dropped from woman's rosiest mouth,
> And tenderer are those azure skies
> Than this world's tenderest pair of eyes!
>
> But ah! beneath such influence
> Thought is too often lost in sense;
> And Action, faltering as we thrill,
> Sinks in the unnerved arms of Will.
>
> Awake, thou stormy North, and blast
> The subtle spells around us cast;
> Beat from our limbs these flowery chains
> With the sharp scourges of thy reins!
>
> Bring with thee from thy Polar cave
> All the wild songs of wind and wave,
> Of toppling berg and grinding floe,
> And the dread avalanche of snow!
>
> Wrap us in Arctic night and clouds!
> Yell like a fiend amid the shrouds
> Of some slow-sinking vessel, when
> He hears the shrieks of drowning men!
>
> Blend in thy mighty voice whate'er
> Of danger, terrour and despair
> Thou hast encountered in thy sweep
> Across the land and o'er the deep.

> Pour in our ears all notes of woe,
> That as these very moments flow,
> Rise like a harsh discordant psalm,
> While we lie here in tropic calm.
>
> Sting our weak hearts with bitter shame,
> Bear us along with thee like flame;
> And prove that even to destroy
> More God-like may be than to toy
> And rust or rot in idle joy!

Our last selection from these later writings, most of which were contributed to the *Southern Opinion* newspaper, at Richmond, expresses that numbness of the heart, if not of the head—that sense of weariness and exhaustion under which in later years he was so frequent a sufferer—a numbness of the hopes, which does not subdue the fancies, but endows them with shapes of doubt, and dread, and terror, filling the brain with such images as come to us in the demoniac dreams engendered by the Incubi.

Sonnet.

> I know not why, but all this weary day,
> Suggested by no definite grief or pain,
> Sad fancies have been flitting through my brain,
> Now it has been a vessel losing way,
> Rounding a stormy headland; now a gray
> Dull waste of clouds above a wintry main;
> And then a banner drooping in the rain,
> And meadows beaten into bloody clay!
> Strolling at random with this shadowy woe
> At heart, I chanced to wander hither. Lo!
> A league of desolate marsh land, with its lush,
> Hot grasses in a noisome, tide-left bed,
> And faint, warm airs, that rustle in the hush
> Like whispers 'round the body of the dead!

The poems and other writings of Henry Timrod, to be dealt with justly, require more space and time than we can accord them here. We trust, however, that even here we have truly described their chief characteristics. We may add that his prose writings, which were mostly essayical, and were drawn forth mostly to meet the demands of a daily paper, were characterized by like qualities with his poetry. They were remarkable for their grace, ease, purity, and polish; for gentleness of thought and manner, frankness of spirit, and a lively fancy. His writings are not numerous; and a single duodecimo of three to four hundred pages would suffice to contain not only his poems, but a fair selection from his prose writings, including one or more lectures, and a few samples of elaborate criticism. The preparation of such a volume might well be confided to his friend and brother poet, Paul H. Hayne, who, with kindred tastes and genius, a loving nature, and a sympathizing attachment, would find the labour of such a work a labour of love.

Henry Timrod was born in Charleston, S.C., somewhere about 1830. He was, we believe, just entered on his thirty-eighth year, at the time of his death.— This event took place in Columbia on the 7th instant. He died a Christian. We are told that, while he clung to life, and to all whom he had ever loved, with wonderful tenacity—as how should it be otherwise in the case of one who was so exquisitely sensible to the charms of life and nature?—yet his faith was firm, and he met the trying hour with unflinching fortitude. Some one remarked to him while he was under the agonies of dissolution—"You will soon have rest, Harry." "Ah! yes!" was the reply, *but love is stronger than rest!*" A little later, and he had found both! His remains were attended at the grave by the leading citizens of Columbia, including some of our most eminent of Southern names. It was a spontaneous tribute of society and country to genius—that genius, so little honoured while it lives, but to which society owes its best and most enduring treasures.—The grave has closed its portals upon the form of the mortal; his immortal nature has its reflex in the everliving song, which was its soul-utterance and beautiful voice on earth. He lies in consecrated soil—in the graveyard of Trinity church, Columbia. It will be for his admirers and friends to see that a graceful tablet shall indicate to posterity the sleeping place of the bard. "After life's fitful fever he sleeps well!"

Southern Society 1 (19 October 1867): 18–19; clipping in Simms's Scrapbook C, folio 30 r, 29 v., CCS, SCL.

Charles Warren Stoddard's *Poems*

Simms corresponded with Stoddard in October 1866, advising him to "study Tennyson less, and the earlier masters more"—especially the poets Milton, Shakespeare, and Dryden (*Letters,* 4: 616). In "California Poetry," Simms wrote that "Stoddard belongs legitimately to the school of Tennyson, who blends, with the contemplation of Wordsworth, the metaphysical subtlety of Shelley and the graceful abandon of Keats; and, as in Tennyson, Mr. Stoddard shows himself a peculiar master in the felicitous choice of phrase and epithet" (Charleston *Daily News,* undated issue of 1868, clipping in Simms's Scrapbook C, folio 2 r, CCS,

SCL). The following review gives important facets of Simms's poetic credo. The models he suggested to Stoddard are all English, an indication of his return to a transatlantic focus.

Stoddard's Poems. **Poems by Charles Warren Stoddard. San Francisco: A. Roman & Co., 1867.**

Here is a very pretty and tasteful volume, in the neatest style of American art, which comes to us from the far away press of A. Roman & Co., San Francisco, California. The work is altogether a surprise to us. It is something curious and creditable to encounter such a fine specimen of typography from so remote, if not uncivilized, a region; and quite as surprising to find a young poet springing upon the very edge of the gold region, who, as poet, should be perfectly insensible to the attractions of gold. Let us give the good word of encouragement to Messrs. Roman & Co., for their most admirable specimen of typographic art; such admirable letter press, such happy illustrations, such creamy smooth paper, and such perfect binding. Verily, the pacific arts are at home on the Pacific. One word for the illustrative artist, who gives us five pictures from the poems. Drawings and engravings are by William Keith, an artist of whom we hear for the first time. His subjects are "Point Lobos," a very spirited and picturesque representation of a land and waterscape of fine effects; "Tamalpais," another like scene, the lands, mountains, blending beautifully and harmonizing with a waterscape. The three other pictures are drawn from the poetry rather than from real scenes in the country. We take for granted that the former are wholly taken from nature, and very beautiful they are, speaking strikingly for that wonderful nature, in the landscape which we know to characterize the country. So much for publisher, printer and artist, all of whom deserve our praise.

And now, face to face with Mr. Stoddard. Of this gentleman, and youthful poet, just twenty-five, we have enjoyed some previous knowledge. We were made acquainted with some of his fugitive poems more than a year ago, and were struck with their delicacy of thought, the picturesqueness of the detail, and the unwonted felicity of expression—that expression, at the same time, implying a certain freshness of phrase and manner of utterance, which showed not only a good knowledge of the language, but a freedom and fine play of fancy. We felt, from the first, like cultivating Mr. Stoddard, and said to ourselves, this boy, if he is wise, if he will work, and try to comprehend what real poetry is, like a true man, a thing of flesh and blood, and strong passions, and bold imagination and generous sentiment, will be very apt to flutter the "dove-cotes in Corioli;" in other words, disturb the self-complacency of the sweet-singing swans of the Hudson and the Charles. He has some of the endowments which will enable him to do it, if he will work steadily, with a will, a purpose, and a thought, which shall keep his fancy in subjection to his thought, and remember always that true poetry is an ever-earnest thing, and must, in all its utterances, be made to express the manhood of the individual. Poetry is not a thing of mere fancy, though it makes fancy a page and keeps it forever in attendance. It is *a thing of thought,* fresh thought, bold thought, ever earnest, ever solicitous of what is the truly living in life; this is the only sort of poetry which is ever destined to a long life. In this flippant age, perpetually in a hurry, and having little earnest purpose except the pursuit of worldly objects, poetry has sunk below her proper mission, and a swallow's twitter contents us, when we should follow an eagle flight. The mere warble of the linnet of fancy is sufficient, when we should invoke the lay of the skylark, singing close to the gates of heaven, or that of the mocking bird, who makes his satirical commentary upon the merely imitative song-birds of the grove. We are in a transition period just now, and our social, moral and intellectual elements are in a somewhat chaotic state. We have lost sight—only for a season, we trust—of the grand old masters of ancient and modern poesy, and creep in song rather than fly—dally with fancy, rather than strive with passion, and play with, rather than woo and worship, the affections and the thought. Our song is much too imitative; and while our man-poets strive to follow tamely in the path of Tennyson, in which he alone is the master, our women-poets are content to follow meekly after Miss Jean Ingelow. We shall have to correct this, and, we doubt not, that in a little while it will correct itself. The *bis repetita,* the twice-baked meats of poetry, will not long suffice to gratify an earnest appetite which is wanting solid food instead of whipt-syllabub.

But we must not digress to such a degree as to lose sight of Mr. Stoddard. He has given us here something over a hundred pages of verse, which exhibits grace, delicacy, sweetness, felicitous phrase, and a descriptive and fine fancy. His eye is nicely sensible to the picturesque in nature, which he describes happily, through an inspiration which is born of a fond contemplation of its objects. He has divided his topics somewhat arbitrarily, classing them as "of nature," "Idyllic and Legendary," "of the heart," "of fancy and imagination," "of aspiration and desire," "of meditation." There was no reason for these distinctions. How, for example, separate aspiration and desire from imagination, or the heart from either, and as if all these subjects did not involve the necessity of meditation? But the objection is a minor one, and doth in no wise affect the claims of the poet in the treatment of either subject. There is a certain uniformity in his manner of dealing with all these subjects, however classed, which at once shows us the proper vein of the author. This, as we have elsewhere said, indicates a strong instinct for the picturesque in the natural world. While all around him are looking about for gold, plunging into gulches and grinding quartz, he is looking upward to the peculiar skies of beauty brooding above the Pacific; to its wild headlands, its murmurous seas, its tinted clouds, that swim in loveliness; and all that is peculiar, the strange and new in the now natural world, in which he is a seeker and observer. He draws his images from the scenery around him, and even from the toils of the adventurous people, who see with other eyes than his own, and look for very different objects of interest.

Southern Society 1 (9 November 1867): 47; clipping in Simms's Scrapbook C, folio 20 v-c, 1 & 2, CCS, SCL.

Putnam's Magazine

Simms often noticed H. T. Tuckerman (1813–1871). In reviewing *A Month in England,* he praised his style but noted the coldly contemplative mood that allowed little beyond mere observation (*SQR* n.s. 9 [April 1854]: 540–41). Simms considered him admirable in the Charleston *Mercury* of 7 September 1859, but in the following notice Simms expressed ire. He did not often hurl the curse of the poet, but here he did it splendidly at essay's end. It is both prophecy given at the termination of his life and a withering condemnation of the victorious North, which he declared was spurning words such as "chivalry" and "gentleman," at its own peril. As *vates,* Simms believed, "Poets, when they are real men, are Prophets, for there is a soul-instinct, which they represent, which is far more profound than any reason" (Charleston *Mercury,* 15 June 1863).

When Trent wrote in his biography of Simms, "While chivalry was a good thing in its day, modern civilization is a much higher thing," he was no doubt attempting to counter Simms's blistering comments that a people who foreswear chivalry and high ideals in their rush to power and materialism will fall into tyranny and commit cultural suicide. Trent elaborated shrilly for three pages in his biography on the "very hackneyed expression, 'Southern chivalry.'" To him chivalry simply meant that the "people of the South were leading a primitive life" (35–37). Picking up this theme near biography's end, he remarked of Simms: "A barbarian he could not be, since he was not an aristocrat by birth" (325). In order to have this crucial last word on chivalry, Trent excoriated the Old South civilization with which Simms was so closely identified. Through him, Charles Dudley Warner, who had chosen this young Virginia native as Simms biographer, would share the final pronouncement. Simms, silenced by death, could not reply. Yet, in retrospect, Trent's was not the final word, after all, if one honors, as did Simms, the traditional meaning of the curse of the poet as a perduring and ultimately successful malediction. After the conquest of Wales, King Edward I ordered the execution of the Welsh bards. In one of Simms's favorite poems, Thomas Gray's "The Bard," a surviving poet puts a blistering curse on the invader. Simms no doubt felt kinship.

In the early twentieth century, G. K. Chesterton had a remarkably similar description of the fate of both the American North and his own native land as he witnessed the triumph of "the heresy of materialism" and the accompanying eclipse of chivalry, courtesy, character, and morals—all summed up in the Latin *mores*. He wrote in a tone as vociferous as Simms's: "An egotistical heresy, produced by the modern heathenry, has taught [Americans] against all their Christian instincts that boasting is better than courtesy and pride better than humility" (523–24).

John McCardell's "Trent's Simms: The Making of a Biography" treats Trent's less than subtle postwar literary politics in his portrayal of Simms. Perhaps Louis Simpson has defined the northern post–Civil War process best as a not so thinly veiled intellectual imperialism following on the heels of military invasion.

Putnam's Magazine for February treats us to an analysis of "Virginia—Old and New," from the pen of that voluminous, but cold-blooded essayist, H.T. Tuckerman, in which we discern the familiar traits of malignity, in respect to all things in the South, social, moral and political, which has so long indicated the jealous antipathies of the North, its envy of our prosperity, and its hostility to our fame and reputation. To so great a degree did these people, in many sections, carry it, that it became painful to them to hear the word "Chivalry" and the title "Gentleman" uttered, as these seemed tacitly to describe the characteristics of the Southern people. "Chivalry" and "Gentleman" finally became a sort of scoff among them, especially as they perpetually heard of these beautiful virtues, from European tongues, as especially belonging to the South. There was an awful consciousness, among too many of them born yesterday, and with no other capital of character than a fashionable tailor could supply—assisted by the stolen crest from some English gentleman's carriage—that there was a very substantial difference in the training and development of the two sections, and they preferred to ignore and ridicule the character which they found themselves unable to acquire, or even to assume. You can see the grin of Mr. Tuckerman, all through his essay, as he exults in the overthrow of Old Virginia, and all the grand virtues of her patriots, statesmen and heroes. May God forgive him the double damning sins of malignity and stupidity. He but follows in the wake of wretches who are destroying his own country, as they have destroyed ours. The end is yet to come. Under the asinine legislation of Congress the gulf between the two sections widens daily, and the uncompromising Secessionist may quietly and silently congratulate himself that the tearing asunder of the Union, and forever defeating the hopes to behold again an united people, are about to be effected by processes and parties very different from those upon which he relied. It is a law—illustrated by every page of history—that usurpation becomes tyranny, and tyranny always commits suicide! The rest of this number is light and lively, as usual, of average merit. "Literature at Home," by Stoddard, seems conscientious, and is probably among the best specimens of the literature of *Putnam*.

Charleston *Courier* (22 January 1870); clipping in Simms's Scrapbook B, folio 86, CCS, SCL.

PART 2

Civilization

The Critical Revolution and the Revolutionary Critic

By David Moltke-Hansen

In the three decades before the Civil War journals became principal sites, and the review essay itself a principal form, of intellectual discourse in the American South. Elsewhere in the Atlantic world and America, they already functioned in this way (O'Brien, *Conjectures of Order,* 1: 529–53; Gardner, *The Rise and Fall of Early American Magazine Culture,* 69–102). Yet the review essay form was relatively new at the time, at once an outgrowth of and a departure from the more familiar occasional essay so popular in the eighteenth century. Where the occasional essay was glancing and brief, the review essay was weighty and long. That fact does not make the subgenre particularly congenial or accessible to twenty-first-century readers. Consequently the scholarship largely has overlooked William Gilmore Simms's voluminous output in the form.

Basic questions about the relationships and roles of Simms's review essay production and editing remain unanswered. Simms, like many of his contemporaries, used the subgenre not just as a venue to comment on literature, but as a platform for broader cultural, social, and political criticism. In doing so, he promoted the elevated expectations of criticism that Romantics held. Although Simms frequently addressed abiding themes and issues in his essays, events also often occasioned and influenced his positions and perceptions. Because his production as a review essayist was bound as well to his other work, both as a writer and as an editor, his use of the subgenre predictably changed over the forty-five years of his writing career

This development took place in a landscape of shifting revolutions. Revolutions were Simms's birthright as an American writer and public intellectual, and he had spent his youth absorbing narratives and implications of them. Other revolutions roiled his adulthood. The interplay of these multiple revolutions shaped his understanding and activities as a critic. Of necessity that understanding did not spring full-grown and armored, Athena-like, from his head. It evolved. Four essays by Simms, printed in this part, show the distance he had come as a chief shaper of the South's cultural awareness and intellectual production by the time he became a fully committed advocate of southern nationalism in the late 1840s.

Multiple revolutions mattered to Simms, but not all positively. Simms embraced three wholeheartedly: the American, the Romantic, and the National. The American Revolution established peoples' self-determination as a primary value. The Romantic revolution asserted the combination of collective and personal self-awareness, together with the "deeply felt" and powerfully imagined, as the purposes and fruit of cultural production. In the process the auteur emerged as a central figure. The National revolution identified the proper form of, and vehicle for, political and cultural self-development—the nation-state and national literature. One positive outcome of these revolutions in Simms's eyes was the transformation of history into the study and story of peoples, their course, and future ("Ellet's Women of the Revolution," p. 303). The auteur helped imagine and capture his people in writing, thus inspiring their further self-awareness and development.

Certain other revolutions struck Simms at different times as either threatening or having mixed results. The Industrial Revolution and the commercial (or market) revolutions disfigured the land and human relations. Yet commerce also fostered the diffusion and exchange of ideas, and industry provided markets for southern crops. The Idealist revolution (whether Socialist, Transcendentalist, or Abolitionist) impelled, through abstract, utopian visions and values, the overturn of organic social relations and historical legacies. The sense of the beautiful and the elevation of art that stemmed from the same philosophical ferment behind Transcendentalism, however, were ideals to embrace. The alternative, Utilitarian revolution marginalized the spiritual and the sublime, so essential to humanity, civilization, and progress—at least when properly conceived.

The Democratic revolution affirmed all citizens' right to political participation and defied oligarchic ambitions. These were good things in Simms's view. At the same time, through promotion of the idea of equality, democracy destabilized social and cultural hierarchies and mores. Indeed, in its extreme form of radical individualism, it had the effect of shattering the "great chain of being." For Simms, as many before him and still during his life time, the chain defined the divinely sanctioned, hierarchical ordering of nature and society. Amplifying the enormous cost of democratic extremism were the lives lost in the French and later political revolutions and the debasement of social and cultural values and relations reflected in the low standards of much popular literature of Simms's day—a source to him of much ire.

The technological revolution fascinated Simms. At the outset of the Civil War, he even proposed designs for marine defenses and paid for the manufacture of a bayonet of his design. At the same time as this revolution facilitated travel and life, however, it tended to abstract people from themselves and each other (Rogers, "Art Ready for Battle," 56–81). When, in the mid-1830s, Simms rode the train to and from the plantation of his friend Charles Rivers Carroll, while courting his future wife, it was on one of the longest railroads in the country. He later would write repeatedly about the benefits of railroads. Neverthelss, in the late 1830s and early 40s, Simms expressed anxiety about, as well as approbation of, the leveling influences of the age, represented by such public transport as the omnibus ("The Philosophy," 106–7; Pearce, "All Aboard!," 83–85). "Railroads—the capacity to overcome time and space, are wonderful things," he told students at the University of Alabama in 1842, but "all the steam power in the world" cannot "carry one poor soul to heaven" (*Social Principle,* 53).

These understandings emerged gradually. Growing up in Charleston, South Carolina, Simms heard frequently from his grandmother about the American Revolution and his family's part in it (Guilds, *Simms,* 7), a point on which he elaborated in the latter part of his review essay "Ellet's Women of the Revolution" (p. 303–31). He internalized the importance, and the stories, of the struggle on behalf of political self-determination—not for everyone (for instance, slaves, women, children, and others under patriarchal authority), but for those men with the presence of mind and capacity to use liberty to advance society and themselves. He also explored the ground and gave narrative shape to the chronology of the Revolution's local unfolding. In the process he imagined and defined the universal ideal, self-determination (about which he later wrote), in a particularized, historical setting that made the ideal real and meaningful but also contingent. The same guiding principle carried over into art as the concretization of beauty, feeling, and morality. It informed Simms's writing from quite early on. Lyrics from his nineteenth and twentieth years already show the impulse.

The next half-dozen years saw Simms enthusiastically dive into Romantic currents flowing from Britain and Germany. He did so as an emulator, a critic, and an editor. Never only an imitator, he quickly moved from the neoclassical form and Augustan sentiment of his 1825 *Monody on the Death of Charles Cotesworth Pinckney,* written in celebration of an American Revolutionary leader and Federalist vice presidential and presidential candidate from Charleston. Quite different was his conception and rendering of the drama and passion of the July Days in the 1830 revolution in France, the subject of his *The Tri-Color; or, the Three Days of Blood, in Paris. With Some Other Pieces* (1831) (Brennan, *The Poet's Holy Craft,* 11–39). In time he would treat the American Revolution with similar passion and dramatic sense, but at this youthful stage the contrast between these two small volumes was sharp.

The earlier American Revolution is measured in heroic couplets and calm and noble abstractions reflecting the influence of Alexander Pope (Brennan, "A Note on Simms and Neoclassicism," 23–25). The latter revolution, which led to the overthrow of the French monarch, was also about "the deliverance of a mighty and an entire people from the worst species of human bondage" as a "result of the highest species of resolution and deliberate manhood." Yet it describes "the way to Freedom" in charged language and with Romantic coloring (*Tri-color*, 6). "The cataracts of vengeance burst" (35) in the face of "The purple hue of slaughter" (39) and "The hoarded wrath of years" (40).

To explain his preference for the tomb of Napoleon remaining on St. Helena Island in the South Atlantic, Simms invoked the "principle of the natural sublime" in one of his related poems in the volume. He did so against the new French government's consideration of the idea, eventually acted on, of returning the late emperor's remains to Paris for reburial in a monumental tomb. His argument was that the island, unlike the teeming metropolis, provided a fit setting for a figure that no crumbling edifice could honor perduringly (51). There, in the remote ocean, sea, sky, and cliffs, together with howling winds and swirling currents, revealed to the inner eye the fate of the most successful warrior of modern history. No one meditating on the tomb under the weeping willows in the Geranium Valley had to be there to see Napoleon memorialized in perpetuity: "For him we make the monument That never can decay; Which, when the wrath of Time is spent, May laugh to scorn, his sway" (53). "The late emperor's 'majesty of self' deserved no less" (54).

The invocation of the natural sublime gestured at once to William Wordsworth and Samuel Taylor Coleridge, to Percy Bysshe Shelley and John Keats. Yet another leading proponent of the sublime, George Gordon, Lord Byron, perhaps was echoed more often in Simms's early Romantic poetry than any other. Simms even had a connection to the Byron circle through his older Charleston friend James Wright Simmons, author of *Inquiry into the Moral Character of Lord Byron* (1826). Simmons probably wrote the 1828 review of Leigh Hunt's *Lord Byron and Some of His Contemporaries,* which summatively judged these poets in the *Southern Literary Gazette,* the journal that Simms and he had launched that year. Clearly, under Simmons's tutelage, Simms also was increasingly attentive to, and under the sway of, the Romantics long before better-known American followers such as Emerson (Brennan, *The Poet's Holy Craft,* 36). As clearly, with time, Wordsworth and Coleridge became the most influential of all. This was especially so when Simms wrote lyrical verse and reflected (also with Shelley's "Defense of Poetry" in mind) on poetry's place and value (Kibler, *Poetry* 1–36).

The sublime—no word evoked better what Simms sought both to render and to find in the works of others. The sublime was not what nature revealed, but what one could see, when looking inward. This was true whether one's inner gaze was stimulated by the elemental wild, in all its terror, grandeur, and power, or by familiar places, in all their sweet, nurturing, pastoral softness, or by human nature, in all its complexity and with all its passions, or by history, with all its drama and movement. *Video Volans*—"I see soaring."—became Simms's Coleridgean motto, inscribed on the crest he created for himself (Kibler, *The*

Poetry of William Gilmore Simms, 33). Sometimes he said it in reverse, as when he gave a version of an often revised and republished poem the title "Volans Video"—"Soaring I see": "Give Fancy freedom, freedom tonight! / Let her soar up in the face of the stars" (*Russell's* 4.1 [1858]: 17; Kibler, *The Poetry of William Gilmore Simms,* 222). The power of inner sight was that of the seer or bard, but also of the lyrical poet of nature and reverie, the gothic prober of the psyche, and the historical tale teller.

Insight was what made criticism important as well. The critic should look for and assess the extent to which the works under consideration successfully convey the sublime and achieve individuality and originality in the process. In addition the critic should strive for insight and be estimated according to the degree of his (or her) originality and individuality. Insight comprised judgment as well as understanding and discernment. Individuality was more than singularity, adhering as well in the voice, tone, and personality projected and in the cast of views and feelings expressed. Originality was a function of perspective as well as of expression and thought, not just a matter of novelty. Indeed singularity, like novelty, was suspect, when not alloyed with these other qualities.

The poet, the historian, and the critic helped others to see. In the critic's case it was both the works under review and the subjects they treated. Scale mattered. What could be done, and what was proper, in a brief book note of a hundred words was different than what could be developed in a full-length review essay of anywhere from five thousand to twenty thousand or even thirty thousand words. As the general introduction to this collection makes clear, the review essay emerged only in the early nineteenth century. It embodied the expanded ambition for criticism as a principal form of cultural discourse and engagement. Although angered by the tendency of review essayists to assert rather than explicate their judgments, even Coleridge "most willingly admit[ted] and estimate[d] at a high value the services which the *Edinburgh Review,* and others formed afterwards on the same plan, have rendered to society in the diffusion of knowledge" (*Biographia Literaria,* 2: 117).

That enhanced valuation of the critical enterprise was recent. Like Coleridge, Simms read German framers of Romantic critical theory, though initially in translation. Over time he would engage many dimensions of that theory. In the 1820s, however, his focus often was on poetry, then his chief literary and critical endeavor. Earlier than most Americans, he looked particularly to Wordsworth, Coleridge, and Keats (Kibler, *The Poetry of William Gilmore Simms,* 8–16; Brennan, *The Poet's Holy Craft,* 41–44). Urged on by Coleridge, Wordsworth, in the preface to the second edition of *Lyrical Ballads* (1800), voiced the importance of feeling in both poetry and its critical appreciation: "Poetry," he declared, is "the spontaneous overflow of powerful feelings . . . recollected in tranquility" (27). Two years later he expanded this preface in a revised edition. There he claimed more: "the poet binds together by passion and knowledge the vast empire of human society" (52). It was on that basis, he argued, that poetry should be judged. He also came to agree with Coleridge that it was imagination that was "the prime agent of all human perception," functioning "as a repetition in the finite mind of the eternal act of creation in the infinite I Am" (Coleridge, *Biographia Literaria,* 1: 295–96). Simms concurred. He told a student audience in 1845, "Man is essentially an artist. . . . He is crowned with invention, and delights in its exercise" (*Self-Development,* 35).

Feeling and perception became general or collective at the level of a society or culture. Simms insisted that "nations are but aggregates of individuals. It is the accumulation of personal character . . . that lays the foundation of national renown." That is why, he held, "the individual is the father of the race, even as the child is the father of the man" (*Self-Development,* 23). Individual expressions of feeling and imagination thus were fundamental to national culture. Yet those expressions could either deviate from or carry forward that culture.

There was a potential tension between the individual poet and society. "The spirit of the age is one thing," Simms declared; "its genius another" ("The New Spirit," 314). In his view, "a man of genius," for instance, a poet, always is ahead of his people and his time. "Succeeding generations," Simms continued, "at length reach the spot where his mantle has fallen. This is the history of social progress" and "is in the experience of every community" (316–17). The effective writer knew the tension and the distance between the individual and the collective. The effective critic knew how to judge.

Because of this tension between the individual and his or her society, Romantic theory went in two directions simultaneously. Some belles lettrists placed themselves in opposition to, or at least at some remove from, the collective, asserting the primacy and the worth either of the individual over the herd or of the prophet and critic over the conventional. This posture, its advocates claimed, gave necessary independence from normative constraints, and this was why the artist could assert, develop, and express the self in its radical individuality. The posture also provided the critical distance necessary to see and render, in order to excoriate and address, the ills and pressures deforming society and culture.

Other writers, those in the National Romantic vein, with Simms among them, instead believed the collective gave a culture much of its value and meaning. The great cause was the nation, to be led by its cultural developers and advocates. "The moral objects of the poet and the historian," Simms insisted, "concern not the individual so much as the race" or ethnic group (*Views and Reviews,* Series 1 42). The man of genius knew this and acted accordingly, lending his prophetic power to the cause rather than to its undermining. At least that was Simms's stance until his hopes for a southern nation were blasted, late in his life, by the American Civil War (Moltke-Hansen, "When History Failed").

As the introduction to this volume notes, Sir Walter Scott was a principal, early influence on Simms's thinking about nationalism's cultural expression and purpose (Holman, "The Influence of Scott and Cooper on Simms," 203–18). Writing during the Napoleonic War and after, Scott embraced the new nationalist ideology that the war fostered. His challenge was not to assert ethnic identity but to foster its development. The Scots and the English were united in a kingdom but not yet as a British people. The promotion of that common sense of identity is what Scott sought to effect in the face of the war's challenges and consequences (Moltke-Hansen, "Southern Literary," 9–13).

After the war French historian-statesmen embraced a similar mission in the effort to rebuild and unite their defeated, war-torn country. Germans, inspired by the slightly earlier thought of Johann G. Herder, the great theorist of nationalism, came out of the Napolenonic conflict fervently nationalistic as well. So did other European peoples—or at least many of their intellectuals and artists (Moltke-Hansen, "Identity Politics and the Civil War," 10–14). Against the memory of Napoleon, the great individualist master of history, the wartime allies were collectively asserting and protecting their national genius, and the French were responding in kind.

In the wake of the European nationalist surge, Americans too started to think and write increasingly of themselves as a people. Yet the diversity of the country, its rapid westward expansion, and dramatic immigration all challenged that growing sense and commitment. In the face of increasing sectional tensions, more and more people in the South started talking of themselves as a people separate from others in America. Henry Timrod, Simms's protégé, sometime coeditor, and unofficial poet laureate of the Confederate States of America, expressed his awareness of this burgeoning commitment and the outcome it suggested in one of his most celebrated poems. He wrote "Ethnogenesis"—birth or origin of the people or the ethnos—early in 1861, as the Confederate government was forming. "At last, we are / A nation among nations," he exulted (*The Poems of Henry Timrod,* 100).

There was as much ambition as reality in the bold assertion (Hutchison, *Apples & Ashes,* 4–13), but there also was history. Simms had been laying the cultural foundations for decades. He did so, however, with a new urgency, starting about 1847. That was when he began acting on the decision that the South should become its own nation and southerners their own people (Moltke-Hansen, "Southern Literary," 15–17). He had anticipated the possibility earlier—for instance, in private correspondence as early as 1838, when he thought it unlikely; in a magazine column in 1842, when it seemed more likely; and in a Fourth of July oration in Aiken, South Carolina, two years later (when it seemed dangerously likely). It was on this last occasion that he declared "the ligaments which now chiefly bind us together are those of our political union" (*Letters* 6: 7–8; *Magnolia* n.s. 1 [July 1842]: 59; *The Sources,* 31). This was before adding: "These ligaments need but little for their rupture" (31). Yet it was not until 1847 that he broke with Young America and his twenty-year commitment to framing the South as a distinct part of the American nation and national literature.

Some scholars argue that this political decision reflected itself in what and how Simms wrote thereafter (Kreyling, *Inventing Southern Literature* 93–104; Charles Watson, Jr., *From Nationalism to Secessionism*). Others contend that Simms anticipated social and, later, psychological realism in his work of the late 1840s, 50s, and 60s but that this was at least in substantial part in response to transatlantic literary currents (Bakker, "Simms on the Literary Frontier"; Wimsatt, "Realism and Romance in Simms's Midcentury Fiction"). In any event, topically Simms still treated people, events, and places because they were either in the South or influential in the South's emergence. This ethnogenesis, as he analyzed and fictively portrayed it, took place in stages. Colonies grew out of the Native American and European imperial contests over the area that would become the region. Then the Revolution transformed America into a national project. The Constitution was a written contract that described the new nation. And, finally, the South's westward expansion in his own lifetime gave his native region the scale and potential of a nation. At the same time, conflicts with the North over the extension of slavery in the new territories and states suggested the necessity of a separate future.

The South, Simms came to conclude, not only had grown enough, but was becoming distinctive and coherent enough and had reason enough to become a country. The idea had appeal, but so did historical associations with the Union. What, in addition to growing sectional political divisions, galvanized Simms and turned him into a southern nationalist was the conviction that the rapidly urbanizing North was increasingly different from a South still dominated by agriculture. Also the growing northern resistance to slavery's further westward extension, after the admittance of Texas to the Union, meant that the North would dominate the national government. The increasing vitriol the northern press directed at the South made that likelihood all the more ominous. So did growing talk of northerners as distinct from southerners and *vice versa*.

For Simms secession and the formation of a southern nation developed as the only viable alternative. Once that was decided, in the midst of the heated discussions over slavery during the Mexican War, the question became one of how to achieve that future. At one level the answer was political, but more fundamentally it was cultural. The South still had to build its own culture, if its people were to develop their own ethnos and civilization successfully and fully. Southerners for too long had been in neocolonial thrall to the North, just as Americans for too long had been in thrall to Europe—particularly Britain.

Cultural ethnogenesis meant that white southerners such as Simms were writing about what they were establishing, a separate nation, and who they were becoming, a separate people. In substantial part this was by interrogating what and who they had been. Many southerners, especially those from Virginia, did so by discovering that they had always been collectively different and had always shared characteristics and values (Ritchie Devon Watson, Jr., *Normans and Saxons,* 34–35, 45–46, 93–109; Grammer, *Pastoral and Politics in the Old South,* 1–97; Taylor, *Cavalier and Yankee,* 145–260). Simms was not so simplistic. He knew the complex diversity in the South's and southerners' antecedents. When writing about the Revolution, therefore, he treated the relationship of ethnicity to political loyalty: those with Scottish and German backgrounds tended to support the crown; those with Irish backgrounds and descendants of the French Huguenots often fought for the Patriot cause ("Civil Warfare," 328; *Joscelyn,* 53, 312–3). Simms also understood the South to have Spanish and French as well as Native American and British roots and wrote at length on them over decades.

That understanding was not the predominant one. In the early Republic, other southerners deferred to Virginians. Yet Virginians were farther from the centers of historic French and Spanish power in the Southeast than were South Carolinians and Georgians. As a result Virginians often were less conscious of these centuries-old continuing influences and conflicts. They also thought of themselves as culturally and socially less heterogeneous and politically and demographically more stable than were people and states farther south. This meant that the South constructed and reflected in the antebellum writings of Virginians was different, at least in degree, from that coming to life in the pages of Simms. It was less of an emergent place and had more tradition. Because Virginia dominated the region demographically and politically until the presidency of Andrew Jackson, it was easy for the Virginians' view to prevail.

Part of Simms's self-appointed task was to change the lenses through which people—southerners among them—saw the region going forward (compare Taylor, *Cavalier and Yankee,* 267–97). He did this by shifting the focus in his writing to the South's formation as a society and culture. As the omniscient narrator observes in Simms's first romance, *Guy Rivers,* this genesis was out of "the incoherent" mixture of people agitated by "strife, discontent, and contention" because of "the wild condition of the country" (613). Simms was clear: "It is our common error to regard the close of our revolutionary contests . . . as settling permanently our institutions. . . . That struggle determined nothing but our independence" (*The Sources,* 30). Yet "independence meant achieving self-definition and self-determination, preconditions for real artistic expression" (Moltke-Hansen, "Ordered Progress," 130). By writing the South, Simms and others would not so much promulgate as foster the South's emergence and development, civilizing from the Atlantic edge a vast hinterland only just leaving behind a frontier condition. In the service of this cause, Simms wrote more than anyone else. Yet he could not do the work alone. He needed allies both to propagate the message and to fuel the campaign's growing and ongoing success.

A principal method Simms used to promote the South's revolutionary ethnogenesis was the editing and encouraging of cultural journals. Over his lifetime he edited or coedited a half-dozen journals and additionally a half-dozen newspapers, which also bore strong cultural content—especially so in the case of the *Southern Patriot*. In addition, as his fame grew, he responded positively as often as he could to pleas from across the region to lend his name and pen to other literary and cultural journals. He contributed as well literary, travel, and political columns to the biggest Charleston newspapers—the *Courier* and the *Mercury*. Yet, as productive as he was, Simms needed additional writers, whom he recruited as the cadres in his cultural campaign.

These circles of writers widened over time. As a young man, Simms had friends and mentors largely in the Charleston area and to some extent among Unionists elsewhere in South Carolin. In the early 1830s he added literati in Philadelphia, New York, and the communities in their ambit. By the early 1840s, he also had a growing number of correspondents and familiars throughout South Carolina and adjacent areas of Georgia, a result of his second wife's connections. Many of these new friends were political and social rather than literary, but the number of writers in their ranks progressively increased. In time the overlapping networks extended still further. By the late 1840s, when Simms was editing the *Southern Quarterly Review*, they ranged across the South.

A nation must be imagined as a community of communities and identity, as Benedict Anderson has reminded us in his *Imagined Communities*, but it also must be socially and politically constructed. Simms was doing that by the end of the 1840s and even more concertedly in the 1850s. The result was that the balance of his ties shifted to the South from the East. Yet this did not mean a parochial narrowing of his focus. He continued to read and imagine the South in international contexts. He understood currents of both thought and influence to be transnational.

Committed to the creation of national culture, Simms did not think that such a culture could, or should, be developed in isolation. Indeed he conceived the potential and necessity of national culture in part through reflection on the histories of the literatures of European nations. In the cases of Germany and Italy, which were not yet unified as states, he saw the nation as aspirational and growing out of the claims to having distinct cultures and being distinct peoples. His reviews let him share elements of those reflections and, in the journals he edited, the reflections of his contributors. His hope was that his readers would be inspired, as were he and his growing stable of writers, to emulation—not imitation.

Simms always believed that, as southerners wrote, they needed to keep in mind what others were producing and had produced elsewhere. American subjects needed to be expressed in American idioms but at the same time employ the universal grammar informing any artistic production. Thus Simms looked to Sir Walter Scott when writing his colonial, Revolutionary, and border romances. This was because "Scott's uses of skeleton history have been to furnish it with life and character, to reclothe its dry-bones" (*Views and Reviews. Series I*, 45). It was also because Scott understood, as Simms put it, that "the true and most valuable inspiration of the poet will be found either in the illustration of the national history, or in the development of the national characteristics" (53–54). Art made history, and thus the nation, live.

Yet too many American writers, Simms judged, "fashion[ed] themselves to European tastes," and this was "to denationalize the American mind" (*Views and Review. Series 1,7*). He continued: "We have our own national mission to perform. . . . The national mind is now free to rise to the consideration of its superior wants" (9–10). The reason this mattered, he maintained, was that, "to write *from* a people, is to *write* a people—to make them live—to endow them with a life and a name—to preserve them with a history forever" (12–13). This did not mean, however, that one should treat people and settings only in North America.

Simms's reasons for choosing the subjects of his writings were complex. He wrote *The Life of the Chevalier Bayard; "The Good Knight," Sans peur et sans reproche"* in 1847, in the middle of the Mexican War. In part he did so to illuminate chivalry and the martial spirit in his own day, as well as at the dawn of the European exploration and conquest of the Americas at the end of the Middle Ages and chivalry's dominance. While writing the biography—the first to appear in English—he also was preparing an oration on self-development for delivery before the literary societies of Oglethorpe University. There he declared that our "true nature is art," but people are endowed with different capacities in the arts, as in other areas of life (35). Therefore, he continued, individuals should develop their natures to the best of their abilities, in appropriate ways, and with appropriate regard for their proper level and station in society.

This argument became the basis in the oration for a justification of the war against Mexico. Reasoning by analogy, Simms drew a parallel between individual and national development. The only way, he contended, for Mexico to "be rescued from that blight and tyranny which have left her people underperforming and worthless" was to tutor the Mexicans. The best method, he continued, was "what we call slavery." That institution "has, in most countries, under God," he reflected, "been made the favorite means by which refractory tribes and races have been conducted to safety and civilization" (*Self Development*, 22–23). He then went on to celebrate the ambition "to be a conqueror,—a discoverer,—a man" (30).

What did the ambition require and how had it been deployed by the Americas' European conquerors? If chivalry was an important legacy of Europe for America, and especially the South, so was the spirit of the Spanish conquistadors. To understand the cultural origins, Simms wrote romances of the Moorish conquest of Spain and the beginnings of the *Reconquista—Count Julian* (1845) and *Pelayo* (1838). He also gave considerable attention, in fiction as well as reviews, to the role of the conquistadors in the Americas–for instance in the *Damsel of Darien* (1839) and *Vasconselos* (1854). After all, the conquistadors and their legatees had impinged on the future South significantly from the early sixteenth to the mid–nineteenth century. Simms made this a central point of his 1842 oration on *The Social Principle: The True Source of National Permanence,* delivered before the Erosophic Society of the University of Alabama.

One reason to emphasize the point was that former Spanish territories in Texas and farther west, as well as Florida, were places for the South to expand. So, in Simms's mind and the minds of filibusters, were Spanish possessions in the Caribbean. Justifying the expansion, Simms insisted, was the different character of the British colonies and the present level of southern development. The conquistadors had been conquerors, not settlers. The South, however, was building on its British settler roots in its westward and southern expansion.

For the conquistadors, manhood had been an attainment as well as a birthright. Yet the spirit of democracy was changing definitions of manhood as understood from Mexico to the South Carolina lowcountry. Given the complex implications of this change, democracy's American history and current impact needed to be seen in the context of other countries' experiences. Therefore Simms and writers he recruited considered, along with what they viewed as Mexico's failures, the consequences of other, more complex trajectories—for instance, in France's revolutions. These revolutions were not just political, but also social and cultural. They played out in people's daily lives as well as in legislative and street battles. Consequently the South's revolutionary, nationalist future required preparation at the level of daily life.

Given the capaciousness of this understanding of relevant subjects, almost any topic could be plumbed for its implications for the nation. To lecture, as Simms did in the early to mid-1850s, on "poetry and the practical" was to talk about the highest aims and values of civilization. To treat Shakespeare, as Simms did recurrently, was to consider the greatest writer in English, who was an endless resource for the nineteenth-century writer in the language. To review contemporary northern and European authors was to help furnish the minds and refine the sensibilities, as well as inspire the cultural production, of southerners.

Thus motivated, Simms wrote reviews and review essays for numerous periodicals besides his own. When drafting in 1845 the "Advertisement" for the two series of his *Views and Reviews in American Literature, History and Fiction,* he indicated that the essays would be drawn from the *American Monthly,* the *American Review,* the *Knickerbocker,* and the *Southern Quarterly Review,* as well as journals for which he had been editor—the *Magnolia,* the *Orion,* and the *Southern and Western.* The review essays printed here were among the several dozen gathered by him and bound in at least three volumes, two of which survive. Simms's first biographer, William P. Trent, explained: "Up to 1851, Simms was in the habit of binding for his own use his longer articles; after this date his contributions, at least to his own review [at the time, he was editing the *Southern Quarterly Review*], are to be determined by internal evidence" (*William Gilmore Simms,* 339). Trent then listed more than thirty of these longer pieces (339–40). Of these, two dozen clearly are review essays. The listing is in chronological order and reflects Trent's style of citation:

1. American Criticism and Critics. (So. Lit. Jour., 1836.)
2. Queen Mary. (Dem. Rev., Feb. 1842.)
3. Bulwer's Genius and Writings. (Magnolia, Dec. 1842.)
4. The Writings of Washington Allston. (S. Q. R. [*Southern Quarterly Review*], Oct. 1843.)
5. The Moral Character of Hamlet. (Orion, 1844.)
6. The New Spirit of the Age. (S. Q. R., April, 1845.)
7. A Year of Consolation. (Review of Mrs. Butler's [Fanny Kemble's] book, S. Q. R., July 1847.)
8. Prescott's Conquest of Peru. (S. Q. R., Jan. and April, 1848.)
9. Stevens's History of Georgia. (S. Q. R., April, 1848)
10. Headley's Life of Cromwell. (S. Q. R., Oct., 1848.)
11. Modern Prose Fiction. (S. Q. R., April, 1849.)
12. Guizot's Democracy in France. (S. Q. R., April, 1849.)
13. Later Poems of Henry Taylor. (S. Q. R., July, 1849.)
14. Recent American Poets. (S. Q. R., Oct., 1849.)
15. Kennedy's Life of Wirt. (S. Q. R., April, 1850.)
16. Ellett's Women of the Revolution. (S. Q. R., July, 1850.)
17. Tuckerman's Essays and Essayists. (S. Q. R., July, 1850.)
18. Sentimental Prose Fiction. (S. Q. R., Sept., 1850.)
19. Summer Travel in the South. (S. Q. R., Sept., 1850.)
20. [William James Rivers's] Topics in the History of South Carolina. (S. Q. R., Sept., 1850.)
21. The Southern Convention. (S. Q. R., Sept., 1850.)
22. Pickett's History of Alabama. (S. Q. R., Jan., 1852.)
23. Domestic Histories of the South. (S. Q. R., April, 1852.)
24. The Baron De Kalb. (S. Q. R., July, 1852.)

The sample is suggestive, no more. Trent did not include many pieces from *Views and Reviews.* He even omitted many written between 1836 and 1850 found in the two surviving volumes of offprints that Simms bound, which are now in the Charles Carroll Simms Collection in the South Caroliniana Library at the University of South Carolina.[1] As Trent reported, he also did not list pieces from later numbers of the *Southern Quarterly Review,* during the latter part of Simms's editorship. That editorship began in 1849 and continued through 1854.

Despite Trent's hesitancy to draw the obvious conclusion, it is clear that the unsigned essays in the volumes from 1852 to 1854 were often Simms's. Frequently there were several in an issue (Guilds, *Simms* 153–61). To those pieces one needs to add those that did not make it into *Views and Reviews* as initially planned and many others scattered in the periodicals that Simms named as publishers of his review essays. When one does so, the total number of review essays by Simms may easily be several times greater than Trent's list. It is not possible to be certain, but a total three or four times the number listed by Trent seems likely—the equivalent of ten-to-twelve volumes' worth written over forty years. Making this all the more remarkable is the fact that Simms's production of shorter reviews and review columns—not counting book notes—was at least as voluminous. Yet the number of titles treated was ten-to-fifteen times greater in these shorter reviews.

In the face of such voluminous diversity, selection of a handful of review essays to represent the totality of Simms's output in the subgenre must be arbitrary. Yet there are guidelines that help explain, if not justify the selection here. Because *Views and Reviews* is also available from the University of South Carolina Press, it is easy to exclude the pieces included there and others in a similar vein and with a similar focus—broadly, Americanism in literature. Because the first half of this volume is devoted to literary reviews, it seems reasonable as well not to concentrate in this second section on literary subjects. This is especially so, given the historical and contemporary topics that in addition attracted Simms's attention. Following the model of the *Edinburgh Review,* Simms understood the review essay as a practice in social, political, and broadly cultural, as well as literary, criticism.

Early on, from the mid-1820s to the mid-1830s, Simms wrote more review essays on literary than other subjects (Kibler, *Pseudonymous Publications,* 46–54, 65, 95). He channeled his political criticism through his newspaper editorship, using a common division between the types of periodicals (Gardner, *The Rise and Fall of Early American Magazine Culture,* 69–102). The early to mid-1830s also saw him producing two more volumes of poetry, five novels, and two miscellanies of fiction and verse, one aimed at women readers. During the Civil War, he wrote poetry, fiction, and drama but little criticism. After the war he returned to reviewing, but less for cultural reviews and more for newspapers. When he did write for magazines and reviews, he produced fiction or poetry or columns on various issues of contemporary or historical concern; these last he also wrote for newspapers (Kibler, *Pseudonymous Publications,* 40, 42, 45, 72, 75, 79). His criticism, which was mostly for newspapers, tended to shorter form pieces or, as in his prewar newspaper book columns, multiple short-form pieces presented together.

The period in which Simms wrote most of his social, cultural, and political criticism therefore was the two dozen years before the war. The first decade,

1837–47, was his Young America period and is represented by *Views and Reviews*, although in those years he also wrote extensively on subjects other than Americanism in literature. For instance his widely known review "Miss Martineau on Slavery" appeared in the *Southern Literary Messenger* in November 1837. His essay "Ancient and Modern Culture" came out in the May 1842 *Magnolia*. Simms contributed these review essays not only to the cultural journals that he edited—the *Magnolia* (1842–43), the *Orion* (1844), and the *Southern and Western* (1845)—but also to many others.

The second portion of this prewar period was just over a dozen years. These were the years during which Simms devoted himself most concertedly to building and articulating southern culture and establishing a southern national cultural identity, essential for the political nationhood he anticipated with growing fervor. He did this in criticism through the nearly six years of his editorship of the *Southern Quarterly Review* and also with prolific contributions to other journals. He additionally wrote widely for newspapers, contributing travel and literary columns especially. One of the most extended of the latter was for the Charleston *Mercury*, where, from late 1854 through mid-1856 (so, after his having surrendered his post at the *Southern Quarterly Review*), he published his review column under the pen name Lorris. Then, from the end of the decade to the eve of the war, he contributed forty columns in the "Our Literary Docket" series, sampled, like the Lorris letters, in the first section of this collection. Earlier, in the fall of 1849, he contributed anonymous political essays in fictional form titled "The Home Tourist." These he gathered in a collection the same year called *Father Abbot, or, the Home Tourist; A Medley*. Published over his name, it framed key political and social ideas and judgments that Simms shared with James Henry Hammond, the former South Carolina governor and future U.S. senator (Guilds, *Simms*, 191).

To get a sense of the range of these series and the comprehensiveness of Simms's cultural agenda for the South, consider the more than two dozen reviews that Simms contributed in the Lorris letters in just the first four months after he quit the editorship of the *Southern Quarterly Review* in late 1854 (Kibler, *Pseudonymous Publications*, 61–62):

"Shakespeare Publications"
"Charles Gayerre's Writings"
"Southern Literature"
"The Poems of the Brownings"
"Bayard Taylor and His Writings"
"Benton's Memoirs of His Own Times"
"Mrs. Stowe and the Negrophilists"
"New Cyclopoedia of American Literature"
"Notes on New Publications"

"Art, Scenery and Philosophy in Europe"
"Cheap Literature"
"A Lounge with the Poets"
"The European Periodical Press"
Untitled column on current books
"The Publishing House of the Appletons"
"Agricultural and Educational"
"Current Literature"
"Anti-Catholic Literature"
"The British Reviews"
Untitled column on current publications
"The Periodicals, Quarterlies and Monthlies"
"Pamphlets and Miscellanies"
Untitled on coast survey report
"Harper's New Publications"
Untitled on Collins, Gray, and Goldsmith
Charles Kingsley and His Writings

During this period Simms averaged a review every four or five days. Indeed this was his average over many years, at least when he was not traveling. No wonder there were twelve thousand to thirteen thousand books in his library before he had to sell many during the war; he then lost the balance when his house was burned in 1865 (Guilds, *Simms,* 296–300). As in the list from the *Mercury,* most of the reviews were of contemporary publications, whether literary or other. A number, like that on Harriet Beecher Stowe, had an apparent southern cast and could be aggressively defensive. Yet many did and were not—at least not overtly. Others reflected broader American attitudes and subjects. Still others were not obviously written from the United States.

The *Mercury* was not just a local paper. Even before the 1850s, it was renowned for its secessionist views and therefore had subscribers through much of the South—especially the lower South. Other newspaper editors frequently borrowed items from the Charleston paper. It will be some time before enough papers from the 1850s are available online to search readily for reprints of Simms's reviews. Yet, even not knowing the extent to which the cultural items—as opposed to the political and news content—of the *Mercury* were recirculated through other papers, one can reasonably consider the newspaper reviews a kind of intellectual and cultural index—at least, outside of religion, which was much more extensively treated in denominational newspapers and journals. The recently published works of the sort Simms reviewed were many of those with which southern readers had at least nodding acquaintance in the run-up to the Civil War (compare Wells, *Women Writers and Journalists,* 57–75).

The majority of those readers, as Simms knew, were not subscribers to or consumers of the literary and cultural journals. Whether issuing from Richmond, New Orleans, or Charleston, the journals typically had at most a few thousand subscribers (Bernath, *Confederate Minds,* 84, 164). Because taverns, coffeehouses, and other public places provided copies of newspapers, even county papers had comparable numbers of readers—and auditors—if not subscribers (Wells, *Women Writers and Journalists,* 57–75). One reason for Simms to write for the papers, in addition to their paying, was that he wanted the broader audiences. At the same time, he believed, as did many literati, in cultural hierarchy and therefore thought it important to address the smaller number of more refined and learned readers in more substantial style (compare Gardner, *The Rise and Fall of Early American Magazine Culture,* 69–102). That was part of the motive for his 1857 founding and frequent subsequent contributions to *Russell's Magazine,* edited by his young friend the poet Paul Hamilton Hayne.

Russell's was quite different from the *Southern Quarterly Review* that Simms had edited several years earlier. Although it included an occasional essay on political questions, its focus was cultural, primarily literary. Nevertheless it featured, in addition to criticism, poetry, and fiction, also biography and history. The *Magnolia* and the *Southern and Western* had a similar mix when Simms edited them in his Young America days. The *Southern Quarterly Review* did too, before Simms took over the editorship. When he did, however, Simms considered that the times required a more political journal. Although "he privately expressed reservations" about this approach, according to his literary biographer, John C. Guilds, he nevertheless forged ahead (*Simms,* 155). Even with this increased southern and political emphasis, however, the journal treated a broad range of writings—particularly literary topics—in the review essays that Simms recruited and contributed.

The four essays that follow are drawn from the *Southern Quarterly Review* while it was edited by Simms. Indeed they all were published in the first year and a half of his editorship. Two of the four appeared in the same issue—July 1850. Only one piece is explicitly on a southern subject, "The Southern Convention," which took place in Nashville in 1850. It anticipates secession and considers the possibility of civil war in the face of what Simms and many of the conventioneers judged to be the failure of American nationalism. In Simms's analysis, democracy was undermining republicanism. Northern growth had made the South a minority. Moreover the North's cultural imperialism marginalized and belittled the South. Rooted in New England, these hegemonic impulses and ambitions made secession, in Simms's view, the only way to maintain southern self-determination.

America was not the only place where democracy challenged foundational order. "Guizot's Democracy in France" is on the French revolution of 1848 and meditates on the excesses and failures of French democracy and the role of leaders in shaping progress. Farsighted and bold leadership had made the American Revolution succeed—but to what purpose? "Ellet's Women of the Revolution" answers that question. It treats a three-volume work, which Simms had suggested to its author, Elizabeth Ellet, the young, northern wife of a University of South Carolina professor. The review essay was the occasion for consideration of the roles of women and the domestic sphere in civilization. If women were essential nurturers of civilization, they were joined in this work by critics. "Tuckerman's Essays and Essayists" gives Simms's reflections on the history of the essay genre and cultural criticism. In doing so, it also considers the Romantic and political revolutions that empowered the critic.

As these essays show, two years after his determination that the American Republic was failing to protect the South's future, Simms was fully launched in his campaign on behalf of a separate southern nation and culture. Shaping his commitment were his twin beliefs in nationalism and self-determination. In considering how to go forward, he asked fellow southerners to reflect on the reasons for and consequences of the American Revolution. He assessed the necessity and cultural limits of democracy and the consequences of both democracy run amok and leadership's failures. He promoted the Romantic spirit in the individual, as in the nation. He also asked how civilizations succeed and then honed in on cultural reproduction in the home through the education of children by their mothers under the patriarchal supervision of their fathers. In doing these things, Simms demonstrated his commitment as well to social, cultural, and political criticism.

Note

1. Among the review essays that Trent did not include from Simms's two bound surviving volumes of reviews and criticism are the following:

"Letters from the South," *Southern Literary Journal* 3 (December 1836): 239–48.
"[Cornelius] Mathew's Poems of Man," *Southern Quarterly Review* (*SQR*) 5 (January 1844): 103–18.
"Halstead's Richard the Third," *Southern and Western Magazine and Review* (*S&W*): 203–8.
"A Passage with 'The Veteran Quarterly,'" *S&W* 1 (May 1845): 297–311.
"Library of American Books," *S&W* 1 (August 1845): 128–32.
"South Carolina in the Revolution," *SQR* 14 (July 1845): 37–77.
"The Siege of Charleston," *SQR* 14 (October 1848): 261–337.
"Slavery and the Abolitionist," *SQR* 15 (April 1849): 165–223.
"Bailey's Angel World," *SQR* n.s. 2 (September 1850): 233–47.
"Reminiscences of Congress," *SQR* (November 1850): 509–27.

Review Essays

François Guizot, *Democracy in France*

François Guizot was born in Nimes, France, on 4 October 1787. It was the eve of the French Revolution, and that event would profoundly shape Guizot's life and thought. In 1794, during the Reign of Terror, his father was executed. Guizot's mother fled France, taking François and his brother to Geneva. François returned to Paris in 1805 to study law, but in 1807 he turned to the study of literature, philosophy, and history. He found an early sponsor in Phillip Albrecht Stapfer, a former Swiss ambassador to France, who directed his study and secured a position for him writing articles for the French journal *Publiciste*. Guizot became a regular contributor and gained entrée into the highest circles of the Parisian intellectual elite. In addition to his work for the periodical press, he collaborated with Pauline de Meulan, whom he later married, on a French edition of Edward Gibbon's *History of the Decline and Fall of the Roman Empire*. In 1812 he began lecturing in history at the University of Paris and later held a chair in modern European history at that institution. Following the Revolution of 1830, he served the July Monarchy of Louis-Philippe de Orleans in various capacities, first as minister of education, then as foreign minister, and finally as prime minister until the Revolution of 1848 toppled the monarchy (O'Conner, "The Historical Thought of François Guizot," 1–6).

Guizot's personal biography suggests many similarities with that of William Gilmore Simms. Both men grew up without fathers; both were public intellectuals who sought public office; and both turned to the study of the past as a means of understanding their present. In their study of history both thought deeply about the course and outcome of revolutions, and they participated in their own revolutionary struggles, which they both ultimately lost. But in 1848 only the Frenchman had experienced defeat. The ouster of the Orleans monarchy of Louis-Philippe in February 1848 embittered Guizot and led him to pen a sharp rebuke of the excesses of French society that he believed had led to his downfall. He published *Democracy in France* in January 1849, nearly a year after he had resigned his post as French prime minister. In it he decried democracy as a destructive passion of modern society. Guizot had long been skeptical of democracy, preferring instead a government modeled closely on a British-style constitutional monarchy, but the events of 1848 disabused him of the idea that the French middle-class was an open, progressive social formation (Crossley, *French Historians and Romanticism*, 97).

While Simms shared some of Guizot's skepticism about democracy and certainly about the socialism and uninhibited individualism that Guizot denounced in his pamphlet, he was not entirely sympathetic to the plight of the erstwhile prime minister. He believed that the Frenchman painted with too broad a brush. The problem was not democracy per se, but rather the particular formation that had taken hold in France. For Simms radical individualism was the issue. "It is very certain that Democracy in France," he opined, "means something which it does not mean elsewhere. Instead of a people's government, it means no government at all, or such a government only as will afford the completest sanction to all the appetites and phrenzies of the multitude" ("Democracy in France," p. 257). Without the reciprocal connections and checks on individual prerogative that were found within an organically ordered, hierarchical society, Simms believed, the centripetal forces of individualism would tear apart the social fabric, as was happening in France. Moreover he rebuked Guizot and the Orleans monarchy for failing to retain proper control of their society.

While Guizot had championed progress, both in his writing and later while a politician, he had failed to direct that progress properly. It was "the feeble ruler" who remained "religiously wedded to the habits of a past generation, as if the progress of a race were to be limited to the barriers reached by those who are about to disappear from the ranks." Instead, "the true governor, as [Thomas] Carlyle calls him—the king man—pursues a nobler and manlier method. He leaps into the car, and seizing its guidance, curbs only its eccentricities, and keeps it in the track decreed by its destiny. To oppose the progress, which, when inevitable is always legitimate, is not conservatism, but destructiveness" ("Democracy in France," p. 227). A man could either direct progress or be run over by it, and, Simms judged, Guizot had suffered the latter fate.

As a historian Guizot thought and wrote a great deal about progress. He shared with Simms a broadly whig view of history and thought the story of Western civilization was that of the steady advance of rationality and order (Moltke-Hansen, "Ordered Progress," 126–47; Crossley, *French Historians and*

Romanticism, 87). "No age," Guizot later wrote in his memoirs, "has ever yet had as many advantages as ours to observe this slow but real progression. . . . Modern history alone, from its vast scope, from the variety and extent of its duration, offers us the grandest and most complete picture which we could possibly possess of the progressive march of civilization of a part of the globe" (quoted in O'Conner, "The Historical Thought of François Guizot," 33). For Guizot the pinnacle of this march of progress was British constitutional monarchy, and he wrote extensively about English history. In 1827 he published his first two volumes on the English Revolution, covering the period between the reigns of Charles I and Charles II. His entrance into political life following the July Revolution of 1830 meant it would be twenty years before he returned to the topic. But for Guizot that revolution represented less a break than a fulfillment of his historical thought. He viewed 1830 as a replay of England's Glorious Revolution, with the Orleanist monarchy filtering its power through representative institutions, just as had occurred in England in 1688.

Simms also celebrated the July Revolution, at least briefly. Within several months of the uprising, he published a collection of verse dedicated to the events in France, entitled *The Tri-Color; or the Three Days of Blood in Paris.* Of course, Simms read events in Paris through a different lens than did Guizot, and, as a young editor in Charleston, he celebrated the power of the free press to bring political reform. Quickly, though, Simms and others in Charleston began to express reservations. They were particularly concerned about the ability of the French people, who lacked experience in democratic government, to establish a stable republic (Fox-Genovese and Genovese, *The Mind of the Master Class,* 43–45). For these observers, the events of 1848 justified their concerns. For southern slaveholders such as Simms, 1848 also validated their own vision of history and their fears about what would happen to a society if individual rights expanded too far.

Guizot's *Democracy in France* was an extended lament on the excesses of French democracy and the toppling of the constitutional monarchy. For Simms the events of 1848 represented an assault on progress and descent into chaos. In his review of Guizot's work, which ran nearly half the length of the pamphlet, Simms was ultimately less concerned with the events in France than with their implications for the future of American civilization. The year 1848 was not only an auspicious moment in Europe, it was also an important year in the United States. In the same month that revolutionaries in France toppled the monarchy of Louis Philippe, American diplomat Nicholas Trist completed negotiations of the treaty of Guadalope Hidalgo, ending the Mexican War and adding more than half a million square miles of territory to the United States.

Yet that territorial expansion also brought renewed controversy on the slavery issue. The debate over the Wilmot Proviso during the war had provided one flashpoint, and the suggestion that slavery be excluded from any territory acquired from Mexico had caused much consternation among southerners, though Simms himself had viewed the chances of its passage as remote (*Letters* 2: 293–97). Yet the Proviso position found a new political champion in 1848, when the Free Soil Party nominated former president Martin Van Buren to head its presidential ticket. Van Buren ran on a platform of "Free Soil, Free Speech, Free Labor, and Free Men," and the third-party challenger polled 14 percent of the popular vote in the northern states (McPherson, *Battle Cry of Freedom,* 61–64). It was in this context that southerners viewed events in France and in which Simms wrote his review of Guizot's *Democracy in France.*

For Simms and other southern intellectuals, the most recent revolution in France, and especially the uprising of the Parisian working classes during the June Days, offered a vindication of their long-standing critiques of free society. Simms's fellow South Carolinian John C. Calhoun had long argued that, in a society where capital had no obligation to, or interest in, protecting labor, the inevitable result was social upheaval and revolution. The eventual response to these disruptions, Calhoun predicted, would be the imposition of dictators, who could maintain order, but at the expense of free political institutions. Thus societies that adopted expansive views of individual freedom, such as France and the northern United States, were politically unstable and ultimately dangerous to liberty (Fox-Genovese and Genovese, *The Mind of the Master Class,* 52–53; Calhoun, "Speech on the Reception of Abolition Petitions," 625–33). In his review of Guizot, Simms offered a similar critique, but in this instance one that lacked the proslavery edge of Calhoun's writings. Simms highlighted the contrast that Guizot drew between the American Revolution and the latest French upheaval. The revolution in France, Simms argued, was "between nobility and commonalty, masters and workmen, the owner of property, and he who has none" ("Democracy in France," p. 239). This class warfare differed sharply from the American example, where, according to Guizot, "it was the work of all, led by the highest and the wealthiest, and the most enlightened, who had often great difficulty in rallying the spirit and sustaining the courage of the mass of the population." Simms said that the last point was one that "neither our historians nor statesmen have been sufficiently found to dwell" (p. 240). For both Simms and Guizot the difference was vitally important. The two men men celebrated progress but also desired order. The key to achieving both was to have controlled progress, directed from above. When power was dispersed too broadly, when "the idol of the self" replaced all other deities, the result was social chaos (p. 258).

Simms expanded his critique of French democracy further and, in so doing, offered his own suggestions about what gave the American republic its vitality. Key among these was the federal system enshrined in the U.S. Constitution. The states had begun as separate communities and in forming their union had ceded only those powers "absolutely essential to national purposes" (p. 259). It was this principle of states' rights, Simms argued, that represented "the grand conservative feature in our system" and that French politicians did not understand. Simms was suspicious of the centralization evident in France and the undue power and influence concentrated in Paris. The latter was what allowed urban mobs to gain control of the government, and Simms had "no hope of any good results, so long as the city of Paris may usurp all the power of the nation" (p. 260). If French or American civilization was to thrive in the future, it would be under the direction of landholders who pursued a conservative program of ordered progress. In this review of Guizot, then, we can see Simms rehearsing arguments that he and others would make with increasing force over the coming decade, and we also see how southern intellectuals such as Simms read international affairs through the lens of national politics, and vice versa.

Ehren Foley

Democracy in France. By F. Guizot, late Prime Minister; author of the "History of Civilization," etc. New-York: D. Appleton & Co. 1849.

What an interesting commentary is the mournful publication before us upon the introductory portions of the famous *History of Civilization,* by the same writer, in which he compliments France upon its being the centre and source of civilization for the world.

"I cannot," says he, in his opening lecture, "but regard France as the centre, as the focus of the civilization of Europe. It would be going too far, to say that she has always been, upon every occasion, in advance of other nations. Italy, at various periods, has outstripped her in the arts; England, as regards political institutions, is by far before her; and, perhaps, at certain moments, we may find

"Guizot's Democracy in France." *Southern Quarterly Review* 15 (April 1849): 114–65 (52pp.)

other nations of Europe superior to her in various particulars; but it must still be allowed, that, whenever France has set forward in the career of civilization, she has always sprung forth with new vigor, and has soon come up with, or passed by, all her rivals."

He proceeds, upon this assumption, to assert that even where the ideas and institutions which promote civilization, first had their birth in foreign countries, they have yet found it necessary, before they could bear their proper fruits, "to undergo in France a new preparation." It is from France, as a second birth-place, more rich and fertile than any other, that they have gone forth for the purposes of general conquest; and this, because of a certain sociableness and sympathy, a something which has the property of greater diffusiveness than is possessed by other nations—an energy and facility in the genius of the people—their language, their manners, their ideas—it matters not exactly what, and M. Guizot does not seek to fix it—which enables her to present the subject more clearly, more agreeably, and to penetrate more certainly the great masses of mankind. "In a word, clearness, sociability, sympathy, are the particular characteristics of France; of its civilization; and these qualities render it eminently qualified to march at the head of European civilization."

A complacency of this description is so peculiarly French, that it scarcely needs questioning; and M. Guizot may easily cover his assumptions, with the difficulty of deciding upon the relative meaning of the word which he employs. A definition which shall show what civilization is, or should be, is not easily attainable; and there is a subtlety about one portion of that which he himself gives, which will require other definitions properly to elucidate and explain it. Fortunately for us, and conclusive as a commentary upon the pamphlet under notice, is the final conclusions at which he arrives, in declaring the true signification of the word. When, rejecting the more remote and metaphysical definition, he tells us, that "civilization in its most general idea, is an improved condition of man, *resulting from the establishment of social order, in place of the individual independence and lawlessness of the savage or barbarous life*"* we accept the explanation, and have only to demand its application, under the guidance of all experience since the period when Europe first claimed to have become civilized, to that region which he has just pronounced to be the centre and focus of European civilization. We entreat him, without designing a sarcasm, to read his own complacent estimate of French civilization, as written in the passage already quoted, by the lights of the pamphlet on "Democracy in France." It will, we apprehend, become necessary, in consequence, that he should revise his lectures by his new convictions. His definition is undoubtedly a correct one, and nothing, we are very sure, but that rose-colored medium, through which the philosophers of France, have invariably seemed to behold the country of their admiration, could possibly

* *History of Civilization,* vol. i, p. 18, note.

have seduced a writer so capable of thought, so searching and sagacious, with his own arbitrary standards before his eyes, into the utterance of an eulogium, to which the experience of all ages has shown itself so directly hostile. With the evidence before him of strifes the most barbarous, governments the most unstable, a people the most capricious and sanguinary,—revolutions that are never natural or gradual—never harmless and never beneficial—which advance the country nothing—which leave its institutions no more settled or secure—its repose no more certain—its hopes no more promising—its virtues no higher, and its self-complacency not a whit subdued—and this, through a period of at least one hundred years;—it is truly wonderful that the scales should not have fallen from the eyes of the philosopher, and that his patriotism, purged of all the blinding self-love which might distract and mislead his judgment, should not have become conscious of these mournful truths, in regard to his country, which are apparent to all the rest of the world. Unless we take the pamphlet before us as, in some degree, a recantation—an admission of past mistakes, and a first step to the adjustment of new and revised opinions—it will certainly be difficult for us to recognize M. Guizot as an authority in a matter, upon which his previous decisions have been so cruelly biased. But, in truth, this essay must be taken as a recantation,—though it is evident the writer has by no means intended it as such. He is at especial pains to assure us, in his preface, that nothing will be found in his pages "which bear the impress of his personal situation." Certainly, he goes into no detail of facts, no history of the events by which his own career, as Prime Minister of Louis Philippe, was cut short in the overthrow of his principal. But there is evident, throughout the pamphlet, an industrious labor to throw the whole burden of fault upon the people of the country, and wholly to acquit the government. This is evinced by the nature of his argument, by his deductions, and by those suggestions which go to show, in fact, that no government, of whatever sort, could possibly satisfy or suit the French people in their present condition;—that they are delivered over to a chaos of wild passions and false philosophies;—which leave conjecture utterly hopeless and blind as to the result. Were this true, there would be an end to the argument, and we should be forced to assign to Louis Philippe and his ministry, the place of honor during those of all ages, who have vainly striven, at every hazard, to save their people even in their own despite. The opening paragraph of this essay, is meant to embody this suggestion. We give it as a key note to the whole performance.

"Mirabeau, Barnave, Napoleon and Lafayette, who died at distant and very dissimilar periods, in bed or on the scaffold, in their own country or in exile, all died under the influence of one sentiment—a sentiment of profound melancholy. They thought their hopes deceived, their labors abortive. They were assailed by doubts as to the success of their cause, and by misgivings as to the future. King Louis Philippe reigned above seventeen years, for more than eleven of which I had the honor to be his minister. If to-morrow it pleased God to summon us into his presence, should we quit this earth very confident in the future destiny and constitutional order of our country."

The inquiry has a twofold object. It is designed to show that, in spite of the labors of the various great men enumerated in the paragraph, nothing, at the close of their separate lives, had been done, to their satisfaction, for the safety and security of the French people. The next inference is, that, as these great men had all worked as patriots, with a single eye to the real good of the nation, a certain fatal incapacity for liberty, security and peace, among that people, was the true secret of their melancholy and despondency. The experiment would seem to have been fairly tried, according to this paragraph, by a sufficient variety of leaders. And yet, with the exceptions of Napoleon and Louis Philippe, neither of the great leaders above named had any control of the destinies of France, at a period when they might have shaped the regular direction and plan of a government. Their powers were exercised in seasons of revolution, while the storm was actually raging. To weather the tempest was the only object, and, this end gained, the future management of the vessel of state was confided to other hands. But Napoleon, according to M. Guizot, was a despot. What was Louis Philippe, and why do we find them in the same category? Their melancholy and disappointment could not arise from the same causes. They were very different persons—they ruled the country after a very different fashion. Their policy and purposes bore no common features of resemblance. They pursued the ends and objects of government, through very different processes. They were both despots; with this difference, that Napoleon was a despot who contrived to enslave, without degrading his people; while Louis Philippe degraded the people whom he had not the capacity to enslave. The distinction is a wide one, and, we ask, why bring them together in a paragraph, which, if it possesses any significance, at all, is meant only to show that the ruler weeps his disappointment with a clear conscience—and that all the defeat of liberty in France is the result of the popular ignorance, passion and superstition—that, whether ruled by the legitimates of the Hugh Capet family,—by the passionate and wild, but generous, Mirabeau; by the despotic Napoleon, deluding the people into servitude, by amusing their vanities and exercising their passions; by the temperate, and rather cold, republican, Lafayette; or by the selfish and cunning merchant-king, Louis Philippe; they were equally incapable of that training which secures to a people an even progress to law, order, and prosperity? Why, else, should the prevailing sentiment of these rulers, when giving up their authority, have been that of melancholy and distrust? Does this distrust lead them to declare themselves doubtfully of the policy they have pursued—does one of them declare that he erred in his administration, and that he should be able to repair its evils, by avoiding his own errors, were the opportunity allowed him for the experiment. Not so!—He has few misgivings, and still fewer self-reproaches;—and M. Guizot, in bestowing this anecdote upon us, errs only in the assumption that such regrets are peculiar to those who have labored for the French people. The regret is one common to the great men of all ages. We have some remarkable examples, scattered broadcast overall the fields of history. Solomon uttered these regrets; Abderrahman, Hannibal, to say nothing of the abundant examples in Roman and Grecian history. But this despondency is by no means confined to political, it belongs also to literary, history. The despondencies of genius, at the close of its career, are characteristic of all its departments. They all regret that so little has been done, that so much remains undone, of that which they had appointed to do. Ambition thus deplores the field that others must reap; and its desires—the ruling passion strong in death—are mournfully mocked by the consciousness that their day of performance is at an end. They weep not that they have labored in vain, but that they can labor no more. And a something of self-disparagement, for past works, will possess the mind, as it contrasts the vastness of the fields left untilled, with the dimensions of those over which they have already gone. These are only the natural doubts of an earnest nature, no longer deceived by the world's applause,—no longer sustained by self esteem; seeing all things through the clearer medium which belongs to a period when the passions are humbled and subordinate, and naturally disparaging their own labors, since the same agents of flattery are no longer nigh to encourage ambitions and vanities, which are no longer active. But M. Guizot has not yet attained this condition, in which the judgment is purged of the clouds of self-esteem. When he asks if Louis Philippe and himself, quitting the earth at this moment, should feel "very confident in the future destiny and the constitutional order of our country?" he insinuates a something beyond the question. How should we suppose the minister to think himself in error, who shall put this question? Clearly, we are to understand, that a calm survey of his past labors has only satisfied him of their perfect propriety. The error, if there be error, is certainly none of his. Yet Louis Philippe had the difficult instances before him of the leaders of France, throughout the past; and M. Guizot had been a profound student in the histories of their career. Terrible examples, sufficient to teach them both the peculiar character, the proper wants, and the various necessities of the French people, had been given them, at the very moment of their ascent to power. The question is, did you govern according to these wants, these necessities and this peculiar character of your people; or did you govern with regard to your own lusts and appetites[?] In due degree with the know ledge which M. Guizot shows, in his pamphlet, of the character and condition of the people he was called upon to sway, will be his difficulty in answering this question.

"Is then," asks our author—" Is then the French Revolution destined to give birth only to doubt and deception?"—to bury all its triumphs under ruins?"

He answers this question for himself, by representing the issue as doubtful— as depending upon the reconciliation of classes and circumstances, which it is not easy to reconcile anywhere, and particularly in France. France he describes as a chaos, and the rank seed of this chaos, we find in the one word 'Democracy.' Democracy is the great hobgoblin of M. Guizot's imagination. It haunts his sleeping and his waking hours. It is at his side, whether he summons it or no. It is the evil principle, as subtle as active, every where busy, and giving the impulse to all that is evil in the nation. He tell us that the monarchist swears by this principle, defining it under conditions of his own,—that the Republicans yield it faith, also with their own definitions—that the socialists strip it naked, and believe in it only in *puris naturalibus.* In short, that the virtue of the word is such that no party, whatever their real principles, but adopts it as the avowed idol of their worship. None could hope for success without its adoption. It is the word, signifying every thing, in perfect faith in which the great body of the French people have been trained for centuries. It owes its power, according to M. Guizot, because, "it is the bainer [*sic*] of all the social hopes and ambitions of man—pure or impure, noble or base, rational or irrational, possible or chimerical."

It is well for the people of France that they have faith in something. But what lesson is taught to M. Guizot by the experience of ages? That it is through the faith of man alone that he is governed, and not in defiance of that faith. When, therefore, he tells us that this faith in the word or thing, democracy, is the insurmountable difficulty in the moral constitution of the Frenchman,—that this principle is his nature, is suggestive to him of a thousand instincts, at once parallel and contradictory—at once good and bad—upholding an "interminable vista" of "infinite promises"—prompting every propensity, speaking to every passion, whether generous or base, moral or immoral, wild or soft, beneficent or destructive;—when he tells us that this faith is universal throughout France—that all classes, however remote, in rank or residence, alike feel and declare it—that it is no transitory impression, but a vital development of the popular nature; and that, henceforth, it is inevitably destined to be the permanent condition, and to make the permanent law of the nation;—we ask, in the name of common sense and common justice, where was the wisdom, or the policy of outraging this universal conviction? Why was it not recognized as a faith by the government, and adopted by the constitutional monarch? By this process, only, could its excesses have been restrained; in this manner, alone, could its virtues have been brought into activity[,] pruned of their vices, and stripped of all that is delusive and pernicious in their atmosphere and attributes. This is the very office of a Government. In this respect it resembles religion. Vice and virtue are inevitable constituents of humanity. In all societies we find them equally distributed. To take the society as it is, with its peculiar faiths and instincts, and, recognizing both, proceed heedfully to develope the good and rein and subdue the bad, without endangering the whole by rash experiments, which threaten the life of the body politic;—this is the true business of government. Its cues are suggested by the people who are governed,—by their characteristics and necessities, rather than their declared wishes—and this is the true meaning of our principle, which requires the consent of the parties governed to the governing power. The consent is implied by the sympathy which shows itself as it submits quietly to the supreme authority. The government which refuses to recognize these popular elements, this faith, these instincts, refuses, in fact, to recognize the national individuality. Each nation has a nature of its own, adapted to its climate, its history and its mission. The instant and constant recognition of those peculiarities which constitute this individuality, is the great essential in knowing how to govern.

He who, profound in books only, looks to the career of neighboring and rival nations, or to foreign and remote systems, and finds in the fine spun theory of an ancient, the proper laws by which to supply the wants of a present government, will be likely to sink into contempt, and be dismissed from authority by rude and sudden overthrow. Still less is he likely to prevail, who apprehends nothing but danger when he is required to pass beyond the boundaries of routine. All progress implies novelty, and he whose prejudices or thoughts make fears of change terrible, was never designed as a leader of the nations. The vulgar idea of conservatism, is quite as much in proof of gross stupidity as of great cowardice. To be incapable of distinguishing between the permanent dilation and growth of the waters, from an ordinary swell upon the surface—to attempt fruitlessly to arrest the upward tendency of that ocean, whose working has its origin in tumults that pervade its uttermost depths—these are the equal proofs, in the ruling power, of an imbecility, that is equally blind and feeble. The true conservatism never lacks in courage or in foresight. It never hugs its delusions when the great necessity becomes apparent, and never expends its powers in a vain conflict with the billows, over which courage and dexterity will enable it to ride in safety. The feeble ruler, on the contrary, religiously wedded to the habits of a past generation, as if the progress of a race were to be limited to the barriers reached by those who are about to disappear from the ranks, may be likened to the efforts of the tottering old man, who feebly thrusts his gold-headed cane between the wheels of the mighty locomotive, in the absurd idea of arresting its advance. The true governor as Carlyle calls him—the king man—pursues a nobler and manlier method. He leaps into the car, and seizing its guidance, curbs only its eccentricities, and keeps it in the track decreed by its destiny. To oppose the progress, which, when inevitable is always legitimate, is not conservatism, but destructiveness. It is always in proof of a worthless policy in the ruler, which owes its birth to the weakness of the head or the vices of the heart;—the worthlessness of the one, or the gross and shameful selfishness of the other.

It is evident from this pamphlet—unless we are to suppose the most admirable of its ideas the result of overthrow and exile—that M. Guizot was neither blind to the popular appetites and need, nor ignorant of the processes by which they might be pacified, without hurt to the commonwealth. He had felt the advent of the new spirit of progress, and was well aware of the true processes of conservatism. Hear what he says on this subject:

"There is but one means of rendering ourselves equal to this mighty task, and of complying with this imperious necessity. All the elements of stability, all the conservative forces in the country must unite closely and act constantly together It is no more possible to extinguish democracy in the nation than liberty in the government. That immense movement which has been communicated to every country and agitates all their deepest recesses; which is incessantly inciting every class and every individual to think, to desire, to claim, to act, to employ his activity in every direction,—this movement will not be stopped. It is a fact in which we must acquiesce, whether it pleases or displeases us, whether it awakens our fears or excites our hopes. But though we cannot extinguish this movement, we can guide and govern it; and if it is not guided and governed, it will throw back the whole current of civilization, and will be the opprobrium as well as the curse of humanity. Democracy, to be guided and governed, must form a considerable ingredient in the state, but it must not be the sole one: it must be strong enough to climb itself, but never to pull down others; it must find issues, and encounter barriers on every side. Democracy is a fertilizing, but muddy stream, whose waters are never beneficent till the turbid and impetuous current has spread itself abroad and subsided into calmness and purity.

"The Dutch, a great people, though in a small country, whose republican glory shone bright, even amidst the full blaze of the monarchical glory of Louis XIV., conquered their country from the ocean, and maintained their conquest, by cutting canals and raising dikes on every side. It is the ceaseless care of the whole community that the canals be never obstructed and the dikes never broken; for on this depend the prosperity and the existence of Holland.

"Let all the conservative elements of France learn from this example; let them unite all their efforts, let them keep a common and incessant watch, that the rising tide of democracy may always find safe channels and indestructible barriers. On the joint and efficient action of these depend the safety of the community, and the safety of each individual composing it. If the conservative elements of French society know how to combine and to form a united body, if the party spirit which prevails among them shall give way to a large and enlightened political spirit, then France, and the democracy of France, are saved. If the conservative elements remain disunited and disorganized, democracy will destroy France, and will perish under the ruins she has made."

Thinking as wisely at the first as at the eleventh hour—as we are permitted to assume—why was this policy so grossly set at nought in the administration of Louis Philippe? Democracy is the great passion of France. This is admitted by M. Guizot—nay, asserted with the utmost emphasis. At all events, democracy is the great pretext of all parties, and this implies the prevailing instinct among the people. Now, what is democracy? It is the people's government. We are not now to ask whether the French people are fit for self-government. It is enough, that, professing to recognize this fitness, and aware of their assumptions in this respect, the government of Louis Philippe is undertaken. How did he seek to render his government the fair exponent of the great body of the nation—the majority of the several classes, from the highest to the humblest? By what process did he seek to satisfy the popular demand, while promoting the substantial interests of the nation? The two should not be assumed to be incompatible. At all events, if not prepared to think so, and to endeavor honestly to realize the desired object, no party should seek the responsibilities of rule. At least, they must not ascend the seats of power, to assume that the experiment, as between several sorts of government, is still open to them. It is not within the province of governor or minister, taking office under conditions such as is here set down, to pervert these conditions at pleasure, and supersede, with his own notions of what is best for the people, their own favorite convictions. He is the minister of the people's government; let him beware lest he makes it the sovereign's. We may content ourselves with simply asking the question, in what manner M. Guizot, under Louis Philippe, rendered that of France the government of the people? The world is ready with the answer. The career of Louis Philippe, as King of the French, was begun in fraud and continued in selfishness. The best friends of the revolution of 1830, the true representatives of the people, were shuffled off from all connection with the machine of state; they were used for the delusion of the people, and then let down the wind with an easy indifference, which showed the power which they had raised, to be as little sensible of gratitude, as it has shown itself of wisdom. The fate of Lafitte and Lafayette, and their compatriots of 1830, were conclusive of the treatment that republicanism and democracy had reason to expect at the hands of either branch of the Bourbon family. It is no plea in behalf of Louis Philippe, that democracy was not a good, wholesome or proper rule for the nation. The conditions upon which he ascended to power— the necessities of the country—the exactions of the people—all estop the inquiry. Nor will it do for those who have defrauded democracy, to insist upon its dangers or impossibilities. To Louis Philippe, any government would have been ungenial, which should lessen his powers and opportunities for absorption and appropriation. We have no such harsh judgment on M. Guizot. He has erred undoubtedly—erred, while hearing the people, to have submitted to the king; but perhaps, erring quite as much, because of the impossibles of his own theory, as in consequence of a too easy yielding to the desires of his sovereign. He undoubtedly prefers, of all living forms of government, that of a constitutional monarchy, such as Great Britain. He indicates this preference in his pamphlet. He would—but for certain intrinsic difficulties—certain popular disabilities—have labored to achieve a similar experiment in France. Any thing, perhaps, of this sort,—any thing which would have given security—would have been more grateful to the really solid portion of the French people, than the uncurbed tyrannies of Louis Philippe. But M. Guizot is rather better at framing, than at working out his problems. His mind passes from practice too readily to theory, when, with a

Prime Minister, the fact should be exactly the reverse. We do not see that he was even the representative of the French nation;—he was only the Prime Minister of Louis Philippe. Where are the measures of his administration, which are calculated to give effect to such a development of the popular wish and strength, as would have quieted—we do not say satisfied—-the cravings of democracy? Take for example, the creation of the Chamber of Deputies, and the popular basis taken and established for the representation. Discard from consideration the gross population of France, and consider those only who are proprietaries. These are about five millions, speaking in round numbers. Yet the right of representation is conferred upon three hundred thousand only, leaving four millions and a half denied all political privilege. The Chamber of Deputies became creatures of the king, and were indirectly an aristocracy. They constituted a packed jury, employed really to register and sanction the edicts of a despot. Knowing, as he did, the popular passion of France for democracy, how does M. Guizot reconcile with honesty, or good policy even, a proceeding which directly conflicts with their desires, and, as he himself has subsequently shown, their unavoidable necessities. Was it the part of good faith thus to set at nought the very principle upon which the government received its powers? Was it the part, of wisdom to outrage the principles—call them passions if you will—of those who constituted the great mass of the people under government? On what principle would M. Guizot justify this proceeding ? Surely not by any argument which considers the claims of the people; and quite as little by any which regards the permanence and safety of the governing power. The truth is, that Louis Philippe equally mistook his own powers and resources, and the position and character of the people. The significant import of the fortifications thrown around Paris, was well calculated, however, to indicate to the people that the government entertained a consciousness that there was a vital quarrel —an issue of life and death—between them. Whence should this consciousness arise? Why this quarrel? It surely needed no oracle to interpret to a people, so superior in intellect, according to M. Guizot, the meaning of these threatening fortresses—to show them that their constitutional monarch had betrayed his trust, was become a despot, and was seeking to strengthen himself by powers he had usurped, against the people, whom he had robbed and wronged. The idea is supremely amusing of a people's government taking such precautions against the people. How strong the sympathies between the parties; how admirably is the one the representative of the other; and how gratifying is that degree of confidence on both sides, which renders it a paternal necessity to place over each man's-cabin, a battery of paixhans [naval guns] trained for use at any moment.

To one recognizing, as M. Guizot so sensibly does, the universality of the Democratic spirit in France, and the necessity of exercising it without seeking to thwart or overcome it, it is wonderful how he should have been content to lend himself to an administration which felt the necessity of such precautions. There was but one method, acting in good faith to the Revolution of 1830;—to have carried out the democratic principle, or yielded the reins of government to other hands. It is unfortunate that all men have their ambition, no less than their price; and the love of power is scarcely less agreeable to the philosopher than the demagogue. Admitting this infirmity, without embracing it, and recognizing, for the sake of argument, the necessity of clothing Paris in fortifications, there is yet one particular, for which we should be at a loss to find excuse or necessity. It may be permitted to a ruler or a statesman to commit a crime. The stern policy, the firm nerve, the deliberate calculation, the requisite audacity—all serve to impart dignity to an offence, which outrages, with the rights of man, the laws of God and the feelings of humanity. But a mere folly—a blunder—has been in all periods confessedly without excuse in statesmanship. Of this description was that backhanded stroke of policy which denounced with proclamations the great Reform Banquet—denying to the democracy, so repeatedly and wantonly defied, the petty pleasure of bestowing one feed upon its lions! It was in the very drunkenness of heart—in the supremest insolence of power—that this decree was issued by the insane despot. The wisest despotism have been usually at pains to confer gratuities, as often as possible, upon those they swayed. To prevent a proceeding in which discontent would expend itself upon champagne, and the excess of popular irritation would find a safety valve in mere parade and uproar, was a sad folly. The people were unarmed, and their sovereign had sixty thousand bayonets at their breasts. Could any weakness have been greater; any cowardice more conspicuous; any policy better calculated to provoke hostilities? M. Guizot is a great admirer of the British government. What a pity it is that he had not studied as deeply the British policy. Government is one thing; a written constitution is something; but the policy which dictates the one, and knows, properly, how to use the other, is every thing. Compare the course of the British with that of the French government in a proceeding precisely the same. The John Bull Reformers announced a great monster procession of Reformers. The design was precisely that of the French democrats. It was to inspirit their faction; it was to overawe by their numbers; and, possibly, it may have been the wish of many, to have seized the occasion for entente, in order to bring about a bloody revolution. The world abroad, as well as at home, was made to anticipate great things from this monster procession, and apprehensions were aroused, throughout the world, for the safety of the fast-anchored isle. A long notice was given, and the preparations and clamours of the factious and discontented were positively awful. The moment was full of peril. Had the British government felt, or shown, the least fear—had it taken the least false step—the probability is, that a terrible trial of strength would have followed, in which it would be difficult to predict the consequences. Had orders been issued to prevent the Reformers in their promenadings, or purveyings, the whole Island would have been in an uproar. But, just providing such an increase of the constabulary, as should keep order in the metropolis, and the ministry wisely fell back upon the confidence of the people themselves. They had no reason to doubt this confidence; they were conscious of no outrages upon the popular faith. They might not have done all that was required of them; but they had never willfully arrayed themselves against the social and political principles, for the maintenance of which they had been called into existence. This very show of confidence not only showed strength, but acquired it. It appealed to all that was frank and generous in the national heart; and how admirably the appeal was answered. The faction sunk into contempt. It had failed in its great object, to provoke the fear of the government, and the laborious demonstration had no consequences which were not hurtful to itself. But the fretful, fidgetty nature of French politicians, always in the tribune and always in a crisis, was capable of no such coolness and magnanimity. They armed the activity of their enemies by their own feverish anticipations of evil; and in solemnly decreeing that the opposition should not insolently feed its lions, in the sight of the public at all events; they wantonly provoked an unnecessary trial of strength, which the opposition, in the present instance, would have earnestly endeavored to escape. The act was one significant of nothing half so much, as the insolence of power, assured, in the possession of the necessary strength, and not satisfied unless by seizing some early opportunity of making its subjects feel it also.

It will probably be admitted by M. Guizot, now, in his retirement, that, if the necessities of public opinion in France, required the recognition of the democratic principle, the government of Louis Philippe was singularly regardless of this requisition and these necessities. It would be difficult to distinguish a single act of his administration which was honestly meant to subserve a popular want, or strengthen the republican spirit in the land. Certainly, to limit the representative vote in France to 300,000, when the number of proprietaries was nearly five millions, was a curious mode of recognizing a people's government. As little appropriate to this object, seems the policy that employs the public treasure in the erection of batteries about Paris, which should blow its honest democrats into the moon, at any hour of the midnight or the morning; and should employ sixty thousand troops to assist in this pleasant performance. We say nothing now, of the bribes and corruptions of Louis Philippe; the contemptuous insolence with which he spoke of public opinion; and his continued assaults upon the liberty of the press. But the whole history is one, in which, so far from recognizing the democratic tendencies—nay, necessities, of France—the labor seems to have been to distress, decry, annoy, subvert, and utterly trample out the life and spirit of democracy. We are afraid that M. Guizot, himself, has something of this folly to account for. Profoundly taught, as he is, in books, and in a thorough appreciation of the social system, he has not scrupled to suffer his own preferences to exercise a tyranny upon the desires and the demands of others; and he has been too ready to forget France, and her peculiar wants, in a favorite system. And this is an easy error, with a philosopher prone to generalization, and who idealizes systems as the poet idealizes passions and fancies. It is always much more agreeable to a fine mind to seek symmetry and order in schemes of a possible perfection, than in mere adaptations of absolute means to ends really available; and it feels a corresponding reluctance to pass from the empire of fine and sublime ideas to a rude chaos of conflicting desires, imperfect hopes, vain ambitions, and that ceaseless struggle, which is inevitable among mankind, from the irregularities in their minds, their strength, their resources, and the supposed conflict between their several interests. Yet the true labor [is to] sustain these in equilibrium—not to crush, but to uphold them—not to neglect, but to feed them,—not still more to render them unequal, but to balance them happily against each other. Were this not the necessity, there would be no necessity for government. But this is not the condition of the race anywhere, and still less is it the condition of that portion of the human family which calls for rule in France. But of this more hereafter.

M. Guizot is not insensible to what we have insisted on. He is willing to concede the question of a government suited to a people, in disregard of that Procrustes method which would stifle or contract the minds of the people to a preconceived plan of government. Satisfied that democracy is from henceforth destined to be the social state and permanent condition of the French nation, he proceeds to ask, "What is the duty of the government with regard to democracy"[?] The answer to this question occupies his second chapter. But the question really remains unanswered. The writer, as is his wont, generalizes largely and eloquently upon certain premises and assumptions, but there is no specific application of his views to the absolute condition of things before him. Carlyle would say, "be honest, at all events. Do not defraud those who trust you. Do not make government a device to ensnare and betray the ignorant, who confide in your promises; and you will probably have as reasonable a prospect of governing securely, as well." The just duty of government is to the governed. The people are in error, doubtless. They have vague notions of their own endowments and resources, and quite as vague and idle notions of what should be the liberties allowed them. M. Guizot expends much of his thought, in this chapter, upon the various opinions of people and politicians. One class, he tells us, is for the widest liberty, having so much confidence in the race, as to believe that a little government will answer, simply for the suppression of extreme disorder, and the control of brute violence: and there is a certain degree of truth in this opinion. There is such a thing as misgoverning by over-governing. Men are but children of a larger growth. Keep the rod perpetually over the boy—punish all his escapades—those which spring only from exuberance of animal spirits, as well as those which are the result of a will deliberately perverse and vicious—and you only drive him into rebellion. The secret of the best government, is that which reminds the subject of his restraints as little as possible—which never shows its teeth except when absolutely necessary to make them felt.

Others, says M. Guizot, believe that man is naturally a good, and not a vicious animal, and that human inclinations will right themselves, when in excess, if you will only give them time. To check the animal, unnecessarily, is to make him mulish; when left to himself, he will subside into equal and even paces. And there is some truth in this proposition, also. That all is not truth, in either case, lessens not the substantive value, of that portion of each philosophy which is really correct. We may reasonably agree with both; though, when we contend for giving a little swing to the head of the blooded beast, we do not argue for releasing him entirely from the reins. To guide him,—which is to govern him—is not wholly to subdue and break his spirit, or to suffer him to run off with the vehicle. The didactic portions of this chapter, which relate to the conflict perpetually going on in the mind of man, between his rival principles—or rather natures—may all safely be admitted; but we take it that the application of his views to the specific business of government, is the point in which M. Guizot and ourselves would disagree. We are not to suppose that because evil and good are equally at work in the bosom of man, that we are to assail the former with a force that leaves nothing for the latter to do. The government that allows nothing to the better nature of the subject, and undertakes to rule him, as if there were no natural auxiliary force, on its behalf, working in his bosom, exhibits a consciousness of a total want of sympathy with his condition, and a disregard equally entire, of all his sympathies. It is in politics as in medicine. Nature must be suffered to do her part. She struggles against the disease, and the true art, in medicine, is to give her only the requisite assistance for effecting her extrication. The principle holds good in politics. Individuals may be utterly vicious, but the conservative principle is in the race, (or it is doomed, already, as was Nineveh,)—and the government needs only to ally itself to the race, to secure full mastery over the individual. It is the error of government, too frequently,—it was that of Louis Philippe,—to substitute a faction for the family, and mistake a fragment for the whole. The fearful picture which our author gives of the wild violence of the roused and reckless multitude, however forcible, lacks wholly in originality. We do not need, at this time of day, to be told how fearful a thing is civil war, and what a terrible tempest is that in which the billows of the human multitude, roll, raging and roaring, through the avenues of the affrighted city. But to show that the masses are ignorant; that they are to he maddened; that, when maddened, they are terrible and irresistible;—is not to acquit the government of indiscretion, or to show that the masses are to blame for the outbreak. It is in great measure because man is ignorant, that he has fearful passions; and that, when awakened, they are unmanageable; that renders government necessary. Were he otherwise, there would be no want of King Philippe, or Minister Guizot—we should need no civil establishment—we should environ Paris with no fortifications.

The wild horse has a fearful power when you goad him to desperation; but is he the less noble and valuable, because of his power and his passions? Are not these necessary to his virtues and his strength; and shall we, who have been wantonly provoking these passions, and stinging the noble beast into the furious exercise of his powers, complain of them when he breaks away from our restraint, and threatens the destruction of the vehicle in which we ride? When M. Guizot dwells thus complacently upon the excesses of the multitude, does he expect us to forbear the question as to the excesses of the government? "Shall the people," said Robespierre, with a fearful significance, "who have been crushed and trampled for centuries, be denied the vengeance of a single day?" Wrong naturally brings its penalties, and the wrong-doer, who has given the provocation to society, should be the last person to complain that vengeance runs into excess. You goad a people into phrenzy, and it is not for you to prescribe when their redress is adequate. The passions which are roused for punishment, rarely carry in their hands the scales which balance claims exactly with the offender. Nay, it is a part of the decree, that the punishment, duly apportioned to an offence so enormous as the tyranny over a race, should not only punish but terrify. The example must be one that is not easily to be forgotten. Such, at least, has always been the history in all ages.

In the passage which follows, will be found much or most of the substance of M. Guizot's answer to the question—'what is the duty of government in respect to Democracy.' There is no portion of the extract to which we can take exception. It is full of truth, and eloquently stated, and embodies a warning voice, almost as necessary to our people as to those of France. It illustrates the vital defect in the democratic principle, when reduced to practice, and shows impressively not only the greatest vice in democratic societies, but the greatest danger to their security.

"Resistance not only to evil, but to the principle of evil; not only to disorder, but to the passions and the ideas which engender disorder—this is the paramount and peremptory duty of every government. And the greater the empire of Democracy, the more important is it that government should hold fast to its true character, and act its true part in the struggle which agitates society. Why is it that so many democracies—some of them very brilliant—have so rapidly perished? Because they would not suffer their governments to do their duty, and fulfill the object for which governments are instituted. They did more than reduce them to weakness; they condemned them to falsehood. It is the melancholy condition of democratic governments, that while charged—as they must be—with the repression of disorder, they are required to be complaisant and indulgent to the causes of disorder; they are expected to arrest the evil when it breaks out, and yet they are asked to foster it whilst it is hatching. I know no more deplorable spectacle than a power which, in the struggle between the good and the evil principle, continually bends the knee before the bad, and then attempts to resume an attitude of vigor and independence when it becomes necessary to resist its excesses. If you will not have excesses, you must repress them in their origin. If you wish for liberty—for the full and glorious development of human nature—learn first on what conditions this is attainable; look forward to its consequences. Do not blind yourselves to the perils and the combats it will occasion. And when these combats and these perils arise, do not require your leaders to be hypocritical or weak in their dealing with the enemy. Do not force upon them the worship of idols, even were you yourselves those idols. Permit them, nay command them, to worship and to serve the true God alone."

This whole passage is pregnant with meaning. It is one that might be amplified into volumes. But the reader must do this for himself. We must content ourselves with suggesting the clues which he may follow at his leisure. Still, the question remains unanswered. All this is vague. Governments do not undertake to teach their people words, or thoughts, or systems. They may contribute largely to these objects, but they must work indirectly to do so. The only true object of government is to protect the individual man from his fellow, and the family against nations from without—to see that no citizen suffers wrong, which it is in the power of the race, to prevent or repair; and that each is permitted to pursue his individual vocation,—for his own good, and unmolested—so long as his pursuit offers no molestation to others. Government, with even less powers in some respects, takes the place of the patriarch. M. Guizot's answer to his own question is one that meets none of its requisitions. It could scarcely have been otherwise, indeed, unless he had gone into a detailed history of the administration of Louis Philippe—which we are sorry he has not done—and applied his principles to his facts, and to the policy which has been overthrown. We may be willing to admit all his generalities, and yet doubt if these were allowed to operate during the administration of the government, which they are now indirectly offered to justify. "Democratic France," says M. Guizot, "owes much to the Emperor Napoleon." He gave her civil order, strongly constituted, and a firmly based national Independence. "But had she ever a government which treated her with greater severity, or showed less complaisance for the favorite passions of Democracy."—As to the political constitution of the state, Napoleon's only care was to raise power from the abasement into which it had fallen, to restore it to all the conditions of force and greatness. In this he saw a national interest paramount to all others, whether the nation "were governed democratically or otherwise." "But Napoleon was a despot." . . . "It may be asked, however, whether he could have been otherwise? Whether he could have tolerated political liberty, and whether we were then in a state to receive it." . . . "There are men, and very great men, who are suited to certain diseased and transitory crises, and not to the sane and permanent state of society. Napoleon was, perhaps, one of these men. . . . He re-established order and authority in the midst of Democratic France. He believed, *and he proved, that it was possible to serve and to govern a democratic society without humoring all its inclinations.*"

There is an occult purpose in the remark which we have here italicized. All this is designed to be an apology for the administration of Louis Philippe. We are to understand that the entire misfortunes of the ex-King of the French, are to be traced to his stubborn sense of propriety, which would not suffer him to minister to merely vulgar and insolent pretensions. It is this one feature, in this pamphlet, which every where pervades it, working silently and unostentatiously upon the mind of the reader, in regard to M. Guizot's own personal interest in the question. It is in these adroit suggestions that we are to discover the justifications of the Prime Minister. But the very fact that Napoleon did not minister to the vulgar idols, and yet succeeded in serving and governing a democratic society, must be admitted to make something against the wisdom of the government of Louis Philippe. How should the latter fail with the successful example of the former in his eyes? The disadvantages were all with Napoleon;—with Europe ar[rayed] against him—a royal party strong and restless within his kingdom—he, draining the nation of its youth in foreign warfare—lavishing their wealth and treasure in a conflict that promised to be perpetual—how various must have been his arts—how heavy the burden of his toils—what anxiety must have weighed upon his eyelids—what perils hung about his footsteps! How few in comparison were those of Louis Philippe. Raised by the people to the throne—with his world at peace about him—Europe content to look on, and suffer him to pursue in calm the experiment of a new government—in possession of unbounded treasure, with nothing to embitter his thoughts, or embarrass his purposes;—he had only to study the character of his people, the resources and necessities of his kingdom, and adapt himself and his government to the requisitions of the two. They were easily reconcilable; and had he been honest—had he not forgotten the kingdom in the throne—his people in his children—his country in himself;—in all probability, his career, if less glorious than that of Napoleon, would have been marked by none of his reverses, and would have left such monuments behind it, of great utility and permanence, as would have entitled him to distinctions quite as lofty as those which grace the memory of the mighty Corsican! But the King of the French was not the king man! This was the secret of his failure in comparison with Napoleon. He reasoned for his people from himself. Napoleon reasoned for himself from his people. He framed his policy in obedience to no theories, and adapted himself really to the genius and the desires of the French people. He appealed to their passions rather than their principles;—their love of glory, their vanity, their pride, their jealous sense of national position, their eager impetuosity of character, their restlessness and their enthusiasm. He gave them a leader as well as a ruler, and this important gift supplied many deficiencies. He exercised their endowments, in employment no less grateful to their impulses than honorable to their fame, and made himself the necessity of their pride, as well as the founder of their republic. Nothing of this was in the power of either Louis Philippe or his ministers. The former lacked enthusiasm, and this failed to represent truly the temper of his people;—he was cold and selfish, and this offended their securities. His ministry, however capable, seem to have been better versed in the theories of government than their proper adaptation to the people; and were, we are afraid, too faithful to the sovereign to have always been considerate of the subject. Democracy, as a thing per se, as read in M. Guizot's books, is an inflexible something which would never have troubled the attention of Napoleon; but we fancy that he could have schooled M. Guizot, in a single lesson, more deeply in the true nature of French democracy, than could all the writings of a thousand years. It is too commonly the error of men of letters, when they become politicians, that they apply arbitrarily their definitions of the schools to the things which seem to correspond with them in their own periods;—disregarding the inevitable changes of phase, which must occur in the natural progress of events and civilization; and never making the least allowance for those peculiarities, in the genius of a people, which must always modify the character of institutions derived from other races and past periods. When M. Guizot tells us that "Democratic societies enjoy no privilege which renders the spirit of government less necessary in them than in others;" he utters what, in this country, would be regarded as a truism. The very fact that recognizes the necessity of a government, proves that society is perfectly sensible that it enjoys no immunities from Providence which renders its vital conditions more secure than those of other communities'. But we contend that the struggle between the contrary impulses of man goes on as constantly under all other forms of government as in that of the Democratic, and that the possessor of power, is, in all, "continually called upon to decide between the contrary impulses by which he is solicited to make himself the artisan of good or the accomplice of evil." But we are not called upon here to decide between the virtues of differing institutions, their requisitions or peculiar disabilities.

We quote the passage, in which M. Guizot, in some degree, contrasts Napoleon with Washington. We owe to M. Guizot, on a previous occasion, a glowing and correct analysis of the character of Washington. What he now says, is no less grateful to our pride. We cannot, however, but protest against the assumptions into which European writers so commonly fall, when they speak of the power of Washington, as having been such as could have enabled him to do as he pleased with the American people;—which assumes, not only that he established our independence, but that it was in his option to have built his throne upon its ruins. This is all preposterous. The notion betrays a gross ignorance of the character of the American people, their intelligence, and the consciousness which they never suffered themselves to lose for a moment, of the long and arduous struggle of their forefathers for constitutional liberty. To Washington, the American people owe an immense deal,—far more, certainly, than to any other one man of the revolution. His virtue, prudence, courage, unbending will, patient endurance, the modesty of his ambition, and the admirable subjection in which all his passions were held, enabled him to give direction in a greater variety of departments—to sway the greater variety of character, and to mould more generally the impulses of the country,—than was the case with any other of our public men. He *contributed greatly* to found the political liberty, and national independence of his country. The words "supreme power," are misplaced in the quoted passage. Washington was never without a powerful opposition during his whole career. An opposition, which, even before his administration was at an end, had begun to show decided promise of rising to that ascendant which it now most certainly enjoys. But this is digression. To the rest of the quotation we offer no dissent:

"Washington has no resemblance to Napoleon. He was not a despot. He founded the political liberty, at the same time as the national independence, of his country. He used war only as a means to peace. Raised to the supreme power without ambition, he descended from it without regret, as soon as the safety of his country permitted. He is the model for all democratic chiefs. Now you have only to examine his life, his soul, his thoughts, his words; you will not find a single mark of condescension, a single moment of indulgence, for the favorite ideas of democracy. He constantly struggled—struggled even to weariness and to sadness—against its exactions. No man was ever more profoundly imbued with the spirit of government, or with respect for authority. He never exceeded the rights of power, according to the laws of his country: but he confirmed and maintained them, in principle as well as in practice, as firmly, as loftily, as he could have done in an old monarchical or aristocratical state. He was one of those who knew that it is no more possible to govern from below in a republic than in a monarchy—in a democratic than in an aristocratic state of society."

Speaking of the democratic republic, which he does respectfully, though without sympathy, M. Guizot proceeds to consider the want which is most imperious in France. This want substantially is "peace." He describes the woful [*sic*] condition of parties in that country. The evil is an old one. It is the history of an old social struggle, not for peace, for order, for government, for equal rights or fraternity—these are all masks and lies—but for ascendancy. The strife between nobility and commonalty, masters and workmen, the owner of property, and he who has none—all of whom, under different specious names and sanctions, are aiming only at positions inconsistent with the rights of their neighbors. The words democratic republic, unity, fraternity—with all these does M. Guizot quarrel, as so many watchwords of civil war. The revival of these cries now, he conceives to be one of the most evil signs in the present government of that country. The democratic republic, he doubts, will hardly give the nation peace. "It did not begin well"—beginning with civil war. That it should be so ardent in insisting upon being officially called democratic, fills him with anxiety. We quote a passage here, as it concerns us, and embodies a fact in our history, upon which, neither our historians nor statesmen have been sufficiently found to dwell. We italicize the portion to which we allude.

"The United States of America are universally admitted to be the model of a Republic and a Democracy. Did it ever enter the head of the American people to call the United States a Democratic Republic?

"No; nor is this astonishing. In that country there was no struggle between aristocracy and democracy; between an ancient aristocratical society and a new democratical society: on the contrary, the leaders of society in the United States, the descendants of the first colonists, the majority of the principal planters in the country and the principal merchants in the towns, who constituted the natural aristocracy of the country, placed themselves at the head of the revolution and the republic. The devotion, energy, and constancy which they showed in the cause, were greater than those displayed by the people. The conquest of their independence, and the foundation of the republic, was not, then, the work and the victory of certain classes over certain other classes; it was the joint work of all, *led by the highest, the wealthiest, and the most enlightened, who had often great difficulty in rallying the spirit and sustaining the courage of the mass of the population.*

"Whenever officers were to be chosen for the bodies of troops formed in the several States, Washington gave this advice: — *'Take none but gentlemen: they are the most trustworthy, as well as the ablest.'*"

M. Guizot apprehends from the democratic republic nothing but a social war. The names it assumes, and the principles it upholds, tend to increase his anxiety. These seem to lead directly to revolutionary despotism. He finds in it "no distinct powers, possessed of sufficient inherent strength to exercise a reciprocal control; no solid ramparts, under the shelter of which, various rights and interests can take root and flourish in safety; no organization of guaranties; no balance of powers in the centre of the state, and at the head of government;— nothing but a single motive force and various wheels; a master and his agents; nothing but the personal liberty of the citizens and the bare will of the numerical majority: the principle of despotism, checked by the right of insurrection."

Neither peace nor liberty, he asseverates, can result from such a condition. Yet, he says, if time be allowed to it, it will restore social peace. It is in no danger of being precipitated into error and rashness by external causes. Europe offers no obstacles to the experiment. It is from within, then, that all the danger is to arise; and this will depend wholly on the character of that people, and their preparedness for self-government, whom M. Guizot, at a happier period, described as being at the very head of European civilization;—civilization signifying, in his own definition, the highest capacities for social order, government and self-subjection. For the success or failure of the experiment, he turns to the "social republic." This is the system of the communists, the progress party of France. He adopts, as the exponent of the system, one M. Proudhom, whom he considers to possess the clearest understanding of the theory he seeks, and the object which he aims at. We give the summary of M. Guizot, without abridgment, desirous that the scheme of the socialists should be fully presented, in all its horrible nakedness, to our readers. We need some counselling [*sic*] on this and kindred topics; for communism has its temptations in our country also.

"All men," according to M. Proudhom, "have a right—and the same right—to happiness. Happiness is the enjoyment (without any limit but that prescribed by the want and the faculty of enjoying) of all the good things existing or possible in this world; whether natural or primitive, or progressively created by the intelligence and the labor of man.

"Certain men, certain families, or certain classes have acquired the exclusive enjoyment of some (indeed the greater part) of the most essential and productive of these good things; or, in other words, these things, or the means of procuring them, are become the special and perpetual property of certain men, families, and classes.

"Such a confiscation of a part of the fund common to mankind, for the advantage of a few, is essentially contrary to justice; contrary to the rights of the men of the same generation, who ought all to enjoy it equally; and contrary to the rights of successive generations, each of which, on its entrance into life, ought to find the good things of life equally accessible, and to enjoy them in its turn like its predecessors.

"Therefore all special and perpetual appropriation of the good things which confer happiness, and of the means of procuring those good things, must be abolished, in order to insure the universal enjoyment and the equal distribution of them amongst all men, and all successive generations of men.

"But how is it possible to abolish property? or, at least, so to transform it, that, as regards its social and permanent effects, it may be as if it were abolished?

"Here the leaders of the Social Republic differ greatly among themselves. Some recommend slow and gentle measures; others urge prompt and decisive ones. Some have recourse to political means—for example, a certain organization of existence and labor in common; others try to invent economical and financial expedients—for example, a series of measures designed to destroy the net revenue of property, whether in land or capital, and thus to render property itself useless and illusory. But all these schemes originate in the same design and tend to the same result; the abolition or the nullification of personal, domestic, and hereditary property; and of all institutions, social or political, which are based upon personal, domestic, and hereditary property."

For the admirable reply of M. Guizot, to all this false philosophy, so equally significant of the stye and the brothel, we must refer the reader to his own pages. We can venture to offer no argument of our own after his—nor is this necessary—and dare not attempt to abridge his pages, at the probable sacrifice of some portion of their eloquence. It is from this shocking system, that M. Guizot fears equally for society and government in France. Such a system, as he shows, is equally destructive of all things which are essential to man, whether as an individual or the member of a race whose duration is destined for continuance through countless cycles of time. The social republic, he describes, as being strong in France. How, he asks, could it be otherwise—appealing to all the desires and passions of the heart, and finding for them names, such as truth and justice, which makes lust and violence boldly challenge all indulgence as a right. "But," he adds with a mournful emphasis, "we have no right to complain. It is we ourselves who incessantly add fuel to the fire,—and this is the most deep-seated of our maladies. It is we who give to the social republic all its strength." And, in explaining himself, the Ex-Minister amply shows that the names are nothing which are so freely used in France; and, being nothing, have been used by those, who, appealing to bad passions under a disguise, for selfish purposes,—have no right to complain that the people themselves have assumed the mask for their own.

"It is the chaos of our political ideas and our political morality—that chaos disguised sometimes under the word *democracy* sometimes under that of equality, sometimes under that of *people*—which opens all the gates, and throws down all the ramparts of society before it. We say that democracy is everything. The men of the social republic reply, 'democracy is ourselves.' We proclaim, in language of infinite confusion, the absolute equality of rights and the sovereign right of numbers. The men of the social republic come forward and say, 'Count our numbers.' The perpetual confusion of the true and the false, the good and the bad, the possible and the chimerical, which prevails in our own policy, our own language, our own acts—this it is which has enfeebled our arm for defence [*sic*], and given to the social republic a confidence, an arrogance, and an influence for attack, which of itself it would never possess."

An inquiry into the real and essential elements of society in France, is a first most necessary process towards the establishment of a government. The chapter which M. Guizot devotes to this inquiry, is full of interest and eloquence. He enumerates the various constituent elements of strength, character and society, such as form the basis in all other countries. "The essential and characteristic fact in French society, is *unity* of laws and equality of rights. All families, property of every kind, labor of every description, are governed by the same laws, and possess or confer the same civil rights." But the diversities of position, founded on property, are necessarily "enough to occasion a radical difference and inequality of social position." The same fact accompanies the degrees and conditions of labor. So, also, of the degrees of success among professional laborers and tradesmen. In brief, throughout the whole circle of civil society in France as elsewhere, "diversity and inequality of situation arise and co-exist with unity of laws and equality of rights." M. Guizot considers this inevitable history at some length. The subject needs no examination here. But the discussion enables us to extract two passages, relating to land and labor, which, though containing little or nothing that is new, are so admirably expressed as to seem so.

"Movable property, or capital, may procure a man all the advantages of wealth; but property in land gives him much more than this. It gives him a place in the domain of the world—it unites his life to the life which animates all creation. Money is an instrument by which man can procure the satisfaction of his wants and his desires. Landed property is the establishment of man as sovereign in the midst of nature. It satisfies not only his wants and his desires, but tastes deeply implanted in his nature. For his family, it creates that domestic country called home, with all the living sympathies and all the future hopes and projects which people it. And whilst property in land is more consonant than any other to the nature of man, it also affords a field of activity the most favorable to his moral development, the most suited to inspire a just sentiment of his nature and his powers. In almost all the other trades or professions, whether commercial or scientific, success appears to depend solely on himself—on his talents, address, prudence, and vigilance. In agricultural life, man is constantly in the presence of God, and of his power. Activity, talents, prudence and vigilance, are as necessary here as elsewhere to the success of his labors, but they are evidently no less insufficient than they are necessary. It is God who rules the seasons and the temperature, the sun and the rain, and all those phenomena of nature which determine the success or the failure of the labors of man on the soil which he cultivates. There is no pride which can resist this dependence, no address which can escape it. Nor is it only a sentiment of humility as to his power over his own destiny which is thus inculcated upon man; he learns also tranquillity [*sic*] and patience. He cannot flatter himself that the most ingenious inventions or the most restless activity will insure his success; when he has done all that depends upon him for the cultivation and the fertilization of the soil, he must wait with resignation. The more profoundly we examine the situation in which man is placed by the possession and cultivation of the soil, the more do we discover how rich it is in salutary lessons to his reason, and benign influences on his character. Men do not analyze these facts, but they have an instinctive sentiment of them, which powerfully contributes to that peculiar respect in which they hold property in land, and to the preponderance which that kind of property enjoys over every other. This preponderance is a natural, legitimate, and salutary fact, which, especially in a great country, society at large has a strong interest in recognizing and respecting.

"What I have just shown with relation to property, is equally true with relation to labor. It is the glory of modern civilization to have understood and proclaimed the moral value and the social importance of labor; to have raised it to the estimation and the rank which justly belong to it. If 1 had to point out the most profound evil, the most fatal vice, of the state of things which prevailed in France up to the sixteenth century, I should say, without hesitation, the contempt in which labor was held. Contempt of labor and pride in idleness are certain signs either that society is under the dominion of brute force, or that it is verging to its decline. Labor is the law which God has enjoined on man. It is by labor that he developes and improves every thing around him—by labor that he developes and improves his own nature. Labor is become the surest pledge of peace between nations. The respect and the liberty enjoyed by labor tend more than any thing to calm the anxieties which we might otherwise too justly feel, and to raise our hopes for the prospects of the human race. By what fatality, then, has it happened that the word labor, so honorable to modern civilization, is become a war-cry and a source of disasters in France? It is because that word is made a cloak for a great and pernicious lie. It is not labor, its interests or its rights, which are the object of the ferment excited in its name; the war which has been declared on the plea of protecting labor, is not in fact waged in its behalf, nor, if successful, would redound to its advantage. It is, on the contrary, directed against labor, whose ruin and degradation would be its infallible result

"Labor, like family, property, and every thing else in this world, is subject to natural and general laws; among which are, diversity and inequality of the kinds and results of labor, and of the stations of those by whom it is performed. Intellectual labor is superior to manual. Descartes, who enlightened France, and Colbert, who laid the foundations of her prosperity, performed a labor superior to that of the workman who prints the works of Descartes, or who helps to produce the manufactures fostered by Colbert; and among these very workmen, those who are intelligent, moral, and industrious, justly attain to a situation superior to that which the same description of labor can secure to the dull, the lazy, or the licentious. The variety of tasks and avocations allotted to man is infinite. Labor is every where—in the house of a father of a family, who educates his children and superintends his affairs; in the cabinet of a statesman, who takes part in the government of his country; in that of the magistrate who administers its laws; of the philosopher who instructs, and of the poet who charms it; in the fields, on the ocean, on the highways, in the manufactories and the workshops; and in every situation, in every variety of labor, in every class of laborers, diversity and inequality arise and subsist; inequality of intellectual power, of moral merit, of social importance, of material wealth. These are the natural, primitive, universal laws of labor, originating in the nature and condition of man, or, to speak more properly, ordained by the wisdom of God. It is against these laws that the war of which we are witnesses is waged; it is this hierarchy of labor, founded on the decrees of God and the free actions of man, which it is the object of this war to abolish; and to substitute—what?— the degradation and the ruin of labor, by the reduction of all labor and all laborers to the same level! Examine the meaning which is usually affixed to the word labor in the language of these enemies of social order. They do not distinctly say that material and manual work are the only real work; indeed they occasionally affect great respect for purely intellectual labor: but they omit to mention the various sorts of higher labors which are performed on every stage of the social scale; their whole attention is absorbed by material labor, which they constantly represent as the kind of labor whose importance throws every other into the shade. In short, they talk in a manner to excite and keep alive in the minds of the men employed in physical labor, the opinion that theirs only has a claim to the name and the rights of labor. Even when speaking not of labor, but of laborers, they hold the same leveling [*sic*] and depreciating language; ascribing the rights of labor to workmen, as such, independently of all degrees of personal merit. Thus the coarsest and most ordinary labor is assumed as the standard to which all the higher degrees are adjusted; and diversity and inequality are abolished, for the supposed advantage of that which is the least and the lowest in the scale!

"Do those who hold such language serve—do they even understand—the cause which they affect to advocate? Is it by such means that we can advance, or even barely keep our ground, on that glorious path of civilization in which labor acquired its proper rank and dignity? Do we not, on the contrary, mutilate, degrade, and disgrace labor, when we strip it of a part of its noblest claims, and substitute in their stead pretensions which are not only absurd and preposterous, but mean, in spite of their insolence? Lastly, does not such language show a gross misconception and violent perversion of the natural facts on which civil society in France is founded? This, though admitting unity of laws and equality of rights, assuredly never pretended to abolish that variety of faculties, merits, and destinies, which is one of the mysterious laws of God, and the inevitable result of the free will of man."

This is all very true and very eloquently said. The generalization of facts is perfect, and the wonder is, that with so just a consideration of the claims of all parties, and the elementary interests of society, in speculation, the practical application to them of the government of Louis Philippe should have been, or seemed, so partial and unequal in the eyes of the French people. The charge against the government of the late King of the French, represents him as concentrating the regards and favors of the national authority, only upon a small portion of these several integrals. The political power was confided, nominally, to some three hundred thousand electors—these were said to be subsidized in great part by the king, and were overawed by a greater number of his placemen and dependants. Writing in 1831, Dumas says:

"We have seen the monarchy descending to our own time, leaning, by turns, on the twelve grand vassals of Hugh Capet, the two hundred great lords of Francis I., and the fifty thousand aristocrats of Louis XV. She now 'makes a halt before us, sustained by the one hundred and sixty thousand great proprietaries and working men, of whom Louis Philippe is the representative. Let us see whether this aristocratic representation will suffice for France, and whether the whole population will be contented with it. We do not believe they will. The number of proprietaries actually existing in France, amounts, according to the highest estimates, to five millions; and, according to the more moderate estimates, to four millions and a half Among these four and a half millions of proprietaries, the copy holders, at two hundred francs and upwards, form a total of 113,000; the patentees of the great cities, such as Paris, Lyons, Bordeax, Marseilles, Nantez, Rouen, &c. complete the number of 160,000 electors—the total amount for 1830. The manufacturing interest is therefore joined to the landed interest, in the proportion of *one to four*. Deduct this 113,000 from the total of 4,500,000, and we have 4,387.000 proprietaries cut off from the right of representation in this chamber. Nevertheless, these political *parias* pay a little more than two-thirds of the national taxes, while the 113,000 electors pay something less than one-third. Let us now take from this 113,000, those who are eligible to re-election; and we have 14,000 copyholders at 500 francs each, and 99,000 at 200 francs. Consequently, but 14,000 individuals are entitled to take an active part in the government; the remaining 99,000 take only a factitious part therein, by voting for men who do not even represent them, since the parties eligible are their superiors in rights and in fortune. Now, among these 14,000 aristocrats of property, who are qualified to become deputies—and therefore ministers, peers, counsellors of state, receivers general and prefects;—and indeed, any thing at will —of which the rest are incapable and unworthy—nearly seven thousand, i.e. one half, are embarrassed with ruinous mortgages, and look to their official position to repair, by the ministerial sale of their votes, their dilapidated fortunes. Thus, the government of Louis Philippe is in reality a representation of the interests of only 14,000 persons—although, at first sight, it appears to rest upon 160,000 electors; and although, its advocates have the hardihood to aver that its basis is the whole proprietary interest of four and a half millions of men."

The change from 1831—a period of administration for which M. Guizot was not, we believe, responsible, and when Louis Philippe was fresh in power—showed a large increase of this nominal total of electors. The year 1848 found this body to number 300,000, instead of 160,000; but the principle of things remained unaltered. It still failed to represent the majority of people, and the majority of interests in France. It was still nothing but the creation of the King, as described by Dumas, half of the members being corrupted and bought, and mere pensioners at the will of the sovereign. Of the residue it would be difficult to say how many could honestly insist upon their independence, and quite as impossible to determine the value of the virtue when notoriously in their possession. How far M. Guizot may have given his sanction to the policy of Louis Philippe, which made the stability of his throne to rest upon the venality of the Legislature, we cannot pretend to say; it is enough for us, that we are at liberty to apply the beautiful and eloquent—and no less true—speculations of M. Guizot,—upon the equal claims of the several interests of parties in France,—to the policy of that administration which was so bountiful and so impartial in their recognition. The question is really one of fact, rather than opinion. The King of the French is the representative of the French people at large—the tendencies of the people are either republican or democratic—they are certainly, the

great body, hostile to monarchy—and the great majority are as certainly democratic in their desires and opinions. That both should have joined for his overthrow, proves that he satisfied neither; yet the bourgeoise, or middle classes,
upon which M. Guizot pronounces so warm an eulogy, were more certainly
republican than monarchical. With them, as represented by Lafayette and others,
a constitutional monarchy implied nothing less than a republic. Its forms were
only not borrowed from the American, for the single and sufficient reason that
it was generally supposed that the popular mind was not prepared for a system
so simple, and which yet required so much previous and gradual training for its
first inception among the people. In other words, the doubt with Lafayette as
well as M. Guizot, was not that the people desired a republic, but that they had
not yet made that progress in the management of their own affairs, which had
accrued to the Americans, necessarily, from the fact that they founded their own
society, at the beginning, when in full possession of the civilization of Europe,
yet free from its vicissitudes and struggles. Something too, of the forbearance
of the popular leaders in 1830, to attempt all that the people desired, may be
ascribed to a wholesome dread of the hostility of the neighboring states of Europe, whose apprehensions they did not desire to provoke. It was, perhaps, well
to conciliate despotism, by preserving a certain portion of its forms; and this,
we take it, constituted the real object of the French, when, in the overthrow of
Charles the Tenth, they adopted a constitutional monarchy. A constitutional
monarchy implied nothing adverse to republicanism in France—nothing at variance with the rights of all citizens, of whatever party; and, it is very certain that
Louis Philippe's government left all the parties dissatisfied, which had raised
him to the chief place in the state. Within a year the overthrow of his dominion
was predicted. Dumas writes—"The present government will fall without any
concussion. It will fall, because it represents and is sustained only by the aristocracy of wealth—which aristocracy is every day weakening itself by partition,
and must soon give way beneath the cumbrous and worthless superstructure."
The prediction may be said to have been accomplished, in some degree, by the
overthrow of the ministry of M. Mole, in which there was agitation enough,
but no concussion. The final overthrow of Louis Philippe was not without its
concussion; and yet, when we contrast the preparation and the power of the Ex-
King, with the small degree of tenacity with which he sought to maintain them,
concussion seems a word of really too much emphasis for the occasion. Never
did a vicious administration offer a more feeble conflict in its dying struggles.
One of the most important of the chapters in the essay before us, is that which
is devoted to the political conditions on which social peace may be restored to
Prance. This is to result from a general conviction of the several parties, that they
are all of them natural elements of society, and are to live together and unite for
the common objects, without arraying themselves perpetually for the overthrow
of one another, as if there could be no life for either, but in the annihilation of

its fellow. They must be taught, that if war is their element, they must war upon the Turks, the Mexicans, the Algerians, the Colombians. They must only forbear one another. In good nursery morality, they must learn, that

> "Their little hands were never made
> To tear each other's eves."

In brief, France must learn that if it desires peace, its people must keep peaceable. They must forego that right, so peculiarly an element of Gallic democracy, the right of insurrection. A not very profound counsel, we should think, but one that M. Guizot labors with much solemnity to inculcate. Their parties, if they cannot coalesce, must not quarrel. Their policy and ambition, henceforth, must not be to extinguish the life in one another, as if their own existence depended on the extinction of a rival. Every pretension of this kind, says M. Guizot, must be withdrawn, not by one only, but by all the contending parties. There must be an end of all radical hostility. They must resign themselves to live together, side by side." But how can this first condition of social peace be satisfied? "I reply, by such an organization of that government, as may assign to each its place and functions; may concede something to the wishes, while it imposes limits to the ambition of all." But here occurs one of the difficulties of French politics, arising from one of the vile and specious phrases of demagoguism. How is this recognition of the claims of all parties consistent with the notion, that "national unity involves political unity. There is but one people, and there can be but one power at the head and in the name of this people." This, says M. Guizot very justly, is the principle of despotism, embodied happily in the well-known sentence, *"L'Etat c'est moi!"* Our author argues the question at some length, in general with justice, though we might except to some of his specifications. But such nonsense is really not to be met with argument. The short way of disposing of a popular catch-word, is to couple it with a commentary, the dimensions of which shall be quite as brief and comprehensive. That men should fetter themselves against facts, by favorite phrases, seems, more than any thing beside, to prove the inequality between their endowments and their assumptions. If they prefer to give up their facts for their philosophies, we see not what any government can do for them. They are only comparable to that astronomer, who would not look at the stars whose appearance was adverse to his system. He had rather the stars should perish than his pet conjecture. A dogma which common experience constantly disproves could only survive by being combatted; since it is more easy to make an ingenious argument in defence of a falsehood, than in support of a truth. National unity involves political unity, only in respect to other nations. The business of the government at home, is first, undoubtedly, to consider the people, since it is with them only, that the diversities of interest and employment can arise. But these diversities require the next consideration, since it would be impossible to adopt a policy which should benefit the nation, without first asking what classes would suffer hurt, or receive benefit, from it; and who else could decide upon these influences, but proper representatives from the class affected. We pass over the whole argument of M. Guizot, in relation to the point, regarding the phrase which he labors to refute, as nothing but the specious cry by which the cunning would delude those who are too ignorant, or too indolent to search for themselves. It is one of the many, of which our author complains, as working mischief among the French people. How they should be so successful, with a people at the head of European civilization, we must leave it to M. Guizot to explain. He has properly remarked upon the peculiar training of the Americans—the favoring facts which, in the establishment of their independence, almost inevitably led to a republic. But he has also to recognize a peculiar fitness among the people themselves, in advance of most other nations, for this self-maintenance and government. Something of this is inherited. The cross of the Normans with the Anglo-Saxon race, undoubtedly contributed to the improvement of both the stocks. It tempered the ferocious adventure of the one, by the somewhat phlegmatic, and patient firmness and capacity for endurance of the other. The effects of the amalgamation are perceptible equally in England and America. Without losing a jot of their original strength and courage, their adventure became regulated, and their ambition addressed itself only to objects which were available to the race. Beyond all others, they were both a people who improved by the lessons of experience,—who were the first to perceive their value, and the last to forego their warnings and exhortations. Words may not delude them. They always like to make sure of their foothold, and this is their first object in all experiments. They move step by step. They feel their way, and take care never to hurry so fast, as to leave any posts unconquered in their rear. They fortify themselves at every advance which they make into an enemy's country, and where the French would plant a banner, they plant a hearthstone. Conquest is no less agreeable to them than to their neighbors; but they must first see that it is such a conquest as is worth the making, and that it does not cost them more valuable possessions. Liberty is no less precious to them than to any other people; but it must be liberty of a certain quality; and it is not every catch word of that popular goddess, which will persuade them of her virtues. They seek for the thing and find it, long before they come to give it an imposing name. Never were two people so wonderfully sensitive to the absurd and ridiculous;— hence their reluctance to any degree of enthusiasm, not strictly warranted by the importance of the occasion. They are hence exceedingly cautious. To use the American back woods proverb, "They never halloo till they are out of the woods." They are never to be taken in by flummery; and this is one of the great secrets of the temperate character and certain progress of both families. Having insisted upon the necessity of recognizing politically all the parties by which France is at present distracted—having insisted upon their equal claims to life, and upon their mutual forbearance upon the lives of one another—M. Guizot proceeds to show the conditions of their legal organization. In this, however, being a practical matter, involving the application to use of the previous theory, we find our author as usual somewhat unsatisfactory. He says:

"But to constitute a real and efficient diversity of powers, it is not enough that each should have a distinct place and name in the government; *it is also necessary that all should be strictly organized, all fully competent to fill and to maintain the place they occupy.*"

Surely,—if M. Guizot here speaks of the regular departments through which the heads of the government act, the Chamber of Peers, or Senate,—Chamber of Deputies, and the Ministry or Executive,—to say nothing of the lower administrative functionaries—it is a matter of course that they should work efficiently in the situation which is allotted them for work. In this sense, the closing member of his sentence is singularly inconsequential. If he speaks of parties, which, embodying certain conflicting opinions, act through their separate energies and strength upon the body politic—affecting its adoption of concurrent policies for the nation under the laws—the answer, in this case, is, that these parties may safely be left to themselves. Their organization must be a thing of their own entirely. Either they have a principle of vitality or they have not. The government does nothing more than tolerate their existence, having no reason, if faithful to its duty, to exhibit distrust of any prevailing modes of opinion which seek only to work out their objects through the legitimate organs of government. There is no existing necessity which should make the government lend itself to strengthen either. Were this policy to find sanction, we should find the doors thrown wide to the worst species of corruption:—to a corruption, which, by absorbing a venal party would soon succeed in the subjugation of the people. But there is a vagueness about this portion of M. Guizot's pamphlet,—indeed, in all those portions in which he seems inclined to pass into the practical—which makes it difficult to determine what are his real processes. The sentence which follows, however, may somewhat assist us. It seems designed as explanatory.

"It is the fashion of the day to think that harmony among the powers of the state, and security against their excess, is to be found in their weakness. People are afraid of every kind of authority; and, in order to prevent their destroying each other, or encroaching upon liberty, they ingeniously endeavour to undermine them all in turn."

We fear that M. Guizot, when Prime Minister, afflicted himself quite too much with the conflicting opinions of factious parties. It is the weakness of a government which betrays too much solicitude in respect to the fluctuations of a crude and transient public opinion. The humours of the public mind, when feverish, and capricious, need no such care. Occasional purging, not blood-letting —would be a sufficient remedy. It appears very like trifling on the part of a government to give more than passing heed to these windy distempers of a party or a season. It exhibits the ruler in an attitude by no means of dignity or authority.

All sorts of notions may be expected to prevail in all societies, more or less ridiculous, and more or less unwise. But they are usually harmless, and serve really as the safety valves of the public temper, and acquire permanence and importance only as they are deemed worthy of opposition. A government wisely smiles or winks at these ebullitions, and freely accords to parties the privilege of combating each other, interposing only to see that the people do not suffer in the collision. This is English policy, and the grim lion of Britannia, confident of his strength, suffers all sorts of liberties to be taken with his claws, short of paring them. Grateful for these privileges, his unruly children, are content to forbear those trespasses which might waken up the beast and find him hungry. But the Gallic cock is forever in a splutter. The emblem is certainly a very appropriate one. He is never satisfied unless he is crowing and flapping his wings, and he is the first to grow jealous of his own younger brood, who naturally endeavor to imitate his sonorous articulations. That they should set up a feeble chaunt makes him tremble for his ascendancy, and his whole life and peace are wasted in the futile endeavour to clip their spurs and silence their voices. We certainly mean no irreverence when we employ such a comparison; but the government of Louis Philippe seems unavoidably to force it upon us. We have already illustrated this puerility in the instance of the Grand Reform Banquet. It was either some such outrage upon the popular mood—some such ridiculous endeavour—to close the safety valves of party—or it was an effort, equally pitiful, to conciliate the very passions which the King despised, as in the instance which decreed a triumphal restoration of the bones of Napoleon to the soil of France; a proceeding, by the way, of which all the benefit enures to Louis Napoleon. The people who are denied the public dinner, are not to be satisfied by a tribute to their vanity, particularly when they feel and know that their idol, thus ostentatiously honored, is, in fact, the detestation of the very government which decrees the tribute. Precisely as they discern the motives of the ruler, they will despise the cunning which assails their affections with a bribe; and will equally loathe the tyranny that would blind their eyes, as that which would destroy their liberties. The very solicitude of the government, in both cases, appealing to the humours of the populace, will endow their factions with a strength which they otherwise would not possess; and this strength will naturally be legitimated by that caprice in the authority which pets and conciliates to-day only that it may scourge and tyrannize to-morrow. An habitually stern government is much more easy to be borne than that which constantly fluctuates in its moods; even though some of these moods condescend to the lowest cajoleries, and appeal to the most ravenous passions of the popular appetite. Consistency was one great merit of the domestic rule of Napoleon, which as M. Guizot admits, never showed any "complaisance for the favorite passions of Democracy."

It is not the business of government or minister to consult or conciliate the passing moods or caprices of the people,—even allowing that it is the whole body corporate that speaks, and not some few of its factions. A government is supposed, in its very organization, to have been framed for the general necessities, and after a due consideration of all the essential elements which were to be conserved and provided for. These necessities, clearly considered, and their interests properly adjusted, a ministry is to pursue the even tenor of its way, precisely as the several orbs of a system, each in its place, revolving naturally around the common centre, and contributing in its progress the required amount of light. The atmosphere may be thick, and the storm may prevail, but they are to keep their places, and endeavour still to make their light penetrate the darkness, without afflicting themselves as to its continuance. The minister who does otherwise, and allows himself to be driven from his propriety, by the vapor that rises, or the wind that drives, is himself likely to be too much impregnated with the same atmosphere over which he is appointed to preside. The small factions of society, are but the atmosphere of government; unavoidable from it, and drawn up by its light and heat even as the vapors of the marsh, or valley, by the sun. They will dissipate if the proper light be brought to bear upon them, or in the language and fine fancy of the poet,

> "Become enshrined in upper air,
> And turn to sunbright glories there—."

Become tributary to the governments' stability, even by their opposition, and honor its reputation as did Pitt, Burke, Fox, Sheridan and others, of Great Britain, as much by the audacity which wrestled with it hourly, as by the strength which maintained it. To attempt to hush and silence all discontent—to induce implicit recognition of all the acts of government among a people—to confound opposition with insurrection, and the desire of change with a disposition to run riot over law,—is really the evidence of a despotic will and not of a paternal government.

M. Guizot shows us too frequently that he is scarcely prepared to distinguish between the insubordinates of a faction, and the merely jealous and suspicious. The very activity of his mind has led him to a restless and feverish desire continually to be doing something. Fear always produces this effect. It lacks patience. The physician who does not wait upon his medicine, but who changes the prescription before its effects are seen, will probably destroy his patient. The true first object of a minister is to know the people for whom he works, to ascertain the policy which their condition needs, and to work honestly in obedience to the suggestions of this knowledge. To waste his time upon all the thousand various speculations which occur to presumptuous or idle minds in a great city, is only to divert his thoughts from vital affairs—to distract his judgment, to enfeeble his decision, and finally to lose himself in a wilderness of errors. The petty espionages of Louis Philippe—his tyranny over parties and the press, by which he made himself particularly odious—may all be ascribable to this petty policy, dictated by his selfish apprehensions. It is not necessary to suggest to the reader, that this sentence of M. Guizot, which we have quoted, covers another of those apologetic hints by which we are to account for the downfall of his administration. You are to understand, by indirection, that the determined performance of the duties of the several departments, was the sole secret of the hostility of factions. The erroneous notion among these was that the powers of a state must not be strong, or they would encroach upon liberty. "People are afraid of every kind of authority," therefore, they quarrelled with ours. "They ingeniously endeavour to undermine them all in turn," and hence the melancholy convictions of defeat and disappointment, and doubt with regard to the constitutional order of France, which afflict Louis Philippe and his minister. It is not the vices of our government—not its tyrannies, excesses or exactions—that led to its overthrow. It was only because our governmental departments were "all strongly organized," and "filled with officials, all fully competent to maintain the places which they occupied." Were it not the object of the minister to convey this impression, would he argue gravely the necessity of organizing the several departments of a government judiciously, and having them filled with capable and energetic persons[?] Who, in employing a swordsman, would seek one deficient in his sword arm; or seeking for a danseuse, would procure one who had been denuded of one of her pedal extremities[?] But for the suggestion of a selfish excuse, all this would be only a grave sort of trifling on the part of the minister. He would otherwise have spared us the novel information that teaches that one of the essentials of office is—the capacity to do its duties,—and that a department or an agency which constitutes a balance wheel and weight in the state, should not suffer itself to become despicable by inefficiency or want of talent. Much of the matter of M. Guizot's pamphlet, in this connection, seems idle and irrelevant. To tell us that weak powers are doomed to perish, by extinction or usurpation, is surely gratuitous. To say to conflicting parties in a state, make yourselves strong, or you will perish, is surely to read them an unnecessary lesson. It is no fault of their will, that they are not strong enough to last till doomsday; and this applies to the several interests of a nation—those of land, labor, art, commerce, and manufactures. Shape these interests into branches of government, such as will represent equally the aristocracy and the commonalty, and the question will depend upon the intrinsic strength of their true sources of power. This, however, is always assuming the intelligence of the people, in the first place, and the freedom of the popular mind from all lusts and passions, which are in conflict with virtue and sobriety. A people, whom you have diseased with falsehoods, whom you have maddened with stimuli, have yet to go through the fearful probation, which is to humble them to the becoming convictions—not of what they desire —but of what they need, and what they deserve! The favorite model of a government, which M. Guizot fancies, is that of Great Britain. For the British people, or even the Americans in England, there could possibly be none better. But we may reasonably question the adaptability of the French nation to the system of their island neighbors. Even were we to allow that there is nothing in the temperament of this people, which would conflict with such an adaptation, still, the condition of things in France,—which has been attained by so many outbreaks and revolutions—seems to oppose inseparable barriers to the idea. How is it possible to re-establish in France a Chamber of Peers, and confer upon it authority and character? Will it represent the landed interest of the country, unassociated with large territorial wealth? And of what avail its influence, even if thus accompanied with wealth, if denied succession[?] The larger portion of the dignity and efficiency of the British peerage is due to its being hereditary. This gives it the element of permanency, and a prescriptive influence, which it becomes habitual in the commonalty to recognize. And this, though necessarily in conflict with all the training and prejudices in America, may be admitted as an important element of security and peace, in a monarchy, and among a people like those of Great Britain. But an hereditary peerage is now one of the impossibles in France. What then remains to a peerage, if it is without the power of transmitting its rank, and lacks the large wealth of the landed proprietor, which alone would save it from contempt[?] Wanting in these properties, from what would it derive that degree of strength and influence, adequate to its contemplated uses, as one of the strong, efficient, co-ordinate branches of a government? Nothing external would be left in the possession of such a body. Its possessions would be wholly intrinsic. Its intellectual strength and pure virtues would secure for it respect; and, in a senate like that of the Americans, and similarly constituted, to represent departments, rather than people, the idea of its establishment would be legitimate,—but not as a peerage. This would be preserving an empty pageant, without uses or object, the additional evil of which would be, that it would incur odium, where it could confer no strength. The matter is one of considerable difficulty, but one which must be adjusted, before the first step can be made to engraft upon a nation, like that of France, such a scheme of government as that of Great Britain. But the speculation itself is idle, as the design must prove, in the present condition of the French, or until they have gone through the fearful trials of another reign of terror. The popular mind, if M. Guizot's pamphlet affords a proper diagnosis, is in no state for any calm experiment, of any description. Nor could such an experiment have succeeded at that period, when, according to our author, "an earnest and sincere attempt was made to establish constitutional monarchy in France." They desired, it seems, "an ancient and historical basis for royalty;" yet where was it to be found, unless in families in which weakness and prejudice were equally at work, for the restoration of all the historical pretexts and privileges of despotism—a passion which must inevitably lead to the renewal of the deadly struggle between the people and their hereditary tyrants. The friends of constitutional monarchy desired, "for the Chamber of Peers, an hereditary seat, in the legislature," of a people, taught, for a hundred years, to regard this privilege as one of the most insensate and prejudicial to the interests and integrity of manhood, that ever could be devised by the arts of despotism. How create such a chamber, how sustain it by prescriptive family influence, as in England, by vast wealth, and by a restoration of the laws of primogeniture? Opinion in France had closed the door, forever, against these projects and prospects. The rise and career of Napoleon and his marshals, had established a wall of storm and fire, impossible to pass, which should have hushed such delusions at the first whisper. A Chamber of Peers, without the large influence afforded by the possession of great landed estates, would possess no strength, beyond that afforded by its own virtues and talents; and a senate, such as that of our country, would afford all the advantages arising from such a Chamber, without incurring any odium with the commonalty, and without embarrassing, as a mere dead weight, the action of the other departments, which it could not hope to control. The scheme of these friends of constitutional monarchy in France, whom, we are to suppose, included M. Guizot, did not overlook a Chamber of Deputies, which was to represent the democratic element. These departments, he tells us, were to be true powers, "efficient and living entities; not words or phantoms,"—but representing, firmly and fully, all the great powers of the state. In other words, they were to be "strongly organized" departments, and "competently filled," in defiance of that "fashionable thinking of the day," which insists upon the "weakness of government," as the best or only necessity for the liberties of the people.

But the thing was not only not done, but it could not be done, and it is worse than vain at this moment to inform us of the impossibilities which have been devised by good intention. That the French, whom M. Guizot and a thousand other politicians and philosophers, have been teaching are at the head of European civilization, should now be persuaded to fall back for safety upon English or American civilization, is a thing entirely out of the question. How should you bring them to a recognition of this necessity? By what process unteach all your previous lessons? To disabuse them of that monstrous self-esteem which you have excited to the condition of disease, and rendered chronic by constant irritations for a hundred years, is a labor that no politician will ever venture upon in France, even if his philosophy shall have taught him its absolute necessity. The government of Louis Philippe no where sought to inculcate a lesson of misgiving modesty, except by a brutal trampling upon the sensibilities of nature. M. Guizot has never, until his exile, spoken directly to the infirmities of his people, in this respect; and he now handles the sore places with all the tenderness and caution of the surgeon, whose patient is not only physically but mentally diseased; and all his lessons will be written in vain. The specific, at all events, which requires the French people to recognize a superior wisdom in a neighboring and rival nation, is one that you will hardly persuade them to tolerate. They will adopt nothing that seems prescribed by the statesmen or the experience of other nations. They will follow in the wake of neither England nor America. In truth, they have no respect for the mental acquisitions of either. For America indeed, they entertain opinions something allied to contempt; and a great part of the democratic experiment, so called, which they have at various periods addressed themselves to make, seems to have had for its object a studious avoidance of all those features of plan or policy, which might most certainly resemble ours. They are not likely to follow any examples, and, least of all, those which command the preference of M. Guizot. His pamphlet offers no other panaceas; and to these he refers only to depict such disabilities in his people, as make it morally impossible that they should be acceptable to those to whom they are commended. This constitutes the objection to the treatise before us. It really conducts to nothing. It has no specific suggestions suited to the exigency. It lacks all practical uses. The moment that the writer seems to be approaching the details of the subject, and when we most look for his plan of operations, he darts away into those wide fields of generalization in which he so much delights to wander; and we lose, in an eloquent dilation, frequently upon a common place, the salutary lesson for which we had looked in the execution of the work before us. We feel, at every page, that we are dealing with a master. Here are profound researches in history—large knowledge of the morals and economies of society—a just moral sense—an acute and philosophic mind—rare powers of eloquence, when the subject is grateful; and a capacity to theorize upon the immediate and systematize the remote. But the power which reduces abstract propositions to present use,—which brings the principle to bear directly upon the subordinate—and which applies the fruit of knowledge and research to the most ordinary necessities of society and man; this seems to be somewhat wanting to the organization of M. Guizot's mind. And this faculty is, of ail others, the most necessary to the statesman and the politician. Here, now, is the pamphlet before us. The pretext for this publication is the present distracted condition of France. The lover of country—the true patriot—may well put himself aside when he beholds this spectacle. M. Guizot professes to do so. He will write nothing of himself—he will utter none of the complaints of dissatisfied egotism. What he writes shall be for France. It will probe her wounds—it will declare their origin—it will suggest all the proper remedies. To some extent, indeed, the wounds and sore places of the country are properly laid bare. We have no doubt that M. Guizot's enumeration of the various evil influences, under which France writhes and suffers, is a tolerably correct one;—omitting only such particulars as it would be scarcely possible to expect that a good Frenchman should remember or unfold. And, after his details— after showing that falsehood, selfishness, infidelity and all sorts of belief and unbelief are common among the parties—that little is really believed but lust, and nothing really desired but the gratification of the most selfish passions, he sums up the entire burthen of his complaint, in the single word "democracy."— With this spectre he begins, and with this spectre he concludes his lamentations. With what propriety, let those say who read the analysis which lays bare to the world, as the true source of all the mischiefs in France, vices and passions which the world elsewhere has always distinguished by very different names. It is very certain that Democracy in France means a something which it does not mean elsewhere. Instead of a people's government, it means no government at all, or such a government only as will afford the completest sanction to all the, appetites and phrenzies of the multitude. This, be it remembered, is the showing of M. Guizot. We are not responsible for it, nor are we prepared to acknowledge its propriety or justice. He contents himself with this. He paints beautifully the conditions of a peaceful community enjoying civil liberty—he describes justly the claims of the several dependencies and interests of society. He shows us where the danger lies in France;—but not the means of avoiding it. The process for rendering Democracy innocuous—for soothing and reconciling the conflicts of parties—for making government stable in spite of them, and for securing to the separate interests, of law, labor, commerce and art, all that they have a right to claim—are unapparent in these pages; the substance of which runs simply, that, unless the French people become pacific, there is no possible hope for peace in France.

We are persuaded that the French incline to democracy, so long as the subject is one for abstract consideration, and while comparing the respective merits of different systems. But democracy implies in a people the capacity to yoke themselves. The history of all the experiments which have hitherto been made by the French people, show their unwillingness or incapacity to do so. They prefer that Napoleon, or some other favorite, who shall most symbolize the peculiar tastes, appetites and ambition of the nation, should shape for than and fit the harness; and, thus fitted, they will jog on after any fashion, though the progress conducts them over the burning sands of Egypt, and the frozen wastes of the Russian, fainting, famished, bleeding at every step, and enjoying neither the peace nor the security which liberty has promised them in the name of democracy. They have thus always mocked the sympathies, and disappointed the hopes, of the democrat or republican of other countries, until the nations smile sorrowfully at their pretensions, and predict nothing but bitter overthrow and new mortifications at every fresh experiment. We do not now ask in America, whether democracy can establish a government in France, but whether there have been any new revelations for the Frenchman, which has rendered his race more accessible to, and increased his fitness for the principle. He has hitherto done nothing but run riot with the novel possession—drunken with its intoxicating power—and in his every prostration, he has had his locks shorn, and his limbs fettered, by that arch Delilah of legitimacy, which he has so recently again expelled. She will not suit him, it is evident, but will democracy answer his purposes? Ours, in America, is the inevitable question, which M. Guizot seems never to have proposed, till he himself had been exiled from power. "Is then the French revolution destined only to give birth to doubt and deception?—to bury all its triumphs under ruins?"

The answer of the same writer might serve our purposes, were it not that such an answer should properly contemplate such details, as would enable the most ignorant to apply its principles. "Yes; so long as France shall suffer the true and the false, the upright and the perverse, the practicable and the chimerical, the salutary and the pestilent, are to be constantly mingled and confounded in her opinions, her institutions, and the government of her affairs, such will be the unfailing and inevitable result." But that such is the evil commixture in her public opinion, is of itself conclusive against any hope but that which looks to a despotism. If the people of France be so intemperate in their desires, so wild in their principles, so conflicting in their impulses, so absolutely untutored by all experience, there is necessarily wanting to her repose, under any government which leaves her to herself, a good and guardian virtue, which further experience and a long course of suffering alone can supply. The lay sermons which M. Guizot has incorporated with his pamphlet, repeated in a thousand shapes, will do nothing with a people, by whom all hopes are exaggerated, all lessons despised, all examples treated with contempt. What are these sermons, but such as they might have read in thousands of volumes, and in their own as well as other histories? They neither embody a novelty, nor do they utter themselves in language so articulate and impressive, as to render them more grateful to, or more compulsory upon, the race which has learned only too many lessons in conflict with those which teach humility. And this brings us to what we conceive to be one of the great difficulties in the way of French democracy. It lacks religion—it scorns Christianity. The lessons of its literature, for a hundred years, have been too frequently hostile to faith, devotion, a reverence for holy things, for the divine laws—for that providence, which still, whatever our wisdom, our strength, our self-confidence,

> "Must shape our ends,
> Rough hew them as we will."

The idol of self in France has overthrown all other deities. The decree which formally declared the absence of any necessity for a Deity, in the wild days of Robespierre and Danton, was based upon the easy convictions of a people, whose faith in their own genius was the prominent feature in their career. The formal decree which restored the Deity to his altars, did so nominally only. His restoration did not overthrow the false god, which the erring hearts of the vain people had set up. The egotistical sentiment which had raised self into the godhead, was not driven from possession. With a host of highly endowed and popular teachers, from Voltaire and Rousseau to the present day, all busy in the inculcation of a most audacious *egoisme,* it was not possible to bring back the erring and blind flock to the fold of the Good Shepherd. This is at the root of all the misfortunes of the French people, bringing with it a confusion of ideas, and a perverse struggle after unreasonable purposes. When the English puritans began their reformation, they began with prayer. With prayer they went into battle. With prayer they went into council. By prayer, they strove to conciliate the wisdom, which is certain never to become familiar with the mind which has not duly made this avowal of humility. But the French Reformers begin with preaching, instead of prayer. With all things in chaos about them—with all experiments failing—with hopes constantly mortified and labor constantly baffled,—they yet commence every new struggle for reform, by the most absurd and insolent attempts at proselytism. The new lessons which they only begin to learn themselves—beginning usually at the wrong end—they set about to teach to others. They must inoculate other nations with French ideas of liberty. They are the only genuine. Let M. Guizot ask himself, in how much he has contributed to this arrogance. We refer him to the complacent estimate of the performances of the French mind, in this very work of civilization, to which we had reference in the opening of this article. Here we see the seeds of that presumption which, ere it struggles out of the pit, goes to work to instruct other nations how to achieve the performance. This is the great infirmity which they must cure, before they can hope for safety. Persuade them that they have every thing to learn, and this conviction will be the first best step to a national progress, which shall give them peace. But, even with this conviction honestly entertained, and with an endeavor, equally honest, to attain legitimately the ends of good and wholesome government, there are certain other respects, purely political, which must still prove stumbling blocks in their way, and which they can hardly be persuaded to put into the fire. The first of these consists in the inevitable centralism which must follow, from the continuance of Paris as the seat of government. The action of Paris gives the law to France. The impulses and rages of her mobs control the agricultural power, which is always conservative. What chance could any legislative assembly, the various departments fairly represented, have in Paris, running counter, by its acts, to the desires of her restless and irresponsible multitudes. They must be biassed [*sic*] by the clubs, overawed by numbers, or in the event of a firm disposition to do their duty, be torn to pieces by the mob. To transfer the seat of government to a place which shall neither be dependant on the government, nor be in sufficient power to coerce its deliberations, seems to us absolutely essential to the safety of any government of France, no matter what principle may constitute the basis. To lessen the tendencies to centralism, by increasing the powers of the departments, and giving them sole jurisdiction of all local and internal matters, is the next great step, by which peace and order might be promised.

M. Guizot has referred to some of the peculiar advantages possessed by the Americans, in the easy establishment of our republic, but he has not dwelt upon the one most important of all—that they were originally separate communities, and that, in forming a league of states, for all purposes which were strictly common, they yielded none to the federal government, which were not absolutely essential to national purposes—to such as maybe held external only. The principle of states' rights, the grand conservative feature in our system, has never sufficiently challenged the regards of the French politicians. Its advantages, at a glance, may be seen to lie in the constant checks which it offers to centralism—in the continual jealousy which it exhibits, and the watch which it maintains—and, in giving adequate employment at home, in the administration of domestic affairs, to such a proportion of its ambitious citizens, as always secures for the state the adequate capacity for the maintenance of its securities, while lessening the host of those who, under any circumstances, will still be found craving the favors of the national government, at any sacrifice of principle or people. In devolving upon the several states the business of the home and municipal departments, the national government secures itself, in great degree, from harrassing [*sic*] local disquietudes—vexing questions, which inspire discontent, and increase the odium of a government—and an accumulation of toils, which properly belong to sections, and should not demand the attentions of a national administration. How to increase the powers of the departments, and to lessen those of the national administration—by what policy to prepare the French people to transfer the seat of government from Paris to a less refractory and less powerful community,—are questions which belong to the statesmen of the country, and which we take to be more vitally important to the safety and success of the national administration than any other. These are practical measures, which conflict directly with such phases as vex M. Guizot—unity, and single powers—and they are such as involve results of the most vital importance. Are they feasible in France? That will depend on two things—the degree of honesty among her statesmen, and the degree of intelligence among her landholders and agriculturalists. We have no hope of any good results, so long as the city of Paris may usurp all the power of the nation.

Tuckerman's Essays and Essayists

Henry Theodore Tuckerman was a well-known critic and essayist. He was born and educated in New England, but in 1845 he moved to New York City, where he gained entrance into the social circle of Anne Lynch Botta and grew acquainted with the New York literati (Duyckinck and Duyckinck, *Cyclopedia of American Literature,* 489; Edens, "Henry Theodore Tuckerman," 237). He contributed to many of the leading journals of the day, including the *North American Review,* the *Democratic Review,* the *Southern Literary Messenger,* and Simms's own *Southern Quarterly Review.* He is probably best remembered today as a critic of literature and art, but he began his career as essay writer, and it was as an essayist that Simms assessed him in the review reprinted below.[1] Though Simms frequently noticed Tuckerman in print, Simms's reviews indicated an ambivalence toward the New England writer. He praised Tuckerman's style, but he suggested that the essayist's tone was alternatively phlegmatic and cold-blooded and that his personal musings and meditations often overwhelmed his subjects (see Simms "Critical Notices" *SQR* n.s. 9 [April 1854]: 540–41). It is also interesting to compare the conditional praise offered by Simms in the 1850s, with the unvarnished condemnation of Tuckerman and his "malignity, in respect to all things in the South," found in one of Simms's final critical notices from 1870, included in part 1 (pp. 191–93). In the review essay reprinted here, however, it is Simms's own meditation on the history and usefulness of the essay as a form that is of most interest.

Tuckerman's first published work was *The Italian Sketch Book,* a collection of travel essays derived from his experience during an 1833 Italian sojourn. In it he included essays that ranged in topic from art to politics (Edens, "Henry Theodore Tuckerman," 238). Another compilation, *The Optimist* (1850), was one of the two volumes that offered the occasion for Simms's review. It gathered together essays on a number of topics, many of which focused on social conventions. There were chapters on social life, dress, hair, humor, and even, in an odd meditation, the human hand. The lack of a defined subject and the variety of material covered meant that the collection was much closer in style to the writings of the eighteenth-century essayists than the more popular review essays that populated nineteenth-century cultural journals, a point that Simms noted in his review. What is particularly interesting about Simms's analysis, and what marks this review as a trenchant literary and cultural critique, is that he located the source of this shift in the evolving nature of American and indeed Western civilization.

The essay as a form had its roots in the development of bourgeois individualism and in the expression and consolidation of new cultural norms. The French writer and statesman Michel de Montaigne is often credited with developing the genre, and his massive volume *Essais* (1580) set the standard of personal and introspective essay writing (Stange, "The Voices of the Essayist," 313). What was so powerful about the essay as a form was that it was formless. It lacked the conventional constraints of a fictional plot or poetic meter and could conform to the needs and style of the author (Gualtieri, "The Essay as Form," 54). While the genre had worthy adherents in the sixteenth and seventeenth centuries, Montaigne and Francis Bacon chief among them, it was the combined power of new innovations in print technology and the wit of new practitioners that led to the popularization of the form in the early eighteenth century.

The names of Richard Steele and Joseph Addison were synonymous with the essay, and the two men's publications, the *Tatler* and *Spectator,* set the standard for the genre. They melded the relatively new technology of the periodical press to the cadences of urban life. Steele's and Addison's journals depicted the variety of characters found in the modern city and placed those figures in juxtaposition and conversation with one another (Black, "Social and Literary Form in the *Spectator,*" 23; Marr, *The Periodical Essayists,* 21–63). The chief purpose, however, was didactic, and the essays sought to set the standard of morals and manners for the emerging urban middle class (Moltke-Hansen, "Fox-Genovese as Essayist," xxii). Steele and Addison attempted to develop a common culture through the use of literature, specifically the formless form of the essay, and it was in this longer tradition that Tuckerman was writing.

Certainly Simms could appreciate the use of print culture to develop a common national—or sectional—culture, though, as he noted in his review, the moral essays of Steele and Addison had lost much of their popular appeal by the nineteenth century. In their place had stepped the review essay, a form that Simms promoted, as both author and editor. While the literary or critical essay served similar ends of cultural diffusion and consolidation, its form was more structured. The critical essay took as its starting point a book or work of art and relied on the specialized knowledge of the author to extrapolate on the given subject further. The author would often use that referent as an opportunity to enter into broad discussions of some aspect of the work under review, but the form itself was far more utilitarian than the wide-ranging moral essays of the *Tatler* and *Spectator* and, indeed, of Tuckerman's *Optimist* (Moltke-Hansen, "Fox-Genovese as Essayist," xxiii–xxiv; Stange, "The Voices of the Essayist," 313–16). Simms expressed appreciation for the older form that Tuckerman's work recalled, but he subtly hinted that it was the product of a bygone era.

It was for the good, ultimately, that the critic had supplanted the essayist, for it was the "inferior aims and achievements of society" that had enfeebled the "earnestness and power" of the latter (Simms, "Tuckerman," p. 272). The critic of the modern age suffered no such disabilities. He instead

> elevated narrative by analysis and suggestion, and borrowed from the imaginative in order to wing the contemplative. . . . The triflings of the club-room gave place to the deliberations of a society resolved on work; and, instead of a conceited group of overgrown urchins, prattling over their petty sentimentalities and tidy humours . . . we have the same talent, properly employed, *pro bono public,* in an arena free to all comers, and exercising itself with subjects at once necessary to the welfare of states, and grateful to all the best interests of a whole people. (p. 273)

Simms clearly saw himself as pursuing this loftier mission, and throughout his review he differentiated himself, as a critic, from the essayists he described. It was, he believed, the free circulation of the periodical press that provided one of the greatest forms of popular education for the nation, and especially for the southern part. Thus it was the periodical press that served as the key element for both generating and consolidating a national culture (Moltke-Hansen, "Southern Literary Horizons," 21–22).

Still Simms lauded Tuckerman's efforts and broke slightly with his friend Edgar Allan Poe by offering at least conditional praise for the New Englander's writing. Simms even invited Tuckerman to visit his plantation home, provided he was "not an abolitionist," and he later solicited Tuckerman's contributions to the *Southern Quarterly Review* (*Letters* 3: 70). Simms also insisted that "Mr. Tuckerman perhaps deserves the highest distinction" among those American writers who devoted themselves primarily to the essay, but admitted that competition in the field was lacking. The backhanded compliment aside, what is most interesting about Simms's analysis is how he connected the decline of the moral essay to the nature of American civilization and, especially, the impatient character of the American mind.

As Simms surveyed the national landscape in the mid–nineteenth century, he saw a nation that was expanding more rapidly than anyone could have imagined. The population had exploded, buoyed by the influx of foreign immigrants, most of them populating northern cities. The landmass of the nation had similarly expanded, augmented by the huge territory just acquired from Mexico at the end of the previous decade. The people themselves reflected this expansionary spirit, as did Simms himself through his boosterism of war and territorial conquest. "The national mind," Simms wrote, "is one of feverish urgency, sanguine, eager for action, restive under restraint. . . . Its mission, at present, would seem to be conquest, not contemplation" ("Tuckerman's Essays and Essayists," p. 280). Americans had no time for the meandering, moralizing essays of the past, because they were a people who valued decisive thought and action. "The Essay belongs to a contemplative rather than an active era. It is not permitted to an age of steam to pause and muse upon the mere forms of a season—the passing moods and fashions of society—the frivolous customs, the temporary tastes, the humours, or even the moral phases of a nice convention, or ordinary life" (p. 266).

Yet for all of those pronouncements, Simms remained conflicted. He wondered if civilization was not the worse for having lost that luxury of contemplation. He worried, ultimately, about the fate of a civilization that lost the stabilizing force represented by the essayist. "We cannot forego this class of writers," he decided, "and we should be grievously distressed if their province should be left neglected for others of more pretension" ("Tuckerman's Essays and Essayists," p. 278). What seems like equivocation in Simms's assessment of Tuckerman and of the essay form—he suggested at one moment that the form had lost its usefulness and the next that the culture could not spare the practitioners of the art—represented Simms's personal conflict about the future of American civilization and rapid change—what many, including Simms at certain times, called progress.

For all his celebration of progress, Simms, like other southern intellectuals, remained ambivalent about the rapid pace of change. He and they were willing to accept progress, but only if it was measured and proceeded on their terms. For Simms the essay was the literary expression of this ambivalence. He admitted that, "in an age like ours, which is so fondly insisted upon as one entirely of progress, and in which we do certainly move with astonishing rapidity, though our advance may well admit of question, the quiet, gentle, persuasive form of composition which characterizes the essay" seems at odds ("Tuckerman's Essays and Essayists"). In the midst of rapid change, it was the essayist who offered a sense of conservatism and moderation, even if his audience was smaller than it once had been. "We should be sorry to see the essay die wholly out of the land," Simms concluded, "and are particularly pleased, at a time when the temper of the race is continually yearning for new fields of conquest, if a mild and graceful circle should still be found, in every community, to whom its gentle amenities shall still be precious."

Yet if Simms remained conflicted about the essay and about the nature of progress, he never wavered in his belief that literature had the power to affect the course of civilization. He questioned the value of the old-style moral essay, but he steadfastly believed in the power of the review essay and the periodical press to shape national as well as regional identity. In that sense he, just as much as if not more than Tuckerman, was an heir of Steele and Addison as well as the extended history of the essay as a civilizing force that he outlined in the review reprinted below. Although his chosen form had evolved to meet the current needs and tastes of society, his goals of generating a broader sense of cultural consensus remained the same.

Ehren Foley

Note

1. Tuckerman's work as an art critic includes most notably his *Artist Life, or Sketches of American Painters* (1847) and *Book of the Artists* (1867). Janice L. Edens, "Henry Theodore Tuckerman," in John W. Rathbun and Monica M. Grecu, *American Literary Critics and Scholars, 1850-1880* (Detroit: Gale Research, 1978): 238.

[Review of Tuckerman, *Characteristics of Literature* (1849) and *The Optimist* (1850)]

1. *Characteristics of Literature, Illustrated by the Genius of Distinguished Men. By Henry T. Tuckerman, author of The Italian Sketch Book, Isabel, or a Pilgrimage through Sicily, Thoughts on the Poets, &c.* Philadelphia: Lindsay & Blakiston. 1849.

2. *The Optimist.* By Henry T. Tuckerman. "That I may show the whole world that we ought to value little joys more than great ones; the night-gown more than the dress-coat; that Plutus' heaps are worth less than his handfuls; and not

"Tuckerman's Essays and Essayists." *Southern Quarterly Review* n.s. 1 (July 1850): 370–406 (37 pp.).

great, but little goodhaps, can make us happy. You perceive, my drift is, that man may become a little tailor-bird, which, not amid the crashing boughs of the storm-tossed, roaring, immeasurable tree of life, but, upon one of its leaves, sews itself a nest together, and there lies snug."—Jean Paul. New-York: Geo. P. Putnam. 1850.

The Essay, so famous in the days of Steele and Addison, constitutes but a small portion of the literature of the present time. The mental characteristics of our period are essentially different from those of their day and season, and demand a more stimulating, if not a more wholesome diet. The Essay belongs to a contemplative, rather than an active era. It is not permitted to an age of steam to pause and muse upon the mere forms of a season—the passing moods and fashions of society—the frivolous customs, the temporary tastes, the humours, or even the moral phases of a nice convention, or of ordinary life. These, in all periods, have usually furnished the topics for that class of writers whom we have, by common consent, recognized as the Essayists. They were such as delighted the genius of the fanciful but phlegmatic Addison, and the sweet and spontaneous Goldsmith; such as gave provocation to the dogmatic temper of Johnson, and roused to satire the lively faculties of Steele. That class of wits seem pretty much to have—"died out" with the dynasty which beheld them in their best perfection; and wit itself, under the accepted definition of their time—when it signified rather a happy variety of resource than a spicy capacity for repartee—is no longer a commodity to be esteemed by ours. The Addison period seems to have been an interregnum, in which there was really no crowned monarch of the Muse. Pope, Gay, and Somerville, in verse, fail to supply the vacancy occasioned by the absence of Milton, Cowley, Butler, and Dryden. In the Drama, the writers of the Queen Anne period, with Congreve, Lillo and Farquhar at their head, compare unhappily with Dryden, Otway and Lee, of the preceding age; and Addison, Steel, Goldsmith, Johnson, and Budgell, as Essayists, with all their merits as graceful limners of society, fall immeasurably short of the power, the freshness, the enthusiasm, and richer thought which distinguished the writings, in this department, of Milton. Fuller, Walton, Cowley, Dryden, and a dozen others. The difference was due to the decline of that intense mood in the nation which usually marks a people engaged in a zealous and earnest progress. It was a season of pause and rest, when, after long and violent struggles, the nation needed a temporary repose before recuperation. Zeal was no longer in harness, and Patriotism had grown too phlegmatic to be roused to passion for any cause. The Genius of Britain, under the chilling authority of a sovereign, cold and tasteless, like William the Third, or peevish and feeble, like Anne—achieving no foreign conquests, and busy only in exhausting strifes at home—was querulous rather than earnest; and, where it strove successfully, strove rather in beaten paths than in any enterprises which could open or discover new. Originality had its perils at such a season, or was in bonds by purchase. The genius of the nation was too much in the market, and the poet but too commonly perished in the pensioner. There is an intimate relation between the political virtues of a people and the literature which they most cherish; and the weaknesses which distinguish the reign of Anne—in a prince, the worst sort of vices—had no precious fruits to boast of, in literature, such as marked a very different soul and spirit in the nation by whose fierce courage and determined will a Stuart was brought to the block, and a Cromwell to the throne. Nor do we fail to perceive a character altogether superior in the English literature of a subsequent period, corresponding with the new-born energies of the people, as displayed in their foreign enterprises, their arts, arms, and the progress of discovery. Compare the writers, during the period of the two first Georges, with those who illustrated the career of the two preceding monarchs. How superiour do they show, in courage, in force, in depth and freshness! These are quite as indicative of the political as of the intellectual history of the nation. The temperament of a people accords the true tone of the national writer, whatever may be the extent and the direction of his genius.

The class of writings generally understood when we speak of the Essay, indicates rather the manners than the morals of a literature. As we have said, it belongs to the contemplative rather than the creative in art. It shows grace, taste, and talent, rather than originality; and, when most encouraged by a people, illustrates a period when the graces and refinements of society stand rather in proof of its past than of its present performances. This is not the case in our day. The world has grown something more passionate: is, certainly, more restless and impatient; and, we think, much more adventurous and performing. It is, decidedly, more in earnest; and this declares equally, perhaps, for a greater degree of strength and a less degree of finish. It sympathizes little with the quiet repose—the soothing harmonies—the graceful amenities—the gentle enthusiasm—which furnish the chief materials of the Essay writer. Literature has assumed a more original aspect. It is a thing of more various flight, and more sleepless energies. It is now, as in earlier periods, required to perform the duties of the pioneer rather than the critic—to work rather than counsel—and this, as a natural result of the fields newly opened to enterprise, and the new status which the race has acquired under the encouraging auspices of the gradually liberalizing institutions. Literature is now, perhaps, more than ever, associated with the great business of life. It becomes an active auxiliar, if not an actual leader, in the current toils of politics and statesmanship. History, under its new necessities, has assumed a higher rank, and shares the honours with Philosophy, The Essayist no longer contents himself with amusing his reader, or with insinuating his lessons, through the medium of fanciful allegory, or picturesque analysis. He takes upon him the toils of the preacher, and his language is rather that of the prophet than the phlegmatic. Instead of the quiet, contemplative chapters of Addison and Mackenzie, we have the passionate and daring speculations of Wilson and Carlyle. In place of the easy, unobtrusive numbers of Goldsmith—rilling on in beguiling murmurs, like a clear, sylvan brooklet, prattling through green leaves and over polished pebbles—we have the fierce rush of Brougham, the sweeping, grasping volume of Macauley, or the deep, antique waters of Talfourd. Even where we do happen, in present times, upon the genuine Essayist, fashioned somewhat, though still faintly, after the days of Addison and Mackenzie—as in the instances of Charles Lamb and William Hazlitt—there is still such a difference in the degree of intensity which marks their writings—there is so much more real earnestness of purpose—so much deeper insight—so much stronger sympathy with the working condition of humanity—that, while we acknowledge their legitimacy as the representatives of a former class, they yet force upon us the conviction of a contrast, which, perhaps, we are yet slow to recognize as a proof of any superiority over their predecessors. We behold these day-workers of the present in very different attitudes from those of the times of Addison. They do not retire to green groves, or silent attics, meditating the scene only as spectators—which was the self-assumed condition of those to whom they are likened—but, stripped to the buff, and wrestling in the ring themselves. They assert no privilege to stand aloof while the conflict is in progress—the mere bottle-holders, or, at best, the eulogists of the rival parties. This constitutes the radical difference between the writers of the two periods. The one wrote as simple lookers-on, and having no interest in the affair, except as spectators; the others write as persons who feel all the enthusiasm of the combat, and who carry away from the field its bruises no less than its honours. It may be admitted, perhaps, that the elder Essayists were more calm and impartial observers. It is, doubtless, greatly to the credit of their temper, the position which they occupied; and, so far as they could be expected to sympathize with the actors and events, as spectators merely, it is, doubtless, quite true that we may more confidently rely upon their reports. But, in this consists the difficulty. Could they sufficiently sympathise with the struggle in which they did not share? They belonged to the same race with the combatants. How are we to esteem that sympathy which looks composedly upon the fraternal conflict, only with the eye of the amateur, and apparently without interest in the result? In truth, for that sort of talent, which was essential to the Essayist of the Queen Anne period, a rare degree of phlegm was as essential as good taste. A certain icy temperature of the blood is necessary to a department in which enthusiasm and energy are never permitted to impair manners or derange costume. To "catch the manners living as they rose" was a faculty which needed vigilance rather than enterprise—which demanded the refining rather than the creative finger, and the step of grace rather than the wing for flight. The Essayists, then, did not often perceive the necessities of society. They had but little relevancy with its cause or progress. They were pleased to behold its exterior only. This they could smooth and polish as they would. It seldom vexed their equanimity. It was not provocative of earnest fears and hopes, nor did it prompt to energetic or passionate exhortation. They smiled, or sneered, or praised, but seldom wept or grieved at what they saw; and, looking down upon the vast wilderness of London—its sinks, its stews, its dens of grief and anguish and destitution—they saw nothing of its sores. Their eyes could detect only the want of graces in the courtier, the arts and caprices of the belle, or the fetches or subtleties of the ingenious idler, whose policy employed life only in tasking society for his maintenance in profligacy. At best, a feeble and pointless criticism—faultless, perhaps, but wanting in strength and thoroughness—like that in which the great master, like Milton, was reviewed by the clever schoolmaster, like Addison—or, an Essay, neatly worded, which arrayed, in just connection, all the commonplaces of some starch morality. These were the themes which but too commonly satisfied the wits of a period when the nation was undistinguished by any really commanding genius, whether in literature or politics. We read their Essays, at this day, with the distressing consciousness, all the while, that we are in communion with the most cold-blooded persons in the world. The tone of their narratives of the struggle which they have witnessed from their "loopholes of retreat," bring to mind the description of that delicate fopling who approached Hotspur to demand his prisoners, when the hero was still raging across the field, covered with dust and blood. They wear the appearance of those well-dressed persons whom we are apt to see at some great conflagration; who stand aside, at a safe distance, and cavil at the performance of those who strive, in smoke and uproar, to subdue the flame. We acknowledge their good taste and good breeding; but, we ask, "What the d—l do they here?" We feel that they are very clever persons, but never forgive them their want of blood. That they have a nice judgment, in many things, we are willing to allow; but we naturally inquire why they do not take a hand with us in arresting the common danger? Critics they are, no doubt; but, their lack of proper sympathy with the subject seems to estop their full claims to a proper judgment upon it. We deny that they can be good judges of a condition in which they allow nothing for the smoke which blinds all eyes but their own, and the danger which assails the performer, and from which, at no moment, do they themselves entertain any apprehensions.

Now, this must not be construed into a contemptuous censure of the department of the Essayists. It is meant only to indicate the humbler position which is their rank in relation to the other workers in an original literature, and to justify that inferior sympathy which, as a class, they seem to inspire among the race of readers generally. We are quite willing to accord them much of the praise which the author before us assigns to them, in one of his prefaces. To "point out and uphold the poetry of life,"— social and ordinary, we suppose, is meant—and to insist upon "the common resources of nature," are clearly within the obvious duties of the Essayist. To illustrate "the scope and gracefulness attainable through wise and kindly comments on society," and to furnish "an appreciative interpretation of the true and beautiful in experience, "are performances, certainly, of very great profit and pleasure to society—perhaps, more peculiarly within the province of the Essayist than any other class of writers. We are not sure that we detect in their writings, generally, that "blended acuteness and *enthusiasm*" of which our author tells us, inasmuch as we are very doubtful of the degree in which they possess the latter quality. But, that they merit the title of "urbane philosophers," which he confers upon them, and that "they are more available to the comprehension of readers than more recondite, speculative inquirers," we cheerfully accord. "They make apparent," he says, in a phraseology slightly vague and stilted, "the compensatory elements of human existence; they indicate the best means of refining our senses and keeping alive our better instincts; they disperse, from familiar charms, the mists of custom, and subdue the unhealthy devotion to what is artificial and melodramatic, by refreshing the mind with the unperverted affinities of nature," &c. After some exaggerations in regard to the offices of the Essayists, and their province—of which, by the way, they only share, in degree, with all other writers—he adds, more temperately, "They quietly suggest available food for reflection, and appropriate objects for sympathy, and, accordingly, minister to enlargement of thought, elevation of taste, and delicacy of feeling." Nicety, perhaps, rather than "enlargement" of thought. But, substantially, we have little cause of quarrel with this definition. The province of the Essayists is even as it is described by our author. They are the philosophers of simple life and society. It is their business to do justice to the humble and subordinate. Tastes, manners, sympathies, culture, dress, homely affections, and the phases of convention—these are their natural topics. To see clearly in their walks—to decide justly upon ordinary things, according to ordinary standards—to indicate becoming tastes—to refine the defects of an untrained manner, and rebuke the excesses of a diseased society—to bring the fancy to play, with a soft and grateful light, about the domain of vulgar necessities, and to cheer the lowly with a hope, drawn from histories in which Providence has sent forth angels, with miraculous powers, unexpectedly to bring comfort to the couch of pain—these, which require art and talent rather than genius—thought and sentiment rather than inspiration—fancy rather than imagination—sensibility rather than power—and the capacity for surfaces rather than interior philosophies—these suffice to show how extensive, how useful, how grateful to society, may, and should be, the office of the Essayist, who, with all the endowments of intellect, possesses a heart for ever expanding with just emotions and generous susceptibilities. Such was Oliver Goldsmith, in a past period, and Charles Lamb, in our own: both possessing, in addition, a vein of mild and genial pleasantry, which has almost got to be assumed as the essential of the Essayist; and both, through this medium, and by the employment of sudden contrasts, attaining some of their happiest effects in the delineation of the opposite moods of the pathetic and conventional.

A bird's eye view at the progress of the British Essayists, in different periods—showing us how completely they represent the characteristics of a time, its tastes and energies—will tend still more to illustrate their uses. We must leave the reader to note this progress for himself. Let him run over the list of prose writers of England during the reigns of Elizabeth, the first James, and the first Charles, and note how admirably the character of court and people are shadowed forth by the Essayists as well as Dramatists. These, far more decidedly than the statesmen of the times, and their histories, remain to teach us what they were, and in how much their social progress contributed to the world's moral capital. How suggestive are the names of Philip Sydney, Verulam, Hooker, Raleigh, James Howel, (one of the most delightful of English Essayists, and but little known,) Owen Feltham, John Selden, and Sir Thomas Brown! And, the next period is like unto it—forming a similar catalogue, worthy of eternal record: Milton, Cowley, Fuller, Barrow, Bunyan, Clarendon, Dryden, Temple, Wotton! We may trace a change—a halting—a falling off—at the close of this period, significant of the social degradation which was to follow: the fruits of the misrule of the reign of the second Charles—enuring with even more evil to a future period than to his own. With Defoe, Pope, Steele, Addison, and Wortley Montague—polished, witty, graceful, spirited—always entertaining, and always solicitous of the proprieties, equally of convention and of art—we are scarcely conscious of the vast transition which has been made from the former to the present period, until we look for the echo, in our souls, of that which has so pleasantly sounded in our ears. The next period in which history records a decided improvement in the condition of the English family—in the greater strength of the third estate, and characterized by the fiercest struggles for British liberty—affords us corresponding proofs of a sterner, a deeper, and a nobler purpose in the writings of the British Essayists—an improvement still more decided than that which might be seen in the parallel histories of the Poets during the same periods. Burke, Johnson, Goldsmith, Henry Mackenzie, Junius, Lowth, Moore, Smollett, Gibbon, Hooke, Hume, &c.: compare these—their intensity—their earnestness of purpose—the variety and importance of their subjects—their greater research and care—their more comprehensive thought, if not purer wisdom—with the characteristics of the race immediately preceding them, and we discover the beginning of a new and wonderful progress, equally in letters and society, which, in fact, substantially changed the character of the Essayist, as an exponent of the new condition of things which his labour was to illustrate. He was no longer the organ of passing moods and mere social caprices—could no longer content himself with the lively sketches of conventional character, which before had employed rather his faculties of observation and his fancies than his thoughts and studies. The age had higher requisitions. It could no longer spare the time consumed in the merely sportive and frivolous; nay, had little leisure even for pleasant portraitures of a character at once agreeable to good morals and the offices of art. Hereafter, he was to address himself to the higher objects of the masses, gradually rising into a political estate, and to recognise their wants, however rudely urged, as quite worthy of notice, when taken into consideration in connection with their daily acquisitions of wealth and power. As a matter of course, under the new regime, the Essayists of the old school of British literature mostly disappeared. The literature of a people instinctively appreciates all the changes in society. Under each fresh impulse of the national heart the organs of its mind receive a new stimulus; and the voice that spoke only in flute-like accents, in its hours of drowse and apathy, is found to pour forth the clamours of the trumpet, when the auditor prepares to arm himself for the battle. In place of the musing and contemplative tribe, whose grace and sweetness—whose sportiveness and delicacy of fancy—had afforded the sufficient charm to the nation, at a period when its court and all the higher classes were under the corrupting influences of a Gallic dominion, the race of critics arose—writers who elevated the simple Essay into a higher rank in letters, securing for it greater authority and ascendancy. They grafted upon it new qualities of earnestness; and, instead of addressing it to the tastes and humours of the times, made their appeal, through this medium, to its ambition and its necessities. The Essay became an introduction to a stern examination of the characteristics equally of books, of arts, of politics, and men. It compassed histories and biographies—it discussed the condition of States and the measures of cabinets—the interests as well as the humours and caprices of society. In place of the pleasant sketch, the fruit of a single sitting, in which little more was done than to pursue a favourite suggestion of the fancy, it delivered treatises which demanded earnest deliberation, close research, and a thought largely exercised in the topics which concern the absolute safety of society. The range was no less wide and various than thorough. "From grave to gay—from lively to severe," they passed, with a rapidity which satisfied moods the most capricious. instead of the single author, who, in serial publications, must needs be monotonous, or the small knot of two or three, having the same habits of thought and similar tastes, the Review subsidized the leading minds in remote sections, and thus secured for its objects a leading requisite—that of an infinite variety. The ancient Essayist was not so much superseded as absorbed. Still contributing to the so-much-desired variety, you might find his quaint fancies, his social sketches, and his picturesque delineations interwoven with topics legitimately associated, the severity of which they contributed to enliven; and, losing its externals, merely, the Essay took a higher rank, and grew into an authority as well as a companion—the natural result of the alliance with more ambitious associates. The Essayist might well become the critic, yet maintain every necessary essential of his former department. It was only his province that was enlarged. The criticism of recent periods—in its great increase of philosophy and force—in earnestness and power—was only the natural and full development of an endowment which was enfeebled, originally. by the inferior aims and achievements of society. Were Addison, now, a writer for the Edinburgh, you would see the most wonderful change in his manners and carriage. He would review

Milton in a different spirit, though his phraseology might not be a whit improved. He would never, at least be permitted to display only the surfaces of his subject; and no degree of delicacy and grace of utterance—no purity of style— would be held an equivalent for frigidity of narrative, or a shallow accumulation of commonplace. Compare the poetry of Byron, Scott, and Shelley, with that of Hayley, Shenstone, and Mickle, and you have no unfair comparison of the reviewers of modern times, in Great Britain, with the Essayists in the time of Anne and George the First. Grace, art, delicacy, and a gentle humour, with a pleasant surface-philosophy, but without thoroughness, marked the one; but it too much lacked the elements of insight, eagerness, intensity, and courage, which give force and freedom to the other. The critic grasped at loftier conceptions than the Essayist; cherished higher considerations of life, which were more important to humanity; opened new avenues to philosophy and history, and enlarged the boundaries of science and art. He elevated narrative by analysis and suggestion, and borrowed from the imaginative in order to wing the contemplative. He did more: He helped to furnish better notions of what virtue demanded, as well from the citizen as the statesman; and, in the very choice of his topics, he opened the eyes of readers to a more just appreciation of what was required of life. The triflings of the club-room gave place to the deliberations of a society resolved on work; and, instead of a conceited group of overgrown urchins, prattling over their petty sentimentalities and tidy humours—selfishly, and, in circles, religiously *tabooed* again! the rest of the world—ambitious only of the reputation of men of wit about town— we have the same talent, properly employed, *pro bono publico,* in an arena free to all comers, and exercising itself with subjects at once necessary to the welfare of states, and grateful to all the best interests of a whole people? What has been the result of this change, in respect to public men? The answer to the question—we are speaking now of Great Britain—affords a sufficient commentary upon the suggestion already made, that the literature of a country, in its morals, must most certainly illustrate and keep pace with the moral of society. The public men of Great Britain have sensibly risen in the scale of character since the days of Pope and Bolingbroke; and the character of men of letters has risen, also, in a corresponding degree. Neither the one nor the other trades upon his talent, after the fashion of Swift and the wits of his period. The social requisitions, steadily increasing, have established standards more severely exacting, in respect to all the professions. Public men feel themselves bound by more rigid laws of duty; literary men have ceased to be the despicable retainers of court and faction; and the pension, which, but a hundred years ago, was the price paid for the soul as well as service of the venal Essayist, or poet, is now, by the imperative decree of public opinion, accorded only to the unquestionable claims of an intellect, which, while it proves its power over the public mind, is never to be found in the public market. The pensions awarded, by the Crown of Great Britain, to Southey, Lamb, Wordsworth, and others, of our day, were bought by achievements wrought for the nation. No venal toils, undertaken for prince, or faction, could, at the present, as in past times, challenge their compensation from the public treasury.

We have no doubt that the changes wrought upon the essay, as it was known in the days of Addison, were all decided improvements. Indeed, we are free to say that no one familiar with the English Essayists of a still remoter period, would ever accord to that of Addison the palm of superiority, or even comparative excellence. The papers of Milton, Sidney, Fuller, Barrow, South, Dryden, and a host beside, all belonging to this category, are immeasurably superior in depth, strength and purpose, to any thing which we owe to the wits and fine writers of Queen Anne's period. There is more vigour of thought, more boldness of flight, and a style, of more force and character, even though it may lack something of the harmony and polish. It is thought by many, who yet yield the question of general excellence, that, in mere point of style, the writers of the Addison class and times have the advantage over those that follow. But, even on this point, we may be permitted to entertain a doubt. There is a good deal of cant and bigotry in respect to this matter of style. At one time, within the memories of the present generation, we were required to build our faith upon Addison, and frame our periods wholly upon the model prescribed by his. Our teachers seem never to have had any misgivings upon the subject of individuality, nor to have been disturbed by any thought of what was due, in the way of original expression, to speculations, conceptions and fancies, entirely original. As for peculiarity of temperament, implying necessarily a peculiar type for language, that was a matter that demanded not a moment; and the man of ardent temper full to overflow with daring and world-wide conceptions, eager to declare his object and impetuous in the pursuit of it, was to train his flight in the school of a phlegmatic. Milton himself was to be modified by Master Addison—Burgundy subdued by milk and water; and, before Dryden could attempt his mighty march with his stately coursers, "the long-resounding march and majesty divine," he must hobble his steeds with neat steel fetters, of uniform size, such as Dryden himself ventured to put upon the horses of the Sun, when he undertook to rhyme the "Paradise." Style is quite as arbitrary as the thought which takes it for a medium. The style belongs to the topic, and to the particular genius of the writer. The temperament, which affects the choice of subject, must necessarily determine also the mode of expression. Men of true ability have really no choice, and cannot have, in matters of style, where the subject matter belongs to the suggestion of a native mood or genius. Addison's style belongs to the quiet temperament, easy good nature, gentlemanly tastes, and a smooth epicurean philosophy. For writers of this class it is probably the perfection of style. But, for writers of a more earnest nature, it will never answer. It would enfeeble the thought; and the consciousness of a regularly recurring cadence, would be fatal to those freedoms of expression, which are natural to the utterance, where the matter urged is argumentative and passionate. We may admit that the style of the present day is more loose than in that of Addison, and perhaps more diffusive,—though that is very questionable. But, has it not gained in freedom, and variety, much more than it has lost in circumspectness and method? Let us take an example, by way of illustrating this inquiry. Compare the copious abundance of Christopher North, in expression, as well as thought and fancy, with the best tuned of all the harmonious periods in Addison. Allow that the sentences of the latter, when isolated, are more correct and even more musical; yet, restored to the paragraph, how monotonously do they read in comparison with the chapters of the modern. They may deserve the credit of greater simplicity, but how greatly do they fail in the compass, the frequent overflow, the vivacity and freedom, which give a nameless charm, and that "infinite variety which nothing seems to stale," to the writings of the accomplished blackguard of *Blackwood's Magazine*. In point of richness, raciness, excursiveness, depth and manliness, the space between them is immeasurable. To borrow a comparison from a sister department of letters, we may safely assert that the style of the Modern Essayists, regarding such writers as Hazlitt, Wilson, Charles Lamb, and Talfourd, possesses a freshness in its very freedom, which the staid and cautious graces of Addison could never possibly attain. They employ a lyrical gush, and an abundance, in their variety, which have wonderfully enlarged the somewhat narrow boundaries, to which, in previous periods, (Milton, Sydney, and a few others to be excepted, who boldly carried the voice of poetry into the province of the humbler form of speech,) prose utterance had been quite too much confined.

We have already remarked passingly upon the great difference between the topics respectively chosen by the past and more recent writers of the Essay. The point is one that deserves a farther reference, as it denotes a more radical change in the thought and character of society, than belongs simply to the caprices of popular taste or the indulgence of its humours. The subjects of the *Spectator*, and other kindred publications of the same and subsequent periods, were quite too frequently of a character most ephemeral. We do not except from this category those essays which treated of morals, the principles of which were already well recognized, and which it was the object of the writer rather to dilate upon and to exemplify, than to introduce or establish;—a labor which, of necessity, precluded, in great degree, the exercise of all originality. If the topic was not some virtue upon which it was the aim of the writer simply to insist, it was some passing habit, some silly temporary custom—a humour of the times—a borrowed fashion—or the portraiture of some well known character about town, who had made himself conspicuous for a simplicity or an impertinence. No doubt, these are all legitimate topics. That archery is praiseworthy which sends its shaft at the "folly as it flies;"— and he is no less useful, *in degree,* who rids the land of its caterpillars, than the Hercules who perils life in assaults upon the hydra. But it is with allowance that our acknowledgments must be made. It is *in degree,* only, and after a long interval, that we recognize the claims of the minute benefactor, with those of him who takes upon himself the purging of the stables of Augeas, or the overthrow of the gigantic brood of public enemies. To divert and amuse, seems to have been the object mostly of the Essayists: and if the style was pure and graceful, the thoughts were apt to be puerile and tame. Our utilitarianism is of a sort readily to recognize the propriety of labours undertaken for the mere purpose of amusing and beguiling society of its cares; but this employment must derive its sanction from the understood fact that society is performing, struggling, and in earnest, at the same time. A frivolous condition of the public mind must not be tampered with by farther contributions to its improper moods and appetites; and even the moral essay, at such a period, affords too little of the necessary caustic to answer the purpose of the reformer. It is in the topic, usually, that we find the provocation for the thought; and if this be not of a sort addressed to the real and pressing necessities of a community, it is doubtful whether any lessons teaching mere amenities are not grievously misapplied. When the city is in danger of violent doom, the prophet must not discourse upon popular manners. Now, our Addisonian Essayists, their master at their head, with Steele, Tickell, Parnell, Budgell, *et id omne genus,* do not seem often to have chosen their topics with regard to the moral of English society in their day—though most grievously in need of it. Their chief care was the manners and externals—the outward carriage, the mere deportment of the fine lady and the citizen. The topic too frequently involved an apparent necessity for trifling, and flippancy very often obtruded itself upon the reader in the place of wit. The treatment of the subject, even where judiciously chosen, was not always appropriate to its real exactions; the writer usually seeming to fear, lest, in giving way to his topic, he should prove too profound for the reader or himself. But the fault lay too frequently in the choice of topic, and this misfortune arose from the deficiencies of society, rather than the Essayist. He took his text from the popular wish instead of its necessity, and this seldom offered sufficient provocation to study. It had no long train of relevant fancies and associations. It conducted to no depths of a fresh and encouraging philosophy. It lifted upon no wings of art to enlivening regions of joy and sun-shine. It was artful and ingenious without exercising any of the nobler offices of art. It seldom prompted invention. Its criticism was mostly of a French and *finicking* kind; pretty and precise; and that it was not pedantic, arose probably from the necessity of making it popular. It was never deep, and never thorough, and its fancies were expended chiefly upon the merest conventionalities, which, in the nature of things, must die out in a brief season, without rendering it necessary to summon any executioner. It might bring us flowers, but if it did so, the poor things seem to have been drawn from the hot-house, not from the healthy fields of nature; and were arranged in the trim, prim, array of the Flemish gardener, so much esteemed in that period. The rows of box and the dwarf elms, and the parallel trees "nodding to each other," as sneered at by Pope—himself an artist too much of the same school—furnished our Essayists chiefly with their materials for rustic delineation, quite as much at the expense of art as nature—a labour in which a feeble fancy occasionally strove to make escape from the confines and confusion of a crowded city sphere.

Let us not be misunderstood. We thus rate much of the essayical writings of a time when the essay itself too disproportionately occupied the literature of the country; but we must not be construed to disparage the performance when devoted to its proper uses and written by the proper masters. No doubt the essay of the time, with all its deficiencies, had its uses for society. One objection is, that, while it belonged essentially to the time, it did not rise sufficiently above it—it did not seek the full exercise of its objects and attributes; the spirit of the writer too often yielding to the paralyzing control of society and of courts that had neither tone nor character, the influences of which seemed daily more and more successful in subjecting English mind to foreign dominion, and in emasculating the genius, if not the language, of the nation. The court was declining in power, and the people not yet in position; a courageous and patriotic talent would have darted between and taken the game out of the hands of the one, while preparing it for the hands of the other. But the patriotism of the essayist is not one likely to lead to martyrdom. His temperament involves no rashnesses. It is seldom sanguine. As a reformer, he aims at manners rather than morals, and you seldom find him where the storm is brewing. How much of this imbecility was due to the dependance of so many of the popular writers of the day upon the court—to the habit, so general among politicians, of buying up the clever pens of ready writers—may readily be conjectured. Our essayists, as hacks of party, had too little sympathy with their vocation ever to seek its elevation; which could best be done only by bringing the full force of their endowments to bear upon their performances. Even as essayists to which their tastes particularly inclined them, we find too much that is cool, frigid, phlegmatic;—they do not often seem to have written *con amore*. Yet Addison and Steele both had presentiments of what the essay might become. Their occasional critiques, and passing reviews of the old writers, are in earnest of those high purposes to which the department has subsequently been advanced. The critique on Milton, for example—to whose full appreciation Addison does not seem ever to have attained—is in proof of an effort, however moderate, to rise above the social atmosphere which he was compelled to breathe. This critique, and others in the same collection, are now absolutely valueless; so grievously do they fall below their subject; yet do they foreshadow the subsequent natural transition, by which the essayist has passed into the reviewer. How truly do these performances illustrate the feebleness and ignorance, the bad taste, and the emptiness of an age, which needed that Addison should teach what was due to Milton, and when such criticisms as that referred to were deemed adequate exponents of his claims.

But, though we see the essayist, in modern times, so generally superseded by the reviewer, his vocation is by no means ended. The essay is a distinct province of literature, quite as legitimate as any other. It is one which holds a proper place in the walks of authorship, and possesses certain claims to our respect and sympathy, which can never be wholly set aside for any other. Its charge is over the amenities, the graces, the tastes and morale of society, and it occupies a field which we should never leave in naked fallow. Its province is especially manners, and those smaller moods, which prevail in society in the absence of its enthusiasm, and during the pauses of its progress. Addison, in his dedication to Lord Somers, of the papers of the *Spectator,* speaks of them as "a work which endeavours to polish and cultivate human life, by promoting virtue and knowledge, and by recommending whatsoever may be either useful or ornamental to society." The definition may be admitted, though by no means one with which the essayists have been always careful to comply. Perhaps that of Mr. Tuckerman, in the second of the works named in our rubrick, will more explicitly declare what is due from the essayists, and what we have a right to expect at their hands. "They describe the genuine sources, both of pleasure and improvement, and eloquently indicate that minor philosophy which cultivates the original and spontaneous resources of human life; which gratefully recognizes natural laws, and seeks to observe them; and which practically maintains that truth is the most satisfactory nutriment for the mind, beauty for the imagination and love for the heart. They hold, as it were, the prism of sympathetic intelligence up to the common lights of day, and cause its warm and brilliant, though latent hues, to re-appear. They analyze daily life to discover truth, and celebrate the reign of beauty in order to kindle the spirit of love. . . . Comparatively humble as this species of literature may be, in the estimation of highly practical or absolutely scientific authors, the intended service is noble, and, if worthily fulfilled, inspires affectionate and endearing regard, as is proved by the household fame such writers enjoy."

This is said, by our author, of the labours of the optimist: but it is thus that he describes the essayist. He is measurably correct. The essayist is the household author—the delineator of daily and ordinary life. He is not creative, but he may be fanciful; and, with moderate art, he may bring the ideal to hallow and embalm the material, and elevate the commonplace. We cannot forego this class of writers—we cannot well spare them,— and we should be grievously distressed if their province should be left neglected for others of more pretension. In an age like ours, which is so fondly insisted upon as one entirely of progress, and in which we do certainly move with astonishing rapidity, though our advance may well admit of question, the quiet, gentle, persuasive form of composition which characterizes the essay,—in which doctrine is to be insinuated rather than taught, and by which error and imperfection are to be beguiled rather than rebuked—the essay will probably command a too limited circle of admirers. Its mild graces will appeal only to that class of persons—not actually forced into the ring—who prefer retiring to cool shades and secure retreats—away from the heat and bustle of the crowd; communing upon what they see, and musing in pleasant reverie upon the struggles of that world, in whose vicissitudes they do not seem to share. They will naturally prefer to linger over those studies, in which the writer, like themselves, appears to look down from some secure loopholes of retreat, upon the progress of the distant masses, and studiously forbear to plunge into the restless moral whirlpools, which excite rather their terrors than their curiosity. A sufficient degree of human sympathy will enable them to look with pity upon the strifes which refuse to the combatants that peace which they are so fortunate as to enjoy; and their humanity will find sufficient exercise and aliment from those meditations which, erringly, prefer to strip man of his passions wholly, rather than be compelled to mourn over their perversion. In the essay of the optimist, students of this class will always be sure of a gentle philosophy, such as is always better pleased to show the race at play than at work; and may now and then, as the cloud and dust of the field disappears, under the influence of some blessed Sabbath of the century, be permitted to enjoy pleasant visions of the reign of Astrea restored to earth. Here, even while his subject treats of strife, his lessons shall be of repose. If he depicts the griefs of the world without, he contrasts them with the peace enjoyed within—a peace depending purely upon the whiteness in which he has kept his soul. If he paints the trials, toils and afflictions of the world, he studiously couples the narrative with gentle portraitures of a ministry forever watchful and busy in the affairs of man; superior to his passions; counselling him and restraining them, and always brim full of promise, teaching sweet assurances of a dawn of better things and times. The essay, in his hands, is thus the fireside mentor. It is a form of composition of peculiar use and propriety in the domestic circle. It is usually brief, to be read and relished at a single sitting. Its style is clear, simple and unaffected; its arrangement uncomplex, and its matter varied in accordance with the caprice of passing events. The essayist, accordingly, furnishes a fit commentary for every changing mood of the family circle. He avoids topics of party or vexation, or, if he treats of these, it is only in such a mode as will quiet the anger of the rival champions. He gives sympathies rather than counsels—soothes the thought to meditation rather than exertion, and, in the employment of a mild tone and a graceful fancy, makes the moral lovely, which the sterner censor, the critic, would only render harsh. He represents a class of writers whose tempers are placid, whose tastes shrink from the world's collision, whose habits are circumspect and shy, whose policy is conservative, who fear the mischances of progress too greatly to attempt it, and who are too well satisfied of the present ever to risk its securities upon a doubtful future; particularly as, in the language of Mr. Tuckerman, their study is "to make apparent the compensatory elements of human existence." They preserve the past, with a reverence which makes them love to pore over its chronicles; and seldom look to the future, whose forests they are unfitted to explore. They prefer

reverie to discussion; and possess,—instead of imagination, which is always combative and adventurous,—a meek, submissive fancy, which proves itself the loveliest handmaid to persuasion. We should be sorry to see the essay die wholly out
of the land, and are particularly pleased, at a time when the temper of the race
is continually yearning for new fields of conquest, if a mild and graceful circle
should still be found, in every community, to whom its gentle amenities shall still
be precious;—who will prefer to linger over the treasury already won by art and
arms, without yearning after newer acquisitions—who will give a secure place to
the possessions already made secure;—who will still present these attractively to
the public eye, and, at pauses in the strife, urge becomingly on its regards, the
subdued temper, the moderate tone, the nice propriety, the pure fancies and the
jealous tastes, which, beyond any other form of literary composition, the essay is
best calculated to promote and preserve.

With these opinions, we rejoice to welcome every production of this class
which issues from the American press. In our world, the essay is really more important, as an agent of civilization and refinement, than in any of the old States
of Europe. If it suffered decline in England, because of the more impetuous
impulses of the national temper, and the freshening stimulus of a new popular
excitement, much more greatly do the same influences prevail, to its disparagement, in America, where all the tendencies are to an increasing restlessness, and
where the necessities of the race are habitually hostile to repose. Here, we need
repose, if only to afford opportunity of meditation to the popular thought. Our
people are passionate, rather than contemplative. The national mind is one of
feverish urgency, sanguine, eager for action, restive under restraint and forever
breaking away from place and form, in search of the rough collision which it too
much loves. Its mission, at present, would seem to be conquest, not contemplation. Its training has rendered it eager in pursuit, hardened it for struggle,
impelled it in the single direction which leads to the camp rather than the altar,
and given it up to passions that goad it forever to performance, rather than to
fancies that beguile it from the path. The nation is living the epic, that other
generations perhaps will write. Its history is a wild romance. It bears the banner
of civilization, though it reaps few of its sublimer fruits, and it will be a long
season before it can possibly settle down into that quiet method, which will
afford sufficient scope for taste, to interpose with her softer ministries, to refine
the vigour which it now exhibits in excess. A nation forever in the dust of the
highway, forever in the melee, with no interval for rest or recreation, is an imposing, but not always the most noble spectacle. It is a nation at war, and the
muses, as we learn from the best authority, are but too apt to be silent at such
periods. Happy, if, in the conflict, we can catch the beguiling music from other
spheres, more in harmony with nature and the soul. Happy, if there be some
among us, content to turn aside from the common progress, and modify its
tendencies, and mollify its rages; who can sing us a song of quiet vallies [*sic*], and

teach more soothing harmonies, and unfold us thoughts of gentle beauty, and warm us with better affections than those which follow from the acquisition of provinces, or in the accumulation of the precious metals. In offices like these, the essayist claims kindred with the poet; and if not wholly prepared for the higher inspirations of the one, it is grateful, at least, if we can be won to listen by the more mortal, but still elevated persuasions of the other. The essayist, indeed, has this advantage over the poet, with an audience such as ours. While he teaches contemplation, and quietly improves the taste, his objects are obviously more practical. He ostensibly speaks to our ordinary necessities, cunningly interfusing with these occasional glimpses of fancy, of a yearning for better things, of a spiritual thirst, which, under his gradual offices, may prepare a partially exhausted, if not a thirsting people, to turn aside to waters of a holier inspiration.

Among the very few writers who, in America, have addressed themselves to the essay, in preference to all other forms of literature, Mr. Tuckerman perhaps deserves the highest distinction. He has, more rigidly than any other, adhered to the particular character of the composition thus described. Without refusing to avail himself of the changes made upon the essay, he has contrived that these "graffings" shall not really alter the form of the production, but shall be tributary to it. He is not a critic, not a reviewer, not a lecturer, yet he employs the agencies of all these in the preferred character of the essayist. His field, speaking of America only, is one which exhibits few competitors. We have, perhaps, already shown good reason, referring to the impatient and restless character of the public mind, why this should be so. We can recall the names of but few who have in this wise distinguished themselves among us. Wirt was perhaps a better essayist than orator or lawyer. He will rise in this character. There has been much boast among us of Dennie, in former times, who appeared in the very first dawning of American letters; but, though a correct and pleasing writer, he has left no decided impression upon the public mind, and there was quite too little force in what he wrote to make his meditations effective. Irving and Paulding are both essay writers, and it is not improbable that future criticism will declare their works of this class to be among the most excellent of their performances. Some of the occasional papers of Dana have a profounder value than belongs generally to the essay; but these form no great portion of his literary labours. Of Jones we have had occasion to speak briefly and approvingly in preceding pages. Emerson is an able essayist, of a school too much on stilts, too ambitious of the mystical, to be always secure of the sensible and true. He is decidedly popular with the transcendentalists, if we may recognize, by a term so dignified, a rather inflated race, who presume somewhat upon the fact that their place of birth is a few degrees nearer the rising sun than ours. Emerson aims to be a reformer, after the fashion of Carlyle; and no doubt has large merits, which might be available to common and beneficial use if they were less clouded and embarrassed with his affectations of the Delphic. We might name a few other writers, who have adopted this form of letters as their medium of communication with the rest of the world. But we can mention none, on our side of the Atlantic, whose claims as an essayist may be more favourably stated than those of the author immediately before us. The volumes named at the head of this article are the last which have been issued from his pen, and are probably among his best performances. They are certainly very fair samples of his style of writing and thinking, and afford us an excellent idea of his mind and character. The first of these volumes—"The Characteristics of Literature"—contains eleven papers,—the subjects of which are "Sir Thomas Browne," whom our author adopts as the model philosopher; "Shenstone," who is his *dilletante;* "Channing," his moralist; "Swift," his wit; "Roscoe," his philanthropist; "Lamb," his humourist; "Macaulay," his historian; "John Sterling," his idealist; "Burke," his rhetorician; "Akenside," his scholar; and, in a review of the final memorials of Lamb and Keats, edited by Talfourd and Milnes, he discusses the biographer. This arrangement is rather an artificial one, since the discussion of the several characteristics is made to depend upon the peculiar qualities of the individuals discussed. These are not always the best, or the most striking samples of the class of writers who represent the subject under discussion. We should utterly deny, for example, that John Sterling should be a chosen sample of the idealist, though every poet must necessarily, to some degree, be such; and we should apprehend that some injustice might be done to the endowments of Burke, by employing his name to distinguish the class of simple rhetoricians. Not that Mr. Tuckerman commits any such injustice in his analyses, respectively, of these and other characters. He accords the fullest credit to the genius and the philosophy of Burke, and by no means overrates the pretensions of Sterling. It is one of the peculiar merits of Mr. Tuckerman, that his view is usually a singularly just one; and, with tastes exceedingly decided, and preferences, which are everywhere apparent for certain departments of writing, yet he comes to the judgment upon his subjects with a mind remarkably free from prejudice and bias, and fully informed upon, and quite accessible to, all the characteristics of the particular subject which he examines. His manner of writing unites the essayist of the old school with the critic of the new. He is the analyst as well as essayist. He treats the system of the author and his performance together, and relieves happily the monotone of the essayist with the argumentative habit of the reviewer. Sometimes he narrates, at others muses and philosophizes, and then, descending to his author, he tests his previous speculations. For this practice, there are few writers more capable than Mr. Tuckerman. He is a devotee to letters. His subjects are almost wholly literary. His mind lives in this realm as in an atmosphere of its own. He is extensively read in English classics, and has evidently drank freely of the fountains supplied by the British dramatists, an acquaintance with whom is absolutely necessary to all those who would realize the powers and compass of the language. In these studies, a general and sympathizing nature has taught him to look below the surface, and not suffer himself to be deceived by a rough outside or an unfamiliar manner. His tastes have fused within his own mind all the purer particles in theirs. He not only understands, but feels them; and his success, accordingly, is singularly striking in all those portions of his articles where his analysis takes the form of narrative, and sums up their qualities. He does not examine his subjects in detail. He realizes their wholeness, and gives their characteristics in a summary, which is entirely his own. The summary is made with the entireness of a charge to the jury, the argument keeping pace with the evidence, and the conclusion being made inevitable by the progress of the statement.

The admirer of the quaint, thoughtful and imaginative old philosopher, Sir Thomas Browne, will be perfectly satisfied with the just and appreciative estimate of Mr. Tuckerman. Without seeking to make a keen analysis of his subject,—without examining his philosophies closely, or taking any one of his numerous performances into nice consideration—he has classed together their most characteristic traits, and illustrated the features of his mind by a soft and pleasing general portraiture. A few brief, judicious extracts, here and there, suffice to exhibit his most prominent aspects, and enable us to give credence to the conclusions of our author, as he carries us forward, step by step, in a narrative at once thoughtful and attractive. His tastes, his fancies, his sympathies, his philosophy, and the general scope of his mind, are all brought out to view, and the *tout ensemble* is one of a harmonious wholeness, which, to the reader already familiar with the writings of the old philosopher, leaves nothing to be desired, and nothing to be complained of;—to those to whom he is unknown, the essay of our author will prove a pleasant lure to his volumes, of which there is a beautiful modern edition.

The portrait of Shenstone is to the life. The general reflections of Mr. Tuckerman upon this feeble but amiable *dilettante* are at once well put and truthful. But, we pass to the paper on Channing—decidedly one of the best in the volume—showing a bolder style of thought, a more comprehensive criticism, and a degree of independence, as well as good sense, which prove Mr. Tuckerman to be capable of more adventurous efforts in the fields of psychological analysis. The purity, the coldness, the intense individuality of Channing—his tenacious egotism—his lark of geniality—his sympathy with the race, too frequently at the expense of the individual—are all pourtrayed [*sic*] with a skill and courage worthy of the highest credit; and we readily concur in the opinion that, while a determined individual will, which shaped out to Channing, almost at the beginning, a certain definite career, was the chief source of his great distinction, it was coupled with a lamentable immobility of character, which took all the geniality out of his nature; which deprived him, though a philanthropist, of almost all knowledge of his fellow man, and thus defeated one of the chief objects in his aim—the capacity to serve him with sympathy and succour him with truth.

Of Swift, Mr. Tuckerman's opinions are just and well detailed. His wit—his directness of purpose—his strength of will—his courage—his indefatigable energy—the native force of his genius—the absoluteness of his sense— are all allowed and insisted upon, in due relation with his cold selfishness of heart, and the earthy tendencies which rendered his character as base, probably, as any that ever commerced with Genius, without being sweetened by its sensibilities, or lifted by its wing. The portrait of Roscoe is a pleasant one, but one of mere eulogy throughout. It serves up the chief particulars in the career, personal and literary, of that amiable man and graceful historian; but, the author seems to have aimed more at a biographical than a critical sketch; and, in this, he was somewhat anticipated, and in a similar vein, by the well-known essay of Irving.

Charles Lamb evokes all the sympathies of our author. This paper, and that devoted to the final memorials of Lamb and Keats, should be read together. They furnish a graceful essay upon an Essayist, whose humour Mr. Tuckerman evidently feels warmly and appreciates fondly, though he does not seek to imitate it. He suffers none of Lamb's traits to escape him—lingers, with pleasure, upon his several attributes of pathos, sentiment, and humour, (in all of which he excelled) and has drawn such a portrait of his life and performances as must satisfy every admirer of the gentle and loveable Elia. In his estimate of Macaulay, Mr. Tuckerman concurs with most of the Reviewers, with this difference, that he joins issue with such of them as deny the philosophical faculty to the historian. On this point, Mr. Tuckerman happily remarks that Macaulay has "so arranged his facts, and related his story in so lucid and emphatic a manner, that the latent and general truths evolve themselves, to a reflective mind, more impressively than if set forth in an argumentative shape."

Of the prose writings of Sterling, we know nothing except from this paper of Mr. Tuckerman. His poetry—a good-sized volume—was published, not long since, in this country. It did not strike us as a very remarkable collection. We noticed some plaintive compositions, here and there an impressive or touching line, and an occasional elegy, that denoted a subdued yet earnest spirit, seeking, as it were, to soar, without absolutely taking flight. Mr. Tuckerman describes him as a writer whose life was incomplete; with a mind appreciative rather than productive, and excelling in mental portraiture. We leave it to him to satisfy the reader in regard to his subject. Of Burke, we are told that "his mind was essentially speculative; he delighted in curious observation; his range of inquiry was broad and refined; yet, to public affairs, he brought a calm, practical judgment, a sobriety of mood, a perception of the actual relation of things, and the absolute claims of an exigency, as if he had been wont to deal in matters of fact, and had drawn every lesson from stern experience." But, Mr. Tuckerman is better at a summary, or a portrait, than a definition, and his narrative would suffer misrepresentation by detaching from it any single sentences. His essay upon Burke's career and character affords as correct an idea, if not a sufficiently ample one, of that great master of argument as we may find any where. His paper on Akenside is equally satisfactory. We think, however, that he overrates him, as a poet. The passages which he quotes, from *The Pleasures of the Imagination,* are not, in our opinion, greatly calculated to impress us with the vigour of his own; and, the continued neglect of this performance, at a period which prides itself upon the unwearied resuscitation of neglected but meritorious authors, would seem to show that neither the world nor modern criticism is prepared to sanction the high estimate which Mr. Tuckerman has set upon his muse. We can understand why our author should make this estimate of Akenside. He, also, was an Essayist. He belonged to the school of the moral-contemplative; and, possibly, had his "Pleasures" taken the form of the Essay, rather than the Poem, its claims would have been much more generally recognized than those of Addison.

We must confine ourselves to a single quotation, only, from this pleasant and instructive volume. We take the passage, almost at random, from the paper on Channing. It is a fair specimen of our author's modes of writing and thinking. It illustrates, equally, the philanthropy and egotism of Channing, which were inseparable from the nature of the man:

"The remark of one of the schoolfellows of Channing, when the latter was cited as an example—'it is easier for him to be good'—at once recognises a peculiar moral idiosyncrasy. We need but to glance over the records of biography to perceive that there is a distinct class of men who represent the saintly, as others do the heroic and poetical character. The retirement in which such natures ripen, was sought of old in the hermitage and convent; and now, as in the instance before us, in a kind of self-imposed monachism. It is, however, a serious question whether, after all, this is a healthful species of moral development. Let any human being, of strong will, live upon a fixed system of meditative retirement, and his passions will grow calm, his interest in outward life diminish, and, with the requisite temperament, he easily becomes rapt in spiritual ecstacies. When a man is endowed with remarkable contentiousness and veneration, as well as gifts of mind, he seems ordained to promulgate truth and quicken in others the sentiments so active in himself. Such was the case with Dr. Channing. Yet, to us his memory is hallowed, because he was so 'clear in his great office,' rather than from an unreserved admiration of his personal example. As a moral rhetorician, his labours have reflected honour on his name and country; as a man—there were peculiarities arising from education, physical constitution, and tendencies of nature, which rendered him a very incomplete representative of humanity. No one more eloquently discoursed of philanthropy; but his interest in man, in the abstract, was no test of his ready sympathy with the individual. Indeed, we have observed one trait in modern philanthropists which has sometimes reconciled us to the culture of humbler virtues. They are, generally speaking, the last men to whom are confided personal griefs, or whose exclusive amity is sought. They generalize with the heart as well as the mind; burn with indignation at the wrongs inflicted on the natives of Africa, while often profoundly indifferent to the true welfare of one of their own household. How often some desolate human being, touched by their written appeals in behalf of a distant class of sufferers, is inspired with the confidence to make them the recipients of secret troubles—to seek from them counsel and encouragement in loneliness and doubt. A benevolent father of the Catholic church, by the mere claim of his vocation—a warm-hearted sailor, by the very candid generosity of his soul, or one of Nature's sisters of charity—encountered, as they are, in all the circles of life—were a surer ark of refuge. The views of the professed lover of his race are too expansive. His benevolence is purely speculative. His sympathy with man is like that which the mere botanist has for a flower, or the surgeon for a human form. It is rather professional than natural; and he who has sought a conference with such, in order to relieve his overcharged heart, finds his utterance choked, his tears frozen, and every hope of recognition die within him! In these remarks, we design no indiscriminate application to the revered subject of the memoir before us. He accomplished good enough in his own way—perhaps the only one in which his efficiency was certain; but we desire to repudiate the common notion that usefulness—in its highest sense—is confined to those broad fields of philanthropic enterprise which an influential class among us seems to regard as the only legitimate arena of benevolence. We remember, as if it were but yesterday, at the close of a winter's day, soon after Dr. Channing's return from Europe, when his slender form all at once appeared before a group of mourners—one of the families of his parish, who were bereaved, during his absence, of their dearest earthly friend. As he stood among them, in the twilight, and the flickering blaze revealed his high and placid brow—the eyes of one of those motherless children—(in whose mind his image was associated with the sweetest counsels of maternal tenderness, and upon whom his priestly hand had been laid in baptism)—instinctively sought his face, with a penetrating glance—a silent appeal for some word of solace in that dark hour. At length he spoke—but it was to exclaim, 'What a mysterious Providence!' The scene had awakened a speculative reverie, and not one tear of commiseration. His mind was busy in the attempt to reconcile to itself a sad visitation; but his heart swelled not at the sight of the young band left alone to the perils of the world. And, when he rose to depart, and looked back upon them, it was only to remark, 'I am going to my solitary home.' His own family had not yet returned from their country residence. In a few days, at least, their presence would brighten his fireside; while those he left were destined for years to a home made solitary by death! This incident illustrates the truth we design to suggest—that the sympathetic and reflective character have distinct provinces of action; and that any one who, from the perusal of these interesting memoirs, should deem their subject a model to be practically adopted, with a view to attain the same moral results, would commit an egregious error. The truth is, the essence of Dr. Channing's life appears in his writings. There he emitted the vital aura of his few days of health. There he embodied the energy of feeling which other and less distinguished men give to the offices of friendship and love. He found, at an early age, that he must decide between the free exercise of social habits and feelings and a sphere of utility based essentially upon contemplation. Had he possessed a greater mobility of character, power of adaptation, and facility of intercourse; especially, had the affections of his nature been as individual as his intellectual processes, he would instinctively have cultivated the social duties and sentiments, and recognised in them no small part of the grace and benignity of life. But, his ill-health, the stern influences of his early years, the habit, so remarkable in New-England, of regarding character at the two extremes of right and wrong, and suspecting all zest of life as intrinsically evil, led him to cherish will beyond sentiment, to feel, with singular force, the responsibility incident to the right of choice in action; and hence to lean towards stoicism and penance. It is true, that, as years advanced, the overstrained chords were a little relaxed, and he began to realize how much innocent delight is attainable through a receptive, truthful, genial spirit. He observed to one of his most intimate companions, as this softer experience dawned upon his mellow faculties, that, perhaps, he had made a grand mistake—perhaps, the most happy and satisfactory life was one passed in the free and earnest exercise of the attentions and sympathies."

With the Essay on the "Last Memorials of Lamb and Keats," the volume closes. We have already briefly referred to this Essay, and can do no more. We have transgressed beyond our limits, and must content ourselves with a simple enumeration of the contents of "The Optimist"—the second under notice, and marked, as in the preceding instance, by nice analysis, great delicacy in discrimination, a gentle taste, harmonious style, and a pleasant, discursive vein of thought. The variety of this volume is not the least of its recommendations. This may be conjectured from the titles of the subjects chosen: "New England Philosophy"—a very sensible and searching paper, from which we shall contrive to appropriate an extract; "Travel;" "Music;" "Conversation;" "Art and Artists;" "Lyric Poetry;" "Social Life;" "Costume;" "Walking;" "A Chapter on Hands;" "New-York Colonists;" "Eye-Language;" "Humour;" "The Gold Fever;" "Profession of Literature;" "Hair;" "Presidential Inauguration;" "Weather;" "Manner;" "Flowers;" "Broad Views;" and "The Rationale of Love." Here is reading for a summer; and, the Optimist, seeking, every where, the greatest good in life, and the pleasantest prospects, will find, in the pages of this volume, a prevailing mood every way favourable to the object of his search. But, for our promised extract from the paper on New-England Philosophy. See how happily Mr. Tuckerman introduces his subject:

"In all communities, there is a pervading theory of life—a set of principles which guide the mass—a few permanent ideas that actuate society. The English, for example, driven by a humid atmosphere to look within doors for cheerful associations, gather about them, with profusion, the means of physical well-being. Continental visitors to Great Britain are astonished at the perfection of domestic machinery, and the ingenious devices to secure ease and warmth, and render the dwelling a castle and a home. They at once recognise in such arrangements the idea of Comfort as the chief element in the philosophy of life. People, on the other side of the channel, instead of concentrating their means of enjoyment, go abroad in search of them. The Parisian finds the glare of a public *café* more agreeable than the snug fire-side of a private room; he reads his gazette under the trees in a public garden, and finds no difficulty in making a companion of his neighbour at the theatre, piquing himself, all the while, more on being one of the French nation than for any individual qualities or possessions. By temperament and habit, he directly seeks Pastime, as the end of his existence. If we pass to Italy, we discover a passion for music, great local pride in the fame of genius, universal taste and enthusiasm for imaginative excitement of all kinds, and realize how largely Art enters into their system of life. The Chinese trustfully refer you to 'Old Custom,' and the Turks to Fate, as the principles by which they regulate their being. It may be a fanciful notion, but I think the ordinary salutations of a people indicate, in a measure, their philosophy of living. The French greeting is, literally, 'How do you carry yourself?'—a query suggestive of egotism; that of the Italians, 'How do you stand?'—which breathes of an existence in the immediate, so characteristic of the South; while our favourite phrase is, 'How do you get along?'—at once calling up an external and distant goal—success."

We greatly regret that the length of this paper, and our own limits, forbid that we should give it entire. We must cut our Essay into bits. Here is a glimpse at American mistakes in training, illustrative of a subject already discussed in our commentary:

"Next to the danger of subserviency to society, the unhealthy prominence of the idea of thrift is the most baneful feature in our philosophy of life. That it should be prominent in a young and commercial republic is to be expected. The great error is that there is little desire to restrain its expression within due bounds. Let it have free scope on the exchange and in the mart, but let it not continually deform our fireside discourse, and usurp the inner sanctuary of the soul. There, at least, let not all be 'base respects of thrift and none of love.' Pecuniary ability is the established criterion of the value of life; circumstances are almost deified; success is exclusively desired, or rather grossly misunderstood; for, if there be a single established principle of human well-being, it is that which defines the successful man as him who is true to himself—to his powers, tastes, and actual need. It is time we not only coldly acknowledged, but instinctively felt, that it is as barbaric to reverence wealth as to overload the limbs with ornament. The philosophy of life, with us, seems based on the faith that man lives by bread alone. Trade and politics completely overshadow literature and art. Invention exhausts itself upon machines and finance; our trophies may be found chiefly at the patent office. Yet, the real end of all these is to procure time; and, what is time, if unprovided with the resources which shall dignify and adorn it? 'Poetry,' says a beautiful writer, 'and the principle of self, of which money is the visible incarnation, are the God and Mammon of the world.'"

Here, we have a picture, the necessary result of our social training, and the inferior objects of national desire:

"The next feature in the prevalent theory of life, to which I would allude, is the want of serenity. In society, business, and education, there is a spirit of urgency, an artificial force, constantly exhibited, as opposed to true habits of mind as it is to real happiness. If enterprise hath her Carnival here, enjoyment often keeps Lent. We accustom ourselves to live in a continual bustle, and make, on all occasions, a parade of action, as if this were the true criterion of success—the only evidence of progress. We do not believe in the wise saying, that 'it is an absolute, and, as it were, a divine perfection for a man to know how loyally to enjoy his being.' There is a true epicurism—the luxury of an existence regulated by the natural wants and higher instincts of the individual—of which we are practically ignorant. Instead of meeting, in the frank simplicity and heartiness becoming republicans, at one another's firesides, in the full and frequent confidence of genuine social feeling, interchanging opinions, and enjoying the delights of sympathy, we deem it better to crowd our small apartments to suffocation—wander, for several hours, over a dwelling which has been disarranged from garret to cellar for the occasion—exchange a word or sign of recognition with some hundred acquaintances—and close the evening's pastime by partaking of an extravagant entertainment. Even the preparation for the conflict of life, to which the earlier years of existence are sacred, is marked by the same ostentatious urgency. The tender brain of infancy is fevered by the spirit of emulation. The child is incited at home by the ambitious views of his parents, and surrounded at school by a system of artificial machinery. Certificates of conduct and studies flutter weekly before his eyes, inspiring the same anxious foreboding that the thought of promissory notes is destined, in after life, to awaken—when the banks suspend specie payments. Then come periodical examinations and exhibitions, for which the pupil undergoes weeks of extra drilling, as if he could not be too early and too deeply impressed with the importance of display. How often is the sensitive New-England youth forced to sympathize in Tony Lumpkin's undutiful remonstrance to his mother's officious and mistaken kindness, which she justifies by the common plea, that it was all for the victim's good: 'I wish you'd let me and my good alone, then. If I'm to have any good, let it come of itself; and don't keep dinging it, dinging it into me so.' And, when he leaves the scene of education, whatever his calling, the same principle of 'affected dispatch,' as Lord Bacon calls it, must be acted upon. If he would succeed in business, he must identify himself with some popular movement, he must contrive to keep his name before the public, with the epithets, 'liberal and enterprising,' appended to it. A hint must now and then be given, in the papers, of his yearly sales, or the amount of hands he employs. Above all, he must keep up in his own person an appearance of business. His rapid gait, hasty speech, and short salutations, must give the world assurance of a busy man. Mrs. Jameson, whose observation was artistic as well as sympathizing, observed, that American faces had an outward look. This extends even to American enjoyments, of which it may be said, as some traveller said of the English, 'they amuse themselves sadly after the manner of their country.' If, on the other hand, a professional life is adopted, the first thing necessary to success is, to do or seem to do something extraordinary. One must advocate some peculiar system, announce some startling novelty, or espouse some public cause, and let it be known, from Maine to Georgia, that he is ready to become a martyr in its behalf. In a word, this trait of our philosophy of life is almost universal. Scarcely a week passes without a celebration, by public dinners and eloquent harangues, of some popular event or local anniversary. The political atmosphere is never quiet, and the social spirit is ever and anon aroused by some bold doctrine or alleged discovery. Now, that there is much that is really desirable in such symptoms, it would be absurd to deny—that they constitute an unavoidable feature in our present stage of progress, is very evident. Still, it is of great importance that the individual should not be deceived or carried away by this universal semblance of activity. In older countries, we often see a graceful repose upon destiny, an absence of care respecting the future, and an instinctive trust like that in which a bird or flower lives; which, to say the least, leaves the mind free to please and be pleased, and renders far less prevailing than with us the idea of self-interest and morbid ambition. Such beings have the requisite sympathy to regard the individuality, and realize the fraternal relation, which make human society endearing. Let us not be so absorbed in the show of things, as to miss their essence and reality. There is no little danger, amid all this exhibition of force, this large promise of results, that we shall be drawn aside from our true position by the stream of multitude. The great duty which such artificial activity imposes upon the individual is to estimate calmly the real value of the objects for which so much sympathy is demanded. His obligations to his own nature are paramount to those which society so constantly urges."

We pass, hurriedly, over some, pleasant passages, which we should greatly like to detach, but dare not, and fasten upon the following, in which the baneful practices of confounding the intellectual nature with the soul, and crushing the heart, in giving the crown and sceptre wholly to what we, vulgarly and improperly, esteem the reason, is justly dwelt upon:

"Another principle in the New-England philosophy of life, which demands attention, is extreme devotion to reason. Franklin is still the personation of the American mind abroad—an honoured name, indeed, but one that serves only as a partial exponent of humanity: the type of the practical, not the ideal man—of useful science rather than the soul. In no other country could Poor Richard's sayings have attained such favour. Our only metaphysician who enjoys a European reputation is Edwards, whose celebrated work on the Will is devoted to a defence of the old popular theology. The pride of the cultivated New-Englander is that he is rational. The first lore instilled into his mind is in the shape of prudential maxims. The favourite term of approbation he bestows upon a woman is *sensible,* and there is nothing so congenial to his ambition as the reputation of talent. The natural consequence is, that his ideal of character is based almost wholly upon intellectual gifts and attainments. Every subject is viewed through the cold medium of expediency; all questions must be tried by the level light of the understanding, and the most hallowed associations and universal precedents wrested into the service of temporary and narrow objects. One of our most distinguished men, in a critique upon Othello—that unrivalled exposition of the power of love, and 'jealousy, that doats but dooms, and murders yet adores'—declares the moral of the sublime drama to be an exposition of the evil consequences of amalgamation and runaway matches! In this tendency to seize upon the rationale of existence—to act upon what are called common-sense principles—there is, doubtless, much to approve. A community, thus characterized, possesses an essential element of advancement. But, when such a theory is exclusive—when it is reposed upon as broad and deep enough for the soul, and becomes, as it were, the standard of life and the mould of character, we are tempted to exclaim, with Charles Lamb, 'Hang them!—I mean the cursed reasoning crew—those blights and blasts of all that is human in man or child.' We do not appreciate feeling. We estimate knowledge far beyond sentiment. We reverence intellect, but look distrustfully upon enthusiasm; for, the love of excitement in which the formal lives of New-Englanders re-act, is not entitled to the name. We crusade, for the most part, against vices of appetite, which are often the overflowings of rich natures, linked with the most generous qualities, and, in most cases, only fatal when habitual and excessive. We do not realize that the moral evils that most effectually despoil the spirit of beauty are those of calculation, to which perverted intellect panders;—these are integral, not incidental. A lapse of integrity—an act of successful fraud, accomplished with consummate skill—is infinitely more detestable than the temporary abuse of any natural appetite; for, it argues the deliberate perversion of the higher faculties—a hopeless barrenness of noble feeling. I know that many will not consent to such a broad distinction between the mind and the heart. Ideas, say they, are but feelings shaped into thought. But, such metaphysical niceties have nothing to do with our present purpose. Every one is conscious of a power within him, which reasons, judges, and infers, and other and far different capacities, whose office it is to awaken, impel, and fill him with emotions. Now, I think it cannot be denied that the reasoning powers are too frequently cultivated, with us, at the expense of those fine sensibilities and warm impulses which exist in every human breast, the sternness of our Puritan origin—the formality of our system of education—the

reserve of our social intercourse—the calculating habits of our national character—all tend to repress in the young the earnest flow of their hearts; they early
acquire a false shame at the expression of feeling, and come to regard the least
manifestation of natural ardour as undignified and weak. And thus the saying of
one of the commentators on our country is verified—our climate has no spring
and our people no youth. One often recalls the exclamation of the afflicted par-
ent, depicted by Shakespeare, to his officious consoler, 'I prithee, peace!—I will
be flesh and blood!' The brave Marquis of Posa, in Schiller's *Don Carlos,* in his
bold and generous appeal to the cruel Philip, exclaims, 'In your great system,
suffer *souls* to ripen.' One is inclined to urge the same plea upon those who are
so active in their cares for the New-England mind. The cares of life and the
scenes of competition into which the New-Englander is early introduced, will do
enough to indurate and pervert the fountains of the heart. Let not our theory
of life, our practical philosophy, second the process which circumstances already
sufficiently insure. The vividness and strength of early impressions every one has
realized. They colour our whole after lot. Now, it is remarkable that, acknowledged as this truth universally is, its actual influence upon education is so slight.
The impression which the child receives will be indissolubly associated with all
his future experience. Should it not, then, be more a matter of conscience with
parents and teachers to minister to the happiness of childhood, to reverence its
freedom, instead of following the example of the sagacious man who clipped the
wings of his bees, and selected for them such flowers as he chose? Let us refrain
from stamping any stern or dark impression upon the young heart, that it may
meet the problem of life in a fresh and original spirit. The discipline to which
we are subject in early life, however kindly intended, too often weaves shadows
for our future lot, and sadly mars our spiritual destiny. Byron breaks off, in the
midst of his glorious lay, inspired by classic scenes, to lament the forced teaching of his youth, which embittered the pages of Horace for ever to his taste; and
how many New-Englanders, from a similar cause, have the painful associations
of a task connected with the best of books, and the gloomiest sense of restraint
associated with the holiest of days! We laugh at the impatient child who daily
digs up the seed to see if it has sprouted; and are content to supply good soil to
the plant, and leave it to the free air, the soft dew, and the balmy sunshine. Why
are we less just to the soul? To guard it from evil, and meet its wants, as far as we
can, is indeed our duty; but a higher power has already ordained its capacities;
to them we can neither add nor take away. Let us show our veneration for God's
holy work, and leave it more to his smile and its own freedom.

"Another consequence of this exclusive faith in reason is, that it disposes us to
repose entirely upon rules, to act too constantly upon arbitrary principles, till the
mechanical triumphs over the spiritual, and mere habit usurps the place of the
spontaneous. Now, I do not deny that roles have their utility; that, in a world of
vicissitude, certain laws of action must be, to some extent, at least, adopted, and

that fixed principles are the best security to virtue. But, this admission does not justify the dogged attachment to certain maxims which is so often boasted of as the distinction of New-England philosophy. Constant reference to precise rules indicates the novice. The artist, at first, is continually measuring; but, as his eye becomes practised, he confides in its accuracy. An instinct developes within him more certain than the dictum of science. And, thus, the soul outgrows maxims, and becomes spontaneously progressive and true. With many votaries of the rational system, I believe, the great idea of improvement consists in nothing more than adding to their stock of ideas. Some, indeed, do not even go thus far, but are chiefly anxious to abide by those they have already acquired. The direct tendency of this feature of the prevalent philosophy is to lead a man, particularly one of passive temperament, to entrench himself in a set of fixed laws—as if the goal of progress was reached— the great end of life achieved. He has established a certain theory of dietetics—a certain system of expense—has chosen a set of companions, and adopted a certain political and religions creed—and, now, all that remains for him is to abide by all these rules, and thus realize Burns's picture:

> 'O, ye douce folk, that live by rule,
> Grave, tideless-blooded, calm and cool,
> Compared wi' you—O, fool! fool! fool!
> How much unlike!
> Your hearts are just a standing pool,
> Your lives a dyke!'"

Here, we must stop. We have said and shown enough of Mr. Tuckerman, as an Essayist, to persuade the reader to seek his volumes. We must now content ourselves with the hurried expression of our thanks to this graceful writer, for memories refreshed and fancies enlivened, in their recourse, under his conduct, to well-known and always-grateful fountains. Mr. Tuckerman, we need scarcely repeat, is a most agreeable and graceful Essayist. He is worthy to associate, honourably, with the ablest of his class. His style is not less pure than free—sometimes, a little too swelling, but never wanting in correctness: happily harmonious, and with periods always well-balanced, yet free from any laboured antithesis. As a critic, he is gentle and generous; as an Essayist, contemplative, excursive, sometimes highly felicitous, and frequently as forcible as fanciful. His thoughts, without being commonplace, are limpid always. His sentences ripple onwards in a sweet, clear, musical undertone—like some forest streamlet, usually in a subdued light, under the shadow of stately trees, with a bright sparkle, ever and anon, upon the waters, that relieves their progress from all monotony.

Ellet's Women of the Revolution

Elizabeth Fries Ellet was a northern woman by birth. She was born in 1818 and spent her early years in Sodus Point, New York, a port town on Lake Ontario that declined in significance after it was bypassed by the Erie Canal. Her father was a physician who saw value in educating his daughter and sent her to a female seminary where she studied English and French. In 1835 she both published her first book, *Poems Translated and Original,* and married William H. Ellet, a professor of chemistry at Columbia College in New York City. Soon after their marriage William accepted a professorship at South Carolina College, and he and his young bride traveled south to Columbia, South Carolina (Mattingly, "Elizabeth Fries Lummis Ellet," 101; "Elizabeth F. Ellet," 610). The couple met then William Gilmore Simms, and Elizabeth Ellet began work on the project for which she is best known, *Women of the American Revolution,* a three-volume collection of stories and narratives related to women's participation in the War of Independence.

Ellet had begun cultivating her reputation as a writer with her poetic contributions to the *American Quarterly Review,* the *North American Review,* the *Southern Quarterly Review,* and *Godey's Lady Book,* among other publications. Her early work consisted primarily of verse, while *Women of the American Revolution* represented her entrance into historical writing. Her work was significant, as Simms recognized in his review, for inserting women's history into the story of the American Revolution. Ellet continued that project with subsequent works, including her *Pioneer Women of the West* (1852) and *Queens of American Society* (1867). It was fitting that Ellet looked to the Revolution for her subject, because she was in many respects a product of the postrevolutionary age.

One of the great social achievements of the early Republic was the closing of the literacy gap between women and men—at least in simple reading and writing, and at least in the northeast and among the southern elite and yeomanry.

Central to this transformation in female education was the belief that women would inculcate future generations with the republican virtue necessary for the new nation to thrive. Ellet was among the beneficiaries of this drive to educate women, though even the best education, such as Ellet received, remained circumscribed and focused on those areas—grammar, penmanship, bookkeeping, geography, history—thought most necessary for producing "wiser wives and better mothers" (Kerber, *Women of the Republic,* 199–222). That Ellet engaged in historical writing, therefore, was not a coincidence. Supporters of educational reform, Benjamin Rush notable among them, emphasized that it was important for women to read history, the study of which would not only make them "an agreeable companion for a sensible man," but would also "subdue that passion for reading novels which so generally prevail[ed] among the fair sex" and was ill-suited to women's role within the household as both educators and bastions of republican virtue (Campbell, "Benjamin Rush and Women's Education," 5–31).[2]

These changes had a transatlantic component as well and resulted in and a number of women turning to the study of history during the Age of Revolution. Many of these women, like Ellet, focused their studies not on the political or military exploits of great men, but rather on the social histories of lesser-known female actors. Notable among these writers were Mercy Otis Warren who, like Ellet, wrote on the American Revolution; Maria Williams, Mary Wollstonecraft, and Germaine de Staël, who wrote on the French; and, later, Marie Catherine Sophie, Comtesse d'Agoult (pen name Daniel Stern), who wrote on the Revolution of 1848. This focus certainly reflected the status that these women held as outsiders to formal political life, but also allowed writers like Ellet to assert the central role played by women and the domestic household in political life (Smith, *The Gender of History,* 40, 50–61).

Simms, who recognized and explored the relationship between politics and the household in much of his historical fiction, lauded Ellet for her exploration of these themes. It was an important corrective, he wrote, to the typical history, which had the tendency to "contribute to the errors of the statesman who sinks into the *doctrainaire,*" because it told "the history rather of the princes than the people" ("Women of the Revolution").[3] Simms was not the only critic to speak well of Ellet's volumes. The work also was generally well received by the literary press, adding to Ellet's reputation as a writer. The notice in the *North American Review* described the care and patience she exhibited in compiling the volumes as "deserv[ing] to be called pious." Evert and George Duyckinck later remembered the work as one that required "not only a special sympathy and literary skill, but much labor and research" ("Ellet's Women of the Revolution," 364; "Elizabeth F. Ellet," 610).[4]

It was not surprising that Simms would offer a favorable review of Ellet's work, because it was conversations between Ellet and him that gave the young writer her initial inspiration to embark on the endeavor (Ellet, "Letter to M.D.S."). While Simms later soured on Ellet, partly because she had not expressed proper gratitude towards him for suggesting the subject and leading her to many of the sources that she used, in the review reprinted here he demonstrated the level of enthusiasm that one would expect from a mentor (*Letters* 4: 148). Moreover Simms viewed his review essay less as an occasion to describe the relative merits and deficiencies of the work under consideration than as an opportunity to expand upon themes that he found worthy of discussion. Among these was the interdependency of the household and the broader society.

Simms saw the household as society in microcosm and asserted that it was impossible to imagine a properly ordered society that did not have at its core properly ordered households. "The nation," he wrote, "is but a community of homes, with the same *Genius Loci* set up for the authority of each" ("Women of the Revolution" below). It was by "the fireside—the source of all the virtues— that the lawgiver must first learn to protect and make grateful to the affections of those who seek warmth upon its hearthstones," where the statesman learned the skills necessary to serve as a benevolent leader. Households not only fostered male authority, but also developed the reverence and loyalty necessary for the maintenance of a successful social state. Women, whose role Simms described as that of "the angel," were both the incubators and the inculcators of virtue, ministry, and love, while children embodied the values of dependence and service.

Though Simms did not mention slaves directly, they would have fallen in the latter category, as dependents in a perpetual state of adolescence. The last point is important, because Simms's vision of social order was distinctly southern and written in contrast to the emerging northern bourgeois ideology of the mid–nineteenth century, which was novel in its radical separation of public and private spheres. Increasingly the northern household and women's role within it were divorced from productive labor, which was taking place more and more outside of the home (Fox-Genovese. *Within the Plantation Household*, 61–63). That distinction, however, was less pronounced within the extended households of the slaveholding South, and this provided Simms with one of the themes that he chose to highlight in his review. Instead of a collection of individuals, he viewed society as an organic hierarchy composed of a collection of individual communities. Ellet's compilation of domestic histories, which sought to demonstrate the interconnectedness of the household and the nation, albeit implicitly, offered Simms the opportunity to expound upon this social vision.

Simms recognized the impact of the War of Independence in politicizing not only the household, but also women's roles within it. The crucible of the Revolution, Simms argued, had the effect of elevating women's roles and had transformed "the mere woman, the dependent, seeking simply to minister," and endowed her instead with "the moral characteristics of the citizen" and allowed her "to assert the higher virtues of her own individuality" ("Women of the Revolution"). Here, then, both Simms and Ellet agreed: the war had permitted women to operate as political actors in a way that they had not done before. It had mobilized the entire household and placed increased importance on women's role as purveyors of virtue and strength. As husbands and sons went off to war, it also provided women the opportunity to develop their own social networks and contribute directly to the war effort (Kerber, *Women of the Republic,* 41–42).

Historians have argued that these developments were Janus-faced, allowing women increased opportunities for political action but also confining that action within domestic spaces (Kerber, *Women of the Republic*). That distinction was less stark in the worldview that Simms articulated. If the division between public and private space was less rigid, if the household was a vital component of political life, then women's role within the household was not only vital to the functioning of the Republic, but also less circumscribed than it might have appeared in northern society. Certainly that is an optimistic view that did not fully account for the disabilities that southern white women faced—and says nothing about enslaved women—but it does illuminate why Simms viewed women's history as such a vital component of the history of the nation.

It is also important to understand Simms's review in the context of his broader project of developing a sense of southern nationalism. He was quick to point out that only 19 of the more than 150 biographical sketches in Ellet's volumes were of New Englanders. This ratio he viewed as "something of a commentary, indeed, upon the large pretensions set up of late by the New-England historians." Despite the fact that the author was "a Northern lady by birth, and education, and residence," Simms noted self-assuredly, "the Southern States constitute fully two-thirds of her three volumes" (Simms, "Women of the Revolution," 334). Yet, while Simms elsewhere rankled at not receiving proper credit for his part in developing Ellet's study, he here failed to report that she had begun her project while a resident of his home state and that he had played an important role in pointing her toward much of her early source material. For Simms that elision, while willful, did not represent a distortion. He had long sought to elevate the central role played by southerners in the fight for American independence, a project made all the more difficult by northern writers and their worship of "their false Gods in our History" (*Letters* 4: 149). If making a strong counter argument in a just cause meant exaggerating some of the evidence, then Simms was prepared to do that. Although his emphasis on the centrality of southern history was a longstanding theme in his writing, the politics of the moment gave new intensity to the project.

In 1850 the United States had recently acquired a vast new western territory as a consequence of the war with Mexico, making the nation a continental empire and opening fierce debates about the future of slavery in those new territories. That summer, as Simms penned his review of Ellet, delegates from nine southern states met in Nashville to contemplate a common position with regards to the fate of slavery in the Mexican Cession. It was a meeting that Simms had wanted to attend and that he would write about at length in a subsequent review essay, one that is reprinted in this volume. By this time he had already begun anticipating disunion, and so cultivating southern identity was a project of dire consequence (*Letters* 3: 8–13). Seen within that context, Simms's review of Ellet appears as a call to action, one meant to highlight the necessity of well-ordered households, and the active role of women within them, to the strength of a nation. To that end he also explored, albeit briefly, a theme that he had earlier discussed in his review of François Guizot's *Democracy in France*.

The one error that Simms pointed out in *Women of the American Revolution* was that Ellet suggested that the revolutionary energy was derived from the great mass of the people. In that argument she was mistaken, he insisted. It was instead the case that "the movement originated with the native intellect of the country. It had its birth among the educated and wealthy classes" ("Women of the Revolution"). A far less diffuse operation than most historians admitted, it was instead a revolution that was led from above. It had thus avoided the social chaos of more democratic uprisings, such as those that had recently occurred in Europe.

While he did not know what course the future would take, Simms was here using history as a medium through which he could contemplate the direction of civilization. He was thinking deeply about revolutions and what made some successful while others faltered. He could not know, though he did have reason to suspect, that he might partake in his own revolutionary struggle; so these meditations were more than just philosophical exercises. The reviews that he wrote during this period, the subjects that he selected, and the themes that he chose to highlight thus offer a window into his broader thinking about southern identity, social order, and the future of American and also southern civilization.

Ehren Foley

Notes

1. Rush's 1787 address entitled "Thoughts Upon Female Education" was particularly influential in shaping the program for women's education in the early Republic, and in it he repeatedly emphasized the importance of women's reading of history. Quotations from Benjamin Rush, "Thoughts Upon Female Education, Accomodated to the Present State of Socity, Manners and Government in the United States" (Boston, 1787).

2. Rush's 1787 address entitled "Thoughts Upon Female Education," was particularly influential in shaping the program for women's education in the early republic and in it he repeatedly emphasized the importance of women's reading of history. Quotations from Benjamin Rush, "Thoughts Upon Female Education, Accomodated to the Present State of Socity, Manners and Government in the United States," (Boston, 1787).

3. Elizabeth Fox-Genvovese and Eugene Genovese have pointed out that southern slaveholders displayed a particular interest in the social history of common people and domestic institutions because they believed that these historical subjects offered support for their own social institutions. For slaveholders such a history provided both moral lessons and support for the political economy of slavery. Histories of the common people, slaveholders believed, showed that the laboring classes had been experiencing steady improvement until the emancipations of the modern era. Slaveholders saw social history as an indictment of free society and reinforcement for their arguments that slave society offered a way to avoid the perils of modern society. Fox-Genovese, Elizabeth, and Eugene Genovese, *The Mind of the Master Class: History and Faith in the Southern Slaveholders' Worldview* (Cambridge: Cambridge University Press, 2005): 170–200.

4. See also "Editor's Book Table," *Godey's Lady's Book* (March 1849) and "Notices of New Books," *United States Democratic Review* 23 (December 1848): 565-6.

[Review of Elizabeth F. Ellet, *The Women of the American Revolution*]

The Women of the American Revolution; by Elizabeth F. Ellet, author of "The Characters of Schiller," "Country Rambles," &c. In three volumes. New-York: Baker & Scribner. 1850.

It would be an inquiry, equally valuable and curious, which, in the history of a popular revolution, would undertake faithfully to ascertain, to what degree

"Women of the Revolution." *Southern Quarterly Review* n.s. 1 (July 1850): 314–54 (40pp.).

the action of the political world was influenced by the emotions of the social;—
which would trace the workings of the politician up, from the feelings engendered by the fireside, and show to us how naturally it is that the domestic nature
informs and influences the decision, the courage, and the enterprise of the patriot. The effect undoubtedly would be, to teach the statesman how much more
deeply a nation is governed by its impulses than by its policy; and might result
in counselling [*sic*] him to a more thorough regard for the humanities of life, in
the adoption of his principles, than is apt to govern him, so long as he confines
his views to a dry analysis of the several economies which are usually supposed
to constitute the entire objects of laws and government. If men were machines,
having a single and simple principle by which to operate, the whole scheme of
government might safely be made to rest upon the inflexibility of their natures,
and the arbitrary necessities under which they are decreed to live. It would then
be required only to ascertain where the motive influence lay, and to give it, by
a single exercise of will, the direction which it was required to pursue. It is, perhaps, the great error of statesmen that, in their practice, they seem to consider
this the case; though none of them, from Macchiavelli [*sic*] and Metternich, to
Guizot and Peel, would ever, in their philosophies, allow themselves to avow
such doctrines. But the doctrinaire, who, in his treatment of society, sets out
with certain preconceived notions of government, and, having made a fine theory in his closet, prepares to accommodate man to his system, in reality proceeds
upon some such despotic assumptions. A man of systems, usually, his thoughts
are commonly employed in making a harmonious combination of principles;—
wheels and balance-weights of doctrine and philosophy. moving along together
as the snuggest of all possible contrivances;—and, so long as his scheme remains
an abstraction, it goes with the greatest regularity, and constitutes one of the
prettiest pieces of mechanism imaginable. But, reduced to practice, and put in
application to society, he soon discovers that its working, in fact, is by no means
so successful, as it has seemed in his philosophy. In truth, he has only made the
slight mistake of leaving out the due consideration of the claims of that very
nature of which the system has the charge. He has forgotten the man in the
machine,—and, as it is not easy to persuade him that his scheme is wanting, the
farther necessity is before him of compelling the man to shape his action to that
of the machine. The fable of Procrustes and his graduating bed, was probably
nothing more than a happy allegory, illustrative of the despotism of a scheme of
government, which required the whole nature of the animal to be subordinate to
laws which have no sort of affinity with its wants and necessities. A large proportion of the lawgivers of the world, must naturally fall into errors such as this, for
the very apparent reason that they do not, in their own natures, properly represent the average natures of humanity. The man who has surrendered himself to
philosophy, has usually suffered some of the more exquisite sources of sympathy
with his fellow creatures to be dried up. He has acquired wisdom at the expense

of sensibility. He has grown profound only as he has grown cold. Passions and feelings, in fact, become the merest abstractions, upon which he will not linger; satisfied, as he is, of the eminent superiority of schemes and systems. The heart of man he will be very apt to treat as philosophically and coolly as the naturalist who impales the insect upon the needle; and he will study its writhings with a deliberation that is perfectly unmoved by its contortions, so long as the victim fails to escape, and is incapable of using his petty sting or proboscis in self-defence, or vengeance. He will mistake the writhings of agony for the legitimate workings of the nerves and muscles, and suppose that the exhibition of suffering is an exhibition only of its proper being. In such an experiment, he will probably arrive at a very fair knowledge of the powers and capacity of endurance, rather than of enjoyment and performance, which the insect possesses. Beyond the one discovery, he will learn nothing. In due proportion as the study is prolonged, will be the increase of his own insensibility; and, just in the same degree, will be his incapacity to ascertain, by any process of study, the true nature of the creature under examination. This, really, is only to be fathomed by sympathies, which never lose their humanities in their analysis. Any preconceived system of human government, which shall fail duly to ascertain what is the real nature of the race to be governed,—which shall study rather what they can bear, than what they may become—which shall look for their character in their sufferings rather than their affections—and shall build upon their fears rather than their hopes,—must admirably illustrate that study of the naturalist which we have described. It may ascertain justly the externals of the victim, but it takes too little account of those affections and sensibilities which constitute its moral property, to conceive any idea of its just government. The very fact that the phlegm of the philosopher enables him to behold the sufferings which he does not seem anxious to abridge, is absolutely conclusive against any claim which he might assert with reference to its government.

Now, the whole history of evil in politics may he traced, in great degree, to the very dissimilarity of the nature existing respectively in the bosom of the persons governed and the persons governing. Naturally, we look for wisdom in the latter; but wisdom is, in truth, so frequently acquired at the expense of sensibility,—at the cost of those vital virtues which keep alive and active every precious human sympathy,—that something of peril must necessarily attend the elevation to power of every mind possessing more than common profundity. The most perfect wisdom is that which, while acquiring knowledge, never loses judgment; and which, while adding daily to its stores of human thought and experience, is specially wary never to forfeit or forget any of those instincts which it imbibed with its mother's milk. But how rarely is such wisdom found. How commonly do we find, with great knowledge, a cold and ascetic philosophy, which, in the plenitude of its own attainments, discovering the deficiencies of its fellows, in proportion as it finds them feeble, believes them vicious! How difficult is it for the commonly wise to forbear contempt for the weakness which should ask for care and kindness only; and how naturally does the inflated intellect, assured of its superiority over its contemporaries, learn to confound with an inferior race that very family, for the tuition and patriarchal guardianship of which, his own superior endowments were specially conferred by Providence. It requires the rarest wisdom to remember that the inequalities of human endowment confer upon the superior no right of sneer, or scorn, or censure; but rather impose upon him the nobler duties of benevolence, sympathy, and an ever watchful and loving philanthropy, which never forgets itself in its possessions, nor despises the virtues which may yet nestle at the heart of the destitute who possesses nothing else.

This sort of wisdom which, in its own fullness, proves its own deficiencies, is of a kind, perhaps, more common to the statesman than to any other class of philosophers. His exercise necessarily brings him into contact with a race over which he is tacitly the master. Let the government be what it will, this is measurably the case. His position of command gives him authority, and the dependance of his fellows necessarily distinguishes their bearing by a deference to his authority which is continually stimulating it. He speaks only to command, they only to obey; and, in due proportion to their dependance and servility, will be the aptness with which he will learn to despise their complaisance and to forget his own. The distance which lies between him and the multitude, will be naturally suggestive of a difference, as well in capacity as in condition; and the very draft which is hourly made upon his intellect, to supply the wants of theirs, will increase the difficulties in the way of that humility which is the first essential, as well of wisdom as religion. How easy for a ruler, thus separate from his people, to lose sight of their peculiar characteristics. How much more agreeable for him to study an idea of his own, than to inform himself of the actual in their condition;— to frame an Utopia, in which the making of government and laws, will not be so much the object as the making of men;— and where the fancy of the ingenious statesman will shape society to his system, in a manner so grateful to himself, that, when he applies his conceptions to the world about him, he will only find cause of offence in that humanity which shows itself insusceptible to the operations of his machine. How easy that such a doctrinaire should err in policy. How natural that revolutions should be the result of his constant offences against humanity. But, the very study of History will contribute to the errors of the statesman who sinks into the doctrinaire. As history has usually been written, it is the history rather of princes than of a people. It is a long series of biographies of men who have attracted the attention of mankind by movements which have shaken kingdoms to their centre, overwhelmed dynasties, and established new usurpations in the blood of armies, and in the sack and conflagration of states and cities. In these narrations, the race has always been made to appear subordinate to its despotisms. Men are only shewn [*sic*] as the creatures of a will so imperative as to seem a destiny. They rise to no commanding position in our eyes. They appeal to none of our sympathies by their actions. They are swarms that would lack significance were it not for their numbers; and assert nothing, by means of character, by which to beguile our interests or affections. The historian has given them the back-ground in his canvas only, where, marked indistinctly, they serve only as foils for the prominent dramatis persona; whom he shows conspicuous in his foreground. He conducts us to none of the abodes of the people, and shows us no personal history, by which the cottage of the peasant, honored by the domestic virtues, might be made to challenge an equal respect with the feudal castle, distinguished rather by its attributes of strength and wealth than its virtue. How naturally, reading such histories, marked by such omissions, do we forget the claims of the race, in the more prominent endowments of the favored individuals; who, assigned as their guardians, have but too frequently preyed upon the flock they were set to watch! How superior must be those endowments of wisdom in that statesman who never suffers his eyes to be dazzled by the pomp and glitter of individual greatness, to a disregard of that race from whose ranks all his greatness must be evolved, and for whose uses only are all the appointments of the superior intelligence. Wanting in this wisdom, he must lack that sympathy with his stock which is the only guaranty of its safety, if not of his own. How should his laws contemplate their necessities—how should his government accord with their conditions! What theory of rule could he frame, suited to their wants, while he refuses to look into the sources of their hope—the seemingly small desires of their hearts—the dreams with which faith compensates poverty—and the illusions with which a confiding nature is allowed to solace the home of suffering and denial!

But, the chronicler of the age reports progress. Not the least remarkable of the achievements of modern civilization is the change which has equally come over the historian and the readers of history. The great moral triumph of recent times is the recognition of the race as well as the individual. Man has risen into an estate, and not the least of estates; and this, perhaps, is somewhat due to his first recognition by the philosopher and the historian. The poets were the only class of philosophers who had recognized him, in his true capacity, a thousand years before. We now read *human* histories. We now ask after the affections as well as the ceremonies of society; and that government which does not take account of the very dreams and fancies of its people, is in danger of forfeiting all its sympathies. When Fletcher of Saltoun reported the famous phrase of the wise man, whom he does not name, (and which has grown into a proverb :) [*sic*] "If a man were permitted to make all the ballads, he need not care who should make the laws of a nation,"* he indicated the necessity for that appreciation of,

* This proverbial phrase is frequently ascribed to other writers; but it is first reported by Andrew Fletcher, Esq., of Saltoun, a very remarkable man, of whom the world should

and sympathy with, the domestic life of a people which was essential to the formation of proper laws for their government. It is the family fireside—the source
of all the virtues—that the lawgiver must first learn to protect and make grateful to the affections of those who seek warmth upon its hearthstones. Hence
spring all the virtues and securities of a nation. Here, in little, are to be found
the germs of those representative principles which, recognizing an equality of
claim, if not of condition, among its people, imposes upon the government a
law of benevolence which takes its rule from that of the Deity—suffering not the
smallest sparrow to fall to the ground without seeking to lift it, heedfully, and
restore it to its perch. The household, in fact, is not only the source hut the true
guardian of the nation. From that high habitation, the race goes forth, spreads
widely, and becomes an empire. Protect that, and all the rest is easy. You are not
to ask which of the sons that emerge from that dwelling is the bravest, or becomes the wealthiest—which has the largest endowments of strength, or talent,
or succeeds most in the accumulation of wealth; for, these by no means represent
the various virtues which take root in the lowly habitation. But, with what affections and sympathies did its numerous sons go forth on their mission of toil
and enterprise? What hopes inspired the restive spirit? What tastes beguiled their
labours? What passions and desires were in the ascendant? And, what was the
class of amusements which appealed most impressively to the domestic genius?
It is in studies such as these that you learn what are the peculiar characteristics,
not only of the family, but the stock. And it is only by a just appreciation of the
character of a race that you can frame the laws, as well for the attainment of their
confidence as for the protection of their interests. The one duty must precede
the other. No foreign power can ever satisfy a people. Substantially, in all ages,
this has been the case, even when the despotism was most unembarrassed by opposition, and most complete in the seemingly-perfect submission of the people
governed. They will always suspect that ruler whose assumptions of superiority
will not suffer him to explore the lowly nature which he claims to govern—enter
into its domestic abodes, in the examination of its necessities, and make just as

---

know something more at length. It is to be found In his treatise, entitled, "An Account
of a Conversation concerning a Right Regulation of Government for the Common Good
of Mankind. In a Letter to the Marquess of Montrose, the Earl of Rothes, Roxbury, and
Haddington: from London, the first of December, 1703. Printed in Edinburg, 1704." The
passage runs thus, and is to be found at page 372 of his works, published in London, 1737,
of which a copy lies before us:—"I said"—it is Fletcher of Saltoun who speaks—"I knew a
very wise man so much of Sir Christopher's (one of the interlocutors) sentiment, that he
believed if a man were permitted to make all the ballads, he need not care who should make
the laws of a nation. And we find that most of the antient [*sic*] legislators thought they
could not well reform the manners of any city without the help of a lyrick and sometimes
of a dramatick poet," etc.

much allowance for its sympathies and sports as for its exterior possessions of soil, commerce, and production.

It is for this reason that the ballads of a people are supposed to possess such a wonderful power over their impulses, beyond that of the laws. It is thus that laws and governments are frequently overturned by the rude ditty of the "blind old crowder." Thus it is that wisdom prefers to write its songs in the vernacular, when stupid or wilful [*sic*] politicians frame them in the obscure dialect of a people that exist no longer; and the great poet thus makes his most successful appeal to posterity, by rescuing the living tongue from the fetters of the dead and past. Chaucer commended his people to the better sympathies of the Norman race by composing his charming stories in the common language, and compelling the sympathies of the superior to descend to the simpler stock, which they had ruled with a rod of iron. He softened the severities of the foreign rule, by showing new attractions in the native language. He thus prepared the way for the restoration of the native tongue to the laws, and to that society which the dialect of the invader had usurped in his usurpation of the soil. Chaucer and Shakespeare have governed, and will govern, England thousands of years after the laws of all her Normon [*sic!*] monarchs shall be forgotten. Their laws were framed in the popular heart, and they were ineradicable in the popular ear. Italy, in the same manner, was rescued from the artifices of a foreign speech by that genius of the household, the native poet; and the Provencal Troubadour has left his voice behind him in a region which no longer knows the people or the princes, the laws or histories, of the races to whom he made appeal. He could rouse its warrior tribes to enthusiastic war for Christendom against the pagan, when his rulers could compel only their sluggish and reluctant submission. In all lands, this has been the common history. The Jew, the Greek, the Saracen, were better ruled by their poets than their statesmen; their poets, indeed, were their prophets, and showed their profound philosophy by seeking the elements of the popular law in the popular sympathies. The Arab acknowledges the wild song of the Desert, when he would yield to no other authority; and the subjects of the Caliphs of Bagdat [*sic*], in the thousand stories of their weird romance, found a solace which could make them forgetful, for a season, even of the capricious tyranny of their suspicious and selfish sovereigns. The song of the Rhine will force the tear down the withered and bronzed cheek of the German pilgrim in far lands; and the music of the shepherd song of the Swiss—the *Rans des Vaches*—was forbidden, on pain of death, in the French armies, because of its effect in producing desertions among their mercenaries—a people, perhaps, as little accessible as any other to appeals of the affections. What has been the effect of Burns's songs upon the people of Scotland? What of Beranger upon the French? What of Dibdin among mariners? And who shall say what has been the degree of influence exercised among our own people, during our two wars with England, by the very rude martial ballads of the native "crowders" of those periods? These, having the key-notes of the heart, were in possession of the best clues which conduct to authority over the people. In the common sentiment, they found their inspiration. They became the voice of the universal heart. They were the true representatives of the things most precious to a people—their tastes, their emotions, their feelings, their peculiar hopes, and the very fears which disturbed their repose and made them set down their feet in trembling and apprehension. How should the balladmonger learn these things, and not the statesman? Perhaps, because he is out of place. All poets may be said to be out of place; and they thus naturally look into the conditions of others. It is the misfortune of the statesman, whose mind is called upon to meditate the government of a people, to undertake these meditations while he is in place. Place disturbs the equilibrium of the soul—power perverts the judgment. Pride and vanity step in to suggest a false medium, through which all objects are beheld; and the sense of authority is apt to beget a grossly erroneous notion of the true relations which should exist between the governor and the governed. In half the number of cases, the world's greatness is a vulgar greatness. It is apt to forget the guardian in the master—to pass from the ruler to the despot—and, in the consciousness of mental superiority, to lose the virtues of magnanimity, without which, the superior sinks rapidly into the inferior. In due degree as we sink the affections, in our progress, do we not only lose our hold upon the race, but incur the danger of being no longer able to serve them. It is then that our toils grow selfish, and worthless, accordingly. We forget humanity in art. Systems take possession of our brains, as the appreciation of man passes out from our hearts; and, in making systematical our philosophies, we only torture the race to whose wants we vainly endeavour to apply them. We forget the vital condition upon which an individual duty and existence are allotted to us—forget that we are evolved from the masses, and have our endowments, intellectually as well as politically, only because of our appointed uses, as the representatives of the stock at large. In the sense of personal elevation, we lose sight of the very condition upon which we receive it—the good of mankind—the true object of the relation between the governed and the governor.

Could this always be kept in mind, to what would it conduct us? To the household, surely! Here, in embryo, are all the interests of society. Here, too, we see them stript [*sic*] of all their artifices. Here is nature, frank and artless, in *deshabille* because *at home*. The secret of good government is in establishing and acknowledging the home;—in making it grow and flourish—in seeing in the home the true guardian of the nation. The nation is but a community of homes, with the same *Genius Loci* set up for authority in each. To find out the native qualities of this Genius of Place, and to acknowledge them and make them safe and confident, is really the great and only business of statesmanship; and fortunate is he who, called to superintend the interests of a people, begins his study of their characteristics in the homeliest fireside of the virtuous, What should he study there? The heart, the social relations, the influence of the same lore upon different temperaments and endowments, tastes and objects,—harmonizing the elements that otherwise might appear in opposition, and forming the true cement which makes safe and strong the social edifice of state. Here will the lesson be before him ever, that the State is durable rather as a social than a political edifice; and in this distinction he finds the secret which will prevent him from such a cold and arbitrary conception of schemes and laws as seem to regard man only as a machine, representing millions of like machines, and not as an individual whose attributes are special, and who resembles his fellow chiefly in his desire of sympathy and his recognition of one universal law, in the need for love. Above all, he will discover, in this region of study, that man docs not legislate for man alone, for the simple reason that man is not appointed to live alone. The philosopher sees three aspects in every household—the husband—the wife, and the child; and, in these, a close study shows him three other aspects—the patriarch, for the husband is scarcely such who is not the father also to the wife—the angel, for the wife is scarcely such if she occupies not a higher rank than that of help-meet—and the servant, for such is the child, who can only pass into the places of authority at last, by having been properly tutored in the delight and readiness to serve. Here, then, are the representatives of the three great securities of the social state, strength, reverence, loyalty, the one implying labour and authority, the other ministry and love, the third service and submission. And these involve all that is good and grateful, wise and necessary, in morals and industry, self-study and religion. Here are the sources of all the humanities—toil that is healthful and cheerful—love that is constant and watchful—obedience that seeks service, and is never so well satisfied as in being useful where its loyalty is due. Let these qualities and possessions fairly represent the household, and what is there that the nation cannot do? It is a nation born for conquest—a chosen nation—with the paternal wings of God spread over it always for protection, and his eye forever guiding it onward, in security and strength, to the daily increase of power.

Suppose such a nation to have provoked the hostility or to have incurred the jealousy and hatred of a rival nation, and what wondrous energies could she command, even at a word, to encounter the iron legions of the invader! Her dwellings will seldom suffer outrage. Her sires, in possession of inborn strength and dignities, to which the love of women and the loyalty of children have alike ministered without ceasing, swell with indignant sensibilities, which nothing can subdue, at the very consciousness of outrage. The son, trained to service and obedience, strengthened by industry and elevated by a sense of parental approbation, possesses a well-tempered enthusiasm, which renders him eager for the encounter and irresistible in the strife; whilst the wife, who has ministered with love and duty, who has been the domestic angel of the sire and the maternal angel of the son, now clothes herself in still loftier attributes of strength and virtue, which suffers the courage of neither to falter, and warms them with an impulse which finds its birth among the very highest virtues. It is at such a period of doubt and peril that she rises to a rank of immeasurable dignity, and puts on aspects at once of counsel and devotion. She is no longer the mere woman, the dependant, seeking simply to minister, in the common walks of duty, as the wife and mother. The new necessities of the social state elevates the moral characteristics of the citizen, in increasing his responsibilities. She shares these with her husband and her son. She has always shared their existence, and now is sharing their necessities. She begins to assert the higher virtues of her own individuality. *She* has not been insensible to the history of her people. She has felt their trials. They have passed into her heart, as a part of its vitality, and her pride in what has been done by the past has prompted lessons to her progeny, which are at the bottom of all the achievements of the future. She has taught the boy at the knee of the achievements of the maternal grandsire. He has listened to a thousand details of early adventure among the Indians, of desperate hand-to-hand fight, and perils passed, which, but for God's favour,—giving courage and strengthening confidence,—could never have been overcome. She has been the one to remember and repeat the ancient ballads which recorded the achievements of her people, and the ear of the boy has drunk in greedily, from her lips, as she sung him to his slumbers, a thousand impulses of courage and enthusiasm, which never go out from his heart—which give him a heart, and make him a thing of courage and resistance, having no fear, whenever events shall recur like those which found a hero in his grandsire. It is the domestic histories which the mother finds it most easy to remember, and which she loves most to repeat. But these domestic histories are really so many keys and clues to the history of the nation. The one is suggestive of the other. What—could we look back to the domestic world of the old thirteen States at the dawn of the revolution—what—had the homestead histories of that time, in our region, been faithfully chronicled, fully and not in doubtful fragments, as we possess them now,—what grateful and improving spectacles might we behold of the maternal lessonings bestowed upon the young, in preparation for the conflict! We should have heard the mother recalling the first sad struggles of her grandsire, as he crossed the dreary waste of ocean to subdue the wilderness to the wants of humanity. She would depict the trials of this destiny, and its final conquest, the adventurer supported only by his own courage, strength of heart and body, and the sanction and approbation of God. She would show the insatiate ambition of the foreign despot, who would seek to wrest from him the small fruits of his hardly earned possessions. Of the power which threatened his security she would speak in equal indignation and apprehension, thus informing her pupil equally in caution and in courage; and, thus teaching, she would send him forth in tears, but with words of cheer and stout encouragement, reminding him of that grandsire whose deeds it had been her favourite pleasure to relate in earlier years. And what schooling could so well as this inform the manhood of the youth—could so stimulate his courage—could so warm his virtues—could make him so confident of God's favour, thus blessed by the counsel and the parting exhortations of a mother who had seen and felt so much!

Thus, too, she warms the heart, of her nearer associate. The husband of her bosom is a man of strength. He has been the patriarch in her abodes. He has preserved her from common dangers. He has always shown himself a man beside her. He has kept foes and poverty alike from the door. He is the sire of her children. He has given them none but brave and noble lessons, and he now prepares to take them under his wing and show them how to achieve their first blows in battle. But his hair is white—his arms have no longer the vigour of their youth. The wife has no misgivings of his heart—only of his strength. She now summons her children to private council. She depicts the feebleness of their father; she counsels them not to allow his confidence to deceive himself or them, but to become his protector, as he has hitherto been theirs. And then she sends them forth, or perhaps attends them, unwilling that they alone should seek for toil and danger, she alone in the enjoyment of security and repose. There, again, she proves the ministering angel of the household, and exhibits a strength, a courage and a variety of resource, which no one had deemed her to possess, and of which she herself had never conjectured the possession until the day of unknown exigency and trial. She stimulates their adventure and enterprise, but without forgetting their moral. Her counsels, which remind them of what is expected by their country, do not forget what is demanded by their God. She prescribes the Bible as their companion. She places the sacred volume in their bosoms— some favourite copy, in which she has written their names and her blessings.

Could we go back, sufficiently far in this scrutiny—had the record been sufficiently well preserved—we should probably discover that, almost unconsciously to herself, she was preparing them for the struggle. The mother of the household has been no indifferent or insensible spectator of public affairs. In our country, it is not usual for her to mingle in discussions, especially of a political character; but she is not heedless of the progress of the argument. She has an interest which is sleepless and unceasing in whatever concerns her family; and she watches, with increasing anxiety, those growing specks of danger which gather on the horizon of her country, to which the fingers of masculine apprehension point with indignation and misgiving. Silently and gradually she prepares against their approach. Sterner cares attend her in her domestic duties. Severer requisitions upon self, abridge her enjoyments, as she anticipates the future. War brings with it a gloomy train of harpies, even more terrible than itself. The good mother provides against the wants of the future by lessening gradually the unnecessary expenditures of the family; and the thousand daily details of duty which are the result of this calm, firm, manly principle of precaution, contribute to strengthen her resolves, and to elevate her spirit. The policy is not lost upon those around her, and the man, always confident, will smile and jest at precautions, which it is only a superior wisdom that adopts. Insensibly thus, day by day, will she train her young Spartans to the trial—to the endurance of privation—cold, hunger, toil—no less than the danger and the brunt of battle.

But the examples are numerous in our country, and in that fearful first period of strife which tried the souls of our people, when she exhibited qualities, which, if not higher than these, were yet more brilliant and perhaps impressive. She made society tributary to Revolution, as did the famous women, beloved of the Girondins, at the period most full of delusive promises for France. She brought the graces, the tastes and the affections to the succour of patriotism, and where she could not charm and beguile the adversary to the side of the country, she overwhelmed him with her satire, and repelled him by her scorn. She was not unequal to the argument: and her wit and beauty made the most of it. She made loyalty to the soil a condition of society. She taught patriotism as the proper creed of love. She made resolution stern in its support, and stimulated courage and ambition by her smiles. Her converts were in due proportion with her admirers, and to desire and deserve her favor, it became necessary to belong to her party. It is not possible to compute the amount of her influence, or to trace, at this day, the thousand persuasions which she brought to the enterprise in that. The whigs found her an admirable ally in preparing the people for the strife; in reconciling them to its privations, and in marshalling them into the ranks of action. Perhaps, it would be safe to assert that, in no country, nor in any period of revolution, did the sex exhibit so deep, so warm, and so imposing an influence. There was one reason in particular why this should be the case,—and here we are brought to one of the errors—few, indeed, which the author of the interesting work before us has committed. She tells us, in her introduction, that the leading spirits of our Revolution derived the sources of their power from the sentiment pervading the great mass of the people. This is a great mistake, and one which is too commonly made in our recent histories. The great mass of the people had really very little sympathy with the movement of 1776. It was neither caused by their dissatisfaction with the existing condition of things, nor did they help it forward by their exertions and self-sacrifice. They felt few of the wrongs which caused the revolution. British taxation gave them little annoyance. On the contrary, it relieved them from some of their cares, and sheltered them with its protection. It is time that the error should be exploded which insisted on this as the impelling influence which led the American people to shake off the power of the foreigner. The tax was a popular pretext, which served to influence, in some degree, the commercial and manufacturing classes. *The movement originated with the native intellect of the country.* It had its birth among the educated and wealthy classes. It was the result of convictions which might be considered instincts, and with which the masses had little sympathy. It arose from the consciousness of strength and right in the native mind, which Britain had subjected to denial and *non user.* It was a revolt of the domestic genius, eager for employment, and restive under the foreign domination, when its own endowments were quite equal to its own responsibilities. The loyalty of the American for the Guelph dynasty was diminished duly with his education and resources. This rendered the struggle so hazardous and so prolonged. This was the source and secret of the civil war which prevailed, in greater or less degree, in all the colonies. The higher classes stood comparatively alone. The sympathies of the uneducated were not with them. The latter openly charged the movement upon the ambition of the other; and this was the accusation of all the provincial governors against the revolutionary party in the several provinces. The people were hostile to the war, in due degree as they were jealous of the superiority of their immediate neighbours. They preferred the remote superior in preference to him whose wealth and education were forever vexing their self-esteem. But for this, the contest, urged feebly as it was, by Great Britain, with inferior and inefficient officers, would have been terminated in two years instead of seven. Had the people everywhere sympathized with their leading minds there would have been scarcely any struggle, particularly after the alliance with France and Spain. But the mother country derived its stimulus to perseverance entirely from its American auxiliaries, and these were generally the least wealthy, the least educated and least intellectual of the people;—but, in one-half of the States, if not in all, they were nearly if not quite as numerous as those who originated and maintained the contest for independence.

This fact being understood, it being unquestionable that the great work of the revolution had devolved on the best educated and most wealthy of the native Americans, it became inevitable that the spirit which governed it had the fairest chances for the support of society. In other words, the highest tones of society were in unison with the action of the *movement* party; and this fact shows us to what an extent the influence of woman must have participated in the event. For where could she be so well informed of the principles and objects of the controversy—how else could she feel them—what other lessons could have tutored her nobler instincts for the appreciation of the condition to which the intellect of the country aspired? It is only where education prevails, where the tastes are refined, where the sensibilities are warmed, where the affections and emotions are duly ministered to, as the excelling attributes of man's condition, that woman rises into an estate of influence and authority. It is only in such a condition that she will presume to exercise a sway over the minds of a circle, and seek to impel its action in seasons of difficulty and extremity. In all other situations she is a subordinate, descending in grade in due degree with the absence of grace, polish, freedom and civilization in society. Here, only, is she the recognized minister to high ambitions, and sensibilities that aim at the attainment of objects which address themselves only to the affections of the noble, aspiring nature. Here, only, will her education and acquisition permit and encourage her to become a counsellor—to take part in affairs that extend beyond the household, and to mingle in interests which, at ordinary periods and in humbler circles, are sup-posed to be totally beyond the province of the sex. No doubt, the influences of such a circle extend, to a certain degree, to other classes which surround it, and into which, by reason of local affinities, its power necessarily penetrates. As the humble neighbour will sympathize with the superior, whose virtues he has learned to acknowledge and to love, so the endowments of the educated woman, tempered by the gentle and persuasive virtues of benevolence and love, will make themselves felt and honoured by the poor and little-hoping of her own sex; and such as these will naturally sympathize with the cares and the strug-gles of those to whom they look with respect and veneration. And then shall we find good and great deeds, and a noble spirit of patriotism, in many instances emanating from among the poorest as well as the proudest circles of the country. But the fact which we allege remains unimpaired. The great movement of the revolution originated with the educated of the people, and did not greatly or fa-vourably influence the desires or the feelings of the masses, full a moiety of which was decidedly and bitterly hostile to a spirit with which they did not sympathize, and in which they beheld little more than the exhibition of an insatiate desire for power on the part of an ambition on which they had already learned to look with equal dislike and suspicion. We repeat, accordingly, that, as the struggle for independence belonged chiefly to the educated circles, so the women of these circles necessarily took a larger part in the proceeding than ordinarily attends the revolutions of a nation. The higher classes could, and did, influence the hum-bler, whenever the local circumstances encouraged or permitted it. Wherever the society had become stable, this was usually the case. In the communities long established, where the various classes had been accustomed to meet and mingle, where they knew each other instinctively, and had learned to respect and confide in one another, the proofs are abundant that they worked harmoniously together to the end, the humbler looking to the higher for counsel and aid; the higher receiving from the humbler the natural tribute of loyalty, that had its roots in the domestic and social affections. Of course we are to understand that there were circles in which no wealth was to be found, which were invariably true to the revolution and earnestly devoted to the cause. This was commonly the case in communities which were wholly of Irish origin, and with most of the Presby-terian settlements, where these were not of the Scotch of the ever memorable '45. But our case concerns not these. The points which we make are invincible: first, that the revolution chiefly originated with the educated aristocracy of the country, and that this fact necessarily implied such a position for its women, as to leave it probable, as the facts seem to show, that they took a more active part in the movement than is commonly the case at such periods in other countries. We may add that, in one respect, it was the misfortune of the nation that the movement was so much the creature of the higher classes; still more that these classes did not take the proper pains always, or proceed in the proper manner, to enlist the sympathies of the humbler. Their very wealth and education seemed to rebuke and keep at distance the pretensions of classes less favourably placed; and they themselves but too frequently aimed to govern rather by dictation than by love. A less elevated condition of aristocracy, and a larger degree of conciliation on the part of the leading minds of the country, might greatly have abridged the length and severity of the conflict.

With the progress of the contest, under its actual privations, the spirit of the American women, who had lent their souls to its support, underwent no abatement. In the siege of cities and the defence of dwellings, dismissing all feminine fears, they sought every opportunity of making themselves useful to the champions of the good cause. They prepared clothes and bandages, melted the bullets, served as spies, and conveyed intelligence, under constant privation and in frequent peril to themselves. They tended the sick and wounded, were the sisters of mercy in hospital and prison ship, shutting their eyes upon the outward world and all its persuasions, and giving themselves up wholly to the cause and the sufferings of those whom they loved. It was in vain that beauty and talent were solicited by the conqueror to appear at his high places of festival. They withstood the temptations which, in the gayer hours of fortune, are usually so persuasive with the sex. The crowded and bright saloon no longer had a charm for the spirit which had risen to the highest sense of social responsibilities. They denied the arts of the tempter—they defied his authority and anger. It was equally in vain that he lured and threatened, and those with whom his arts proved influential were at once driven into Coventry by their nobler and firmer sisters. The latter cheerfully gave up the gaudy, but rapidly failing attractions of the ball room; having an eye on the nobler fame which follows from the grateful "well done" of posterity and country. How copious are our chronicles of the South in details illustrative of this patriotism. The venerable Major Garden* has done little more than furnish samples of this history. Every little community, from the Potomac to the Savannah, may yield its thousand anecdotes of the self-denying patriotism, the deep devotion, the ardent activity, the firm courage, and the unwearying love with which our women gave themselves up to the cause upon which their countrymen had staked life, fortune and sacred honour.

It was a happy thought which suggested to the compiler of the three pleasant volumes before us, to supply, as well as might now be done, the deficiencies of this history. Unfortunately, with all the industry of talent and patriotism, the work can only imperfectly be done. The period is past, or is rapidly passing, when these details of tradition can be obtained; and what are available serve rather to provoke an anxiety for what we cannot now possess, than to satisfy us with what is in our keeping. There has been a criminal neglect among our old families, of the written correspondence, the memoranda and the diaries of the revolutionary

---

* Garden's *Anecdotes [of the American Revolution]*, First and Second Series.

period. Boasting, and with becoming pride, of their ancestors, our people have but too commonly deserved the censure of the historian for that vanity which, while it makes the boast, has failed to provide the monument; and a strict justice must declare that, where the descendant has failed to preserve and take due care of the memorials of his family, it betrays a melancholy evidence of his own degeneracy and decay. But the diligence which works, under the influence of patriotism and love, may achieve many things—may discover many hidden treasures—may still rescue from time many valuable possessions: and the work of our author we regard rather as the pioneer of other volumes, than as exhausting the quarries into which she has so successfully penetrated. She will add to these volumes, and her example will be followed by others.* They will address themselves to the task with the ardor of such a feeling as possessed "Old Mortality," and by extending their inquiries into the ancient settlements, personally visiting ancient families and places, ransacking old stores of manuscript and parchment, and waking up half-slumbering memories, will enrich themselves with resources which shall yet unfold ample pages of delight, and noble lessons for the education of the future. What has been done by Mrs. Ellet has been done with much ability and success. The work has been properly undertaken by a female. She can best enter into those quiet details of the household, the small lurking hopes, affections, sympathies, which inform the peculiar nature of the sex, and warm it to great endurance and great performances. She can better appreciate the delicacy, the tact, the grace, the ingenuity, the purity, which constitutes, in particular, the character of woman, and which are all discoverable in traits of conduct and expression which the masculine writer would wholly overlook, unless evolved in connexion with striking and impressive action. Thus far, we have every reason to be satisfied with the performance of our author.

The volumes before us contain, besides a well written and interesting introduction, notices of one hundred and seventy women of the revolution, who were distinguished by their virtues, their character, and their direct agency in the struggle. These notices are, in many instances, biographies, giving complete lives

---

* *The Sketches of North-Carolina,* by the Rev. W. Henry Foote, deserve honourable mention in this connexion. Though prepared from a narrow point of view they are yet useful, and may provoke other researches. They contain much suggestive material. It would not become us to forget, while on this subject, the labours, still continued, of the venerable Judge O'Neall, of South-Carolina; of the no less venerable Joseph Johnson, M.D. of the same State, whose researches in our domestic history are equally valuable and various; nor must we pass without due acknowledgment the efforts of the Hon. Benj. F. Perry, of Greenville, South-Carolina, who has done much to gather the unwritten histories of our forest country. The duty before those gentlemen, and others, also busy in this ample field of study and exploration, is to digest those materials into a complete whole, while yet the feeling which first prompted them to these researches, is yet stirring warmly in their bosoms.

of the subject; but, in the greater number, they are sketches only, embodying anecdotes of their conduct at particular periods in their career. Our author has sought for them in all parts of the Union, not merely in the old thirteen States, but sometimes in the territories, as in the case of Kentucky, denominated the "dark and bloody ground," at the very time of the revolutionary conflict. It does not appear that she has been equally successful in prosecuting her researches throughout the States. It is something of a commentary, indeed, upon the large pretensions set up of late by the New-England historians, who have not tarried sufficiently long at Jericho for the growth of their beards, but who would claim the whole revolution to have been the work of "the Saints" of Yankeedom purely—that, but nineteen of these biographies or sketches are afforded by the New-England States; New-York, New-Jersey and Pennsylvania furnish thirty-six; while the researches of the author—who is a Northern lady by birth, and education, and residence—in the Southern States constitute fully two-thirds of her three volumes. Assuming that she designs to prosecute her inquiries, she owes it to Maryland, Pennsylvania and Delaware, which were among the most patriotic States of the revolution, to extend her inquiries into these regions. Georgia, too, deserves and would reward research; and to Virginia, as one of the chief maternal States of the nation, it is due that her resources be explored, in deference to her power and performances in the revolution, her great statesmen, and the high tone which distinguished her society. South-Carolina and North-Carolina contain thousands more of such memorials as these volumes contain, which only need the help of the domestic historian, and from which a body of literature may be compiled, at once quite as valuable, and much more grateful to the reader than all the historical collections of all the States. It is not doubted that Massachusetts, a State of peculiar sectional temper, of large intellect, and, even in the revolution, in possession of a good educational establishment, would amply and admirably compensate the diligent inquirer, who would find it not difficult to assign its volume to each of the old Thirteen. Nor would the peninsula of Florida, the place of refuge for the Southern loyalists and their families, the place of captivity for so many of the most noble of the Southern whigs, fail to afford considerable materials of interest and value. But we need not indicate more closely the regions in which this sort of research might be urged with profit. Let us confine ourselves to what is before us, and especially to its most valuable portion, —that which illustrates the contributions made by female virtue and patriotism to the revolution, in the Southern section of the Union. We need not go beyond this, assured that our Northern neighbours will never suffer judgment by default, in consequence of any bashfulness or backwardness in the assertion of their claims.

The wife and mother of Washington have properly a conspicuous place in this collection. Of these, Mrs. Ellet gives us two graceful and interesting biographies, affording us all the facts which are now available, and all, perhaps, which are necessary to a just appreciation of their character. The great performance by which the mother of Washington was mostly distinguished lies in the domestic education of her son. From her he acquired the dignity and simplicity of his character, his veneration, his love of truth, his patience, and all the virtues which sublimed his courage and rendered his performances successful. Her family name was Ball. She lived to the age of eighty-five, and, to the last, appeared among her visitors clad in the homespun of her own manufacture. Of the wife of Washington the history is well known. She was a Dandridge, but was the widow of Col. Curtis when she married the great American chief. She was young, rich and beautiful when she won his eye. Her abilities were considerable; she conversed with spirit, thought with caution and wrote with judgment. Her equanimity and cheerfulness were conspicuous under all circumstances. She lived till 1802, and died at the age of 71. In the intervals of the campaign, during the revolution, she lived with Washington in the camp, possessed his inmost confidence, and, no doubt, contributed to strengthen his character by the noblest virtues, the firmness and the integrity and sweetness of her own.

A chapter is given by our author to Elizabeth Clay, the mother of the great statesman. She was born in Hanover, Virginia, in 1750. Her husband, John Clay, was a preacher of the Baptist denomination. She was eminent for her piety, her energy and industry. Marrying a second time, she removed with her husband to Kentucky, leaving her son, Henry, at school in Virginia, when he was but thirteen years of age. She died in 1827, having survived most of her children. Our author includes in her collection one single other subject from Virginia. She owes it to the "Mother of States" to enlarge her chronicle. We pass to North-Carolina. Twelve chapters are gathered from the traditionary [*sic*] memoirs of the "Old North State." That of Elizabeth Steele, who furnished Greene with a couple of bags of money, at a moment of his greatest necessity, is probably familiar to all our readers. It may be found in Garden and in most of the Lives of Greene. Of Mary Slocumb, of Wayne County, N. C, we have an interesting chapter. She managed her husband's plantation while he was in the army of the Americans. Tarleton quartered his troops upon her plantation, and her spirited dialogues with the famous British partisan are given at some, but not a fatiguing length. It was at this time that she received a visit from her husband, whose ignorance of the presence of the enemy led him almost into their clutches. His escape affords the author an opportunity for an exciting passage, which we are half tempted to copy, for the benefit of our readers, but dare not—the length of the chapter discourages our desire. It is enough for the future romancer, who would seek for a heroine, to know that Mary Slocumb was one of the bravest-hearted women in the world—a sort of Di Vernon—a good shot, a fearless rider, of great coolness in the moment of danger, and of desperate intrepidity. A brief paragraph devoted to Esther Wake, represents her as a politician, one who exercised large influence in State affairs. But she and her sister, Lady Tryon, were both loyalists. They helped to sustain Governor Tryon when his power was on the wane. It is honourable to the people of North-Carolina that they valued Esther Wake in spite of her politics. When it was proposed, after the revolution, to alter the name of Wake county, the proposition was rejected by acclamation. Thus, says our author very prettily, "the county in which the city of Raleigh is located is consecrated to the memory of beauty and virtue."

Margaret Gaston was the mother of the distinguished Judge Gaston, and deserves to be celebrated as such. She had rare virtues of her own. She was of English birth, a catholic, and was educated in France in a convent. In visiting her brothers, who had emigrated to America, she married Dr. Gaston, a Huguenot. He was one of the most zealous patriots of North-Carolina, and took an active part in the revolution. He was butchered by the tories in her arms. The noble training which the young widow gave her children, with some sweet anecdotes, furnish the materials chiefly of the chapter which is devoted to her name. To this succeeds that of one already known to fame. Flora McDonald is celebrated as the fearless damsel who contributed to the successful escape of Charles Edward, the Pretender to the throne of England, after the terrible battle of Culloden, which prostrated his strength and fortunes. Her agency in this escape is elaborately written by our author. Flora removed to North-Carolina in 1775. Her kinsman, Donald McDonald, became a general of the loyalists in the war which followed. She herself espoused the royal cause; since, curiously enough, the Scottish Highlanders, who hated the House of Hanover when in England, very generally proved devoted to it when they were transferred to America. They had paid too many of the penalties of disobedience at home to peril anything in behalf of a doubtful cause in America; and, in fact, the very virtues of loyalty, which made them faithful to the House of Stuart, made them cling to the now established throne of that family by which it had been superseded. The new affinities of Flora became as unfortunate as the old. The Highlanders found a new Culloden at the battle of Moore's Creek, in North-Carolina, and Flora became a fugitive and an outlaw in America, as she had been in Scotland, after a variety of fortunes, quite as eventful as the past, which afford our author the materials for a very interesting narrative. Flora returned to her native country, where she died in 1790. Her residence, destroyed by fire, stood upon the spot now occupied by the town of Fayetteville. Mrs. Willie Jones, Mrs. Allen Jones, and Mrs. Nicholas Long, also of North-Carolina, derived some of their prominence from their husbands, who were all active and influential workers in the great cause of American independence. They shared the toils and sympathized with the patriotism of their lords. They were women of education, taste and intelligence. One of them has been long since known for the sarcastic witticism with which she replied to the sneering remark of Tarleton in regard to Col. Washington. "He would like to see that officer." "You might have had that pleasure," was the answer," had you looked behind you at the battle of Cowpens."

There are but two chapters given to Georgia, at that time the youngest, the feeblest and most exposed State of the confederacy. We shall give these chapters at length, preferring not to abridge the narratives of our author. The first of these relates to Mrs. Spalding. It illustrates the calm, dignified virtues of one who represented society in its higher classes.

"A tribute is due to the fortitude of those who suffered when the war swept with violence over Georgia. After Colonel Campbell took possession of Savannah, in 1778, the whole country was overrun with irregular marauders, wilder and more ruthless than the Cossacks of the Don. As many of the inhabitants as could retire from the storm did so, awaiting a happier time to renew the struggle. One of those who had sought refuge in Florida was Mr. Spalding, whose establishments were on the river St. John's. He had the whole Indian trade, from the Altamaha to the Apalachicola. His property, with his pursuits, was destroyed by the war; yet his heart was ever with his countrymen, and the home he had prepared for his wife was the refuge of every American prisoner in Florida. The first Assembly that met in Savannah recalled him and restored his lands, but could not give him back his business nor secure the debts due; while his British creditors, with their demands for accumulated interest, pressed upon the remnant of his fortune. Under these adverse circumstances, and distressed on account of the losses of her father and brothers, who had taken arms in the American cause, Mrs. Spalding performed her arduous duties with a true woman's fidelity and tenderness. She followed her husband with her child when flight became necessary, and twice during the war traversed the two hundred miles between Savannah and St. Johns River in an open boat, with only black servants on board, when the whole country was a desert, without a house to shelter her and her infant son. The first of these occasions was when she visited her father and brothers while prisoners in Savannah; the second, when, in 1782, she went to congratulate her brothers and uncle on their victory. This lady was the daughter of Colonel William Mcintosh, and the niece of General Lachlan Mcintosh. Major Spalding, of Georgia, is her son.

"Mrs. Spalding's health was seriously impaired by the anxieties endured during the struggle, and many years afterwards it was deemed necessary for her to try the climate of Europe. In January, 1800. she, with her son and his wife, left Savannah in a British ship of twenty guns, with fifty men, built in all points to resemble a sloop of war, without the appearance of a cargo. When they had been out about fifteen days the captain sent one morning, at daylight, to request the presence of two of his gentleman passengers on deck. A large ship, painted black and showing twelve guns on a side, was seen to windward, running across their course. She was obviously a French privateer. The captain announced that there was no hope of outsailing her should their course be altered; nor would there be hope in a conflict, as those shifts usually carried one hundred and fitly men. Yet he judged that if no effort were made to shun the privateer the appearance of his ship might deter from an attack. The gentlemen were of the same opinion. Mr. Spalding, heart sick at thought of the perilous situation of his wife and mother, and unwilling to trust himself with an interview till the crisis was over, requested the captain to go below and make what preparation he could for their security. After a few minutes' absence the captain returned to describe a most touching scene. Mrs. Spalding had placed her daughter-in-law and the other inmates of the cabin, for safety, in the two state-rooms, filling the berths with the cots and bedding from the outer cabin. She had then taken her own station beside the scuttle which led from the outer cabin to the magazine, with two buckets of water. Having noticed that the two cabin boys were heedless, she had determined herself to keep watch over the magazine. She did so till the danger was past. The captain took in his light sails, hoisted his boarding nettings opened his ports and stood on upon his course. The privateer waited till the ship was within a mile, then fired a gun to windward and stood on her way. This ruse preserved the ship. The incident may serve to show the spirit of this matron, who also bore her high part in the perils of the revolution."

The other chapter is illustrative of the masculine spirit of a brave, fierce, old lady of a humbler rank in society. It belongs to another section of the same State, where the politer influences of life had then only in part made their appearance.

"At the commencement of the Revolutionary war, a large district to the State of Georgia, extending in one direction from Newson's Ponds to Cherokee Corner, near Athens, and in the other, from the Savannah River to Ogeechee River and Shoulderbone, had been already organized into a county, which received the name of Wilkes, in honour of the distinguished English politician. At the commencement of hostilities, so great a majority of the people of this county espoused the whig cause that it received from the tories the name of the 'Hornets' Nest.' In a portion of this district, near Dye's and Webb's ferries, on Broad River, now in Elbert County, was a stream known as 'War-woman's Creek'—a name derived from the character of an individual who lived near the entrance of the stream into the river.

"This person was Nancy Hart, a woman entirely uneducated and ignorant of all the conventional civilities of life, but a zealous lover of liberty and of the 'liberty boys,' as she called the whigs. She had a husband, whom she denominated a 'poor stick,' because he did not take a decided and active part with the defenders of his country, although she could not conscientiously charge him with the least partiality to the tories. This vulgar and illiterate, but hospitable and valorous female patriot, could boast no share of beauty—a fact she would herself have readily acknowledged had she ever enjoyed an opportunity of looking in a mirror. She was cross-eyed, had a broad, angular mouth, was ungainly in figure, rude in speech and awkward in manners; but having a woman's heart for her friends, though that of a tigress or a Katrine Montour for the enemies of her country.

She was well known to the tories, who stood somewhat in fear of her vengeance for any grievance or aggressive act, though they let pass no opportunity of teasing and annoying her when they could do so with impunity.

"On the occasion of an excursion from the British camp at Augusta, a party of loyalists penetrated into the interior, and having savagely massacred Colonel Dooly in bed in his own house, proceeded up the country, with the design of perpetrating further atrocities. On their way, a detachment of five from the party diverged to the east, and crossed Broad River, to examine the neighbourhood and pay a visit to their old acquaintance, Nancy Hart. When they arrived at her cabin they unceremoniously entered it, although receiving from her no welcome but a scowl, and informed her that they had come to learn the truth of a story in circulation, that she bad secreted a noted rebel from a company of 'king's men' who were pursuing him, and who, but for her interference, would have caught and hung him. Nancy undauntedly avowed her agency in the fugitive's escape. She had, she said, at first heard the tramp of a horse, and then saw a man on horseback approaching her cabin at his utmost speed. As soon as she recognized him to be a whig flying from pursuit she let down the bars in front of the cabin and motioned him to pass through both doors, front and rear, of her single-roomed house, to take to the swamp and secure himself as well as he could. This he did without loss of time, and she then put up the bars, entered the cabin, closed the doors, and went about her usual employments. Presently some tories rode up to the bars, calling vociferously for her. She muffled up her head and face, and opening the door, inquired why they disturbed a sick, lone woman. They said they had traced a man they wanted to catch near her house, and asked if any one on horseback had passed that way. She answered no—but she saw some one on a sorrel horse turn out of the path into the woods, some two or three hundred yards back. 'That must be the fellow!' said the tories; and asking her direction as to the way he took, they turned about and went off, *'well fooled,'* concluded Nancy, 'in an opposite direction to that of my whig boy; when, if they had not been so lofty minded, but had looked on the ground inside the bars, they would have seen his horse's tracks up to that door, as plain us you can see the tracks on this here floor, and out of other door down the path to the swamp.'

"This bold story did not much please the tory party, but they would not wreak their vengeance upon the woman who so unscrupulously avowed the cheat she had put upon the pursuers of a rebel. They contented themselves with ordering her to prepare them something to eat She replied that she never fed traitors and king's men if she could help it, the villains having put it out of her power to feed even her own family and friends, by stealing and killing all her poultry and pigs, 'except that one old gobler you see in the yard.' 'Well, and that you shall cook for us,' said one who appeared to be the leader of the party, and raising his musket he shot down the turkey, which another of them brought into the house and handed to Mrs. Hart, to he cleaned and cooked without delay. She stormed and swore awhile—for Nancy occasionally swore—but seeming at last disposed to make a virtue of necessity, began with alacrity the arrangements for cooking, assisted by her daughter, a little girl of ten years old, and sometimes by one of the party, with whom she seemed to be in a tolerably good humour, occasionally exchanging rude jests with him. The tories, pleased with her freedom, invited her to partake of the liquor they had brought with them—an invitation which was accepted with jocose thanks.

"The spring—of which every settlement has one near by—was just at the edge of the swamp, and a short distance within the swamp was hid among the trees a high snag-topped stump, on which was placed a conch-shell. This rude trumpet was used by the family to convey information, by variations in its notes, to Mr. Hart and his neighhours, who might be at work in a field, or 'clearing,' just beyond the swamp, to let them know that the 'Britishers' or tories were about, that the master was wanted at the cabin, or that he was to keep close, or 'make tracks' for another swamp. Tending the operation of cooking the turkey, Nancy had sent her daughter Sukey to the spring for water, with directions to blow the conch for her father in such a way as should inform him there were tories in the cabin, and that he was to 'keep close' with his three neighbours who were with him, until he should again hear the conch.

"The party had become merry over their jug, and sat down to feast upon the slaughtered gobbler. They had cautiously stacked their arms where they were in view and within reach, and Mrs. Hart, assiduous in her attentions upon the table and to her guests, occasionally passed between the men and their muskets. Water was called for, and our heroine having contrived that there should be none in the cabin, Sukey was a second time despatched [*sic*] to the spring, with instructions to blow such a signal on the conch as should call up Mr. Hart and his neighbours immediately. Meanwhile, Nancy had managed, by slipping out one of the pieces of pine which formed a 'chinking' between the logs of a cabin, to open a space through which she was able to pass to the outside two of the five guns. She was detected in the act of putting out the third. The whole party sprang to their feet, when, quick as thought, Nancy brought the piece she held to her shoulder, declaring she would kill the first man who approached her. All were terror-struck, for Nancy's obliquity of sight caused each to imagine himself her destined victim. At length one of them made a movement to advance upon her, and, true to her threat, she fired and shot him dead! Seizing another musket, she levelled it instantly, keeping the others at bay. By this time Sukey had returned from the spring, and taking up the remaining gun she carried it out of the house, saying to her mother, 'Daddy and them will soon be here.' This information much increased the alarm of the tories, who perceived the importance of recovering their arms immediately; but each one hesitated, in the confident belief that Mrs. Hart had one eye, at least, on him for a mark. They proposed a general rush. No time was to be lost by the bold woman;—she fired again, and brought down another of the enemy. Sukey had another musket in readiness, which her mother took, and posting herself in the doorway called upon the party to surrender 'their d— tory carcasses to a whig woman.' They agreed to surrender, and proposed to 'shake hands upon the strength of it.' But the victor, unwilling to trust their word, kept them in their places for a few minutes, till her husband and his neighbours came up to the door. They were about to shoot down the tories, but Mrs. Hart stopped them, saying they had surrendered to her; and her spirit being up to boiling heat, she swore that 'shooting was too good for them.' This hint was enough; the dead man was dragged out of the house, and the wounded tory and the others were bound, taken out beyond the bars and hung. The tree upon which they were suspended was shown in 1828, by one who lived in those bloody times, and who also pointed out the spot once occupied by Mrs. Hart's cabin, accompanying the mention of her name with the emphatic remark: 'Poor Nancy! she was a honey of a patriot, but the devil of a wife!'"

The spirit and interest of this little memoir needs no comment.

We pass now to the heroines of South-Carolina. These have long since been known to fame. Their distinctions were acknowledged during the progress of the Revolution, and many of the noble women of that State have already sate to the painter and the poet, as they have done to the Historian. Of Sarah Reeve Gibbes, Eliza Wilkinson, Rebecca Motte, Mrs. Brewton, Sabina Elliott and others, of the same family, we have memories, sketches and anecdotes almost without number. They have been grateful subjects for the admiration and study of posterity, some of them combining the graces and beauties of Aspasia, with the high virtues of the mother of the Gracchi. We are not permitted to do more than accord to these, as we pass, the tribute of our unfeigned and grateful admiration. The industry of Mrs. Ellet has added to this fair list of fine women,—a collection such as might afford to some of our native poets, "a dream of fair women," which might prove more ennobling to song than those chosen for his muse, by the luscious Tennyson. We can only give the names of these, detaching one or more instances for the reader, as samples of the rest. Here are sketches or anecdotes of Martha Bratton, of York District, a fine Roman portrait which the true woman will love to study; of Jane Thomas, of Fairforest River, who rode sixty miles in one day to warn the Americans of the approach of the loyalists; a copious and highly interesting narrative.— Isabella Sims, Mrs. Otterson, and Nancy Jackson, of the same region, afford pleasing anecdotes of devotion and patriotism;—Dorcas Richardson, of Clarendon, occupies worthily an entire chapter;—Elizabeth, Grace, and Rachel Martin, of Ninety-Six, furnish some remarkable instances of valor as well as patriotic endurance. The two eldest, disguised in their husbands' garments, and well armed, actually succeeded in capturing a British party. Dicey Langston, of Laurens District, furnishes a lovely specimen of maidenly devotion, with masculine firmness and enterprise;—Mrs. Dillard, of Spartanburg, was a heroine of like mould and performance. Of Mrs. Potter, Mrs. Beckham, and

Mrs. Brevard, there are interesting anecdotes; and a paragraph is properly assigned to the mother of Andrew Jackson, who died by the wayside, returning from Charleston, whither she had gone to carry clothing to one of her sons, then in a British prison ship. To the virtues, the patriotism, and strength of character of Behethland Foote Butler, the mother of Pierce and Pickens Butler, and allied with so much that is precious in Carolina history, a chapter is fitly given; and we note with pleasure the several anecdotes which belong to the names of Hall, Shubrick, Heyward, Izard, Geiger, and Gaunt. That of Emily Geiger, of Orangeburg, is in proof of equal intelligence and patriotic devotion on the part of a young damsel, scarcely in her teens.

"At the time General Greene retreated before Lord Rawdon from Ninety-Six, when he had passed Broad River he was very desirous to send an order to General Sumter, then on the Wateree, to join him, that they might attack Rawdon, who had divided his force. But the country to be passed through was, for many miles, full of blood-thirsty tories, and it was a difficult matter to find a man willing to undertake so dangerous a mission. At length a young girl—Emily Geiger—presented herself to General Greene, proposing to act as his messenger, and the General, both surprised and delighted, closed with her proposal. He accordingly wrote a letter and gave it to her, at the same time communicating the contents verbally, to be told to Sumter in case of accident. Emily was young, but as to her person or adventures on the way, we have no further information, except that she was mounted on horseback, upon a side-saddle, and on the second day of her journey was intercepted by Lord Rawdon's scouts. Coming from the direction of Greene's army, and not being able to tell an untruth without blushing, she was shut up, and the officer in command having the modesty not to search her at the time, he sent for an old tory matron as more fitting for the purpose, Emily was not wanting in expedients, and as soon as the door was closed she ate up the letter, piece by piece. After a while the matron arrived. Upon searching carefully, nothing was found of a suspicious nature about the prisoner, and she would disclose nothing. Suspicion being thus allayed, the officer commanding the scouts suffered Emily to depart whither she said she was bound. She took a route somewhat circuitous to avoid further detection, and soon after struck into the road to Sumter's camp, where she arrived in safety. She told her adventure, and delivered Greene's verbal message to Sumter, who in consequence soon joined the main army at Orangeburg, Emily Geiger afterwards married a rich planter on the Congaree. She has been dead thirty-five years, but it is trusted her name will descend to posterity among those of the patriotic females of the revolution."

Here are other specimens of the virtues of strong courage, and a noble will, overcoming the ordinary weaknesses of the sex.

"A man named Hubbs, who had served with the bloody tory and renegade, Cunningham, in South-Carolina, was an 'outlier' during the war. At one time he proposed, with two confederates, to rob an old man of Quaker habits—Israel Gaunt—who was reputed to be in the possession of money. The three rode up one evening to the house and asked lodging, which was refused. Hubbs rode to the kitchen door, in which Mrs. Gaunt was standing, and asked for water. He sprang in while she turned to get the water, and as she handed it to him she saw his arms. Her husband, informed of this, secured the doors. Hubbs presented a pistol at him; but his deadly purpose was frustrated by the old man's daughter, Hannah. She threw up the weapon, and, being of masculine proportions and strength, grappled with and threw him on the floor, where she held him, though wounded by his spurs, in spite of his desperate struggles, till he was disabled by her father's blows. Gaunt was wounded through the window by Hubbs' companions, and another ball grazed his heroic daughter just above the eye; but both escaped without further injury. Hannah afterwards married a man named Mooney. The gentleman who relates the foregoing incident has often seen her, and describes her as one of the kindest and most benevolent of women. She died about the age of fifty, and her grandson, a worthy and excellent man, is now living in the village of Newberry.

"The same company of marauders, with Moultrie, another of Cunningham's gang, visited Andrew Lee's house, at Lee's Ferry, Saluda River, for the purpose of plunder. Moultrie succeeded in effecting an entrance into the house. Lee seized and held him, and they fell together on a bed, when he called to his wife, Nancy, to strike him on the head with an axe. Her first blow, in her agitation, fell on her husband's hand; but she repeated it and stunned Moultrie, who fell on the floor insensible. Lee, with his negroes and dogs, then drove away the other robbers, and on his return secured Moultrie, who was afterwards hanged in Ninety-Six."

The third volume of these biographies, just issued from the press, affords us no less than fifteen subjects from the domestic history of South-Carolina, out of forty-four which form the collection. These are all highly interesting portraits of character, accompanied with details which greatly serve to illustrate a portion of our history in the upper country, which our historians have but too greatly neglected. We have no space, however, for any thing beyond a mere register of the names of these noble women, Katharine Steele affords an exciting chapter. She was a model of firmness, courage and patriotism; Nancy Green, Esther Walker, Mary McClure, were of the same region, the Catawba Country, and owned hearts and heads of the same moral strength and sympathies. Isabella Ferguson was a Chester woman of wonderful vivacity and spirit; Mary Johnston was of Chester also; so were Jane Boyd, Jane Gaston, Sarah McCalla, Mary Adair, Mary Nixon, Mary Smiley, Isabella Wylie, and Jane White: each of whom affords material for a graceful chapter. Rebecca Pickens, wife of the General, was a Calhoun, a very noble woman, and, with her biography, the share of South-Carolina women, in this volume, terminates. But an Appendix contains a narrative of the surprise of General Sumter, by Tarleton, at Fishing Creek, and as our historians have generally contented themselves with briefly stating this fact, and giving no details, we propose to extract the account before us, premising that Mrs. Ellet has foreborne to tell us from what source it was derived. It was evidently drawn originally from the lips of one who had witnessed something of the transaction; and may have been derived from several, at second or third hand.

"After the fall of Charleston, May 12th, 1780, the British overran the State, establishing posts at Georgetown, Camden, Rocky Mount, Ninety-Six and Augusta, with others on the line from those to Charleston, to serve as places for rest, or to keep open their communication. The province was thus, to all appearance, conquered, the people generally having submitted; but a few resolute spirits, scattered over the country, could not be subdued by the severest measures. The 'outlyers,' gathered under the command of Pickens and Williams, did service, while, in the upper country, the battles described were fought, and Marion harrassed the enemy from the recesses of his swamps. This was the state of the war during May, June, July and August: the patriots endeavouring to supply their lack of numbers by laborious service and rapid marches. The news of the approach of Gates gave a new impulse to their zeal, and brought recruits to the standard of Sumter, enabling him to commence an aggressive warfare. By August 13th Gen. Gates rested at Clermont, thirteen miles from Camden. The mistake he committed in sending four hundred regulars to aid Sumter in the taking of Carey Fort was productive of a train of disasters. Had he, instead, ordered Sumter with his riflemen to join him, he might have advanced on Camden and fought the battle before aid arrived from Georgetown; or had he still delayed, and commenced the night march when he did, such an addition to his force, and of such men, might have turned his defeat into a splendid victory. Sumter's attack on the convoy and Carey Fort was crowned with success, and with his three hundred prisoners, and forty four wagons loaded with munitions of war, he hastened to join Gen. Gates, on the way receiving the news of his defeat, Encumbered with prisoners and baggage wagons—many of the regulars and country militia being on foot—his march on the retreat was slow, though kept up during the nights of the 16th and 17th August It was not more than forty miles above Camden that he pitched his camp on the ill-fated morning of the 18th.*

"A strong guard could have disputed the passage from Fishing Creek up the valley, for half a mile from the place where the road passed on the ridge. The enemy could only have kept the road in file, and a few discharges of artillery would have demolished them. Had they taken the open field, lying a few hundred yards from the camp, they must have passed in column over parts of the ground—the ravines narrowing one pass into a mere strip of land. General Sumter had occupied this very ground on the night following his attack on Rocky Mount, having chosen it as a stronghold, in the expectation that the British, reinforced

* (See Katharine Steel, page 101.)

from Hanging Rock, would attack him. They did, in fact, march for this purpose; but the creek was too much swollen by the heavy rains to be crossed. This strong military position was guarded by the Catawba on the east, and the creek on the west, with ravines in front and rear, and on either hand a narrow strip of ground affording the only space for occupation; while at the place of encampment the ground was so spread out that he could have used his whole force, or if driven from that position could have taken a similar one at almost every hundred yards distance on the ridge, for miles up the river. Its great natural advantages, therefore, justified his selection. When his army halted and struck their tents, the guard, being mounted, repaired to their posts, Major Crowford, of the Waxhaws, being the officer in command. The men in camp who had no duty to do, and were not too hungry, were soon fast asleep in their tents, having had no rest for two nights. Some were engaged in slaughtering beeves, and every few moments the crack of a rifle might be heard, while those awake would call out 'Beef!' to one another. The sentinels posted down the road towards the ford of the creek were marching up and down the line appointed, while others of the guard made the the river, desirous of a bath, as the weather was oppressively warm, and intending to be back at the station in time to take their turn. It is said that Major Crowford gave them permission to go; in any case, it is likely that these forest hunters, unaccustomed to military discipline, would have exercised their own discretion. Just as the army halted, Sarah Featherston, a young woman of a tory family, passed the road. Many of Sumter's men gave her the credit of having informed Tarleton of their situation, and some thought she had guided the British up the creek to what was called McKown's ford. This, however, she did not do, for they came up the road from the stream. The sentinels did their duty, delivering their fire in turn; but there was no guard to oppose the advance of the enemy. Each dragoon had a foot soldier posted near him, and these dismounted near the camp. In front, a short distance from the tents, Mrs. Pray, of Fairfield District, was seated upon a log feeding her two children. Her husband had gone into North-Carolina, after Gates' defeat, to join his force, and she having to leave home because her neighbours were loyalists, thought it safest to travel with the army. She had with her a negro boy and two horses. As she sat upon the log, the British dragoons charged past her, and she would have been run over, had not the log been large and furnished with branches, so that they were obliged to pass round it. She sat still, her eyes fixed on the terrible spectacle, and saw the defenceless or slumbering men shot down or cut to pieces, till she turned sickening from the scene of massacre. She saw a few of the regulars rallying behind the wagons and returning the fire, and presently the bullets whistling near brought her to her recollection. Slipping down from the log, she pulled the children after her, and kept them close by her side till the firing ceased. When the British left the ground they took her servant and horses, and she was left with her children, alone with the dead and wounded. Next day she went with the little ones, who were crying for food, to the house of Nat Rives, a tory living in the neighbourhood, to beg some food for them. He coolly told her there was the peach orchard, and she might take what she wanted; it was good enough for a rebel. This Rives afterwards accompanied Mrs., Johnston to the ground. When the British made their onset on the camp, Mrs., Pray's brother, John Starke, mounted his horse and made for the river. Plunging in, he reached an island, and spurred his horse from a high bank into deep water, rising in a few moments and effecting thus his escape to the opposite shore. The dragoons had pursued several of the men into the river, and were shooting and stabbing them. Starke, indignant at the sight, rose from his saddle to call the attention of the enemy, and made them a gesture of defiance. They were nearer than he calculated, and their fire wounded him severely in the thigh. Some of the whigs who had escaped across the river procured a cart and carried him to his mother's house, where he lay helpless a long time, exposed to ill usage from the tories, whom in after life he could never forgive.

"At the time of the surprise, it is supposed that between one and two hundred young men were bathing in the river. The dragoons, pursuing those who fled, came in among them, and an indiscriminate slaughter ensued. One William Reeves had his hair cut with a bullet, and was so stunned he would have been drowned, had not George Weir dragged him upon a rock. John Nesbit, Richard Wright and Stephen White were making for the opposite bank, when White called out that he was shot. His companions dragged him to a rock, and then hid themselves till the British had left the river. When they came back they could find nothing of White, nor was it ever known what became of him. Many of the soldiers stood on the east bank of the river, with no covering from the burning sun. Some of them went to the house of McMeans, whose wife gave them all her husband's clothes, and even exhausted her own wardrobe, so that more than one of the survivors of that disastrous day went home in petticoats. Ben Rowan, 'the boxer of the army,' heard the firing of the sentinels in the direction of the creek, but supposed it to be the killing of beeves a little further from the camp. The men had just, brought in some of the meat, and were cooking before the tents. Ben, on his way to the next tent, had in his hand a piece of buckskin, of which he meant to have a pair of moccasins made for his blistered feet. He was startled by the enemy's broadside, and seeing in an instant that all was lost, ran for safety to the place where the three hundred prisoners were under guard. They were shouting for joy and flinging up their hats, when with his Herculean strength he forced himself a pathway through and over them. Just as he got through them, he saw a loose horse grazing, and flung himself upon the animal without saddle or bridle, slapping first with one hand and then with the other to direct his course. The horse went off at a brisk pace through the woods, and Ben made good his escape, to be an actor in every subsequent battle of the South. Joel McClemore, as he ran through the camp, picked up a rifle, not knowing if it were loaded or not. He was presently pursued by a dragoon, and after dodging from tree to tree for some time got near the fence and succeeded in crossing it. It then occurred to him that the open field was not so safe as the woods in case of continued pursuit, and turning round, he said to the dragoon in his Virginia vernacular, 'I'll eat fire if you cross that fence but I'll shoot you!' The dragoon put spurs to his horse, and as he leaped Joel drew trigger at a venture. The gun went off, and the man fell, while the horse leaped the fence. Joel lost no time in mounting, and thus escaped with a fine horse, holster and pistols. William Nesbit was in his tent asleep at the first alarm, but taking a horse from one of the wagons escaped up the river, and was with the foremost at McDonalds ford. On another part of the field the brave Capt. Pagan was rallying his men, among whom were the brothers Gill; he was shot and fell down the hill, while his company scattered. Archibald Gill, though but a stripling, showed so much indignation at what he witnessed at this defeat that he was afterwards called 'mad Archy.' A few regulars, who contended for a time against overpowering numbers, were forced to yield. Gen. Sumter was saved in the manner already mentioned. Near the spot where James Johnston was wounded after lulling one of the British dragoons, John Reynolds shot another and secured his horse. Everywhere up the river and creek the woods were filled with men flying for their lives, while some who escaped butchery were driven back to the camp by the troopers.

"The prisoners were placed under a strong guard, having to do without dinner as well as breakfast, with the prospect of the gibbet before many, who had taken British protection, when they should reach Camden. Among these were Col. Thomas Taylor, (distinguished afterwards in the war,) and his brother, Capt. John Taylor. Tarleton remained master of the field of slaughter, for it could not be called a battle. By his order the wagons for which they could not find horses were collected together and consumed, with such articles as could not conveniently be taken away. Long before sunset the British commenced their march towards Camden, leaving the dead unburied and the wounded, who could not be removed, to perish. The march was continued several hours after dark. Thomas Taylor advised those among the prisoners who expected no mercy to effect their escape, and showed them how this was to be done. The guard could not long keep on the edge of the road, but must march in the front and rear of the prisoners; they were to get as near the centre as they could, drop off on the side, and lie down till they were passed. Many escaped in this way. It was near midnight when Tarleton halted to encamp on the bank of Wateree creek. While the men were reposing, Col. Taylor watched his opportunity and proposed to his brother and a Mr. Lake to attempt escape, by jumping down a steep bank, fifteen or twenty feet in height, sliding gently into the water and swimming down the stream. The feat was accomplished, though it was very dark, and in leaping down they fell one over the other. Col. Taylor profited by the lesson of this surprise at the Fishdam, Nov. 7th, when the same corps of Tarleton, under Major Wemyss, attempted to steal a march on Sumter's army at dead of night, and were repulsed with much loss.

"The scattered men of Sumter's army, with one accord, made their way to Charlotte, as if their destination had been previously appointed. Those who went home stayed only long enough to procure such articles of clothing as they had lost, and went on. They might be seen the next day upon every road leading towards Charlotte. Sumter himself went on the same night, and Capt. Steel, as already mentioned, returned to the battle ground.

"Capt. Berry, who, with some of his men, had escaped after the defeat of Gen. Gates on the night of the 17th, wandered up the river as far as George Wade's house. Wade, who came home in the night, gave him three hundred pounds of flour for his soldiers, and informed him that Gen. Sumter would be on the other side of the river next morning. Berry crossed the next day with his command, and had not been an hour in camp before the surprise took place, in which he was captured; thus leaving one disastrous field to meet misfortune in another.

With these samples, we conclude our selections. We are not prepared to say that they do full justice to the manner or matter of our author. They are quite too limited to do so. It is in the more elaborate notices, where the mind of the writer gets fairly under weigh, that she shows the grace, felicity, good sense, and general spirit of her productions. But, we aim at nothing more than to provoke curiosity and invite attention to this highly-useful and entertaining collation, at once honorable to the female character of the country and valuable as constituting no inferior portion of our history. As we have already said, it will pave the way for other volumes, and by other writers. We trust, however, that Mrs. Ellet, who has succeeded in fixing the public curiosity upon herself, will not give way entirely to the new gleaners in these profitable and pleasant fields of search. Though not expected to reap them entirely herself, there are yet many sheaves which she can most fitly gather—many other volumes, perhaps, which will be doubly worthy as companions to these before us. Nor must other workers in this goodly vineyard be discouraged when they regard the success which has followed her exertions. They will each, if they devote themselves to familiar sections of country, possess one advantage over all competitors, in the appreciation of the genius loci—in the knowledge of details, scenery, and the social characteristics. These qualities will make amends for many deficiencies of the writer. But, the work must not be delayed. Old memories are rapidly failing us. The oldest inhabitant will soon mutter over these matters, even as a dream, scarcely as a reality, which it afflicts him to recall, yet which he would not entirely lose. We must fix these dream-like memories now, or never. We, who are in possession of all the fruits of that fearful struggle of our sires, and the mothers of our sires, owe it to the old, noble workers of the past, man and woman, to put on record the history of their achievements. The truly patriotic mind—which is the only truly grateful—will mourn, with frequent self- chiding, the treasures of history which we have suffered, and are suffering, daily, to escape us. Nobody, more than the writer of this article, can more deeply regret the indifference which has made him heedless, until too late, of what he might have secured for his posterity. He had his lessons at the knees of those who were young spectators in the grand panorama of our Revolution. Their souls were imbued with its events, as with one great and sole-absorbing history. This was their favourite topic; and each had details of the local struggle, which were as interesting as they were certainly veracious. How the boy brooded over these narratives!—and, how strange, that, to the man, they should appear only as bright glimpses of a wing hurrying through the sun-light, and leaving no traces of its pathway through the thin empire of air! There was scarcely a personage, British or American, Whig or Loyalist—scarcely an event, mournful or glorious—scarcely a deed, grand or savage—occurring in the history of the low country of South-Carolina, which has not been conned, for his benefit, at the writer's fireside, by venerable friends and loving kinswomen, now voiceless in the dust. How the world—always "too much with us" as Wordsworth emphatically teaches—has obliterated these histories—not stricken out their broad features, their general characteristics, their breadth and depth and shadow—all of which necessarily become fused in the mind and absorbed in its permanent convictions—but spoiled it of those inferior but important constituents—the dates, the names, the details—without which, no valuable record of events can possibly be made. He has been taught to see the first kindlings of the torch of revolution, borne, by eager and enthusiastic hands, throughout the country, and warming the multitudes to passion wherever they were carried. He has seen the first gatherings of the rude militia, under their young and gallant, but inexperienced leaders. He has been shown the summary punishment of the treacherous spy, or the faithless tory; and, as the strife grew, and great clouds of war rolled towards the shore, he has seen the citizens thronging the wharves to behold the first wrestle of the young country, at Moultrie's fortress, with the powerful, insolent monarch whom it had ventured to defy. The vicissitudes that followed this victory were not forgotten; and he was shown, step by step, the progress of the invader to the conquest of the city, and, finally, of the State. Nor was he suffered to hear this narrative with a cold and peevish attention. It was made life-like, to his imagination by personal histories, which appealed to his nearest affections and fondest sympathies. The venerable narrator spoke of his grandsire, or her own. The old man, then in the vigour of his youth, was to be seen, day and night, at the lines of Charleston, armed with the rifle, which past experience had rendered a fatal implement in his hands. From the beleaguered city, he had sent his wife and child, at the first approaches of the enemy; but the woman belonged to a Spartan school, and found it easier to brave the enemy than the safety of the solitude, embittered by the ceaseless anxiety which left her doubtful of his fate. In an open row-boat, she descends Cooper river, from its sources; and, with mufiled oars, passes, at midnight, though in the midst of a fearful cannonade, through the thronging barges of the British. The roar of the incessant cannon—the wild Might and explosion of the bursting bombs—lighted up, as with a sulphurous thunderstorm, the gloomy empire of the night. The random shot sullenly plunged about them into the water, as, dropping with the tide, they moved noiselessly along the river, concealed only by the dense atmosphere of smoke which shadowed the scene, lightened only, at moments, by the meteoric flight of shot or shell. How vivid was all this picture to our eyes, unfolded by the native art of that brave old grand-dame! And, how flowed the tear, as she described the soldier's glad surprise in the unlooked-for embraces of his fearless wife! What a picture then followed of the wreck which presented itself every where in the beleaguered city! How the streets were torn up to form banks of earth before the most exposed dwellings: how the women and children found refuge in the damp and gloomy recesses of vault and cellar. We still see the narrator, a little girl, stealing forth with her mother, at intervals of the cannonade, to gather parsley for the porridge, at the bottom of the garden—flying back, with all speed, as the batteries from James Island, or the British galleys, once more opened their fire on the beleaguered city. A mournful spectacle of conflagration and famine succeeds, and the place ceases to be tenable. We are shown the capitulation—we see the old grandsire flinging down his rifle in the pile, and, turning away, hardly reaches his dwelling before the pile explodes in thunder, rending and riving all within reach of the explosion. The captivity that follows is equally pregnant with a personal interest. We see the old grandsire put in chains, and hurried, with forty others, to the prisons of St. Augustine, as a hostage for the good behaviour of his comrades. The scene changes, and the persons. Other kinsmen have their fortunes shown in colours similarly glowing. One brave ancestor was in the brigade of Marion. We see him on a scout, environed by the Black Dragoons. He leaves his horse, and seeks to bury himself in the forest. He ascends a tree and shrouds himself in the branches. They discover him, and he is brought down, wounded with a heavy sabre-cut over the brows. Brought to the gates of Charleston, he asks of the Scotch officer commanding, that his further escort to prison shall be a white one. "Hoot awa', ye d—d ribbel! A black guard's too good for ye!" He had reason to be satisfied. Thus far, the negro escort had been more courteous than the superior. And thus he is conducted to the provost, where he lies, cold, lone, suffering, for many weary months. How many thousand such histories, with details sufficiently ample for the reader's curiosity—not mere glimpses and generalities, such as these—may be gathered by loving patriotism from still lingering memories of the past, and made precious possessions to the future artist and historian! What glorious histories may be gathered of man's valour and woman's devotion—man's daring and woman's endurance—man's passionate love of country, and the fidelity and love with which woman recompenses all! How impressively, with such chronicles well studied and preserved, should we learn how much society contributes to government, and how idle is that system of the statesman which frames theories and laws for a people, yet disdains to borrow his lessons from the fireside—there, where the true nature alone speaks with a perfect freedom, and, in revealing the full measure of its attachments, reveals the necessities which alone constitutes the care of society.

The Southern Convention

The Southern Convention, also known as the Nashville Convention, was a congress of delegates representing nine Southern states—Virginia, South Carolina, Georgia, Mississippi, Texas, Alabama, Arkansas, Florida, and Tennessee. The body met at two separate occasions, both times in Nashville, Tennessee, with the first meeting beginning on 3 June and the second on 11 November 1850. The first meeting took place prior to the passage of the bills collectively referred to as the Compromise of 1850 and the second after.[1] The review reprinted here, which was originally published in the *Southern Quarterly Review* in September 1850, refers to the first meeting.

The germ of the Southern Convention is often traced to the congressional caucus of sixty-nine southern congressmen held on 23 December 1848. John C. Calhoun, the senior senator from South Carolina and the state's leading political theorist, orchestrated the caucus and composed "The Address of the Southern Delegates in Congress to their Constituents" as a collective statement for the group, representing his final attempt to unite the South across party lines. This impulse to develop a unified South had deep roots in South Carolina, and Simms noted in a letter to James Henry Hammond that Calhoun's calls for a Southern Convention were derivative of long-standing suggestions that "old Union men" such as Simms had "preached to him 20 years ago" (*Letters* 2: 293–97). Indeed, in late 1844 Simms had submitted resolutions to then-governor Hammond's "Message No. 1, as relates to the Tariff, to Texas, and the Abolitionists," which included a call for the governors of all "slave-holding States of this Confederacy" to send delegates to meet at Asheville, North Carolina, for consultation as to their mutual defense of their vital interests within the Republic, namely the acquisition of Texas.[2] By the time Calhoun organized the southern caucus in December 1848 the United States had annexed the Republic of Texas and had also acquired the vast tract of land that included the territories of California and New Mexico. It was the debates in Congress over how to organize those territories, and, most importantly, the fate of slavery in them, that made the Southern Convention such a pressing concern for both Calhoun and Simms.

For most southerners, whether they were Whigs or Democrats, the most immediate issue was stopping the Wilmot Proviso, a bill proposed by Pennsylvania Democrat David Wilmot to prohibit slavery from any territory acquired from Mexico.[3] Allowing that measure to pass Congress would represent a severe rebuke of southern honor and would clearly indicate that the South was not considered an equal member of the nation. While Simms did not view the proviso as a legitimate threat, calling it at one point "rather more offensive than dangerous," he did believe that it offered an opportunity to make political headway toward a unified South (*Letters* 2: 293–97).[4] By 1849 Simms strongly supported the proposed convention and had ambitions of attending as a delegate from Charleston (*Letters* 2: 574–77; 3: 8–13). Although he ultimately did not go to Nashville, he used his position as editor of the *Southern Quarterly Review* to support the work of the men who gathered there, a group that included both James Henry Hammond and Nathaniel Beverley Tucker, two of Simms's close confidants. The printed remarks of the two men before the convention were, not coincidentally, included in the review reprinted below.

Simms's review and analysis of the convention displays a boosterism that belies the political difficulties that hampered the meeting. Despite his best hopes, existing party rivalries undermined the convention's efficacy. Though it had appeared possible that tensions over slavery's future in the territories would spark party realignment along sectional lines, that possibility had waned, at least temporarily, by the time the delegates convened in Nashville. Most southern Whigs denounced the Nashville Convention and attacked their Democratic opponents for preaching disunion. Henry Clay's efforts to shepherd a compromise package through Congress sapped much of the support that had existed among southern Whigs, and, by the time the convention met, only nine of fifteen slaveholding states sent delegates. Many Whigs, who had been chosen as delegates, simply refused to attend (Holt, *Political Crisis,* 68–73, 86–88; Holt, *Rise and Fall,* 459–64, 517).

As a young editor in Charleston, Simms had remained a staunch unionist throughout the Nullification Crisis of 1831–32, but he had little faith in the future of the Union by 1850. "I have long since regarded the separation [of the sections] as a now inevitable necessity," he wrote in a letter to Beverley Tucker at the beginning of that year, adding "I have no hope, and no faith in compromises of any kind; and am not willing to be gulled by them any longer" (*Letters* 3: 8–13). Simms extended his rebuke of the compromise position in his review of the convention. He instead endorsed the Calhounite position that slaves, being property, were protected under the Constitution and could not be excluded from the federal territories. Barring that, Simms supported the compromise position offered by the delegates, which would have extended the Missouri Compromise line to the Pacific Ocean and divided the California territory along the thirty-fifth parallel, creating in the process two states, one slave and one free ("Southern Convention"). It was a position supported by southern Democrats in Congress, but one that lost out in the final compromise, which admitted California as a free state and organized the remaining territory on the basis of popular sovereignty.

Simms's positive portrayal of the convention functioned more as polemic than as a reflection of the political reality. Yet his support for the meeting's results was not surprising and operated on multiple levels. What is perhaps most interesting about Simms's discussion of the Southern Convention is that in his view the implications of the meeting were far greater than the fate of the territories: it was the future of American civilization itself. What was at stake was not only how the nation would expand through space, but also how it would move through time. Simms's thought about how societies progressed, and ultimately decayed, was stadialist, drawing on the Scottish historical school. The stadialist model postulates that human society progresses through a series of historical stages, from the savage to the civilized. The theory, also evident in the writings of James Fenimore Cooper and Sir Walter Scott, is not merely progressive; it also suggests historical time is cyclical and that societies, like people, begin to decay after reaching the end of their historical development.

Looking at contemporary American society, Simms already saw the signs of the decadence, vice, and luxury that had preceded the collapse of the great empires of antiquity. He located the root of that decay in northern free society. "We are rioting in all the rankness and emulating all the vices, the excesses, and the luxuries of Europe," he lamented. "The Northern States of the confederacy have reached their highest points of power and civilization. . . . Affluence has corrupted their hearts; pride and vanity have sapped their virtues; they have reached that point in their progress when the warning of the wise, and the teachings of experience are equally vain to arrest the ambition which strives beyond its reach" ("Southern Convention"). The disease had been festering for the better part of a generation and, according to Simms, had infected the northern mind with the "fanaticism and excess which had usually characterized the decay, and prepared the downfall of older nations."

Abolitionism was the core of the problem, but the infection went deeper and penetrated all aspects of society. Free labor, lacking the organic ties between slave labor and capital found in the South, devolved into chaos, and "Mobs, riots, murders, mark the daily events in their progress." Assaults on human property represented merely the leading edge of a more general assault on property rights, which were "held by a doubtful tenure." "Marriage is denounced, as hostile to the proper exercise of the legitimate passions—a doctrine which really seeks to legitimate prostitution—and societies are actually formed, whose sole aim is to abolish the Christian Sabbath."[5] What Simms described was an epochal clash of civilizations similar in magnitude, he suggested, to the conflict between England and the American colonies. In both moments the threat came from an imperial power that had "become arrogant in strength and power" and whose affluence had bred vanity, luxury, and corruption ("Southern Convention"). The current danger, however, was all the more threatening because of its proximity. At stake was the survival of the founders' republic and, indeed of republican values as properly understood.

Simms did not stop with a comparison to the Revolution. His sense of historical time was religious as well as secular. He framed his critique of northern society in biblical terms, with an allusion to the Old Testament story of Belshazzar's feast. Like the Babylonian prince, Simms suggested, too many in the North had forgotten God and were worshiping at the alter of the self, and, as it had been in ancient times, the writing was on the wall: "Mene, mene, tekel, upharsin" (thou art weighed in the balances and found wanting; "Southern Convention"). Here Simms was reacting against the other side of the Romantic revolution, the peculiar amalgamation of Romanticism and revivalism that gained traction primarily in the northern United States and that emphasized the central importance of the empowered and perfectible individual. It was this intellectual movement, much of it driven by the religious fervor of the Second Great Awakening, that spawned the many –isms and –ologies that Simms decried: "Communism, Fourierism, Agrarianism, and other isms of the family of Abolitionism."[6] For more orthodox adherents these social utopian movements, and the broader context in which they arose, threatened the sanctity of divine sovereignty. They were blasphemous because they celebrated human reason and relied on the ability of humanity to perfect both itself and its society. Simms's heavy reliance on biblical allusion, especially at the beginning of the essay, is indicative of the grounding of his anxiety in an orthodox interpretation of Christianity.

Simms's reference to Belshazzar was also tied to his deep concern about the United States' role as an imperial nation. He concluded the section by connecting the present state of its society to the decay of ancient empires, warning that, "Hebrew and Egyptian, Greek, Persian and Roman, they were all peoples who had scorned, in the day of their prosperity, the source and policy to which it was due . . . and, in their vanity and lusts . . . set up the false god of their own hearts, in place of the true, the maker of heaven and the earth" ("Southern Convention"). Simms feared a similar situation was at hand in the United States.

Allusions to antiquity were a common device for Americans of the age, especially those who were thinking about the development of their civilization as it grew to encompass the greater portion of the North American continent. It was especially to ancient Rome, and particularly the transition from republic to empire, that these Americans looked and from which they tried to draw lessons when they thought about their own nation's imperial growth. This impulse was especially strong among members of the master class, who were well-read in ancient history and literature. They had read Oliver Goldsmith's *Roman History* (1769) and *History of Greece* (1774), both of which had attributed the downfall of the great civilizations of antiquity not only to their opulence, but also to their imperial aspirations (Fox-Genovese and Genovese, *The Mind of the Master Class,* 264). The question was whether American civilization would suffer the same fate as those ancient empires, and southerners were not the only Americans asking those questions. The painter Thomas Cole posed the same query in his series *The Course of Empire* (1833–36), in which he traced the development of a Roman-like civilization from the savage, to the pastoral, to its height in decadence, and finally to its destruction. The series offered a critique of the unbounded optimism and belief in infinite progress that permeated much of American society during the first half of the nineteenth century (Allen, *A Republic in Time,* 47–53).

Simms also saw signs of societal decay when he looked at the North's free society. Yet he was not necessarily convinced that the stadialist pattern of recurring cycles of the rise and fall of civilization would repeat itself in America. He believed that it was possible to arrest historical time and thus forestall the civilizational decline that had befallen all previous empires. Here he adopted an outlook that closely paralleled one held by the Jeffersonians of the previous generation. They too had believed that the great expanse of the American West could sustain the vitality of the republic, allowing it to remain "young" and not succumb to the decadence and corruption that accompanied the movement from the pastoral to the civilized phases of historical development. It would be in the West, they maintained, that abundant land would allow generations of yeoman farmers to till the soil and maintain a virtuous and independent republican citizenry (McCoy, *The Elusive Republic, passim*).

Simms recited many of the old Jeffersonian fears in making his case that the American Republic was in peril. He worried that the agrarian South suffered economic disabilities and threats from free trade that favored northern manufactures. He expressed deep suspicion of urban mobs and unchecked majoritarianism, and he indicated a strong preference for the agricultural, rather than the industrial, organization of production. Yet he was not merely presenting the old Jeffersonian arguments anew. His social vision had a hard proslavery edge that was largely absent from that earlier formulation. Simms took to task Jefferson and his generation of southerners, primarily those from Virginia, for misunderstanding the core strength of their political economy. They were too quick to assent to Enlightenment ideas of natural rights and universality and too quickly accepted that slavery was a problem that required a solution. Jefferson himself "was inoculated with French opinion on the subject," and, Simms lamented, "it has been the unhappy distinction of our sister State of Virginia, to have furnished from her own armory of debate, most of the arguments which the abolitionists have so desperately wielded since" ("Southern Convention").

Virginians had ignored their own history and failed to see "that African slavery, in the hands of the Anglo-American people, was really an element of strength rather than a weakness" ("Southern Convention"). It was the organic hierarchy offered by southern slavery, Simms argued, that was the key to a properly ordered society and provided the remedy for the "deafness and blindness which have invariably prepared the way for the disasters and defeats of older nations." Slavery provided the foundation for an agrarian republic and offered a check to the chaos of mobocracy that accompanied the political empowerment of the laboring classes. By uniting the interests of labor and capital together, slavery also protected against the urban riots and social upheaval that invariably led to the imposition of dictatorships and the destruction of republican liberty, as recent events in Europe could attest. In short, slavery offered, in Simms's view, the basis for a properly ordered, hierarchical society, which was the only civilization that could long endure.

That was why the territorial and the slavery questions, the two issues of deepest concern to the delegates of the Southern Convention, were of such great importance to Simms. "Slavery will be the medium & great agent for rescuing and recovering to freedom and civilization all the vast tracts of Texas, Mexico &c.," he had told Hammond in an 1847 letter, "and our sons ought to be fitted out as fast as they are ready to take the field, with an adequate provision in slaves, and find their way in the yet unopened regions. . . . The acquisition of Texas and

Mexico secures the perpetuation of slavery for the next thousand years" (*Letters* 2: 330–33). In the perpetuation of that social order lay also the key to maintaining another millennium of American civilization.

Ehren Foley

Notes

1. For an detailed overview of events at the convention, including useful excerpts from letters written by key figures and some of the resolutions passed at each session, see Dallas Tabor Herndon, "The Nashville Convention of 1850," *Transactions of the Alabama Historical Society, 1904* (Montgomery: Alabama Historical Society, 1906): 5: 203–37.

2. The resolution read as follows: "5. *Resolved*, That as the interests involved in these previous considerations are, in the opinion of this House, equally important to all the slave-holding States of this Confederacy, it becomes us to invite their co-operation with us in grave and circumspect deliberation upon them: To this co-operation and consultation, therefore, be it further resolved, that the Executive of the State of South-Carolina be requested, by communication to the Governors of the several States aforesaid, to meet us, by their Delegates, in Asheville, North Carolina, on the fourth day of March, one thousand, eight hundred and forty-six." (reprinted in *Letters,* note 16, 1 January 1845, 2: 10).

3. For more on the politics of the Wilmot Proviso, particularly in the northern states, see Eric Foner, "The Wilmot Proviso Revisited," *Journal of American History* 56 (September 1969): 262–79.

4. See also Simms to Calhoun, 10 February 1847, and Simms to Hammond, 2 March 1847 (*Letters* 2: 267–68, 278.

5. For an extended discussion on marriage, see Simms, "A Year of Consolation," *Southern Quarterly Review* 12 (July 1847): 191–236 (review of Fanny Kemble, *A Year of Consolation,* 2 vols. [New York: Wiley & Putnam, 1847]). Simms's statement about anti-Sabbatarianism was both overstated and oversimplified. As Richard John demonstrated in his discussion of nineteenth-century debates over a seven-day mail service, anti-Sabbatarianism cut less along sectional lines than economic ones, with merchants in port cities such as New Orleans, who relied on timely delivery of information about fluctuations in European demand, lining up against attempts to stop the Sunday mail. Moreover many anti-Sabbatarians were drawn from religious organizations that opposed evangelical reform—for instance the Alabama Baptist Association. The anti-Sabbatarians, however, also did include figures such as feminist Frances Wright and utopian socialist Robert Owen, individuals who better fit Simms's characterization of the movement (John, *Spreading the News*, 169–205).

6. Simms here used "Agrarianism" to mean plans of land redistribution rather than the valorization of the agrarian life. Simms may have had in mind George Henry Evans's National Reform Association, which in 1844 declared a three-point program for land reform in the West calling for free distribution of public land, but only to those ready to settle it immediately and only as much land as a family needed for its own subsistence. There were other calls for land redistribution during this time as well however (Levine, *Half Slave and Half Free*, 131–35). Evans's was a far different vision for western settlement than the one expressed by the delegates to the Southern Convention or by Simms in his review essay.

[Review of *Resolutions and Address, adopted by the Southern Convention*]

1. *Resolutions and Address, adopted by the Southern Convention,* held at Nashville, Tennessee; June 3d to 12th, inclusive, in the year 1850. Published by order of the Convention. Nashville, Tenn.: Harvey M. Waterson. 1850.

2. *Remarks of the Hon. Beverly Tucker,* of Virginia, addressed to the Members of the Southern Convention, during its session at Nashville. Reported for the Augusta (Geo.) Republic, July 9th, 1850.

3. *Speech of the Hon. R. Barnwell Rhett,* delivered at Hibernian Hall, in the City of Charleston, June 21st, 1850. Reported in the *Mercury* newspaper, Charleston, July 20th, 1850.

4. *Remarks of Judge Goldthwaite, of Alabama, Judge Mackey, of Mississippi, and Ex-Governor Hammond, of South-Carolina, at Nashville.* Reported in the Courier newspaper, Charleston, June 21st, 1850.

5. *Remarks of Hon. Mr. Gholson, of Virginia, and Judge Wilkinson, of Mississippi,* addressed to the Southern Convention at Nashville. Reported in the *Courier* newspaper, Charleston, June 22nd, 1850.

It seems to be the fate of most nations to perish in consequence of a prosperity which is beyond their capacity to bear. It is in the full flush of all their wealth and splendour, when most stately in their pride and most glorious in their promise and performance, that the seeds of ruin are planted in their hearts, and that the insidious worm eats into their green honours. A poor and humble nation thrives in its humility. It is because of its humility that it thrives. Its step cautiously, while it remembers its own feebleness, and entertains natural misgivings of that strength, which has not yet been deluded into an exaggerated self-estimate by too frequent successes. The reverse is true of more prosperous nations. They first forget God, and next forget themselves. They forget that they are mere men; and, in the unvarying tide of fortune which has hitherto so proudly borne them forward, they refuse to see that small speck upon the horizon, no larger than a man's hand, in which the storm prepares itself for the business of destruction. They go forward vauntingly, and with an insolence that, at last, outrages heaven. They cease to pray, and set up, as Gods for themselves;—their own brazen images, being, in plain terms, fit likenesses for the overweening vices which are working in their souls. They forget justice, in losing veneration; and, no longer fearing God, they no longer honour man. The evil becomes incurable, the fate inevitable, when, in the insolence of their pride and vanity, they cease to give ear to the counsels of experience.

"The Southern Convention." *Southern Quarterly Review* 2 (September 1850): 191–232 (42pp.).

These counsels are written on all the pages of human history, and every nation possesses its own sufficient records for the instruction of the race. We have but to read the writing on the walls before us, luminous in mysterious light. "Mene, mene, tekel, upharsin:"—thus the inscription runs on all the crumbling walls and towers of the past. "Thou art weighed in the balances" is the mysterious language of the inscription, which mere vanity and presumption never stop to decypher. What balances? is the question; and it loses none of its terrible significance, when the answer, "Those of God!" prepares us to comprehend the solemnity of the trial which is to gauge all our performances. It is only the deaf and inaccessible sense that finds the import of this answer lessened, when told that the standards of these eternal balances are simply—right and justice! What familiar words—how freely spoken—how commonly abused—lispingly uttered as the commonplaces of the orator and the demagogue, yet of what noble significance, and, of all others, the most vital to the safety of the race. To be weighed in the balances, according to these standards, and to he found wanting, is something of deep and awful concern to nations as well as men. It was as a king, a royal governor, the representative of a race, as well as the ruler of a people, that these words were spoken to Belshazzar. It was no unmeaning language. "Thou art found wanting. Thou hast forgotten God—thou hast forgotten right and justice. Thy vanities, thy pride, thy insolence and bold presumption, have eaten thee up, and thy days are numbered. They have only been evil in the land. Thy sway is taken from thee; thou hast abused it by thy many wrongs and usurpations. Thou hast forgotten reverence and justice; thou hast forgotten the first, last, and always best lesson, which should have kept thee in due remembrance of thy humble first beginnings—which counsels to be always distrustful of thy own securities, and, thus distrustful, never to forget the truth which teaches that it is only by a constant regard to God's power, by unwearied obedience to his law, by a studious putting aside of self from the high places of our worship, that a race can ever hope to preserve the blossom of all prosperity, which is security and peace!"

No matter what the history, or where—in what land or nation—the same eternal laws are written, in records made indelible by storm, flood, fire, famine, war and pestilence; and the final blank which follows, tells us not only where the nation lived and swayed, but where it outraged the laws of heaven, and was punished accordingly. The history, and the event, are still the same. These were, all of them, nations which forgot God! Hebrew and Egyptian, Greek, Persian and Roman, they were all peoples who had scorned, in the day of their prosperity, the source and policy to which it was due—the humility and patient working, and the modest, God-fearing virtues, which alone achieved it; and, in their vanity and lusts, their pride of heart and folly, they set up the false god of their own hearts, in place of the true, the maker of the heaven and the earth. They mocked at heaven and defied earth. They said, "where is the power which shall say us nay?" They meditated conquests on every side. They scorned the supplication of the weak for justice, and they measured their strength with the strong for conquest; and if their madness did not actually grasp at the heights of Heaven itself, as Isaiah relates of the Babylonian, it was rather because they had ceased to think these heights desirable, and not because they held them to be inaccessible to their attempts!

These histories are not confined to the pages of the sacred volume. What are improperly termed *profane* histories are equally copious in the same unvaried lessons. The experience of all the nations has been the same. If they did not behold the immediate hand of God in the work—if they did not read his mysterious characters of fire upon the walls—if they did not hear his accents in thunder from the mountain,—still, the disasters which conducted to their overthrow were the acknowledged fruits of their vanity and insolence—their pride and lusts— which made them deaf to all the warnings of their prophets, and made them blind to all the dangers which threatened them, equally from the heavens and from the earth! They grew besotted with power. They ceased to be grateful or content with their possessions, and, while they forgot the prayer for help, they still urged on the march for conquest. To such a people, engaged in such a progress, it is usually found to be impossible to teach any lessons of a saving caution, or a moral prudence. You cannot persuade them that the empire which they have so wonderfully constructed—which has grown so lofty and so wide—which is the fear and admiration of all other nations—is one which may be overthrown in the twinkling of an eye, by the simple decree of that Will which, hitherto, has only seconded their achievements while these were urged in a full concurrence with the standards prescribed by its own unerring laws. They deceive themselves by false notions of their own stedfastness. They shut their senses against the warnings and entreaties of the wise, and fall into that condition, ripening daily for destruction, which makes them disdainful of the experience that would tutor them from all the pages of the past. Hearing, they do not heed—seeing, they will not believe; and it is only when the tempest descends, thick and terrible, upon them, that they spread their hands aloft in supplication, and call for the help of the prophets whom they have driven in mockery and scorn from their counsels, Their repentance comes too late; and the fear and feebleness in which they succumb to the storm, renders only more shameful that overthrow which their vanity and insolence have made inevitable. It is a sufficient proof that a nation is thus doomed and ripening for the sickle, that it ceases to take these histories into consideration—that it ceases to regard the Deity as the controlling power of the earth—that it relies on mere human agency, and the temporary policies of society—that it contemns the inflexible laws which bind the spheres together in harmony, and rejects those standards of right in government, of justice and humanity, which, if not stedfastly [*sic*] adhered to, as the only true models for human institutions, must avenge themselves on the perverse insolence which has dared to set their authorities at nought. History abounds with parallels, which show the same results from the same perversity; and, even if we reject the sacred volume wholly—if we no longer call God to our counsels—if we set up our own intellects—we have but to study the events which marked the career and overthrow of all the nations, to perceive that the end of such reliance is the same. There is nothing more singularly uniform than those events which produce the downfall of the empire; and the statesman who shall disregard the parallels thus available to all his studies, is but the agent of that overthrow which he unprofitably seeks to avert. To follow with calm and scrutinizing judgment the course of nations and races, throughout all the known periods of time, is to see where they have faltered or fallen in their march, and by what means they have prospered or been overthrown. The application of the knowledge thus obtained, to the affairs and the necessities of present times, is that philosophy, teaching by example, which is said to be the true office of history; and the politician who disdains this study, for this object, foregoes the advantages of a lesson such as no schools or training can impart, and exhibits a morbid self-esteem, whose pernicious influence, wherever he exercises a present power, must necessarily, for a long period, survive himself. There is scarcely a necessity or a progress of the present, that cannot find its apt likeness in the past. The passions of men are every where the same;—their hopes and fears—the vanity that goads them to excess—the presumption that prefaces overthrow. Head as you will, you see that the same seeds bear the same fruits, and the vices that run riot with arrogance, are the certain parents of a corruption that inevitably provokes the hand of punishment.

The history of our country, however brief, is already written in characters which all may read. Let us contract our view of its chief features, and ask in what they consist. We see, at the outset, a few bands of hardy adventurers, settling in a new world. They are all, more or less, the victims of despotism in the old, against which they found no remedy at home. In their feebleness began their virtues. They began with humility, and they exercised their toils with patience. They brought with them the fear of God, and were diligent in the proper work of man. Their progress was smiled upon by heaven. They grew glad in the possessions of earth. They became prosperous in due season, and excited the envy and ambition of the usurping power from which they had gone out into the wilderness. They were pursued with insolence and fury. They were strengthened for resistance; and the arrogance of Britain received its monitory lesson, in the loss of provinces which it sought to conquer rather than to cherish. The race was shown to be not to the swift, nor the battle to the strong. God reared up armies in defence of the feeble. "The stars in their courses fought against Sisera." Gnashing her teeth in hopeless fury, full of shame as well as hate, the gigantic power of Great Britain was compelled to yield, and forego a conflict which she had mocked with a spirit such as Goliath boasted when he advanced against the shepherd boy of Israel. Britain had been warned in all the usual modes by which the Deity counsels, through means of human wisdom. Already she reaped large harvests of profit from her colonies. But she grasped at all. Nothing short of unconditional submission would satisfy her lust and insolence. Her own wise men strove to lead her back to the paths of justice and moderation. The colonies implored, in attitudes of humility, and then urged their entreaties in the bolder attitudes of warning. But the besotted power, drunk with affluence, is seldom accessible to the prayers of justice and humanity, and only acknowledges the necessity of such counsellors in the hour that beholds its complete downfall.

In the triumph of the colonies over Britain they themselves grew strong. Maturing into States, they became a noble empire. Their alliance was the result of their fears of the external enemy. In the consciousness of their feebleness they bound themselves in a compact, which was studiously framed to afford protection to all the parties. In this compact they prospered to a degree unparalleled in history. It was *because* of this compact that they so prospered. The alliance, framed in their humility, with a mutual sense of danger and self-respect, so long as it was maintained in good faith, became the talisman of safety, and the sure guaranty of affluence and power. What would seem necessary to maintain this affluence and power? The continued exercise of the same good faith, the same spirit of justice, in which it had its origin—the same moderation, mutual respect, and harmonious co-operation, to which we owe our unmixed benefits. Were it not for the parallels of history, which show man to be never in greater danger than when in the zenith of success, one might well wonder at the infatuation which should put in peril, by any departure from the ancient usage, such a rare condition of social prosperity. But the deafness and blindness which have invariably prepared the way for the disasters and the defeats of older nations, are already upon us. We are rioting in all the rankness, and emulating all the vices, the excesses, and the luxuries of Europe. Our great cities are rapidly becoming the mere sinks and sewers of civilization. Their crimes and shames cry aloud to heaven, while the tyrannies that flow from their overgrowth and insolence, are rousing the anger, and provoking the vengeance of earth. The Northern States of the confederacy have reached their highest points of power and civilization. They have had a fungus growth, like the gourd of the prophet, in a single night, and may well apprehend a brevity of term corresponding with such prematureness of growth. They have become arrogant in strength and power. Affluence has corrupted their hearts; pride and vanity have sapped their virtues; they have reached that point in their progress when the warnings of the wise, and the teachings of experience, are equally vain to arrest the ambition which strives beyond its reach, and so loses its present securities; and the arrogance which they exhibit is that which always goes before a fall! They are a doomed people. *Quos Deus vult perdere, prius dementat* [those whom the gods wish to destroy they first make mad]. It was under the Constitution that they grew vigorous and powerful: it was as agents, chiefly, of the slave States that they grew wealthy;

yet they scorn the guaranties of the constitution, and seek to destroy the very institution by which they have been fattened into insolence. Wantonly, they set at peril all the possessions they have gained, and all the strength and permanence of position which might have guarantied their securities for a thousand years.

Were the spirit which they thus manifest a recent exhibition, we might hope that it would be temporary only. Were it a sudden impulse of the moment, originating in a mistake of fact, position or philosophy, a reasonable hope might be entertained that wisdom would find an early opportunity to speak, with some chance of being heard—that the lessons of experience might be again brought home to the erring parties, in season to prevent their realization of that fate upon which they are rushing with such desperate blindness. But, unhappily, this is not the case. The madness is a disease of long duration. It has been growing upon them every year, and exhibits every form of fanaticism and excess which has usually characterized the decay, and prepared the downfall of older nations. There is, in the Northern States, a growing and monstrous disregard of all the usually recognized securities of society. Mobs, riots, murders, mark the daily events in their progress. Wild philosophies, vague and vicious, penetrate the better informed circles. The venerable ties to which antiquity owes its most noble triumphs, are either sundered, or about to become so. Property is held by a doubtful tenure, and God alone knows how long it will remain secure. Marriage is denounced, as hostile to the proper exercise of the legitimate passions—a doctrine which really seeks to legitimate prostitution—and societies are actually formed, whose sole aim is to abolish the Christian Sabbath, No institution seems secure from threatened overthrow and desecration; and the licentious industry of these marauders, upon the peace and hope of the human family, is busy in the endeavour, not only to demoralize their own particular homesteads, but to extend their pernicious sway to the hearts of other communities. When, to this looseness of doctrine, and recklessness of practice, in the moral world of the Northern States, you add the systematic immoralities of political parties, and the utter shamelessness with which they grasp at power, in the teeth of principle, you see a terrible condition of society, which shows it ripe for the destroyer. All is uncertainty and clouds hanging over their prosperity. Rottenness and corruption are seated in their marble palaces; insolence and ambition, bloated with power and reckless in a blind security, reign pre-eminent among them. They no longer ask what is right, but what it is in their power to perform; and, in the very breath which clamours most loudly for the Union, they repudiate the Constitution, which is at once its source and living spirit.

Now, if they could be really brought to believe that the Union was vitally essential to their prosperity, and had been the source of it all, and that this Union was endangered by their reckless progress, there is no doubt that they would gladly retrace their steps. Of the first fact they have but an imperfect consciousness. It is one of the evils of a diseased vanity, that it believes only and wholly in itself. It believes itself the source, and not the recipient, merely, of the power which it enjoys. The Northern people take counsel from no other teachers than their own; and these teachers, by the same growing influence of popular vanity, are false prophets, who gloze in the ears of their people the most lying histories. In New-England, the popular belief, engendered by their orators and historians, teaches that the establishment of American independence was wholly due to that section. The vulgar notion is, that their statesmen furnished all the thought, and their soldiers all the valour of the country. They claim the wisdom of the nation, and assert a right to all the battle-fields. We need not state that all this claim is absurd, false and impertinent, and that the New-England States did far less than their share in the great drama of the American Revolution. But the falsehood serves the purposes of those whose egregious vanity needs a daily supply of this treacherous aliment. They have learned, by repetition, to believe the falsehood which they themselves have manufactured; and assume, accordingly, the possession of resources, in wisdom and weight of arms, which precludes any thought of successful resistance to their objects. Another of the falsehoods which have grown into a faith among them, is that the South is too weak, in consequence of her slave institutions, for her own defence. They actually believe that they have assisted us in our battles for liberty before, and that, in the moment of emergency, they would be required to assist us again. All this is equally false and foolish. Their ignorance of their own deficiencies, and of our resources in the South, is partly the secret of that insolence which is hurrying them on to extremities, which must test both in such a manner as shall effectually seal all the frauds of future history.

It is another misfortune of the Northern people to be really ignorant of politics. The great masses by which their society is every where controlled, have no leisure to study; and their politicians are not the persons, from principle, to teach them any better. The vulgar notion is that our policy is to be swayed always by majorities; and a reference to the constitution, as an arbitrary pact which precludes the will of the majority, is almost a matter of offence, in reasoning with a people who derive all their strength, courage and information from the conviction that they belong to the masses. Where this ignorance does not exist, the morals of the persons better informed, are not sufficiently strong to resist the force of numbers. If they struggle, they are overwhelmed, and they make the temporary necessity a sufficient excuse for an habitual deference to a power which they despair of successfully resisting. The difficulty of resistance is annually increased by an influx of two hundred thousand foreigners. These crowd to the Northern States especially, as being the best theatres for the exercise of their peculiar virtues. Of the merits of our revolution, they know nothing; of the intricate doctrine of State Rights, and a sovereignty reserved to the separate States, over which the General Government has no authority, you can teach them nothing; and it is their special policy to insist upon a doctrine which resents every principle that seems to stand in conflict with a self-esteem suddenly brought into existence, and a lust for power which is duly precious from the fact that it has never been enjoyed before.

They have brought the country to a fearful peril. The fate of the Union hangs upon a hair. One rash step, one fearful collision, one overt act which shall force the trial of strength, between any portion of the separate sections, and there is an end to the confederacy. There is a blind confidence in the integrity of the Union, which makes thousands unwilling to believe in this peril. Still more reluctant are these hostile sections to believe in an event which shall cut them off from the pleasant pastures in which they have so long fattened. The worshipper who cried "Great is Diana of the Ephesians," at the very moment when the image of the goddess, her shrines and temples, were about to perish by storm and fire, was not a whit more blind and deaf to the signs of danger—not a whit more loth to believe in such danger—than is that blatant priesthood at the altars of the Union, whose ministry is chiefly shown by their appropriation, to their own purposes, of all the rich gifts and treasure of its worshippers. If, by insisting the more earnestly upon the preservation of the temple—if, by cries of sacrilege against all those who denounce its abuses and their selfish spoliations—they can, not only avert its fate, but its reform, they will not, we may be assured, be sparing of their voices. They cry aloud when they behold the besom spread which would only purge the shrine of its pollution. It is to them much more important that they should still spoil the altars than that the temple should continue in existence.

Such is the Union to the Northern States. It is their place of pleasant pasturage. There they feed and fatten free of charge. The labours of the South, through this medium, are made to enure almost wholly to their advantage. Our fruits pass into their granaries. The toll which is assessed upon Southern productions, pays their taxes, builds their fortresses, crowds their marts with shipping, and clothes their barren hills with marble cities. Will they peril these goodly spoils, gathered at the shrine of Union? Not if they know it. That they do not believe in the peril, is only the natural result of that assurance which springs from habitual successes, which belongs to minds rioting in power, and wholly forgetful of the vicissitudes of earthly things. If, in moments of calm and reflection, they apprehend a danger, they do not seek to avert it by doing justice, for that would be a surrender of the privilege of spoliation. They prefer to alarm the fears of the discontented sections—they prefer to appeal to the superstitions of the people. They throw up their hands and eyes in holy horror, as they insist upon the sacredness of the Union; precisely as the gambling Jews in the temple must have done, when our Saviour cast down the table of the money changers, denouncing the crime which had converted the altar of the Father into a den of thieves.

To make and preserve the Union, the South has done many things at her own grievous charge and loss, and has made a thousand concessions. In the original acts of confederation, there were no social affinities which brought the two sections together. They were by no means of congenial temper. The Union contemplated the mutual weaknesses as of the parties, and their protection against common dangers from without. The dread was still of Great Britain, her power, her ambition, and her natural resentments. Had there been a sufficient degree of sympathy between the sections, the confederacy would have been the act of a single people. But a prudent jealousy insisted upon maintaining the individuality and independence of the several States. The bond of Union was one designed for the common safety against foreign pressure, rather than the promotion of any common objects of interest at home. The more perfect union, contemplated by our ancestors, was one which regarded their securities simply. It was the error of the South, at that season, to undervalue her natural securities, and, through this self-disparagement, to show quite too much anxiety for the formation of the confederacy. She was too heedless of the proper conditions of the Union. It was, perhaps, natural enough that such should be the case. Sparsely settled, recovering slowly and painfully from the exhausting effects of the war with Great Britain, which, for the last three years of the conflict, had fallen almost exclusively upon her unassisted shoulders,—the most perilous period of the war—marked with the most bloody battlefields—when the resources of the country were mostly exhausted, and when the enemy, concentrating all his strength for a last effort, was urging his assaults with greatly increased ferocity and earnestness— she exaggerated the dangers from without, and made a disparaging estimate of her own resources in the encounter with them. This same feeling, to a greater or lesser extent, prevailed with all the sections. But, in the South, it was naturally increased by what was there supposed to be an especial element of weakness— her slave population. Her Statesmen overlooked their own experience of seven years war, which should have taught them that African slavery, in the hands of the Anglo-American people, was really an element of strength rather than of weakness. They preferred to reason from the histories of slavery in ancient nations, where the subject race was one fully equal in natural intellect with the conqueror, and without any distinctive marks of colour; rather than to look at their own facts, occurring beneath their own eyes, during a conflict in which all the circumstances were against them. This was a natural error, since men, in general, reason rather from habit, and from principles imbibed in memory, than from the absolute facts in their own experience. The South underrated its own strength and its own resources, exaggerated its own weaknesses, and included, in the category of the causes of apprehension, certain speculative dangers, which time has shown to be wholly imaginary. It was thus prepared, from the outset, to make sacrifices for the establishment of the Union, referring to the importance of the tie, in a conflict with external pressure. It did not perceive, as it might have done, that all expectation of support from the New-England States, in the event, of war, was utterly futile. Their course, in the war of 1812, in that of Florida and Mexico, might well have been anticipated by a reference to their history in the war of the revolution. From the moment when the troops of Great Britain were withdrawn from the absolute territory of New-England, the people of that region lost all interest in the struggle, and left their Southern brethren to get through the conflict as they might. Their regiments were unfilled, and the hosts which they had on paper were only known to the country through means of the pension list.

Thus selfish from the beginning, they have continued selfish to the end. They have never made, as a section, a single concession to the confederacy for which they have not exacted ample and direct recompense; while they have grasped tenaciously at every concession of the South, without according any thing like a return. In this business of concession, the South has been as spontaneous and frank as if they had fashioned their public policy wholly upon the individual and personal character of their people. Governed by a sincere desire, which has sometimes looked like an absolute passion, for the general welfare, and the dignity and glory of the Union, they have yielded rights, lands and securities, without pausing to consider consequences. Their earnest wish to establish the confederacy, too precipitately indulged in action, led to the commission of the first great error, that of suffering the Northern States to class our population for us,—degrading a certain portion of our numbers to a rank in representation greatly inferior to that which was asserted for the corresponding race living in Northern territory. This exaction of the North was sufficiently significant of what we might expect from their tender mercies, whenever the power to compel and control should pass into their hands. By what right did they presume to look into our domestic arrangements, and reject from representation altogether, two-fifths of our servile population? What was it to them, in what manner, for local purposes, we classed our people; and how did it affect our foreign relations, that we insisted on keeping in a condition of minority, and under guardianship, even as we did our women and children, a certain portion of our population, whom we could not but see were inadequate to the duties of their own government? In what moral or human respect was our negro of the South inferior to the same race in New-England and New York, that he should have been denied like recognition with them, man for man. In moral respects, indeed, as more fully complying with God's first law of labour, his claim was essentially far superior, and he was more legitimately a human being. Here was the first grand error of our Southern Statesmen, conducting to all the rest. It yielded up a vital portion of our political strength without any equivalent,—the loss necessarily increasing annually with the due increase of the population whose claims to representation were thus degraded. We should have made their recognition the *sine qua non* [without, then not], and have better struggled on alone, than have yielded on a point so dangerous in its probable results to our safety and independence. That we did not exhibit sufficient tenacity on this point, arose chiefly from the fact, that too many of our Southern Statesmen were morbidly diseased in opinion touching the institution of slavery. Mr. Jefferson was inoculated with French opinion on this subject; and, even to a later day, it, has been the unhappy distinction of our sister State of Virginia, to have furnished from her own armory of debate, most of the arguments which the abolitionists have so desperately wielded since. Had our Statesmen, at the formation of the confederacy, been as sound and sagacious in regard to the morals of slavery, as the people of the South have since become—had they examined the question *per se,* according to intrinsic standards, and to the exclusion of all the formulas and pet phrases of French fraternization and equality—they would have become fortified in its behalf, regarding it, indeed, as the great medium through which all inferior nations have been raised from barbarism to civilization, and the only means for the exaltation of the African, to a christian [*sic*], from a savage condition. Any events which shall render necessary a revision of the American Constitution, will find the people of the South prepared to insist, as an absolute preliminary essential to any Union, upon the recognition of the Southern slave, without qualification, according him a representation, man for man, on equal terms with any other people of the confederacy. Another of the great evils to the South, constituting one of the causes of her present disparagement and lack of strength, arose again from the liberality of her own concessions. Virginia voluntarily ceded to the United States, without equivalent, the whole of that immense territory, out of which Ohio and Indiana, Illinois, Michigan, Wisconsin and Minnesota, have been erected into States. Here she planted the teeth which were to spring up dragons, seeking to devour the generous mother to whom they owed their birth. Even this liberal grant has been openly abused. The absolute condition of her grant required that no more than five States should be framed out of this territory. They have contrived to manufacture six; which, having covered them with a New-England population—restless, envious, exacting and insolent—they have converted into vast instruments of annoyance to the maternal State, which has so unwisely surrendered her soil to the possession of her enemies.

In like manner, South-Carolina and Georgia yielded up the territories of Alabama and Mississippi, without equivalent, for the formation of these States. Very far different, if we remember rightly, was the conduct of Connecticut. She, it appears, had some territorial rights to surrender also; but she required and received two hundred thousand dollars for the cession. This we believe to be the fact, but we speak now from memory, and cannot lay hands upon the proper authority. The contrast will illustrate fully the degree of attachment which the two sections have uniformly shown in respect to the Union. The war of 1812, a strictly national necessity, was treacherously and bitterly opposed by New-England, who refused her succour to the Union, and gave her sympathies to the enemy. It was the South from which came the declaration that flung out our flag in defiance to the insolent foe; and her patriotic sacrifices were accompanied by the exhibitions of a spirit that never once faltered or failed throughout the struggle. In the war with the Indians of Florida, the North, which had cut oft' her domestic savages with a tomahawk as ruthless as their own, interposed for the protection of ours—encouraged them in resistance to the Southern people, and fomented the ill temper which made them refuse all the efforts of Government at conciliation, and finally beguiled them into the attitude of hostility. The same spirit was manifested by the North upon the proposed annexation of the State of Texas. The North which had eagerly grasped at all acquisitions of territory, which has been long lusting after Canada, encouraging insurrection among the people of that foreign country, strenuously toiled to defeat the alliance of the South with a kindred people, and prevent our possession of a territory which otherwise must have fallen into the hands of a hostile power. The war with Mexico was but another chapter in the same history. The volunteers from the South numbered twice as many as those from the free States. New-England denounced the war, denounced the few troops that offered from her own borders, refused them all sympathy and assistance, and dealt in terms of moral rebuke in regard to the conflict, worthy of that saintly period in her history, when Puritanism, with the Bible in one hand and sword and scourge in the other, robbed the Indians of their soil, slaughtered them without mercy, and scourged the Quaker and the imputed witch, with the same instruments of torture. Yet, thus saintly in denouncing the war with Mexico, her people were the first, the conquest made, to rush in, seize upon and monopolize the golden spoils of California. The virtues that were proof against all temptations to the conflict, yields, without scruple, when the division of the spoils is to be made! And throughout the whole history of the confederacy, every page is thus distinguished by a base and slavish selfishness, which makes no sacrifices itself, yet continually exacts them at the hands of its neighbors. The revenues of the country, two-thirds of which are drawn from the Southern exports, are three-fourths consumed in the Northern States. In possession of the majority, the North is wholly unrestrained by principle, moderation, justice or the constitution, in the exercise of it. Taxes are raised for the two-fold object of appropriation among themselves, and for the stimulation of their domestic manufactures. In the adoption of tariff laws, their simple rule, if less bold than that of Rob Roy, the outlaw—

> "That they should take, who have the power,
> And they should keep who can—"

is not more barefaced and unscrupulous. Not content with these spoliations, they deny protection to the very regions from which they make their levies. Instead of protecting us, the government becomes the instrument of our degradation and ruin. Our institutions are threatened with continual overthrow; and, too feeble for our protection, the Government of the United States is made the medium through which to destroy our securities, prejudice our property, and deprive us of all the benefits which the constitution was expected to afford. No one in the South can blind himself to the fact that we have no worse enemies without, than those which assail us from within;—that the States, professing to be sisters, which appeal to us continually in behalf of the Union, are daily using the Union for our detriment—organizing schemes and parties by which to rob us of our property, abridge our provinces, and cut us off from all the advantages and all the securities of our government,—the government itself, being too little able, or too little willing, to interpose its ægis for our shelter.

Our space will not suffer us to go into details; nor is this necessary[.] The facts from which we draw our conclusions, are already the convictions of the great body of the Southern people. They have been arrayed, time after time, by our first Statesmen, equally before the eyes of North and South; and here we have but to pursue the parallels of history, to show how equally do all nations receive the warning, which, failing to heed, they rush headlong on their own ruin. So far, the history of our relations with the Northern States is a precise counterpart of the case of the whole of the colonies of Great Britain, prior to 1776, with the mother country. In both cases, through means of unjust legislation and continual encroachment, the more powerful States endeavoured to rob and to oppress the weak. Vainly did the colonies appeal to the constitution, and implore the sense of justice in the superior power. Appeal and entreaty were alike scorned, until the colonies began to look to one another. It was a common cause, forced upon them against their own will, by the foreign oppressor. They took counsel together; they met in convention; and, for the first time, began to comprehend their own resources, their own power of resistance and defence. In the first conference of the colonies together, was the germ of the future Congress. In the first moment in which they compared notes, and took the hands of each other in friendly grasp, the independence of the country was determined! The South, after long years of argument, appeal, entreaty and expostulation, have been brought to the necessity of a convention of the threatened and the injured States. They have been as slow to this meeting as were their fathers during the long interval from 1756 to 1776. In South-Carolina, a convention of the Southern States was urged in 1830. In 1850 it is obtained; twenty years of gestation, just about the same period of time occupied by our fathers in opposing the pretensions of Great Britain, before the sense of wrong ripened to a sense of the necessity of resistance. Is the parallel to be pursued? Will the wisdom of the North take counsel from the experience of the past, shown in this parallel passage from our own history; or must the future chronicler, mourning over the downfall and complete defeat of one of the most glorious political experiments in the history of humanity, pursue the gloomy record through other chapters, distinguished by the disruption of all the ties of States, and marked in characters of strife, captivity, of blood and desolation? Fortunately, the action of the Southern Convention has been so moderate, so reluctant to precipitate events, so full of forbearance as well as firmness, so willing to afford an opportunity to the assailing States to return to the paths of peace and justice, that, unless utterly deaf to the counsels of wisdom, to the appeals of kindred, to the experience of seventy years of a prosperity utterly unexampled, to all the parallels of history, the North has still the power to avert the omens of evil that threaten her future progress. She may avoid the catastrophe that belongs to the parallel we have employed; and the perilous and fearful chapters that seem now unavoidably to belong to the close or the history, may yet remain unwritten!

The proceedings of the Nashville Convention are of less importance than the assemblage of that body. Whatever may be the intrinsic value of the address and resolutions adopted, their significance is not to be weighed for a moment in comparison with the great fact, that the South has met in Convention, with the view to a redress of its grievances, and a remedy to its wrongs—that nine States have been assembled, in their sovereign character, duly sensible of the dangers which threaten their peace and safety, and with a spirit that, so far, does not show itself unequal to the crisis. They have met in a ten days session, and have resolved, unanimously, to meet again. In these two respects we find a more grateful promise than in any thing in their absolute performances. The act of meeting was a solemn one. It was one slowly determined on, and encountered a vigorous resistance. It had the prejudice of faction to encounter, the hate of enemies, the scruples of party to overcome, the fear of demagogues, and the natural hostility of all those who regard with a vague apprehension every thing that looks like change, even while they acknowledge the necessity of seeking a remedy against evils that have taken the worst shapes of danger. The South was not united. It could not be united so long as two powerful parties divided the country, North and South, upon issues which were studiously made to obscure others of the most vital importance to the latter section. The strictness of party drill, and the absorbing exercise of party machinery, completely occupied the popular mind, and produced an habitual disregard to all other concerns, not absolutely necessary to the party argument. So long as the conflict remained doubtful, it was scarcely possible to bring back the attention of the multitude to our geographical danger. While the contest of free trade was pending, a question of next importance to that of slavery, the subtle and rapid progress of the abolition party was never justly felt. It was the wish of party politicians to elude all topics, and to depreciate their importance in the popular mind, which might, by any possibility, bring disorder into their ranks; and, with this bias, they found it quite easy to insist upon the absolute worthlessness of the faction, which they nevertheless too frequently sought to conciliate, even when they most professed to hold it in contempt. The measures of the abolitionists, they alleged, were mere *brutum fulmen* [empty threat]. Their several encroachments upon law and Constitution were declared to be of no practical moment. The Wilmot Proviso received the sanction of a democratic president, in respect to the supposed importance of the measures upon which it was insultingly grafted; and while outpost after outpost was thus yielded up, at the requisition of party, to the hands of this equally bold and insidious assailant, until abolition stood in absolute possession of the Capitol, the South was lulled with a syren song of peace and safety, and led to underrate the importance of its own losses. But events were rapidly tending to results which were fatal to the bondage of party organization. It was in vain that leaders on both sides, whig and democrat, strove to maintain their factions—with a selfish object—along the barrier lines which originally separated them. The time had come when these barriers were to be overpassed. The two parties had survived their uses. Two of the three great questions of national policy upon which they had divided, were at an end. The Bank of the United States was an obsoletism. The protective system was almost equally crushed, under the daily increasing intelligence of merchants and farmers, alike; and the only remaining issue between the parties, that of internal improvements in the States with the funds of the general government, found the representatives of the two parties, Cass and Taylor, equally corrupt and profligate. It was evident to all men of sense, to whom mere party organization, involving a struggle without a principle, was something worse than useless, that a new formation of parties, upon a geographical division, was now absolutely essential to the safety of the South. To all but the slavish partizan, or the selfish demagogue, it was evident, that the two parties were mere agencies, by which to emasculate the South, and leave it at the mercy of the majority. Through these leaders, we were distracted by questions which were no longer questionable—kept in bonds to ancient banner cries, which were of no sort of significance. Of what matter to the South, the cry of free trade—a free exchange of our commodities with those of other countries—when the fanaticism of the North was preparing, with axe uplifted, to hew down the very tree upon which our products grew—to tear from us utterly the very labour whose hands were essential to the increase of our fields? The more imperative necessity demanded that all minor cares should be discarded from consideration, and that we should embody, as one man, in the defence of things which were of the last importance, not to our success, simply, but to our very safety and existence as a people.

But few of our politicians taught this necessity. They opposed its consideration to the last moment. Many of them, no doubt, deceived themselves. Others only deceived their people. They believed, or affected to believe, that things would right themselves—that abolition would really prove itself the impotent thing which they described it;—and they submitted to daily insult in the halls of Congress, to daily encroachment, until they became quite too much reconciled to this treatment to feel either its indignities or dangers. But for the overweening insolence of our enemies—had they left to our benighted leaders the slightest plea upon which a doubt could have depended—we should still hear the same dulcet notes of the syren, which would carry us, with a drowsing song of peace, down the steeps, and over the rocks, of ruin and destruction!

It is, perhaps, fortunate for the South that the insolence of the abolitionists, reckless and wanton in their confidence of strength, left our partizan leaders without pretence or plea. There was no longer room for evasion. They could no longer deceive themselves or their people. The language of our assailants, throwing off all pretexts and disguises, distinctly announced to us that, whatever might be our acquisitions of territory, it was to become the exclusive property of the Free States. The Slave States might conquer, but they were not to occupy or possess it. They were no longer to be admitted to equal rights in the confederacy. The policy was to degrade them from all power; and, once certainly in a minority, with institutions odious to the majority, they had nothing to expect but the fate of any other conquered people. *Væ victis* [woe to the vanquished]*!* was the open cry of our assailants. We will surround the Slave States with a cordon of Free States, all eager to overthrow a hateful institution. We will rob them of their property, or so act and legislate as to make it profitless and dangerous! This was the avowed policy. And this was to be done under the countenance of a union of brotherly love—under a government which guaranties us safety and protection! That the Southern States, with this experience before them, these threats, these continual assaults, and these dangers, should have been quiescent so long, only proves how complete was the party drill, how blind or selfish were their leaders, how easy is encroachment upon the rights of an agricultural people, the sparseness of whose settlements prevent frequent interchange of opinion, and how abiding was their attachment to, and how great their habitual confidence in, the Union itself. A history of similar aggression, upon the rights of the Northern people, would have found them cutting loose from the connection more than twenty years ago.

Assuming the most ordinary degree of intelligence and character among the people of the South, a convention of the Southern States had become inevitable. The suggestion finally came from Mississippi. The measure instantly awakened the fears of party leaders everywhere, and was denounced bitterly by the *habitués* of the party press. It threatened to close the fat pastures against those who had hitherto fed without restraint. All those public men, of inferior virtues and endowments, who can only obtain position through the means of a party organization, were dreadfully apprehensive of the results. Their patriotic outcry was great. They beheld in it all sorts of dangers. It threatened the Union. It implied famine, pestilence, and civil war. We were cautioned to submit, lest we should be kicked; to yield, rather than be crushed under the tread of Northern hosts— that terrible infantry which had shown so much coldness in the Revolution— so much reluctance in the war of 1812—so much moral revoltings at the very thought of war, when that of Mexico was in progress—we were warned not to provoke their ire, lest we should be swallowed up in their rage. "Moderate your demands," said Mr. Clay, and he moderated them for us with a vengeance, guaging [*sic*] the condition of our future existence, as a partner in the confederacy, not by any reference to our rights and our securities, but by a nice calculation of what might be assumed to be the degree of toleration accorded us by the dominant faction, conscious of the power which they held, and regarding the South with a degree of hatred, which, already, in the language of their orators, held the knife to our throats. In other words, the Compromise Bill was so framed as to yield all the substantial issues to the abolitionists, and, through a specious phraseology, to enable the Southern politicians, trading on their position, for national office, to gloze over the matter to their people. The most specious of these pretexts, was that for the recovery of fugitive slaves. Now, there is not a member of either house in Congress who does not know that any such measure, in the present temper of the Northern people, will be wholly inoperative unless sustained by a United States Army; and, throw out the idea of such an army, to such a people, in regard to such an object, and their response of scorn and indignation will be a sufficient commentary upon the excellent speeches of the same people, when threatening the anticipated rebellion of the South with the same terrible agency. The wonder really is, that the Compromise Bill of Mr. Clay did not pass. It was so satisfactory to Mr. Clay himself—to his curious Irish echo, Mr. Foote, and to that veteran of the party press, Mr. Thomas Ritchie. The assurance of the latter to the South, that this bill was "the best that could be got"—thus, virtually telling us that we were sold and sacrificed, and proceeding on the assumption that the spirit of the country had so completely gone out, that we could conceive of no manly alternative against the shame of such a sacrifice—was sufficiently characteristic of the counsellor. The suggestion that we should take the best that could be got, certainly comes with a proper grace from one who has made it his own invariable maxim, not only to take the best that he could get, always, but as much of it as possible. The Compromise Bill should have been quite satisfactory, as a temporary measure, to the abolitionists also. It had but one disadvantage. It gave the South a little time; and fanaticism makes no concessions, and regards the smallest matters as essential. The Southern Convention was probably among the final causes of its defeat. It strengthened the decision of those Southern statesmen who had resolved against the bill—it determined the doubtful—and served to isolate from the ranks of the South, those politicians, Clay, Houston, Foote and others, who, professing the cause of the South, were yet always unwilling to recognize this cause, unless through the medium of a national party. As a matter of course, all this class of persons were sufficiently sagacious to perceive that the very organization of such a Convention was calculated to take the game out of the hands of the party politicians. It was, in effect, an appeal to the people, against those among their leaders who had been sacrificing the South to the policies of parties and their own. Southern politicians, who had lived by party only—whose hopes were founded upon anticipations of its future favours and employments—who looked to be Presidents, Vice-Presidents and Secretaries—and who had made Congress the mere stepping-stone by which to secure these offices—they at once beheld the complete overthrow of all their hopes, in the disorganization of their parties. "If"—they soliloquize—"the South concentrates its strength, upon a sectional necessity or interest, there is an end to all our pretty little arrangements." It became their policy to denounce the Southern Convention, as factious, insurrectionary, and dangerous to the Union; and, but that the Southern people were too intelligent, at such a juncture, to be frightened from the path of necessity and duty, by the Raw Head and Bloody Bones conjurations of these small magicians, their hideous outcry would have defeated the assemblage of the Southern States in Convention. On some of them it had its evil effect in full. In most of them, it paralyzed, in some degree, their courage and patriotism. But nine States were represented, and several of these inadequately. We are told that delegates from Louisiana were en route for the place of assemblage, but were told that nobody had assembled, or would assemble. It was even rumoured, by those whose "wish was father to the thought," that the Union-loving people of Nashville would rise en masse, and expel from their city these supposed traitors and disorganizes, whose great offence—peculiarly odious in free America—was the determination to find some means for resenting a wrong, which all the South acknowledged—and for resisting encroachments, which, none doubted, were sapping all our sectional securities. There is no doubt that Nashville, itself, was not, at first, favourable or friendly to the objects of the Convention. The State of Tennessee, it is true, sent a noble body of delegates, who proved themselves as true to the feelings and interests of the South, as those of any section. But there were still especial reasons why the State, and the city of Nashville, in particular, should be slow to apprehend, in full, the dangers which threatened us through the agency of the general government. Tennessee had given two Presidents to the Union. One of these had but recently retired from power, having passed through a term of four years, and an administration as singularly brilliant as that of any by which it had been preceded. The other, Andrew Jackson—*clarum et venerabile nomen* [he of illustrious and venerable name]—had been always an authority in behalf of the Union; though, at periods when no such warfare as that which now prevails, was waged upon the Constitution and the rights of the South. Opposed to the protective tariff and the bank, Jackson only forebore to see, *in these measures,* a sufficient degree of provocation to force the South to extreme issues. He was spared the present spectacle—the insolence of the North on the one hand, and the too hesitating spirit of the South on the other; when the language of safety must needs be one of the most united and decisive resolution. His influence, while he lived—this crisis unforeseen—was cast in favour of the confederacy. Its effects naturally remained among the Tennesseans. In Nashville itself, a courtly city, where, through long-continued political affinities, the intercourse was constant and intimate with Washington, the influence of the latter place was always immediately felt, and almost as immediately responded to. What the influences of the city of

Washington have been in this controversy—that city of partizan politicians, restless labourers in the search for office, pensioners, bondholders, claimants and beggars—busy from night to morning, at all hours and in all places, in the manufacture of opinion favourable to each selfish object—we sufficiently understand and know. The effect of their selfish industry, their clamours and falsehoods, in respect to Southern rights and the Southern Convention, were felt in Nashville when the delegates first assembled. Their reception was a cold one. They were under the ban of the trading politicians; and each of these politicians had his petty newspaper, labouring at the dirty work of defiling his opponent and making clear his patron. The Convention was a body to be watched and suspected. They were in a false position, from which they could work themselves right, only by the clearest proofs of moderation and truth, courage and patriotism.

They succeeded in the endeavour. In the delegates sent, the South was particularly fortunate. Most of them were men of experience, as well as thought. Upon many the mantle of years had fallen, as well as wisdom. They approached their duties with a due sense of their solemnity, and possible importance to the future. Patient discussion followed, and the fruits are before us in an address which embodies, in temperate language, a history of the wrongs and injustice under which the South has been made to suffer in the confederacy, and such as yet threaten her peace, safety and future securities. The resolutions adopted are in like temperate spirit with the address. Their declaration, that the territories of the United States inhere with the people of the several States, and that these, all, possess an equal right to occupy them, with their property, so long as the government shall remain territorial—that Congress has no right to exclude from this territory the property of any citizen, no matter what shall be its form or character—that Congress is bound to provide proper governments for the territories, and that all foreign laws are void within them, from the moment when they pass under our flag—that the slaveholding States will not submit to any enactment of Congress which shall discriminate against slave property in its passage into the territories—that in the event of such discrimination being insisted upon by a dominant majority in Congress, then, that the territories shall be treated as property, and so divided between the North and South, according to the line already in part established, of 30 degrees, 30 minutes, north latitude, extending to the Pacific ocean;—these were the chief resolutions. There were others, in respect to the Texas boundary, and declaratory of opinion, with regard to the powers of the government, and the rights of the States, which our limits will not suffer us to give. But they have already found full circulation in the newspapers. These resolutions passed with rare unanimity. There were but few dissenting voices, even to the address, to which there was most opposition. In the progress of debate, there was neither strife nor confusion. The body was one of marked eloquence, as well as ability. Of the speeches made, few have been reported in full, and but one or two of them by their respective authors. Virginia, the Mother of States, spoke ably and with great influence, through Gordon, Gholson, Goode and Tucker. Mr. Gholson was opposed to the address, but concurred with the resolutions. He was not willing to commit the Convention against the Clay compromise—the amendments to which, he thought, might yet make it acceptable to the South. He was for caution. He did not wish any step to be taken which it would be difficult, yet necessary, to recall. We make the following extract from a rude report of his remarks in the newspapers:

"Mr. President, I am one of those who desire to use every effort under heaven to preserve the Union. I trust—I believe it may be preserved—preserved without the sacrifice of rights or honour. I agree that firmness is indispensable—but moderation is not less so. I love the Union—I love it for all that is glorious in the past, or bright in the future. I love it because of the blessings it has conferred on the civilized world. I shudder at, the contemplation of its destruction. I dare not calculate its value. It has blessed the inhabitants of earth, while its influences have extended to heaven. Strike down the Union, and the trembling thrones and tottering crowns of the old world will again become steady. Despotism, that has been quailing before the march of free principles, will again rear its head, and fasten the chains that fetter the minds and body of men. He would pause before he would take any step involving the perpetuity of such an Union.

"He loved the South more than the Union, and would never agree that she should be subjected to shame or humiliation. He loved the South as he did his own hearth or fireside, and gentlemen would find, when the necessity came, which he prayed a kind Providence might forever avert, that those whom they may now regard as timid, will be found the first where danger calls. Let no man think that the South—any part of the South—will ever yield to the arrogant pretensions of the Northern fanatics. We must have peace, security, and equal rights, or this Union cannot endure. It was an Union of equality into which these States entered, and that man deceives himself, who thinks that the South will submit to see the Constitution, which formed the terms of the compact, perverted and abused, and instead of continuing the source of protection and blessings, converted into an engine of wrong and oppression. Every man in whose bosom there beats a Southern heart, is resolved—determined—to stand by Southern rights; our duty to ourselves, to our children, requires it."

His speech called up Beverley Tucker, that "old man eloquent," who, to the peculiar powers of wit and sarcasm possessed by his near kinsman, John Randolph, possesses a classical force, fulness, and beauty of utterance, peculiarly his own. His speech, on this occasion, has been fully reported by his own pen, and does it and himself great honour. It is a brilliant and powerful performance, rich, copious and keen, with a lightning-like sarcasm. We have not space for the frequent extracts which we had marked for quotation. Fortunately, the publication has been largely circulated, and is to be easily had. When his colleague spoke of the anticipated amendments to Mr. Clay's bill, rendering it acceptable, he answers, "Ay, but who shall have the mending of it?" "Give me the mending of that bill," said he, "and I will mend the breach in the Constitution, and cement the Union, and restore mutual friendship, and confidence, and brotherly love, among all the States of this great confederacy." Despairing of such amendments, and assuming that the work of Southern overthrow and degradation still goes on, in the hands of a blind and violent majority, he answers the apprehensions of those of the South, who look to the consequences of a dissolution of the confederacy. We cannot do justice to this portion of Judge Tucker's speech by any abridged report. We must give the extracts.

"And now, sir, let us look at the dangers which are to attend disunion. Let us suppose a case, and consider the influence which will be brought to bear on those on whom the peace of this continent will depend. Let us suppose but five State?—the States of Florida, Georgia, South-Carolina, Alabama and Mississippi—to withdraw from the Union, and form a Southern Confederacy. Their policy would be clearly pacific. What would be the policy of the rest of the world? Would the manufacturing States wish to rush into a war, which, while it lasted would shut them out from the best market in the world? Would the shipping and commercial States wish to rush into a war which would throw the carriage of our rich and bulky productions into the hands of Europe, until our own commercial marine should have become adequate to our wants? I say nothing of the fatal consequences which would attend the loss of a supply of cotton to the spindles and looms of New-England, because, although war should prevail, the laws of trade would be sure to carry the needed supply to the place of demand. This, indeed, must be on a circuitous route, and at enormous expense. But on this I lay no stress. It would, indeed, prevent the Yankee from hoping to compete with the English manufacturer in markets open to both, while war would shut him out from this, the chief and best market.

"'And how long would such a war last?' asks Mr. Webster, with a scornful scowl. 'How long would it be before the fleets and armies of the North would sweep the coasts, and blockade the ports, and overrun the desolate territory of the South, and turn the knives of the slaves against their masters' throats?' How long? Sir, such a war will never be waged until Massachusetts shall have lost her senses, and be prepared to rush on self-destruction. Whence, but from the Southern States, comes the cotton that keeps in activity the spindles and looms of the North? Sir, the north would not dare to prosecute war with such activity as even to *diminish* the supply. Obtaining it, as she must do, from neutral ports, the North could only get what was left after supplying the demand of other countries, and any essential diminution would leave her nothing. But a war of desolation! Why, sir, such a war would re-act upon the North like the bursting of a cannon in a crowded ship, working ten times more mischief there than on the enemy. Do gentlemen consider the nature of great manufacturing establishments, kept in operation by what they call *free labour*—the labour of those whose daily bread is the purchase of daily toil and who, left without employment for a week, must starve, or beg, or rob? The mind of man has not conceived the wretchedness which the failure of one cotton crop would produce. Universal bankruptcy—universal ruin—the prostration of the wealthy, and the uprising of the suffering mass, violently snatching from their beggared employers a portion of the scanty remnant of former abundance, to satisfy the wants of nature. Sir, when the overwhelming force of France threatened to invade and subjugate Holland, the Dutch cut their dykes and let in the ocean; the enemy withdrew, and all thought of again invading the soil of a people capable of defending their liberty by such sacrifices, was abandoned forever. Here was a self-inflicted suffering, which did but warn the enemy, without wounding him. But what if the people of the Southern States, goaded by insult and wrong, should determine on a much less sacrifice? What if, with one accord, they should agree to make no cotton for a single season, except for their own factories, and apply all their labour to laying up a store of grain for another year? The South could bear it, sir. It would incommode many. It would enrich some. It would ruin nobody here. And what would be the effect elsewhere? The mind of man cannot calculate it. The imagination of man cannot conceive it. *Horresco referens* [I shudder to tell the tale]. An earthquake shaking the continent, from the Potomac to the Lakes, swallowing up the British Isles, and overturning all that revolution has left standing in France, and Germany, would be hardly more destructive. Sir, the pillars of the world would be shaken—and here stands the South grasping them in her strong arm. Here she stands, like old blind Sampson, set to make sport for these Philistines, who mock her degradation. Will she not make her prayer to God, and bow herself in her might; not, like him. to die with the Philistines, but to overwhelm them and stand unhurt amid the ruins? No, she will not. But this is always in her power, and this she will do, if ever her loathing detestation and scorn of her oppressors equals in acrimony and malignity their fierce philanthropy and insidious friendship.

"Something like this would be the consequence to the North of *any war* with the South. Worse, if possible, than this would be the consequence of a *war of desolation and emancipation*. In that case the mischief would not be confined to the North. It would overspread the civilized world, in aggravated horror. In New-England we can calculate it. The seven hundred millions of which the South has been robbed by the unequal operation of the Federal government, has been *realized,* as they call it. It has been built into ships and factories; it has been paid out for barren lands, at high prices, only justified by these establishments; it has been built into palaces, where merchant princes and manufacturers dwell in marble halls. There are no other objects of investment, and the boasted, heaped up wealth of New-England is just that—no more. Now take away the cotton and commerce of the South, and what do you see? The ships lie rotting at the wharves; the factories tumble into ruins; and, skulking in corners of their marble

palaces, the merchant princes, like those of Venice, live meagerly on contributions levied on the curiosity of travellers. As to the labouring classes, the far West
is open to them. What violence and rapine may practice for a while, under the
teachings of Communism, Fourierism, Agrarianism, and other isms of the family
of Abolitionism, it is not possible to say. But they will soon see that Communism
is of little worth where there is nothing to divide, and that what they call the
rights of labour cannot be enforced against those who have nothing to pay. They
will off to the West, sir, there to found a new Ohio on the banks of Wisconsin
and Minnesota. And Boston—? Look at Venice, sir. The history of Boston is, so
far, the history of Venice. Venice enriched herself by the oppression and plunder
of her subject provinces. Boston has done the same. Venice concentrated her ill-
gotten wealth on the marshes of the Adriatic. Boston has heaped up hers upon
a barren rock. The poisoned chalice has been commended to the lips of Venice,
and she has in turn become the victim of misgovernment, while the trade of the
world has found other channels—and behold she in a wilderness of marble in
a waste of waters. Even such would be the mischiefs which Boston would pull
down upon herself, by the suicidal step of warring against the South.

"But look across the Atlantic, and suppose the madness and malignity of the
North to hurry them into a desolating war against the cotton-growing States.
Other countries have more various resources than New-England, and might have
something to fall back on. England, for example, insular as she is, has land. But
England has a superabundant population, and there are there not less than three
millions of labourers whose very existence depends on cotton. They have no
western country to fly to, and while the land of England is sufficient to feed them
all, they will not starve, whether there be work for them to do or no. There is
something there for Communism to divide—something for Fourierism to experiment on. Let but the loom stand still for one month, and there will not be
one stone left standing on another, of the whole political and social fabric of
England.

["]The statesmen of England know this, sir, and this it is that governs the
foreign policy of England, and determines her to oppose her veto to any war that
might disturb her commerce, and, through that, her manufactures, on which
her very existence depends. The play of the shuttle is the pulse of life to her. Let
it once stop and it beats no more. Nor is that confined to her. The same cause
operates on every powerful nation of Western Europe, and hence that long, un-
natural peace, which, for more than thirty years, has covered Europe as with a
death pall, and produced and prepared more suffering and more causes of mischief than half a century of war had ever done. But the evil is upon them, and
they dare not shake it off. However, the angry spirit of rival nations may chafe
at the restraint; however the plethora of redundant population may call for the
letting of blood, the immense fixed capital invested in manufacturing establishments, and the multitudinous population whose bread depends upon them,

compel the world to peace. It is indeed but a peace of suppressed hostility, of stifled envy, of insidious rivalry; and its confluences make us feel the full force of the woe denounced against those who cry "peace, peace! when there is no peace." But there is no escape from it. In the cant of the day, "the spirit of the age demands it—the spirit of the age is essentially pacific."

["]What then, sir, would all Europe say to any attempt on the part of the Northern States, or of every power upon earth, to lift a hand against the cotton growing region, and interrupt the production of that article The power of wealth would oppose it—the cry of famine would forbid it—the universal nakedness of mankind would forbid it—the united voice of the civilized world would command the peace. The Southern States of this Union are confessedly the only cotton growing country in the world, and slave labor the only means by which it can be produced. Whatever may be their spite against us, and however they may cant about slavery, they will be careful to do nothing to interfere with the production of cotton. Had Orpheus been the only man in the world, sir, the nymphs, however enraged, would never have killed him.

["]All this time I have spoken as if our dear *sister* Massachusetts, and the rest of that sisterhood, were to have the matter their own way. I have taken no notice of the fact, that, although North-Carolina and Virginia, Tennessee and Kentucky, might not be at once prepared to join the Southern confederacy, they would feel that their interests were identified with it, and refuse to join in a crusade against the defenders of their rights. They would have a voice in the question of peace or war. They might indeed be out-voted, but would a vote restrain them, and would the North press a measure which would be sure to force them into the Southern confederacy? The exemplary patience of Virginia is a proof that she fondly recollects, that to her, more than to any other State, this Union owes its existence. She will be the last to dissolve it violently, because she will be the last to forget the proud and endearing recollections of the past, and to lift her hand against those she has so long cherished as brothers. But, let her be told she must fight somebody, and she will not be long in deciding whom she will fight. Tell her to regard and treat as enemies the Southern States, peopled mainly by herself—to imbrue her hands in the blood of her own children— and her answer is ready in the words of Harry Percy:

> "Not speak of Mortimer!
> Forbid my tongue to speak of Mortimer!
> Yes, I will speak of him: and may my soul
> Want mercy if I do not join with him!"

Sir, Virginia did not approve the attitude assumed by South Carolina in 1833. What then? Was she prepared to lift a hand against her? On the contrary, she remembers now with pride, that the Governor then declared, that, before one foot should cross the Potomac on a hostile errand against South-Carolina, he would lay his bones on its shores. That was old John Floyd, sir, a man "who never promised, but he meant to pay;" and, thank God, there stands now another John Floyd in his fathers place, to repeat and make good his father's words.

["]But, suppose the few remaining Southern States not to be driven to the necessity of choosing their enemy. Suppose, as would be the case, that no war-like attempt should be made—how long would those States be content to re-main under the grinding misgovernment which taxes them for the benefit of their masters in the North, unite witnessing the prosperity of their Southern brethren living under a revenue tariff and enjoying the blessings of free trade? With a modest, economical government, such as a mere central agency for in-dependent States ought to be, a moderate revenue would suffice, and nothing would prevent the acceptance of the overtures for free trade, now made in all commercial nations. These are not accepted now, sir, because mainly beneficial to the South. And who cares for the South? What is the South? An ass of the tribe of Issachar, "bowed down between two burthens;" thirty millions to be paid into the treasury, and twice as much more to go into the pockets of the Northern manufacturers. What if Lord Palmerston should offer now, in return for a reduction of our Tariff to a revenue standard, to take off the English duty of seventy-five cents on our tobacco. Would it be accepted? No, sir, no. It would but enrich the tobacco States; and what do our masters care for them? On the other hand, let a Southern confederacy, in adopting the free trade overture, ask a differential abatement of ten per cent of this duty in their favour, and how long would Virginia and North-Carolina, Tennessee, Kentucky, and even Maryland and Missouri, delay to avail themselves of the arrangement? Depend on it, sir, such a confederacy as I have supposed would hardly be formed before every slaveholding State in the Union would seek admission into it. The *prestige* of Union once dispelled by a partial secession, the Middle States would be at no loss to choose between union with their Southern brethren, or with their North-ern enemies, persecutors and slanderers.

"But the thing would not atop here, sir. Pennsylvania, at this moment, with all the advantage of a protective tariff, finds her manufacturers often on the verge of bankruptcy. A tariff may protect her against the competition of European manufactures, but not against the superior skill and capital of New-England. Against this she contends as well as she can in the markets of the South. Take that away, and she will sink at once. Even now, Massachusetts grudges her the benefit of the protection which, only, enables her to hold up her head. But let the Southern victims of that oppressive system emancipate themselves from it, and, my life upon it, five years will not pass over before it is abolished. What, then, will be the condition of Pennsylvania, placed on the border, between a Northern confederacy, in which she is overshadowed by superior capital and skill, and a Southern confederacy, of which she might become the workshop? A revenue tariff of ten per cent, would be worth more to Pennsylvania, as a member of a Southern confederacy, than forty per cent is now—more than all that protection could do for her, were the South withdrawn from the Union.

"Let us look a little to the West. sir. I begin with Illinois, because she reaches farthest South; because she is nearest to New-Orleans and farthest from New-York; and because she begins to be aware that slaves are wanted in the Southern part of the State, and seems not quite insensible to the propriety of letting such of her people have them as have need of them. Now, what will be her situation? No man admires more than I do that noble system of inland navigation that connects the waters of the Mississippi with the lakes. But tolls and tow paths are extensive things, and canals are sometimes broken by floods, sometimes laid dry by drought, and winter rarely fails, with his icy breath, to close up the navigation of the lakes. But the Mississippi, broad, deep and full, is ever open to bear on its flowing bosom all the bulky and weighty products of Illinois, at the lowest possible rate of expense. I am aware, sir, that the law of nations would secure to the States, on the waters of that river, a free passage to the ocean. But that law would not exempt them from imposts and from export duties, and from all the inconveniences which must be encountered by those who necessarily pass through a foreign country to get to their own. A great river, such as the Mississippi, like an iron cramp, holds together all the country penetrated by its tributaries; and no amount of human perverseness can long prevent them from blending into one, 'like kindred drops.'"

This long extract materially abridges our limits. Fortunately, it is of a character sufficiently to compensate the reader for the space occupied. It was one of the most admirable efforts made in the Convention. To these we are by no means able to do justice. Nothing can be more meagre than the newspaper reports. Judge Sharkey, of Mississippi, one of those with whom the Convention originated, is said to have spoken well; but his position, at first, in consequence of a too hasty committal in behalf of Mr. Clay's compromise, was an awkward one. With proper manliness of character, however, as soon as the real features of the measure became known to him, he renounced the opinion given in its favour. He also opposed the address, while he subscribed to the resolutions reported to the Convention. We quote a few extracts from his speech:

"Judge Sharkey took the floor. *He said* he was not much in the habit of public speaking, and should adopt a conversational tone; had few flowers of rhetoric to offer, and should confine himself wholly to matters of fact. He should vote for the resolutions, but against the address, whatever shape it might assume—that portion of it, at least, which treated of the compromise. It is true that he might have said he favoured this compromise. He should go against it now, however. His reasons might be easily gathered from this circumstance. He was one of those with whom the Convention had originated. The movement began with a small meeting in Mississippi. There was no dictation from any quarter. That meeting called the October Convention. It was charged that it was gotten up by those who were in favour of disunion. Those who favoured it were denounced as guilty of treason. He started from home in fear and trembling, not knowing that he should meet a man here. Under these circumstances, he would have taken any compromise at all. But he found that the spark of public patriotism burnt bright and strong, and he again, therefore, took his stand. He did not fear a charge of inconsistency, for his reason was given to guide him in such cases. He was against the report, and cared not what name sanctioned it. He held it to be impolitic to pursue a course calculated to throw off men, and that report was calculated to divide us. We should not arm those who were opposed to us, and when you armed the opposition you armed the abolitionists. . . .

"The compromise bill was discussed as a grievance; the other was a plain, straight forward stricture on Congress. He came here to discuss grievances, but not to discuss the bill in question as such, until it was carried out. The address could not set up a bill as a grievance—it was our own proposition, to some extent, and we could reach it by the usual channels of legislation. The Convention sat for a higher purpose—to do that which could not be done by ordinary legislation. It was when the people could not find redress through the ordinary means, that they must try others. . . .

"When Congress proposed to exclude, slavery from California, it was an evil to be reached by extraordinary means. When we could have redress by the ordinary means of legislation, it must be resorted to. . . . The abolitionists might say to us, they were as opposed to the compromise as we were, and would assist us to put an end to it. They were discussing matters here which might be put an end to at any time. He was not sent here to advise Congress. It was for the people to advise their members. They were here on higher grounds—to make the issue with the Northern people. If the evil is in Congress, the power is not here to arrest it. The North does not present the compromise bill as an issue—it is our own. The opposition is so decided there, that he considered the proposed measure as at an end. He did not believe it would be unconstitutional to admit California—other gentlemen might differ with him; but they ought not to send forth debateable [*sic*] matter. He believed Congress had power to admit California. It was contended in the address, that it would be unconstitutional; and yet it said that it might be assented to! How could we assent to it, if it was unconstitutional? Why, too, discuss the compromise bill in the address, when it was not in the resolutions? The one ought to be based upon the other, and the Convention ought not to put forth any thing on which it could not stand. There were differences of opinion abroad and at home; and unless you strip the proceedings of objectionable matter, you might call Conventions forever, but it would be like 'calling spirits from the vasty deep,' they would not 'come.' The compromise bill had never been an issue before the people of Mississippi, and he did not feel that he had any authority to act upon it. If it was a grievance, it was a grievance supplied by people of all portions of the country, North and South, by some of the people of Mississippi, and some of those of Tennessee, as well as by members of Congress. Whether, in what he had said, he bad expressed his views exactly, he did not know; but he would say to all, in conclusion, that this should be a Convention of compromise."

General Hammond, of this State, replied to Judge Sharkey. He had fought the address through the committee, and, though not its author, was, in some degree, responsible for it. There is none but a wretched newspaper report of this reply, which is described as very able.

"*Gov. Hammond said,* that, as one who had acted in trying to get the address through the committee, he, perhaps, ought to speak; and he should endeavour to answer objections, in the calm temper and spirit which had characterized the address of the gentleman who had just taken his seat. The committee had had a hard duty to perform, in the great mass of matter laid before them. He did not feel disposed, at the present stage of the question, to say what should be done. The sole object, at this time, was to unite the South. What was to be done—what looked to? Why, to the action of Congress on the compromise bill now before that body, as the remedy for all the wrongs now suffered by the South. It was of no consequence who permitted it—men of the North or South. Every thing dear to us was at stake, and were we to stand trembling on the verge of ruin, awaiting the pleasure of this or that member? The committee were anxious to conciliate all, were anxious to put it in such a form as that all might be pleased; but no proposition could be advanced to which some men would not have to give way, and, after twice considering all the matter brought before it, they had presented what is now before the Convention. He was never more astonished than he was to hear a gentleman, of the wide reputation of the gentleman from Mississippi, say that it was unconstitutional to examine into a measure before Congress. Of what grievance do we complain? Was it not the legislation of Congress which had driven us to this? It was the privilege of any member to examine the measures of Congress, and to attempt to arrest oppressive legislation.

"Judge Sharkey explained. He only meant to say that when ends could not be obtained by ordinary means, other means must be resorted to.

"*Gov. H resumed.* The explanation does not alter the matter. What were we attempting now? Simply concentrating public opinion, to influence the ordinary legislation of Congress. It would be perfectly constitutional to denounce the legislation of Congress, if we disagreed with it. All of us had the right to do this. He was astonished at the obliquity of intellect evinced by the gentleman, and he could not account for it, unless it was caused by the fears with which (as he had admitted) he had started from home, and which must have clouded his intellect. Was not the chairman of that compromise committee now writing and eliciting letters to and from all directions, to try to influence public opinion? He did not, until now, understand the position of his Mississippi friends. This had furnished a key to it. He could not conceive, until this moment, what they were driving at. He did not see it in committee, but he saw it now, and with amazement. He could not imagine how the j could be influenced to mar the report to so great an extent.

"*Judge S. again explained.* He did not wish to send out a report to condemn men.

"*Gov. H.* If they deserve condemnation, condemn them. He was for no master, Northern or Southern; and it made no difference whether he was Northern or Southern, if he was a master. He was for the principle *libres homo* [free to decide ???? *yes*], as was said yesterday. He did not care who was the author of the compromise: it was enough that it was wrong. He now understood how the matter was. They would discuss abstract principles, and not measures. He thought we were here to discuss the application of principles to measures. If abstractions must be discussed, merely, we must recommit the resolutions. A good deal had been said as to what they came here for. They were not here to trail in the rear of public sentiment;—they were the leaders of the South—the appointed leaders—not to hunt up public opinion at grog shops, courts, mills, etc., but to act, and act as leaders. They had been sent here with a generous confidence, and the high duty was devolved upon them to point the way—to lead the people in the way—to equality and independence.

"He would say, that, although he came here with no apprehensions as to what would be done, he did apprehend a small meeting. But now his apprehensions were scattered to the winds. Nine States had met together, to consult upon the rights and interests of the South, and it was utterly impossible for any fragment to divide itself off upon any platform so insignificant as that which was just presented. We had nothing to do but to march forward in one unbroken column, to equality in the Union, or independence out of it."

Col. Pickens, of South-Carolina, was another efficient speaker, whose addresses to the Convention have not been reported. We regret this the more, as we learn that his speeches were among the most powerful and effective which had been made before that body. Colquitt, of Georgia, is reported also to have delivered a very powerful address; and the Georgia delegation is admitted to have been as efficient as that of any other State; yet we have not a single paragraph in print from one of them.

Judge Goldthwaite, of Alabama, is the only delegate from that State of whose speech we have a report; and this a bald newspaper summary, such as affords but an imperfect idea of the full scope and character of the performance. We give portions of it, only.

"*Judge Goldthwaite, of Alabama, said,* he felt some delicacy in occupying the time of the Convention, as his delegation had already occupied a good deal of its time. If he did not feel the necessity of harmonizing, he should not think of imposing his remarks upon them. . . .

"It could not be disguised, that the civilized world was leagued abroad against us. Revolutionary France had, the first thing, set free three hundred thousand slaves, who had vindicated their claim to freedom by rapine and murder. England had done the same thing, and other nations of Europe the same also. The whole of continental Europe, with the exception of the weaker powers, had taken the same ground; and on this continent, we had seen, in the last few years, fourteen States deliberately instructing their senators and representatives in Congress to restrict slavery to its present limits; thus endangering the institution. . . . Party ties at North had been sundered and scattered to the winds, in favour of this action. We had seen the compromise, when passed in the Senate, promptly repudiated in the House; and the mean, infamous and contemptible party, whose members, a few years since, were mobbed in the houses and churches of the North, was now countenanced, its views adopted in the pulpits and in the philosophy of the schools, and sanctioned by men high in position there. Circulated largely by their presses, their views had been felt even in the territories of Nebraska and Minesota [*sic*]. Whilst our slaves were increasing, our territory was decreasing, and although the period could not be defined, the time would come, under this condition of things, when we should have to give up our property. Seeing this, we must prepare for this action of the North. The only true principle is, to force upon the minds of the *Northern* people, the idea that, if this is persevered in, the effect must be, ultimately, to dissolve the Union. It should be done temperately, but firmly; and it could not but have a good effect there. What the effect of the Union had been, was well shown by the venerable gentleman from Virginia. It has given importance to the trade of the North— has contributed to their eminence. . . . It has been customary to depreciate the resources of the South. No country ever was richer in all the resources which constitute wealth. We have mines of lead and coal. Once separated, strong hands would bring these resources into action. . . . Did any suppose that the mere abstract slavery would fall with more force on the ear of the North than a question of interest? It was not their interest to let that idea have any weight; but let the idea he had advanced be once impressed upon them, and could it be doubted that it would have its effect? He knew that the horrors of dissolution, as mentioned by the gentleman from Virginia, were held up before us—were pourtrayed by glowing lips and in eloquent language. But he believed, with him, that it was done only to arouse our fears. He could see no reason why secession should produce war, either in relation to the navigation of the Mississippi, or the division of the public lands. Suppose it did. Suppose it produced, not only war, but famine and destruction. Suppose the fertile fields around this beautiful city were deluged in blood! Is that any reason why we should ignominiously submit and put off the evil day? Would gentlemen be willing to avoid war upon the terms put upon us by our Northern brethren— terms involving degradation and disgrace? He would pursue that course which should prevent all this. The only objection he had to the resolutions was that they did not go far enough; but as they were adopted—believing that the utmost harmony was necessary to our success—he was willing to see them adopted

"Did gentlemen suppose that the report went far enough? He did not think it, and he believed that, in consequence, it would fail to have the effect antici-pated. Although he so differed, he was ready to give his vote for the resolutions and address, believing there could be no wrong in that degree of concession. He put forth no peculiar views here. He did not believe he should ever go deranged in favour of the Union. It was true that his pulse might beat faster—that his blood might flow more quickly—when Yorktown, Monmouth, or Trenton were mentioned; but no longer than when the Constitution was preserved was he in favour of the Union."

Judge Goldthwaite had several able associates, among them, in particular, Col. J. A. Campbell, of Mobile. We may perceive that the Judge refers to a want of unanimity among his colleagues. We are told that this was wholly due to the fact that, these delegates were chosen very equally from rival parties in the State, upon whom the party trammels hung too heavily to be shaken off, even when they had survived their uses. To rise to the dignity of the occasion—to see that the necessity of the South requires the equal overthrow of whig and democrat, and an abandonment of all minor issues—is not easy, with the drilled and prac-tised partizan. We note, within a short time past, the lugubrious outcries of an editor in Alabama, who laments bitterly that the session of the Southern Con-vention has materially diminished the chances of Mr. Cass for the presidency! And it is this sort of grief which has made the Convention so odious to the petty trading politicians.

The only other speaker before the Convention, whose remarks have reached us in any shape, was Judge Wilkinson, of Mississippi.

"He spoke for the purpose of harmonizing matters in debate— to find out where they were, so wide had been the latitude of discussion. Like the vener-able gentleman from Virginia, (Tucker,) he would vote for the address, or any thing which would promote harmony and make all agree when they left here— although he did not agree with all that the address contained. There were gen-tlemen here, believing that, when the time comes for the appeal to the *ultima ratio* [last resort]—to secession, or whatever it might be termed—they would not be justified in opposing the federal government, unless the Constitution was openly and directly violated. He took higher ground, although he would yield something to the prejudices of those who differed with him. There were great cardinal principles of ethics, reserved rights—the right of political justice, for instance. This right had been repeatedly impugned. If it was impugned by the admission of California, or in any other way, he was disposed to resist it. Are we to be deprived, by the great code of political ethics, of our rights, because certain rights were not *named* in that instrument? Let the address, if it be necessary, be remanded to the committee. He would like to see it recast, although he could receive it as it was. But it had been compared to a bed quilt, and there was something apt in the comparison. It ought not to appear with a piece of broadcloth here, a piece of silk there, and a piece of damask in another place. He would vote for the address in either of the forms, but he would prefer to have it recast. . . . He was not there to praise the Union; much less to disparage it. It had wrought its benefits. It had covered us with glory, and the North with power. . . . He should not specify the mode of resistance."

These are but meagre specimens of the free and highly spirited debates urged in the Convention, during its ten days session. It is our misfortune that we cannot amend them. We are told of other, and very able speakers—of Erwin and Chapman, of Alabama; of Pillow, of Tennessee; Colquitt, McDonald, and others, of Georgia; Gordon, and Newton, of Virginia; and Henderson, of Texas. The committee to which was confided all resolutions, consisted of, *Virginia,* General Gordon and Mr. Newton; *South-Carolina,* Messrs. Barnwell and Hammond; *Georgia,* Messrs. McDonald and Benning; *Alabama,* Messrs. Campbell and Murphy; *Florida,* Messrs. Pearson and Forman; *Tennessee,* Messrs. Nicholson and Brown; *Mississippi,* Messrs. Clayton and Boyd; *Arkansas,* Messrs. Powell and Brown; *Texas,* Gen. Henderson.

The delegations were far from full. The doubts which assailed Judge Sharkey were very general. Tennessee had a full representation, and a very noble one; but she was almost alone in the former respect. Virginia deserves reproach for the meagreness of hers. Our own delegation was quite full, and with such names as Cheves, Hammond, Barnwell, Rhett, Pickens, Jamison, Trenholm, Chesnut, Gregg, etc., every interest in the State was not only honourably, but most ably asserted. Judge Cheves was silent, mostly. The South-Carolina delegation, indeed, were studious in yielding precedence to all others. Hammond and Pickens spoke only when there was a general conviction that they should be heard, and Rhett, by whom the address was written, very properly yielded its discussion to other persons. His views of the condition and the duties of the South have been fully and ably given in the speech in Charleston, which has drawn down upon his head the censures of Mr. Clay. He will survive them. We should gladly quote from this truthful and forcible performance, but that it has already been secured a much greater circulation than our own. It is a speech which should offend no freeman jealous of his liberties and rights;—no Southron, feeling as he does, and must, that these rights are outraged and these liberties in danger;—no justly minded person, reasoning properly, according to the facts, when he sees that, when Mr. Rhett refers to the *ultima ratio,* he does so only in the sense of an alternative to an intolerable oppression, for which no other remedy is to be found. It is only in view of certain contingencies that Mr. Rhett insists upon extreme measures. He counsels nothing which should put South-Carolina in an attitude of bad faith to her sister States. She has gone willingly into Convention with them, and, though prepared for issues such as few of the States are yet willing to contemplate, she will adhere strictly to her guaranties to her sisters, so long as the common action, through the medium of the Convention, shall hold forth any promise of remedial results. We are, thus far, in possession of their action. They have declared their ultimatum in regard to the boundary line which separates the territories North and South. Will the Southern States sustain this ultimatum? Will the Congress of the United States give any heed to this decision? We can more easily respond to the last than the first question. But we have no hope that the North will show more moderation, or a better sense of justice, than has hitherto marked her career. In the supposed possession of all the power for aggression, we do not see the proofs of a wisdom which should shape her action safely. And

> "What is strength, without a double share
> Of wisdom!—Vast, unwieldy, burdensome,
> Proudly secure, yet liable to fall,
> By weakest subtleties."

Her course is destined to be reckless. She will provoke all the fatal parallels which marked the career of Great Britain, in respect to her colonies. And she will provoke these results without any such relative superiority as Great Britain possessed. It was said in England, in 1775, by way of warning, "Three millions of freemen, with arms in their hands, are not to be enslaved." Five millions of Southrons, not only with arms in their hands, but practised in their use, and with a host of gifted warriors to lead them, the sons of the soil, will never submit to such tremendous acts of legislation, as will make a blank of their prosperity, and convert their country into a desert. The hand-writing is upon the wall, where the North, in her high places, may read it if she will. Unfortunately, her Daniel is not the man to decypher it, with that peculiar sense of the truth, that asks only what God wills, and not what man requires. It is the most melancholy history in the progress of the nations, that their Clays and Websters, commissioned by heaven with endowments for a great work, will yet waste themselves upon petty work—will forever substitute man for God, in the objects of their solicitude; and will narrow the province, which they might control, to the base and little ends of vulgar and temporary power. It is in the falsehood of such men to their high trusts—it is in their selfishness, or their cowardice—their fear of men and factions—that they lose themselves and mislead their people,—so that a judicial blindness overspreads the faculty, that, kept clear, and purged by constant and humble reference to the Great Master, in whose hands lie all the destinies of empire, would enable them, with unsealed eyes, to decypher, in season for the safety of their people, the terrible denunciations of an outraged deity, and the fiery warnings, which the benevolence of God still vouchsafes to the offender, so that, seeing, he may repent and live. The signs of warning are before them,— the writing is luminous upon their walls, and they still have time for safety. But—!

Allen, Thomas M. *A Republic in Time: Temporality and Social Imagination in Nineteenth-Century America.* Chapel Hill: University of North Carolina Press, 2008.

Anderson, Benedict. *Imagined Communities.* London: Verso, 1983.

Bakker, Jan. "Simms on the Literary Frontier; or, So Long Miss Ravenel and Hello Captain Porgy: *Woodcraft* Is the First 'Realistic' Novel in America." *William Gilmore Simms and the American Frontier.* Edited by John C. Guilds and Carolina Collins, 64–78. Athens: University of Georgia Press, 1988.

Beckwith, Francis, and J. P. Moreland. Preface to David Jeffrey, *Christianity and Literature.* InterVarsity Press, 2011. i–ii.

Bell, Malcolm, Jr. *Major Butler's Legacy.* Athens: University of Georgia Press, 1987.

Bellows, Barbara. *A Talent for Living.* Baton Rouge: Louisiana University Press, 2006.

Bernath, Michael T. *Confederate Minds: The Struggle for Intellectual Independence in the Civil War South.* Chapel Hill: University of North Carolina Press, 2010.

Berry, Wendell. *Standing by Words.* San Francisco: North Point Press, 1983.

Black, Scott. "Social and Literary Form in the *Spectator.*" *Eighteenth-Century Studies* 33.1 (1999): 21–42.

Blake, William. *The Poetical Works.* Edited by John Sampson. Oxford: Oxford University Press, 1961.

Brennan, Matthew C. "A Note on Simms and Neoclassicism." *Simms Review* 17.1/2 (2009): 23–25.

———. *The Poet's Holy Craft: William Gilmore Simms and Romantic Verse Traditions.* Columbia: University of South Carolina Press, 2010.

Brophy, Brigid. Introduction to Lady Morgan Sydney, *The Wild Irish Girl.* London: Pandora, 1986. V-XI.

Burke, Edmund. "Reflections on the Revolution in France." In Paul Langford, general editor, *The Writings and Speeches of Edmund Burke,* vol. 8, *The French Revolution: 1790–1794,* edited by L. G. Michell, 53–293. Oxford: Clarendon Press, 1989.

Calhoun, John C. "Speech on the Reception of Abolition Petitions, February 6, 1837." In Richard K. Crallé, ed., *The Works of John C. Calhoun: Speeches Delivered in the House of Representatives and in the Senate of the United States,* 625–33. New York: D. Appleton, 1853.

Campbell, Jodi. "Benjamin Rush and Women's Education: A Revolutionary Disappointment, a Nation's Achievement." *John & Mary's Journal* 13 (2000): 5–31.

Cantrell, James P. *How Celtic Culture Invented Southern Literature.* Gretna, La.: Pelican Publishers, 2006.

Cawthon, William Lamar, Jr. "The Mother Land: The Southern Nationalism of William Gilmore Simms." *Simms Review* 8.2 (2000): 3–19.

Chesnut, Mary Boykin. *Mary Chesnut's Civil War,* edited by C. Vann Woodward. New Haven: Yale University Press, 1981.

Chesterton, G. K. *The Collected Works of G. K Chesterton.* San Fransisco: Ignatius, 1990.

Cisco, Walter Brian. *Henry Timrod: A Biography.* Madison, N.J.: Fairleigh Dickinson University Press, 2004.

Coleridge, Samuel Taylor. *Biographia Literaria: or Biographical Sketches of My Literary Life and Opinions.* 2 vols. London: Rest Fenner, 1817; rpt. Menston, U.K.: Scolar Press, 1971.

Cothran, Bettina F. "The Reception of Goethe in Charleston before the Civil War," *South Atlantic Review* 59 (January 1994): 87–106.

Crossley, Ceri. *French Historians and Romanticism: Thierry, Guizot, the Saint-Simions, Quinet, Michelet.* London: Routledge, 1993.

Duyckinck, Evert A., and George M. Duyckinck, eds. *Cyclopedia of American Literature: Personal and Critical Notices of Authors and Selections from their Writings.* Vol. 2. New York: Charles Scribner, 1856; rpt. Philadelphia: W. M. Rutter, 1875.

Edens, Janice L. "Henry Theodore Tuckerman." In *Dictionary of Literary Biography. American Literary Critics & Scholars,* 1850–1880, 236-41. Detroit: Gale, 1978. Edited by John W. Rathbun and Monica M. Grecu, 236–41.

"Editor's Book Table." *Godey's Lady's Book* 38 (March 1849): 196.

Eidson, John. *Tennyson in America.* Athens: University of Georgia Press, 1943.

"Elizabeth F. Ellet." In *Cyclopedia of American Literature: Personal and Critical Notices of Authors and Selections from their Writings.* Vol. 2. Edited by Evert A. Duyckinck and George M. Duyckinck, 609–10. New York: Charles Scribner, 1856.

Ellet, Elizabeth Fries. "Letter to M.D.S. by E. F. Ellet, Author of 'Women of the Revolution.'" *Godey's Lady's Book* 38 (January 1849): 3–6.

"Ellet's Women of the Revolution." *North American Review* 68.143 (1849): 362–88.

Foner, Eric. "The Wilmot Proviso Revisited." *Journal of American History* 56.2 (1969): 262–79.

Fox-Genovese, Elizabeth. *Within the Plantation Household: Black and White Women of the Old South.* Chapel Hill: University of North Carolina Press, 1988.

Fox-Genovese, Elizabeth, and Eugene Genovese. *The Mind of the Master Class: History and Faith in the Southern Slaveholders' Worldview.* Cambridge: Cambridge University Press, 2005.

Gardner, Jared. *The Rise and Fall of Early American Magazine Culture.* Urbana: University of Illinois Press, 2012.

Grammer, John M. *Pastoral and Politics in the Old South.* Baton Rouge: Louisiana State University Press, 1996.

Greenspan, Ezra. "Evert Duycinck and the History of Wiley and Putnam's Library of American Books, 1845-1847." *American Literature* 64.4 (1992): 677-93.

Greer, Fred Warren, III. "An Index to 'Our Literary Docket.'" Ms. thesis, University of Georgia, 1991.

Guilds, John C. "The Literary Criticism of William Gilmore Simms." *South Carolina Review* 2.1 (1969): 49–56.

———. *Simms: A Literary Life.* Fayetteville: University of Arkansas Press, 1992.

————. "Simms and the *Southern and Western*. In James B. Meriwether, ed., *South Carolina Journals and Journalists*, 45–59. Columbia: Southern Studies, 1975.

————. "Simms as Editor and Prophet: The Flowering and Early Death of the Southern *Magnolia*." *Southern Literary Journal* 4.2 (1972): 69–92.

————. "Simms's First Magazine: *The Album*." *Studies in Bibliography* 8 (1976):169–83.

————. "William Gilmore Simms and the *Cosmopolitan*." *Georgia Historical Quarterly* 41.1 (1957): 31–41.

————. "William Gilmore Simms and the *Southern Literary Gazette*." *Studies in Bibliography* 21 (1968): 59–92.

Herbert, Edward Thomas. "William Gilmore Simms as Editor and Literary Critic." Ph.D. diss., University of Wisconsin, 1958.

Herndon, Dallas Tabor. "The Nashville Convention of 1850." *Transactions of the Alabama Historical Society, 1904* 5 (1906): 203–37.

Higham, John. "The Changing Loyalties of William Gilmore Simms." *Journal of Southern History* 9.2 (1943): 210–23

Holman, C. Hugh. "The Influence of Scott and Cooper on Simms." *American Literature* 23.2 (1951): 203–18.

————. Introduction to William Gilmore Simms, *Views and Reviews in American History and Fiction. First Series*. Cambridge, Mass.: Belknap Press, 1962. vii–xliii.

Holt, Michael. *The Political Crisis of the 1850s*. New York: Wiley and Sons, 1978.

Hutchinson, John. *The Dynamics of Cultural Nationalism: The Gaelic Revival and the Creation of the Irish Nation State*. London: Allen & Unwin, 1987.

Hutchison, Coleman. *Apples & Ashes: Literature, Nationalism, and the Confederate States of America*. Athens: University of Georgia Press, 2012.

John, Richard R. *Spreading the News: The American Postal System from Franklin to Morse*. Cambridge: Harvard University Press, 1995.

Johnson, Jason. "'Dazzling Outlawries of the Imagination': Simms and the 'Americansim' of the Sonnet." *Simms Review* 14.2 (2006): 5–13.

————. "A Southern Victorian: William Gilmore Simms's Reconstruction of Robert Browning." *Simms Review* 18.1-2 (2010): 35–44.

Justus, James. *Fetching the Old Southwest: Humorous Writing from Longstreet to Twain*. Columbia: University of Missouri Press, 2004.

Kerber, Linda K. *Women of the Republic: Intellect and Ideology in Revolutionary America*. Chapel Hill: University of North Carolina Press, 1980.

Kibler, James Everett, Jr. "*The Album*." In Edward E. Chielens, ed., *American Literary Magazines*, 8–11. Westport, Conn.: Greenwood Press, 1986.

————. "*The Album* (1826): The Significance of the Recently Discovered Second Volume." *Studies in Bibliography* 39 (1986): 62–78.

————. "Bryant Borrows from Simms." *Simms Review* 1.1 (1993): 39–40.

————. "Donald Davidson, the Simms Legacy, and a Reminiscence." *Simms Review* 10.1 (2002): 25–30.

————. "The Eagle Unhooded: Poetic Technique in Simms's *Poetry and the Practical*." *Simms Review* 17.1-2 (2009): 27–34.

————. "The First Simms Letters: 'Letters from the West' (1826)." *Southern Literary Journal* 19.2 (1987): 81–91.

————. Introduction to Augustus Baldwin Longstreet, *Georgia Scenes*, vii–xxii. Nashville: J. S. Sanders, 1992.

———. "Perceiver and Perceived: External Landscape as Mirror and Metaphor in Simms's Poetry." In John C. Guilds, ed., *"Long Years of Neglect": The Work and Reputation of William Gilmore Simms,* 106–25. Fayetteville: University of Arkansas Press, 1988.

———. "Poe's Poetry: A New Simms Essay." *Simms Review* 1.2 (1993): 20–25.

———. *The Poetry of William Gilmore Simms: An Introduction and Bibliography.* Columbia, S.C.: Southern Studies Program, 1979.

———. *Pseudonymous Publications of William Gilmore Simms.* Athens: University of Georgia Press, 1976.

———. Review of William Elliott's *Carolina Sports. Mississippi Quarterly* 48.1 (1995): 337–42.

———. "Selections from Simms's Docket." *Simms Review* 13.2 (2005): 5–12.

———. "Simms's Celtic Harp." *Studies in the Literary Imagination* 42.1 (2009): 164–80.

———. "Simms's Editorship of the Columbia *Phoenix* of 1865." In James B. Meriwether, ed., *South Carolina Journals and Journalists,* 611–75. Columbia, S.C.: Southern Studies Program, 1975.

———. "Simms's Irish: An Address at Hibernian Hall, 14 January 1999." *Simms Review* 10.2 (2002): 1–7.

———. "Simms's Last Poems and the Artifice of Eternity." In David Moltke-Hansen, ed., *William Gilmore Simms's Unfinished Civil War: Consequences for a Southern Man of Letters,* 149–58. Columbia: University of South Carolina Press, 2013.

———. "Simms's Prophetic Muse." *Mississippi Quarterly* 49.1 (1995–96): 109–13.

———. "Sound and Sense in Simms's Poetry." *Southern Literary Journal* 31.2 (1999): 12–18.

———. "The *South Carolinian.*" In David Sloane, ed. *A History of American Magazines: American Humor Magazines and Comic Periodicals,* 264–67. Westport, Conn.: Greenwood Press, 1986.

———. "Stewardship and Patria in Simms's Frontier Poetry." In John Caldwell Guilds and Caroline Collins, eds. *William Gilmore Simms and the American Frontier,* 209–20. Athens: University of Georgia Press, 1997.

———. "Trelawny in Charleston." *Simms Review* 8.2 (2000): 20–21

———. "William Elliott." In *Dictionary of Literary Biography.* Vol. 248, *Antebellum Writers in the South. Second Series,* 109-17. Detroit: Gale, 2001.

———. "William Gilmore Simms." In *Dictionary of Literary Biography.* Vol. 73, *American Magazine Journalists,* 275–92. Detroit: Gale, 1988.

———. "William Gilmore Simms." *Dictionary of Literary Biography.* Vol. 248, *Southern Antebellum Writers,* 329–51. Detroit: Gale, 2001.

———. "William Gilmore Simms." In S. Serafin, ed., *Encyclopedia of American Literature,* 1039–43. New York: Continuum, 1999.

Koch, Theodore Wesley. *Dante in America: A Historical and Bibliographical Study.* Boston: Ginn, 1896.

Kreyling, Michael. *Figures of the Hero in Southern Narrative.* Baton Rouge, Louisiana State Press, 1987.

Levine, Bruce. *Half Slave and Half Free: The Roots of Civil War.* Revised ed. New York Hill and Wang, 2005.

Marr, George S. *The Periodical Essayists of the Eighteenth Century.* London: J. Clarke & Co. 1923.

Mattingly, Carol. "Elizabeth Fries Lummis Ellet." *Legacy* 18.1 (2001): 101–6.

McCardell, John. "Trent's Simms: The Making of a Biography." In W. J. Cooper et al., eds. *Master's Due: Essays in Honor of David Herbert Donald,* 179–203. Baton Rouge: Louisiana State University Press, 1985.

McCoy, Drew R. *The Elusive Republic: Political Economy in Jeffersonian America.* Chapel Hill: University of North Carolina Press, 1980.

McPherson, James. *Battle Cry of Freedom: The Civil War Era.* New York: Ballentine Books, 1988.

Meriwether, James B. "Augustus Baldwin Longstreet: Realist and Artist." *Mississippi Quarterly* 35.4 (1982): 351–64.

Miller, Perry. *The Raven and the Whale: Poe, Melville, and the New York Literary Scene.* New York: Harcourt, Brace and Co., 1956.

Mingura, Corey Don. "'Cash Is Conqueror': The Critique of Capitalism in Simms's 'The Western Emigrants' and 'Sonnet—The Age of Gold.'" *Simms Review* 17.1-2 (2009): 87–96.

Mitchel, John. *Jail Journal.* Dublin: Gill, 1914.

Moltke-Hansen, David. "Elizabeth Fox-Genovese as Essayist." In David Moltke-Hansen, ed., *History & Women, Culture & Faith: Selected Writings of Elizabeth Fox-Genovese,* xix–xxxiv. Columbia: University of South Carolina Press, 2012.

———. "Identity Politics and the Civil War: the Transformation of South Carolina's Public History, 1862–2012." *Historically Speaking,* forthcoming.

———. "Ordered Progress: The Historical Philosophy of William Gilmore Simms." In John Caldwell Guilds, ed., *"Long Years of Neglect": The Work and Reputation of William Gilmore Simms,* 126–47. Fayetteville: University of Arkansas Press, 1988.

———. "Southern Literary Horizons in Young America: Imaginative Development of a Regional Geography." *Studies in the Literary Imagination* 42.1 (2009): 1–32.

———. "When History Failed: William Gilmore Simms's Artistic Negotiation of the Civil War's Consequences." In David Moltke-Hansen, ed., *William Gilmore Simms's Unfinished Civil War: Consequences for a Southern Man of Letters,* 3–31. Columbia: University of South Carolina Press, 2013.

Montague, John, ed. *The Faber Book of Irish Verse.* London: Faber and Faber, 1974.

Moss, William. "Vindicator of Southern Intellect and Institutions: The *Southern Quarterly Review.*" *Southern Literary Journal* 13 (Winter 1980): 72–108.

"Notices of New Books." *United States Democratic Review* 23.126 (1848): 565–66

O'Brien, Michael. *Conjectures of Order: Intellectual Life and the American South, 1810–1860.* 2 vols. Chapel Hill: University North Carolina Press, 2004.

O'Conner, Mary Consolata. "The Historical Thought of François Guizot." Ph.D. diss., Catholic University of America, 1955.

Pantusa, Nancy Anne. "An Index to the 'Lorris' Letters of William Gilmore Simms." Ms. thesis, University of Georgia, 1975.

Parks, Edd Winfield. "The Three Streams of Southern Humor." *Georgia Review* 9.3 (1955): 147–59.

———. *William Gilmore Simms as Literary Critic.* Athens: University of Georgia Press, 1961.

Pearce, Colin D. "All Aboard! 'The Philosophy of the Omnibus' and the Problem of Progress in William Gilmore Simms." *Simms Review* 18.1/2 (2010): 71–91.

Quinn, Arthur Hobson. *Edgar Allan Poe: A Critical Biography.* Baltimore: Johns Hopkins University Press, 1998.

Raine, Kathleen. *William Blake*. London: Thames and Hudson, 1970.

———. *Blake and Tradition*. Princeton: Princeton University Press, 1968.

Rogers, Jeffery J. "Art Ready for Battle: William Gilmore Simms and the Civil War." Ph.D. diss., University of South Carolina, 2004.

Rush, Benjamin. *Thoughts upon Female Education, Accommodated to the Present State of Society, Manners and Government in the United States*. Boston, 1787.

Scott, Patrick. "Genre and Perspective in the Study of Victorian Women Writers: The Case of Elizabeth Missing Sewell." *Victorian Newsletter* 66 (1984): 5–10.

———. "Martin F. Tupper." *Dictionary of Literary Biography*. Vol. 32, *Victorian Poets Before 1850*, 288–98. Detroit: Gale, 1984.

Simms, William Gilmore. "The Civil Warfare in the Carolinas and Georgia, during the Revolution." *Southern Literary Messenger* 12.5–7 (1846): 257–65, 321–36, 385–400.

———. *Count Julian; or, The Last Days of the Goth. A Historical Romance*. Baltimore and New York: William Taylor, 1845

———. "Guizot's Democracy in France." *Southern Quarterly Review* 15.29 (1849): 114–65.

———. *Guy Rivers*. Rev. ed. New York: A. C. Armstrong and Son, 1855.

———. *Joscelyn*. Columbia: University of South Carolina Press, 1975.

———. *The Letters of William Gilmore Simms*. 6 vols. Edited by Mary C. Simms Oliphant, Alfred Taylor Odell, and T. C. Duncan Eaves. Columbia: University of South Carolina Press, 1952–82. Vol. 6 reissued and supplemented in 2012.

———. *The Life of the Chevalier Bayard; "The Good Knight," "Sans peur et sans reproche."* New York: Harper & Brothers, 1847.

———. "A New Spirit of the Age." *Southern Quarterly Review* 7 (April 1845): 312–49.

———. *Pelayo: A Story of the Goth*. New York: Harper & Brothers, 1838.

———. "The Philosophy of the Omnibus." *Godey's Lady's Book* 13 (September 1841): 102–9.

———. *Poetry and the Practical*. Edited by James Everett Kibler. Fayetteville: University of Arkansas Press, 1996.

———. "Reviews and Criticisms." 2 vols., collected and bound by Simms. Charles Carroll Simms Collection, Manuscripts Division, South Caroliniana Library, University of South Carolina, Columbia, South Carolina.

———. *Selected Poems of William Gilmore Simms*. Twentieth anniversary edition. Edited by James Everett Kibler. Columbia: University of South Carolina Press, 2010.

———. *Self-Development. An Oration Delivered Before the Literary Societies of Oglethorpe University; Georgia; November 10, 1847*. Milledgeville, Ga.: Thalian Society, 1847.

———. *The Social Principle*. Tuscaloosa, Ala.: Eurosophic Society, 1843.

———. *The Sources of American Independence*. Aiken, S.C.: Town Council, 1844.

———. "The Southern Convention." *Southern Quarterly Review* 2.2 (1850): 191–232.

———. *The Tri-Color; or, the Three Days of Blood, in Paris. With Some Other Pieces*. London: Wigfall & Davis, 1830. [Charleston: James & Burgess, 1831.]

———. "Tuckerman's Essays and Essayists." *Southern Quarterly Review* 1.2 (1850): 370–406.

———. "Volans Video." *Russell's Magazine* 4.1 (1858): 17–20.

———. *Views and Reviews. First Series*. Edited by C. Hugh Holman Cambridge: Belknap Press, 1962.

———. *Views and Reviews. Second Series*. New York: Wiley and Putnam, 1845 [1847].

———. *The Wigwam and the Cabin.* 2 vols. New York: Wiley & Putnam, 1845 [1846].

——— Watson, Charles Jr. *From Nationalism to Secessionism: The Changing Fiction of William Gilmore Simms.* Westport, Ct.: Greenwood Press, 1993.

———. "Women of the Revolution." *Southern Quarterly Review* n.s. 1.2 (1850): 314–54.

———. "A Year of Consolation." *Southern Quarterly Review* 12.23 (1847): 191–236.

Smith, Bonnie G. *The Gender of History: Men, Women, and Historical Practice.* Cambridge: Harvard University Press, 1998.

Stange, G. Robert. "The Voices of the Essayist." *Nineteenth-Century Fiction* 35.3 (1980): 312–30.

Taylor, William R. *Cavalier and Yankee: The Old South and American National Character.* Cambridge: Harvard University Press, 1961.

Thierauf, Doreen. "Ancient Wisdom versus Material Progress in William Gilmore Simms's 'The Hunter of the Calawassee.'" *Mississippi Quarterly* 63 (Winter/Spring 2010): 135–44.

Thomas, J. Wesley. "The German Sources of William Gilmore Simms." In Philip Shelley, ed., *Anglo-German and American-German Crosscurrents,* 1: 127–53. Chapel Hill: University of North Carolina Press, 1957.

Timrod, Henry. *The Poems of Henry Timrod.* Edited by Paul Hamilton Hayne. New and rev. ed. New York: E. J. Hale & Sons, 1872.

Trent, William P. *William Gilmore Simms.* Boston: Houghton Mifflin, 1892.

Watson, Ritchie Devon, Jr. *Normans and Saxons: Southern Race Mythology and the Intellectual History of the American Civil War.* Baton Rouge: Louisiana State University Press, 2008.

Weaver, Richard. *The Southern Essays of Richard Weaver.* Ed. George Curtis. Indianapolis: Liberty Press, 1987.

Wells, Jonathan Daniel. *Women Writers and Journalists in the Nineteenth-Century American South.* New York: Cambridge University Press, 2011.

Welty, Eudora. "Must the Novelist Crusade?" *Atlantic Monthly* 216 (October 1965): 104–8. Collected in Welty, *The Eye of the Story,* 146–58. New York, Harcourt, 1978.

Widmer, Edward L. *Young America: The Flowering of Democracy in New York City.* New York: Oxford University Press, 1999.

Wilbur, Richard. Introduction. In Richard Wilbur, ed., *Poe: Complete Poem, 5-30.* New York: Dell, 1959.

Wilson, Edmund. *Patriotic Gore: Studies in the Literature of the American Civil War.* New York: Oxford University Press, 1962.

Wimsatt, Mary Ann. "The Evolution of Simms's Backwoods Humor," In John C. Guilds, ed., *"Long Years of Neglect": The Work and Reputation of William Gilmore Simms,* 148–65. Fayetteville: University of Arkansas Press, 1988.

———. *The Major Fiction of William Gilmore Simms.* Baton Rouge: Louisiana State University Press, 1989.

———. "Realism and Romance in Simms's Midcentury Fiction." *Southern Literary Journal* 12.2 (1980): 29–48.

———. "Simms and Southwest Humor." *Studies in American Literature* 3.2 (1976): 118–30.

Wordsworth, William. *Literary Criticism of William Wordsworth.* Edited by Paul M. Zall. Lincoln: University Nebraska Press, 1966.